Islamic State's Online Activity and Responses

Islamic State's Online Activity and Responses provides a unique examination of Islamic State's (IS) online activity at the peak of its "golden age" between 2014 and 2017, and evaluates some of the principal responses to this phenomenon.

Featuring contributions from experts across a range of disciplines, the volume examines a variety of aspects of IS's online activity, including their strategic objectives, the content and nature of their magazines and videos, and their online targeting of females and depiction of children. It also details and analyses responses to IS's online activity – from content moderation and account suspensions to informal counter-messaging and disrupting terrorist financing – and explores the possible impact of technological developments, such as decentralised and peer-to-peer networks, going forward. Platforms discussed include dedicated jihadi forums, major social media sites such as Facebook, Twitter, and YouTube, and newer services, including Twister.

Islamic State's Online Activity and Responses is essential reading for researchers, students, policymakers, and all those interested in the contemporary challenges posed by online terrorist propaganda and radicalisation.

The chapters were originally published as a special issue of *Studies in Conflict & Terrorism.*

Maura Conway is Professor of International Security in the School of Law and Government at Dublin City University, Ireland, and the Coordinator of VOX-Pol.

Stuart Macdonald is Professor of Law at Swansea University, UK.

Islamic State's Online Activity and Responses

Edited by
Maura Conway and Stuart Macdonald

Routledge
Taylor & Francis Group
LONDON AND NEW YORK

First published 2020
by Routledge
2 Park Square, Milton Park, Abingdon, Oxon, OX14 4RN

and by Routledge
52 Vanderbilt Avenue, New York, NY 10017

Routledge is an imprint of the Taylor & Francis Group, an informa business

First issued in paperback 2021

British Library Cataloguing-in-Publication Data
A catalogue record for this book is available from the British Library

ISBN13: 978-0-367-85865-0 (hbk)
ISBN13: 978-1-03-208179-3 (pbk)

Typeset in Minion Pro
by codeMantra

Publisher's Note
The publisher accepts responsibility for any inconsistencies that may have arisen during the conversion of this book from journal articles to book chapters, namely the inclusion of journal terminology.

Contents

Citation Information

The chapters in this book were originally published in *Studies in Conflict & Terrorism*, volume 42, issues 1–2 (2019). When citing this material, please use the original page numbering for each article, as follows:

Introduction
Introduction: Islamic State's Online Activity and Responses 2014–2017
Maura Conway and Stuart Macdonald
Studies in Conflict & Terrorism, volume 42, issues 1–2 (2019) pp. 1–4

Chapter 1
Mujahideen *Mobilization: Examining the Evolution of the Global* Jihadist *Movement's Communicative Action Repertoire*
Maxime Bérubé and Benoit Dupont
Studies in Conflict & Terrorism, volume 42, issues 1–2 (2019) pp. 5–24

Chapter 2
Competition and Innovation in a Hostile Environment: How Jabhat Al-Nusra and Islamic State Moved to Twitter in 2013–2014
Gunnar J. Weimann
Studies in Conflict & Terrorism, volume 42, issues 1–2 (2019) pp. 25–42

Chapter 3
A Dialectical Approach to Online Propaganda: Australia's United Patriots Front, Right-Wing Politics, and Islamic State
Imogen Richards
Studies in Conflict & Terrorism, volume 42, issues 1–2 (2019) pp. 43–69

Chapter 4
Grading the Quality of ISIS Videos: A Metric for Assessing the Technical Sophistication of Digital Video Propaganda
Mark D. Robinson and Cori E. Dauber
Studies in Conflict & Terrorism, volume 42, issues 1–2 (2019) pp. 70–87

Chapter 5
Women's Radicalization to Religious Terrorism: An Examination of ISIS Cases in the United States

Lauren R. Shapiro and Marie-Helen Maras
Studies in Conflict & Terrorism, volume 42, issues 1–2 (2019) pp. 88–119

Chapter 6
"The Lions of Tomorrow": A News Value Analysis of Child Images in Jihadi *Magazines*
Amy-Louise Watkin and Seán Looney
Studies in Conflict & Terrorism, volume 42, issues 1–2 (2019) pp. 120–140

Chapter 7
Disrupting Daesh: Measuring Takedown of Online Terrorist Material and Its Impacts
Maura Conway, Moign Khawaja, Suraj Lakhani, Jeremy Reffin, Andrew Robertson, and David Weir
Studies in Conflict & Terrorism, volume 42, issues 1–2 (2019) pp. 141–160

Chapter 8
Informal Countermessaging: The Potential and Perils of Informal Online Countermessaging
Benjamin J. Lee
Studies in Conflict & Terrorism, volume 42, issues 1–2 (2019) pp. 161–177

Chapter 9
Social Media and (Counter) Terrorist Finance: A Fund-Raising and Disruption Tool
Tom Keatinge and Florence Keen
Studies in Conflict & Terrorism, volume 42, issues 1–2 (2019) pp. 178–205

Chapter 10
A Storm on the Horizon? "Twister" and the Implications of the Blockchain and Peer-to-Peer Social Networks for Online Violent Extremism
Gareth Mott
Studies in Conflict & Terrorism, volume 42, issues 1–2 (2019) pp. 206–227

Contributors

Maxime Bérubé is a SSHRC Postdoctoral Fellow at the Université de Montréal, Canada, working with Project SOMEONE to create social education strategies on jihadism in order to prevent radicalization and violent extremism. He holds a PhD in Criminology and is also a Lecturer at the School of Criminology at the Université de Montréal, Canada, where he teaches a master's seminar on terrorism and counterterrorism. Maxime has completed a research internship at the Canada Research Chair on Conflicts and Terrorism in the Department of Political Science of the Université Laval, Quebec City, Canada, and also completed a certificate in Arab Studies at the Université de Montréal, Canada. He has published many scientific articles in top tier journals, such as *Studies in Conflict and Terrorism* and the *Canadian Journal of Criminology and Criminal Justice*. He has also published an edited book entitled *Délinquance et innovation*.

Maura Conway is Professor of International Security in the School of Law and Government at Dublin City University, Ireland, and the Coordinator of VOX-Pol.

Cori E. Dauber is a Professor of Communication at the University of North Carolina at Chapel Hill, USA, where she is also a Research Fellow at the Triangle Institute for Security Studies (TISS.) She is a co-editor of *Visual Propaganda and Extremism in the Online Environment* (2014), and the author of *YouTube War: Fighting in a World of Cameras in Every Cell Phone and Photoshop on Every Computer* (2010). She has been the Visiting Research Professor at the Strategic Studies Institute of the US Army War College. Her research focuses on the online visual propaganda strategies of terrorist groups, particularly the Islamic State and Al Qaeda and its affiliates.

Benoit Dupont is a Professor in the School of Criminology at the Université de Montréal, Canada, and the Scientific Director of the Integrated Network on Cybersecurity (SERENE-RISC). He is also Holder of the Canada Research Chair in Security, Identity and Technology.

Tom Keatinge is the Director of the Centre for Financial Crime and Security Studies at RUSI, UK, where his research focuses on matters at the intersection of finance and security, including the use of finance as a tool of intelligence and disruption. His research on finance and security considers a number of themes including terrorist financing, human trafficking, new approaches to tackling financial crime, and corruption. He also co-leads RUSI's work on the following: counter-proliferation finance, the design and implementation of financial sanctions including the related impact on transatlantic relations, the role of finance and financial investigation in disrupting wildlife crime, and the illicit trade in wildlife products. Tom Keatinge has contributed to a variety of publications and media outlets; he has given evidence to parliamentary hearings and spoken at a range of high-level forums.

Florence Keen is a Research Fellow at the International Centre for the Study of Radicalisation, specialising in far-right extremism and violence. She is studying for her PhD in War Studies at King's College London, examining the interaction of individuals and social movements from extremist ideologies to understand what is fuelling far-right violence in the UK and internationally. Florence was previously a Research Fellow at the Royal United Services Institute where her work focussed on terrorist financing.

Moinuddin (Moign) Khawaja is a PhD student at the School of Law and Government, Dublin City University (DCU), Ireland. He previously worked as a multimedia journalist in the United Kingdom, the United Arab Emirates, and Sultanate of Oman.

Suraj Lakhani is a Lecturer in Criminology & Sociology (Sociology) at the University of Sussex, UK. Suraj joined the University after completing his doctorate at Cardiff University, UK. During this time he was also employed as Researcher for the Universities' Police Science Institute and lectured at the School of Social Sciences. Prior to his doctorate, Suraj worked as Researcher for the National Security and Resilience Department within the Royal United Services Institute. Suraj regularly provides expertise on the topics of radicalisation; violent extremism; counter-terrorism; and policing to a variety of print, radio, and television outlets.

Benjamin J. Lee is Senior Research Associate in the Centre for Research and Evidence on Security Threats (CREST) at Lancaster University, UK. Before joining CREST, Benjamin was a Research Associate on the European-funded project on far-right populist communication – e-Engagement Against Violence – at the University of Leicester, UK, and an oral history interviewer collecting archival material on anti-fascist campaigning at the University of Northampton, UK. His research interests include political communication, campaigning, digital media, and the far-right.

Seán Looney is a joint PhD Candidate at Swansea University and University Grenoble Alpes studying government surveillance of social media. He obtained his BA from Dublin City University, where he was also an intern on VOX-Pol, and his MA from the University of Amsterdam.

Stuart Macdonald is Professor of Law at Swansea University, UK.

Marie-Helen Maras is an Associate Professor at the Department of Security, Fire, and Emergency Management at John Jay College of Criminal Justice. She is also part of the faculty of the MS program in Digital Forensics and Cybersecurity and PhD program in Criminal Justice at John Jay College of Criminal Justice. She is the author of *Cybercriminology* (2016); *Computer Forensics: Cybercriminals, Laws, and Evidence* (2014); *Counterterrorism* (2012); *CRC Press Terrorism Reader* (2013); and *Transnational Security* (2014), among other publications. Furthermore, Dr. Maras is the creator and co-editor for a monograph and edited volume series titled *Palgrave Studies in Cybercrime and Cybersecurity*. Prior to her academic post, she served in the U.S. Navy for approximately seven years gaining significant experience in security and law enforcement from her posts as a Navy Law Enforcement Specialist and Command Investigator. During the early stages of her military career, she worked as an Electronics and Calibration Technician.

Gareth Mott is a Lecturer in Security and Intelligence at the University of Kent, where he has appointments in both the Department of Politics and International Relations and the Institute for Advanced Studies in Cyber Security (SoCyETAL). He graduated from Nottingham Trent University in 2018 with a PhD in International Security prior to which he received an MA in International Security and a BA in International Relations and Modern History from the University of East Anglia.

Jeremy Reffin is Research Fellow (Informatics, Data Intensive Science Centre) at the University of Sussex, UK. Since 2010, he has co-founded two AI research laboratories at the University of Sussex, the Centre for Analysis of Social Media at the think-tank Demos, and a R&D-focused consulting firm, CASM Consulting LLP. He is co-founder of Text Analytics Laboratory (TAG Lab) with Prof David Weir and co-founder of Predictive Analytics Laboratory (PAL Lab) with Dr Novi Quadrianto. His current area of expertise is in the analysis and interpretation of language by machines. He works extensively with companies, NGOs, and government, addressing practical problems using leading-edge AI techniques.

Imogen Richards is a Lecturer in Criminology at Deakin University, Australia, specialising in the areas of surveillance, social media, and counter/terrorism. She has published on issues related to online extremism, with a focus on comparative and cross-disciplinary approaches to online criminological research. Her wider research interests include the performance of security, theories of violence, and drugs and crime.

Andrew Robertson works in the Texts Analytics Laboratory (TAG Lab) at the University of Sussex, UK.

Mark D. Robinson is the Director of the Multimedia Labs in the University of North Carolina at Chapel Hill Communication Studies department, USA. His extensive technical expertise encompasses the making and assessment of multi-media particularly those involving computer, Internet technologies, standard, high definition and above, video formats.

Lauren R. Shapiro is an Associate Professor at the Department of Security, Fire, and Emergency Management at John Jay College of Criminal Justice. She had been teaching Criminal Justice courses as Full-Time Faculty at King Graduate School of Monroe College for several years prior to joining John Jay College in the spring of 2015 as an Adjunct and as Full-Time Faculty in the fall of 2015. In 2015, Dr. Shapiro co-published a book with Jones and Bartless entitled, *Multidisciplinary investigation of child maltreatment*, with Dr. Marie-Helen Maras. She is currently co-editing *Encylopedia of Security and Emergency Management*, which covers multiple chapters ideal for students and new professionals. Dr. Shapiro has done pro-bono work consulting with officials in the police, sheriff, and district attorney departments and with psychologists, as well as in-service workshops for those who work with children, including child care and social service workers.

Amy-Louise Watkin is a PhD Candidate in Criminology at Swansea University, UK, researching the regulation of terrorist and extremist content from social media platforms.

Gunnar J. Weimann is a Research Fellow at the Institute of Security and Global Affairs at Leiden University, the Netherlands. He holds a PhD in Islamic Studies from University of Amsterdam, the Netherlands, for a thesis on the application of Islamic criminal law in northern Nigeria. After completing his studies in Arabic and French at Leipzig University, Germany, he has worked extensively on Muslim discourses regarding law and violence in Africa and the Middle East.

David Weir is Professor of Computer Science (Data Intensive Science Centre) at the University of Sussex, UK. He is also Co-Director (Sussex Humanities Lab), Co-Director of the Text Analysis Group, Co-Founder of the Centre for the Analysis of Social Media, and the Head of Data Science Research Group.

INTRODUCTION

Islamic State's Online Activity and Responses, 2014–2017

Maura Conway and Stuart Macdonald

The ten articles in this special issue were selected from those delivered at an international conference on terrorism and social media (#TASMConf) held at Swansea University, U.K., on 27–28 June 2017. Organized by Swansea University's Cyberterrorism Project (www.cyberterrorism-project.org), the conference was attended by 145 delegates from fifteen countries across six continents. In addition to academic researchers, these delegates included representatives from a range of nonacademic stakeholders including Facebook, Tech Against Terrorism, law enforcement, the North Atlantic Treaty Organization's Cooperative Cyber Defence Centre of Excellence, the U.K.'s Home Office, the U.S. State Department, and the BBC. Six keynote presentations were delivered, videos of which are available free-to-access online.[1] The keynote speakers were Max Hill QC (the U.K.'s Independent Reviewer of Terrorism Legislation), Dr. Erin Marie Saltman (Facebook Policy Manager for Europe, the Middle East and Africa on Counterterrorism and Countering Violent Extremism), Sir John Scarlett (former head of MI6), and Professors Maura Conway (Dublin City University), Philip Bobbitt (Columbia Law School), and Bruce Hoffman (Georgetown University). In addition, a total of fifty-three other speakers presented their research into terrorists' use of social media and responses to this phenomenon. These speakers were drawn from a range of academic disciplines including law, criminology, psychology, security studies, politics, international relations, media and communication, history, war studies, English, linguistics, Islamic studies, and computer science. This emphasis on interdisciplinarity is evident in the articles in this special issue. A number of the speakers were also early career researchers or postgraduate research students; this emphasis on nurturing young researchers is also reflected in the contents of this special issue.

The articles chosen for inclusion in the special issue have a focus on the so-called Islamic State (IS) and their online activity. Not all the articles have IS as their exclusive focus, but all those with, for example, a comparative remit have IS as one of the comparator cases. The TASM conference took place at around the same time as IS's loss of their Iraqi "capital" of Mosul, but some months prior to the loss of their Syrian "capital," Raqqa. A slight but steady overall downward trajectory in IS's online content output could be apprehended over the course of 2017, with a precipitous decline on the October loss of Raqqa.[2] Output quantities have since rebounded, although not (yet?) to the levels of 2015 and 2016.[3] Many of the articles in this special issue treat aspects of IS's online activity, including the content and nature of their magazines and videos, their online targeting of females, strategies of online disruption targeted against them, in the period 2014 to 2017. Together therefore the collected articles supply a useful accounting of IS's online "golden age."

In the opening article, doctoral candidate Maxime Bérubé and Benoit Dupont draw from social movement theory, particularly Charles Tilly's concept of "action repertoire," to devise the concept of "communicative action repertoire," which is then elucidated through an analysis of the evolution of the global *jihadist* movement's network of actors, the contexts in which its communications are undertaken, and its adaptation to new communication technologies. The role of Twitter is, of course, mentioned in the latter and is the core subject of the second article in the collection. In this article, Gunnar Weimann details how and why Jabhat al-Nusra and IS shifted from their previously heavy reliance on online forums to Twitter in the 2013–2014 period. His argument, based on Arabic language statements by the two groups, along with those by *jihadist* forum administrators and other online activists, is that the "real world" conflict playing out at that time between Jabhat al-Nusra and IS accelerated the migration to social media. Despite their schism, Jabhat al-Nusra and IS clearly share a set of core commitments. Less obvious perhaps are the overlaps between IS and a group such as Australia's United Patriots Front (UPF). Nonetheless, in her article, early career scholar Imogen Richards examines how UPF has attempted, since its establishment in 2015, to legitimize itself through dialectical interactions with domestic and international politics, including IS. In particular, she analyzes publicly available online content produced by prominent UPF members and posted to their Facebook pages, YouTube channels, and Twitter accounts, through the lens of dialectical theory. She finds both implicit and explicit conflation by UPF of the Islamic religion with IS terrorism.

Into her TASM Conference keynote speech, Prof. Maura Conway underlined that more research needed to be conducted in extremist visuals, including especially video productions. In their article, Mark D. Robinson and Cori E. Dauber seek to provide researchers with a template for accomplishing exactly that. Robinson and Dauber, a media production professional and Professor of Communication respectively, describe their method for systematically grading the quality of extremist videos based on technical production criteria, which they then apply to a number of IS video productions, revealing periods when IS production capacity was debilitated (Fall 2015) and when it rebounded (Spring 2016). They advocate use of their method for, at a minimum, evaluating propaganda video output across time for not just IS, but a variety of other extremist and terrorist groups. Women are largely absent from IS videos, but were nevertheless an integral component of the overall "caliphate" project. Lauren R. Shapiro and Marie-Helen Maras apply social learning theory to data gained from open sources, largely court transcripts, in order to examine how thirty-one American females were radicalized by IS and their actions thereafter. Included in their findings are that a majority of the women used the Internet to begin (77 percent) and throughout (68 percent) their radicalization processes with, in terms of social media, Facebook and Twitter being the most heavily used platforms. Not only women but also children were a key component of the IS project. In their article, Ph.D. students Amy-Louise Watkin and Seán Looney report the findings of their analysis of the ninety-four photographic images of children that appeared in four terrorist groups' online magazines published between 2009 and 2016. The magazines were Al Qaeda in the Arabian Peninsula's *Jihad Recollections* and *Inspire*, IS's *Dabiq*, the Taliban's *Azan*, and Somali Al-Shabab's *Gaidi Mtanni*. *Dabiq* contained the largest number of child images, with their focus changing over time from an initial emphasis on child victims of Western-backed warfare to portrayals of "fierce, prestigious child soldiers." *Dabiq* was, furthermore, the only publication to exploit both genders in their images, using photographs of girl children to represent the "caliphate" as a safe and agreeable place to live.

Much of the content described and discussed in the first six articles in this collection is no longer as easily accessible as it once was. Significant pressure has been brought to bear in recent years by policymakers, media, and publics on Internet companies to "clean up" their platforms. The most significant disruption activity has been targeted at IS, as evidenced in Conway et al.'s article. The focus of the latter is the levels of disruption experienced by IS supporters on Twitter as compared to that experienced by "Other *Jihadists*." According to Conway et al., Twitter is no longer a conducive space for pro-IS accounts and communities to flourish. They also point out that not all *jihadists* on Twitter are subject to the same high levels of disruption as IS however, but that there is differential disruption taking place. IS's and other *jihadists*' online activity was never solely restricted to Twitter, of course; it is just one node in a wider *jihadist* online ecology, which is addressed in the article too. Content and account take-down is certainly not the only, and perhaps not even the best, way to respond to extremists and terrorists' use of the Internet. CREST's Benjamin J. Lee advocates for informal or grassroots countermessaging in his article, some of the benefits of which, including increased legitimacy and more aggressive messaging, he highlights. Lee is cognizant of the perils of such informal approaches too, however, and draws attention to, for example, serious potential backlash against its producers.

So major social media companies increasingly recognize the importance of preventing violent extremist and terrorist content from proliferating on their platforms, but less attention is paid to their fund-raising role. As well as presenting a threat, say RUSI's Tom Keatinge and Florence Keen, the movement of terrorist fund-raising activities online creates a disruption opportunity. Their article argues that social media companies need to do at least two things to capitalize on this: (1) display greater awareness of their vulnerability to supporting terrorist financing and (2) collaborate more with law enforcement and financial service providers to improve the system in the face of abuses. Finally, a common question for researchers interested in the terrorism–Internet nexus is "what's the next big thing?" Or "where are we going from here?" Extremists and terrorists' use of crypto-currencies is often now raised in this regard—as it is by Keatinge and Keen, admittedly to point out its little use to-date—although less attention has been paid thus far to blockchain technologies more generally. Gareth Mott seeks to remedy this by reflecting on the implications of "the blockchain" and peer-to-peer social networks in violent extremism and terrorism, including mitigation of the latter. He focuses, in particular, on the potential uses and abuses of the micro-blogging platform known as Twister. The latter's users operate a blockchain combined with DHT = Distributed Hash Table- and BitTorrent-like protocols to make posts, receive entries from other users, and send private messages. The uptake of this or similar decentralized social networks by extremists and/or terrorists would present significant challenges for current counterextremist practices, such as content takedown.

Notes

1. Recordings of the keynote presentations are available at www.cyberterrorism-project.org/tasm-conference-2017.
2. BBC Monitoring, "Analysis: Islamic State Media Output Goes Into Sharp Decline," *BBC Monitoring*, 23 November 2017, https://monitoring.bbc.co.uk/product/c1dnnj2k.
3. BBC Monitoring, "IS Media Show Signs of Recovery After Sharp Decline," *BBC Monitoring*, 23 February 2018, https://monitoring.bbc.co.uk/product/c1dov471.

ORCID

Stuart Macdonald https://orcid.org/0000-0003-4216-8592

Mujahideen Mobilization: Examining the Evolution of the Global *Jihadist* Movement's Communicative Action Repertoire

Maxime Bérubé and Benoit Dupont

ABSTRACT
Drawing on Tilly's notion of "repertoire of action," this article shows how the evolution of the global *jihadist* movement's communicative action repertoire has increased the potential resonance of its discourse. It foresees the construction of the global *jihadist* movement's discourse of mobilization as the result of the evolution of its network of actors, the context in which its communications are undertaken, and its adaptation to new communication technologies. Accordingly, it argues that the decentralization of the global *jihadist* movement has led to a widening of its communicative action repertoire and a diversification of its discourse offering.

Communication and transmission of ideological discourse is of paramount importance to collective mobilization.[1] Such communication is critical to "how entities are formed, how people come to share a political cause and mobilize around it, as well as how political action can turn to violence."[2] In recent years, the communication activities of the organizations that mobilized under the global *Salafi-jihadist* social movement umbrella have been widely studied.[3] As other researchers have done, the radical organizations mobilizing around this ideology are herein considered part of a broader movement that can benefit from using social movement theory to better understand its evolution.[4] Today, this movement is commonly known as the Global Jihadist Movement (GJM),[5] and is dominated by the social movement organizations (SMOs) Al Qaeda, Islamic State, and their multiple sub-organizations. Although the GJM has been identified as a social movement in numerous studies,[6] there is no consensus around its identification as such in the literature. Also, while the ideological orientation of this movement tends to be global, it is worth mentioning that each of these SMOs also has different local considerations, and that they do not define themselves in exactly the same ways. In terms of communications, the content of the movement's diverse discourses has been widely studied,[7] as have the differences between these discourses,[8] its use of "new" information and communication technologies (ICT),[9] and its targeted audiences.[10] Given the importance of new ICT in these works, it would be tempting to fall into technological determinism and seek to explain the evolution of the GJM's communications only with respect to the advent of the Internet and social media. In fact, none of these works manages to satisfactorily explain the evolution of the GJM's communications. Moreover, while some refer to the decentralization that has characterized the GJM over the last decades, they do not rely on this decentralization to explain the evolution of the GJM's communicative apparatus and the diversification of its discourse over time.

Tilly introduced the concept of "collective action repertoire" as "a model where the experience of actors intersects with the authorities' strategies, creating a limited number of actions more convenient, more attractive, and more frequent than many other means of action that could, in principle, serve the same interests."[11] Despite the significant contributions of this concept to understanding collective mobilization, it mainly pays attention to protest actions when, in fact, social movements can deploy many other actions, such as the construction of persuasive narratives to convince new members and to encourage their participants to actively engage themselves in protest actions. Accordingly, this article focuses on the evolution of the GJM's communicative apparatus and aims to contribute to the sociology of both terrorism and social movements by introducing the concept of "communicative action repertoire." Furthermore, it seeks to fill a gap in such literature by asking what the relationship between the decentralization of a social movement, its repertoire of communicative action, and the diversity of its discourse is. It will be shown that, in the case of the GJM, these three components are interrelated. It is worth mentioning here that for the purpose of this study, only oral and written forms of discourse transmission were analyzed, but that communication is not limited to these dimensions and can obviously also include nonverbal communications, such as images or behaviors. Indeed, many argue that collective actions themselves, including acts of violence, are forms of communication.[12]

This article is divided into three sections. The first section describes the theoretical approach behind the concept of communicative action repertoire. The second section supplies a historical look at the evolution of the GJM's communicative apparatus, with a specific focus on Al Qaeda and Islamic State, in order to better understand the widening of its communicative action repertoire and the diversification of its discourse. This allows for discussion, in the third section, of the implications of such changes in the GJM's communicative action repertoire and discourse offering.

Communicative action repertoire

It is generally understood in the literature that, as is the case for several other objects of study, social movement theory alone cannot manage to explain collective action. There has been much effort to understand collective mobilization, on the one hand, and SMOs' action repertoires, on the other, but without considering how these two approaches can enrich each other in order to better understand collective action.[13] Since resource mobilization theory has its origins in economics, it carries the assumption that a well-structured organization with abundant resources should normally thrive.[14] Nevertheless, studies show that social movements are not always well-structured and have variable levels of resources.[15] Indeed, numerous studies have shown heterogeneity in various SMOs and have suggested that heterogeneity can serve a number of adaptive functions for social movements and facilitate collective actions.[16] However, some also argue that beyond a certain threshold, the heterogeneity of participants' interests may polarize a movement and undermine collective action,[17] and even resulting in fractions within movements that may be detrimental to them.[18] This uncertainty regarding the effects of heterogeneity within social movements points to a requirement for further digging this aspect of mobilization.

In a similar vein, according to "new social movements" theory, modern social movements are usually more decentralized and diversified.[19] New social movements theory was developed in the 1970s, as researchers sought to describe and analyze those social movements that emerged in the 1960s, which were thought to be different from the workers and trade union movements. More specifically, researchers were interested in the alleged decentralization and diversification of feminist, ecologist, consumerist, nationalist, and student movements.[20] However, this paradigm was somewhat neglected by social movement researchers after a number of studies showed that "old" and "new" social movements were more similar than different. Nevertheless, in the case of terrorist movements, some still adopt this position, claiming that a "new terrorism" began to emerge from the early 1990s.[21] Of course, this "new terrorism" designation is hotly debated in the literature,[22] but whether one agrees with it or not, there is no doubt that the GJM has significantly decentralized since the early 2000s.[23] Therefore, it seems appropriate to study this particular case in order to learn more about the effects of the diversification and decentralization of a social movement on its repertoire of action.

Collective action repertoire is a well-known concept in social movement studies. Originally suggested by Tilly,[24] it is drawn on here to underline the range of protest actions in which participants can engage in order to accomplish their SMO's objectives. In this way, one can see that substantial efforts are being made by the participants in social movements to empower their ranks by creating an engaging rhetoric. Specifically, it has been shown that the GJM's communication apparatus has greatly evolved and is no longer only the work of a specific branch of the organization or its high-ranking officials.[25] Members and sympathizers from all levels are now engaged in various communication activities on behalf of the movement. Therefore, this article focuses on the communicative actions undertaken by a social movement, both to mobilize collective action and to communicate their narrative. It is agreed herein that certain collective actions can be spontaneous, but assumed that most have to be planned and that communication is required beforehand, at least between the action's initiators. It is also important to understand that communication remains central to the development of a social movement. An SMO's intentions, whether real or purported, must be communicated to its adherents or potential adherents, as well as toward a larger public that can make the desired social change happen. The very essence of a social movement is to defend a cause and to rally an audience to it, so it is considered that all of their communications have the purpose of obtaining a preselected behavior from a specific population. Again, not every communication has this explicitly persuasive component, but it nevertheless always remains part of an overall project of persuasion. Like collective actions, these communications can take various forms and vary from one organization to another. So, in order to allow for a better understanding of the communication practices of social movements, the concept of "communicative action repertoire" is introduced. As the concept of collective action repertoire suggests, focused on are the experience and capacities of the actors involved and the strategies of the SMO's leaders for purposes of assessing the conditions under which social movements' communicative actions are constructed and thereby better understanding the relationship between the evolution of a social movement, in this case the GJM, and the development of its communicative action repertoire.

The case of the global *jihadist* movement

As underlined earlier, there is no consensus around identifying the GJM as a social movement.[26] Indeed, significant ongoing structural changes, including uncertainty about the organizational structure of its core organizations, Al Qaeda (AQ), tend to challenge its social movement status.[27] The fact that this movement was very centralized around bin Laden and his associates was also a reason why some researchers were reluctant to define it as a social movement, due to it not being conceived and activated "from below."[28] The widening of the GJM, which will be discussed in the following section, and the rise of homegrown terrorism from the 2000s, has resulted in a broader identity than that of bin Laden's core organization.[29] For those who identify the GJM as a social movement, several parallels can therefore be made in order to justify this epistemological posture. In this regard, Filiu suggests two ways of comparing the GJM.[30] First, he maintains that the terrorist nature of the GJM makes it comparable to other social movements, such as the Italian Red Brigades, the German Red Army Faction, or the Japanese Red Army, particularly with respect to its organizational structure and methodologies. Second, he emphasizes the "global" nature of the GJM and the "us" versus "them" identity that forms part of its ideology. Of course, not every SMO composing the GJM defines itself in the exact same manner, but they all agree that they are *mujahideen* waging *jihad* in order to protect the Muslim *ummah* (community). Whether we agree with this epistemological posture or not, it seems appropriate to address this object from this phenomenological perspective.

Decentralization of the GJM's communication network

The GJM has its roots in the 1980s Afghanistan, where the *jihadists* were opposing the Soviet invasion. At that time, before the movement expanded to other conflict zones and took on a greater international dimension, it was mainly structured around a core Afghan-based SMO, AQ, which is sometimes also referred to—even today—as Al Qaeda Central (AQC). It was also structured as what Arquilla and Ronfeldt call a "hub" network,[31] with communications mainly issued under AQ leaders' responsibility and released through an entity especially designed for this purpose: their official media production house known as as-Sahab Foundation for Media Production. It later became common for every *jihadist* organization to have its own official media production house. At that time, however, this centralized structure and the way Osama bin Laden and his associates controlled it was one of the factors that favored the development of AQ's reputation over those of other organizations within the nascent GJM. It also enabled the execution of numerous large-scale projects, such as the 11 September 2001 (9/11) attacks against the United States of America.[32]

On the morning of 9/11, the world witnessed a major demonstration of strength from AQ when the organization claimed the deadliest single attack ever on US soil. This date was a crucial turning point in the history of the GJM. These actions provided AQ with significant credit within the GJM, but also resulted in an overwhelming resource deployment against the whole movement. Among other things, the response to these attacks was the beginning of the U.S.-led "War on Terror" that triggered the wars in Afghanistan (2001–2014) and Iraq (2003–2011). McAllister shows how these efforts against the GJM forced AQ to adopt a complete "all-channel" structure, essentially an even more decentralized network.[33] Indeed, the GJM has expanded considerably since that time, with AQC-affiliated organizations emerging in a variety of different locales. The GJM's organizational structure is therefore now more decentralized than ever, but with the nature of this decentralization varying from one organization to another. In this regard, there was a debate between two prominent terrorism researchers who sought to determine the remaining hierarchical influence within the GJM. On the one hand, Sageman argued that the GJM represented a "leaderless jihad"[34] as if hierarchical influence no longer existed. Hoffman maintained, on the other hand, that following Osama bin Laden's death, and the uncovering of the relationships he was still maintaining within his network, there would always be "leaderless jihad's leader."[35] This leader would be like a central power influencing other actors in the movement, but to a lesser extent than within a purely hierarchical organization.

This structural decentralization had some later impact on the GJM's communicative action repertoire, as it affected its network of actors.[36] Indeed, between 2003 and 2010, new media production houses appeared in several branches of the movement. Al-Andalus Media Foundation, al-Malahim Media, and al-Furqan Media, associated with Al Qaeda in the Islamic Maghreb, Al Qaeda in the Arabian Peninsula, and Al Qaeda in Iraq (AQI), respectively, were among the main media production houses established during this period. These new actors—whether they were under the control of a central power or not—brought new considerations into play because of the context in which they operated. Thus, this structural decentralization considerably modified the communication action repertoire of the GJM.

A number of external events also had a major impact on the GJM's communicative action repertoire, particularly in terms of their human resources, communication capacities, and the framing of local objectives for its SMOs. In general, events that had a significant impact in terms of the decentralization of the GJM and expansion of its communicative action repertoire were events related to conflictual relationships between the Muslim and Western worlds, or within the GJM itself. If events such as these result in changes to the communicative action repertoire, these changes may in turn be the source of other subsequent events. As an example, the Syrian conflict was an important turning point in the network's decentralization, which then led to further conflictual relationships within the GJM. When the civil war broke out in Syria, AQ had a Syrian branch with the name *Jabhat al-Nusra* (JAN).[37] At around the same time, the leader of AQI, Abu Bakr al-Baghdadi, wanted to take advantage of both the Syrian conflict and the Sunni-Shia confrontation in Iraq to expand its organization to Syria.[38] Tensions had existed between its sub-organization and AQC since Abu Musab al-Zarqawi had begun a reorganization of AQI in 2006, after which it was renamed the Islamic State of Iraq,[39] but it was nonetheless still affiliated with AQ. In 2013 however, al-Baghdadi sought to integrate JAN into his organization, so he could rename it Islamic State in Iraq and the Levant, but Abu Mohammad al-Julani, the leader of JAN, and Ayman al-Zawahiri, the leader of AQC since the death of bin Laden, refused this proposal. Al-Zawahiri wanted al-Baghdadi to concentrate his efforts in Iraq, and leave control over Syria to JAN. Despite al-Zawahiri's disapproval, al-Baghdadi announced the establishment of an Islamic caliphate overlapping the border between Syria and Iraq in June 2014, which he called Islamic State (IS), and over which he became caliph. This split the GJM into two large factions, with all active *jihadist* organizations having to choose to ally with either AQ or the new IS.[40] It undeniably marked the evolution of the GJM, since two major groups were now fighting for the governance of a dominant representation of *jihadism*.[41] While AQ had a well-established reputation within the GJM, some researchers argue that IS's communication skills and resources have enabled it to make itself a dominant player in the GJM:

> ISIS is following an unprecedented and sophisticated audiovisual strategy, consisting on the massive elaboration and distribution of audiovisual images that are highly salient and resonant in the culture of their targeted audiences. ISIS's audiovisual campaigning is massive in scale. According to the data I have analyzed, the terrorist group released 845 audiovisual campaigns between January 2014 and September 16, 2015, or more than one every day for a year and a half.[42]

This rivalry led to an increase in communications issued by the GJM since 2014[43] for purposes of ensuring their organization's legitimacy within the movement. While AQ's media houses were primarily associated with each of its major franchises, every city or area under IS's control had its own official media house. According to a June 2017 Yaqeen Media report, IS had forty-six official media production houses in operation at that time. The proliferation and complexity of IS's media apparatus was underlined by Winter who stated: "there are the less regular but more prominent releases from its three central propaganda video production branches, the al-I'tisaam and al-Furqan Foundations, and the al-Hayat Media Center,"[44] and there are also those of its various provinces in Iraq,[45] Syria,[46] Iraqi–Syrian border,[47] Yemen,[48] Saudi Arabia,[49] Egypt,[50] Afghan–Pakistani border,[51] and so on. In addition to these, another media entity related to IS is worth mentioning: the Amaq News Agency. Unlike other components in the IS media machine, this one was presented for some time as an independent entity akin to any official state news agency, which lent it a greater degree of objectivity and legitimacy.[52] Communications issued through this channel therefore offered a different rhetorical representation of IS activity than the movement's other media production houses

It should be clear at this point that the conflictual interactions between the West and the GJM, as well as those resulting from its internal disputes, ensured the decentralization of the GJM. Yet if it was initially the structural decentralization and conflictual interactions that affected the GJM's communicative action repertoire, the relationship between these elements is far more complex. In fact, changes in the communicative action repertoire also allow for more decentralization and generate new conflicting relationships, because not every actor agrees with every other's actions and strategies.

Furthermore, recent technological shifts that have affected communication in all spheres of modern society are another important factor that has favored the diversification of the actors involved in the GJM's communication practices. In effect, social media has "democratized" the GJM's communications,[53] by increasing the number of foot soldiers, participants, and sympathizers engaged in this activity,[54] which opens the door to a broader technical expertise within the movement's communicative action repertoire.[55]

Diversification of the Sociotechnical instruments mobilized by the GJM

Ours is the digital era; a historical look at the evolution of the *jihadist* communication apparatus reveals that its SMOs have adapted well to this digital environment. Nevertheless, it would be wrong to believe that all *jihadist* communications are taking place in this environment. Traditional communication strategies still exist in this movement, and many researchers argue that they remain essential to the process by which individuals join this type of movement.[56] Having said this, digital communication, particularly social media, has revealed itself as a core component of the GJM's communication action repertoire, particularly in the last decade.

In the 1980s, Abdullah Azzam attempted to convince Muslims from around the world that the Afghan *jihad* was an individual obligation. He mainly did so by writing letters to influential Arab *imams* and distributing pamphlets in Afghanistan and Pakistan.[57] Today's communicative landscape is totally different. Social media considerably altered the communicative dynamics of *jihadist* organizations, especially by making them less dependent on traditional media for dissemination of their narratives. [58] In the social media age, there is no need for *jihadists* to have, for instance, Al-Jazeera Television act as an intermediary in order for them to reach a large audience. They can count on their sympathizers to share their material online, which is often then picked-up by mainstream media. Stern and Berger described this as the outsourcing of *jihadist* communications sharing. [59] Of course, the preaching of Salafist *imams* in mosques and the "real world" efforts of various "moral entrepreneurs"[60] are still relevant to convince people to wage *jihad*, but one can see that beyond speeches, images have become a major communication and persuasion channel. Although audio recordings are still an important type of media production, video recordings, electronic magazines, and short image-messages are now of greater importance in *jihadist* communication strategies.[61] Mass online distribution of these image products is one of the most frequent techniques within the GJM's communicative repertoire.[62]

The GJM's contemporary online communicative action repertoire can be classified into two distinct types: one-way communications and two-way communications. One-way communications refer to the sharing of audio/video recordings and digital magazines. These are hosted on a wide variety of websites and online platforms and their download links massively disseminated through online forums, social media, and instant messaging applications. As for two-way communications, this refers to the use of the three latter instruments for interactive communication, including discussions between members of the GJM, its sympathizers, and the interested public.[63] Most of the one-way communications produced by *jihadists* are made by their various official media production houses. Depending on the organization's resources and their objectives, the material's quality and format vary, as can the languages in which they are made available. As the "War on Terror" also manifested online, many websites that originally hosted *jihadist* content are long closed. *Jihadists* have been quite innovative in their use of new ICT to multiply their dissemination channels.[64] The distribution of media material was initially diverted to online *jihadist* discussion forums and subsequently to social media platforms and instant messaging applications.[65] At one time, material could be directly uploaded to social media platforms such as Facebook, Twitter, or YouTube. This enabled *jihadist* SMOs not just to diversify their dissemination routes, but also gave them access to a much larger audience —Facebook has more than 1.2 billion users, for example. Many Internet companies have, more recently, begun to remove as much content violating their user policies as possible, which means some *jihadists*—particularly IS—instead upload their material to content-hosting or archiving sites whose owners are oftentimes committed to protecting freedom of expression and/or a free and open Internet.[66] A problem from the *jihadists*' perspective however is that many content-hosting and archiving sites are not well known to potential sympathizers or wider publics; it is thus required for the *jihadists* to share the download links through other channels, such as social media, in order to ensure their distribution. Once content reaches these online platforms, SMOs' sympathizers ensure its further dissemination.

The second type of online communication, two-way communications, is well-described by Carter and his colleagues:

> Official accounts tend to only make announcements and spread news, making their flow of information unidirectional; that is, they tweet information and their followers receive it. These accounts do not tend to engage followers in conversation by answering questions or responding to queries, which makes them less appealing. Disseminators, by contrast, *not only* replicate the material coming from official accounts but also engage with their followers, taking the time to explain ambiguities or engage in polemics. This enhances their reputation and, over time, allows them to demonstrate their importance as both accurate and valuable contributors to the proliferation of jihadist material on social media.[67]

Unlike the previously described top-down communication that requires no return from a given audience, this is a type of dialogic communication. Many different instruments, which are more or less secure depending on the needs and capacities of the interlocutors, are used by *jihadists* and their supporters to communicate with each other. *Jihadist* online forums witnessed a decline in popularity from circa 2010 at around the same time as the migration of *jihadists* to social media.[68] A similarly significant shift is occurring at the present time with the use of instant messaging applications, popular with young people in general, gaining popularity also within the GJM. Unlike online forums, social media are greatly more accessible. Compared to most instant messaging applications, which offer the ability to encrypt the content of communications, social media content tends to have a much greater level of publicness attached to it, which means its users can be easily identified. To avoid this, *jihadists* can use privacy protecting online tools, such as, for example, TOR (The Onion Router), which anonymizes both the source of messages and their recipients. Of course, these specific communications tools and techniques offer more security to *jihadists*, but they also require greater technical capabilities, which is why they are oftentimes not employed even in high-risk situations such as attack planning.

The usefulness of ICT for social movements' internal communications and other forms of social mobilization is also relevant to highlight. It has been established that social media are helpful to mobilize sympathizers and encourage them to participate in a variety of forms of traditional protest.[69] Further to this, it has also been shown that, within the GJM, ICT can also serve as a digital mode of protest action. For instance, one could think of the planning of "Twitter storms," which are coordinated dissemination campaigns of several hundred messages on Twitter, or the hijacking of a highly popular or so-called trending hashtag on social media to multiply the recipients of a message.[70] The following example, supplied by Stern and Berger, clearly illustrates how these tactics form part of the GJM's collective action repertoire:

> "One mujtahidun complained that no one had showed up for a Twitter storm he announced. 'Where are the others? Let's terrorize the kuffar on #Twitter. Is it too much difficult? Kuffar is doing their best to fight us. What about us?'"[71]

Highlighted by this is the diversity of the GJM's communicative action repertoire and the variety of relationships among the movement's participants. Moreover, a significant number of communication practices take place in a digital environment having a whole set of features distinctive from a traditional context. Addressed thus far has been how the GJM's communication practices are now decentralized and diversified. In the following sections, the focus shifts to the context in which these communication practices take place.

The Internet as a communicative social space for *jihadists*

The Internet and social media are viewed as optimal communication vehicles for social movements. The use of the Internet as a social space has undoubtedly changed the dynamics of *jihadist* organizations, as well as their communicative action repertoire.[72] The new means of communication available in this environment have caused important changes in the GJM's dynamics of persuasion, including significantly increasing the potential audience they can reach and the speed of their communications.[73] Contemporary Internet-based communication is low-cost, but with the possibility of reaching a much wider audience than via traditional mass media (i.e., television, radio, newspapers, etc.).[74] The Internet now allows anyone—even those without technical skills—to send messages that can be received anywhere in the world at very low cost in just milliseconds, with the potential consumers of a given message possibly reaching billions or micro-targeting resulting in tailored messages for more specific audiences, all while cutting out mediators between the message sender and their audience. Having said this, "potential consumers" is utilized here because, as Wolfsfeld, Segev, and Sheafer argue, this view is still being challenged.[75] For them, studies that support this idea are most often based on observations made in environments where new technologies are easily accessible. Thus, the fact that messages can be received anywhere in the world does not mean they actually are.

As already pointed out, subsequent interactions can also occur through online communication channels, which also increases the proximity of the interactions between GJM participants.[76] Wright and Bachmann claim that "today's social media rhetoric incorporates a concentration of iconic images, graphics, and text,"[77] and the information to which individuals are exposed on social media, unlike other means of communication, comes mainly from their peers, and not from more distant communicants whom they would be less likely to follow.[78] According to Jowett and O'Donnell,[79] this communicative proximity is one of the important amplifying factors to consider when assessing the persuasiveness of a communication. Despite the physical distance between an individual in Syria and the home of some young person, social media and instant messaging applications create an environment where these individuals can communicate directly, including by videophone calls, while still engaging in their own normal daily activities. Social media did not, of course, exist when Azzam was trying to recruit from Afghanistan, and such communicative proximity was impossible. With social media and messaging apps, *jihadist* recruiters can establish direct and secure contact with potential recruits in order to inspire, instruct, or guide them on how to join a group, travel to a conflict zone, or participate in collective actions. The line between the "real world" and digital environments is becoming less and less tangible; interactions are now possible twenty-four hours a day, seven days a week, in an environment that is very close to traditional social interaction. Turkle goes so far as to suggest that a radical change has occurred in the nature of our social relations and that societies are now increasingly connected to the world but less and less to those physically close to them.[80] A consequence of this is that digital social relations can partially substitute other types of social relations historically predominant in our societies. In effect, there has been a transformation in social relation spaces, such that the digital space is no longer complementary to and distinctive from our "real world" social environment, but rather an integral part of it because of its omnipresence in present-day social relations.

The evolution of the Internet's functionality impacted on the development of the communicative action repertoire of the GJM, providing additional resources for the SMOs and modifying the strategies and tactics favored by the movement's leaders seeking to adapt to the interests of their target audience.[81] This review of the actors, sociotechnical instruments, and environment of modern *jihadist* communications reveals a significant evolution of the communicative action repertoire of the GJM. Moreover, it shows that this repertoire varies depending on the different SMOs. The decentralization of the GJM has resulted in a downscaling of its hierarchical media structuring and a decrease of its control over many organizational aspects, including its communication practices. It is also relevant to underline that a democratization of certain technical tools—video capture and editing for example—has led to a drastic reduction in entry costs and thus allowed the multiplication of local production efforts, and ultimately the diversification of contributors and messages. In sum, the number of actors involved in these practices has increased and each of these actors contributes to the movement according to its resources and the strategic context in which it operates. Thus, this review of the GJM's evolution reveals how the decentralization of a social movement can affect its communicative action repertoire. Consequently, the next section challenges the impact of the widening of the GJM's communicative action repertoire on the diversity of the mobilization discourse collectively constructed by the GJM's various SMOs.

Diversification of the GJM's discourse

The GJM's communicative action repertoire is now wider than it used to be. The changes in this repertoire do not necessarily represent a paradigm shift in the GJM's media campaigns, to the extent that the communication methods used in the early days of the GJM are still used, simply now also in conjunction with new ones. However, these changes had significant impacts on the homogeneity of the GJM's discourse. It is well established in the literature on social movements that the latter are rarely as unified as they may first appear.[82] As already discussed, the GJM's discourse is now issued in various formats by a range of actors. However, since the presence of IS in the field is relatively new, most studies analyzing the diversity of *jihadist* discourse explore that of AQ. To give an example, Holbrook made clever use of collective action framing theory to highlight the public discourse of two AQ leaders, Ayman al-Zawahiri and Osama bin Laden.[83] His analysis of 260 statements made by them between 1990 and 2014 clearly describes the evolution of AQ's ideology during this period. In a similar vein, Kepel and Milelli, with the contribution of other researchers, analyzed more than seventy-five AQ source documents in order to better understand how the organization tries to mobilize its sympathizers by using politico-religious arguments.[84] They detected some inconsistencies in AQ's discourse. Among other things, they argue that al-Zawahiri's and bin Laden's speeches are characterized by an ideological shift between the fights against the far enemy and the near-enemy—mainly Western countries and dictatorial Islamic regimes, respectively. They also note divergent views on the legitimacy of the use of violence against Muslims. Interestingly, these observations also fit with some of the ideological differences between AQ and IS.

Based on Charaudeau's typology, built to categorize various types of propagandist discourse, it seems that the initial strategy of AQ was often a form of promotional speeches. For Charaudeau, a promotional discourse does not attempt to sell an idea or a product but rather seeks to demonstrate the moral need to be actively involved in the prevention of specific injustices or grievances.[85] Accordingly, the rhetoric of AQ brings to the forefront Muslim populations whom they say are oppressed by Western invaders and local apostate regimes.[86] For example, they describe the American occupation of Iraq or Afghanistan, various Western forces bombings over Arab soil, or an international conspiracy against Islam, as evidenced by the following quote from material produced by the as-Sahab Foundation for Media Production:

> It is a hateful Crusade. And what does it mean when Iraq is reoccupied through deception and lies and grotesque acts are committed there, including bombing, destruction, murder, displacement, and imprisonment and torture, and massive military bases are set up to tighten their control of the entire region. So pay attention to what is being said to you. It is a Zionist/Crusader war against the Muslims.[87]

IS, conversely, tends to adopt an advertising type of discourse with a strategy of triumphalist violence. Charaudeau suggests that advertising discourse often contains charitable claims and is characterized by its superlativity.[88] It is presented to the receiver as an ideal, an imperative that cannot be contradicted. In this way, it is similar to various commercial companies' product sales strategy. Along with the establishment of an Islamic caliphate overlapping Syria and Iraq, IS launched a media campaign demonstrating its local power and control. Rather than focusing on the defeats suffered by the organization and the GJM, they underlined their strengths and weapons arsenal—heavy machine guns, tanks, ground-to-air missiles, and so on. They demonstrated, further, an unlimited violence against those who opposed the movement. This was a strategy completely different from that offered by AQ. These major strategic trends are not necessarily representative of the entire communications of both organizations however.

Although IS's general strategy has been described as advertising-like, an important branch of the organization stands out for adopting a different media discursive strategy. Most of the Amaq News Agency's discourse does not attempt to persuade and is rather limited to the dissemination of more or less objective information. This media is part of the IS organization, but tries to show a certain independence in order to give itself a greater appearance of objectivity and legitimacy.[89] Also in contrast with most other IS media agencies, Amaq has both online and offline elements. Amaq has, for example, street kiosks in Iraq and Syria where it provides information to local populations; it also makes significant efforts to disseminate its news on various digital platforms, especially on Telegram's public channels.[90]

It thus appears that a variety of rhetorics continue to be implemented by the GJM. In addition, it shows that a strategic diversity is reflected in the heterogeneity of the GJM discourses. Other examples of the GJM's discourse diversity can also be pointed out, especially with respect to what Snow and Benford call the "framing dilemma."[91] This dilemma occurs when the leaders of a social movement are constructing their mobilization discourse. On the one hand, they often have an exhaustive knowledge of the ideology they are defending, which they seek to share with their audience in order to forge a certain credibility for themselves. Therefore, they tend to use complex and technical vocabulary to spread their knowledge, but oftentimes this vocabulary is not accessible to everyone. As a result, this type of discourse may only reach a limited audience and thus may not fully benefit the movement. On the other hand, they also have the opportunity to simplify their discourse and to leave technical vocabulary aside in order to allow a larger number of people to access the discourse. Within the GJM, it can be seen that even though AQ tends to shift over time from a complex technical discourse to a simpler one, the latter still retains a more elitist approach than IS does.[92] In particular, they remain dedicated to the production of long theological discourses, seeking to instruct their followers on their own interpretation of the Quran.

IS produce many short items and make extensive use of images. Theirs are more familiar and less esoteric representations in which certain populations can more easily identify themselves. For instance, in order to reach youth specifically, they often refer to video games or expressions from youth culture. The left-hand side of Figure 1 shows what looks like a geared-up *jihadi* fighters, and says: "This is our call of duty and we respawn in Jannah." In this example, they are using the popularity of the video game *Call of Duty* to convince young people that it is their duty to join the global *jihad* and die in the path of Allah, which will give them the right to enter Paradise (*Jannah*). In the same vein, the right-hand side of Figure 1 shows how IS utilized the popular hashtag "YOLO—You Only Live Once" for its own purpose, to rather suggest "YODO—You Only Die Once," in order to make an appeal for martyrdom. The message transmitter's intention is very easy to detect in these examples; further, although the religious

Figure 1. Simplified representations of *jihad* by IS.

dimension may appear to be of minor importance in these representations, its simplistic delivery does not undercut, but instead sharpens, its complex message.[93]

Conclusions and discussion

This article aimed at bringing together various social movement theories in a communication-focused approach to illustrate the development of communication practices in social movements. In this regard, it is suggested that the notion of communicative action repertoire can help us to understand how communication practices evolve within social movements, by interweaving the possibilities of contributions from movement actors and the leaders guiding them. As the notion of repertoire of action comes from resource mobilization theory, emphasized in this reflection is the role of technological resources and sociotechnical instruments in communication processes. In order to illustrate this, the focus was on a movement, the GJM, that gained significant notoriety over the last years, including as a result of its significant efforts in improving its mobilizing rhetoric and strategies. Considering the perspectives of "new social movements" and "new terrorism," the decentralization of the GJM was examined in order to understand the relationship that may exist between the evolution of a social movement and the development of its communicative action repertoire. It was found that this decentralization was made possible due to the widening of its communicative action repertoire. The GJM's decentralization led to a relative decrease of the hierarchical control within the movement and to the diversification of the discourse offering that is also linked with each SMO's specific objectives. In turn, these changes also affected the structure of the movement.

Unlike McAdam's findings regarding resource mobilization, in this case the diversification of the actors involved in a decentralized network is linked with a proliferation of its communication resources.[94] In fact, the flattening of the hierarchical structure and the adoption of a network structure led to a redefinition of the roles of the different actors in the movement. These changes ensured that the actors had more freedom and that there was more space for low-level participants' initiatives. In other words, it opened the door to grassroots militant initiatives and leaders' influence became less palpable.[95] In the case of the GJM, there is a significant recent increase in the involvement of militants and sympathizers in communication activities.

It is not because the widening of the communicative action repertoire allows a greater diversity of means of communication that the target audience is necessarily reached. However, it is still worthy to mention that the actors involved in this decentralized network have various capacities, that they target different types of audience, and that the diversity of discourse they promote is interconnected with the target audiences. Furthermore, the new ICT facilitate a massive dissemination of these discourses toward a wider audience. The use of all the movement's resources, therefore, proposes an increase in their capacities to reach a more extended and more distant range of potential recruits. Indeed, their discourses are constructed to appeal to different audiences, and they are propagated and transmitted by multiple channels. Moreover, we have seen that more SMO members can be involved in the movement's communication practices and that this role is no longer exclusively played by SMO leaders. As the proportion of activists involved in communications has significantly increased within the GJM, the audience has now within its reach a diversity of discourse that can fit with their interests. In addition, *jihadist* communications are now featuring different figures with which potential followers can identify. For example, while AQ's communications are most often issued by their leadership, IS tends to portray young foreign fighters from sociodemographic circles that fit the audience they are trying to appeal to, including delivering the message in the language usually spoken by the target audience.

Considering all these major rhetorical distinctions within the GJM, various audiences are exposed to promotional, advertising, and media discourses given by *jihadist* leaders and young foreign fighters, sometimes under a very paternalistic dynamic, or in a peer relationship. There are also theological and complex discourses, and very simplified ones calling on familiar referents from different generations. Each discourse producer testifies to different realities, different considerations, and different objectives depending on the context in which they evolve. In the end, it is clear that we are facing a discourse that is much more diverse than it seemed at first sight. Therefore, it would be necessary to develop research on the specific reception—or the resonance—of each of these forms of discourse. This would also allow understanding of the effectiveness of each of the means of communication mobilized in this repertoire.

From a more general perspective, it appears that fractions can have a positive effect on a social movement, and this is reflected here in the development of its communications. Indeed, the decentralization of a social movement can contribute to a widening of its communicative action repertoire and a diversification of its offering to potential followers. The wider offering is the result of a greater diversity in its discourse and an expansion of the audience that could be exposed to it. However, in order to clarify our position, we do not claim that the widening of the communicative action repertoire of a social movement gives it a greater mobilization capacity, but rather that it is the diversification of its narrative, combined with a multiplication of the media of diffusion, that would increase the potential resonance of its discourse. Nevertheless, before assessing the degree of resonance of a discourse, we believe that it is imperative to further explore how the various discourses are constructed, and more specifically how the various discourses' content are actually constituted. Of course, this has to be done in a systematic way and it also has to go beyond the major trends we have underlined.

In the end, by avoiding any technological determinism and by opting for a broader look at the evolution of the communicative action repertoire of a social movement, this article, in addition to contributing to the literature on terrorism, also contributes to the understanding of the dynamics associated with the decentralization and diversification of social movements.

Notes

1. Charles Tilly, *Stories, Identities, and Political Change* (Lanham, MD: Rowman & Littlefield, 2002).
2. Cristina Archetti, *Understanding Terrorism in the Age of Global Media: A Communication Approach* (Basingstoke, UK: Palgrave Macmillan, 2012), 33.
3. More specifically the global *Salafi-jihadism* introduced by Abdallah Azzam, Osama bin Laden, and Ayman al-Zawahiri in the 1980s in Afghanistan.
4. Donatella della Porta, *Social Movements, Political Violence and the State. A Comparative Analysis of Italy and Germany* (New York: CUP, 1995); C. Beck, "The Contribution of Social Movement Theory to Understanding Terrorism," *Sociological Compass* 2, no. 5 (2008),1565–1581; Jeroen Gunning, "Social Movement Theory and the Study of Terrorism," in *Critical Terrorism Studies. A New Research Agenda*, ed. Richard Jackson, Marie Breen Smyth, and Jeroen Gunning (London, UK: Routledge, 2009), 156–177; Olivier Fillieule, "Le Désengagement D'organisations Radicales. Approches Par Les Processus Et Les Configurations," *Lien Social et Politiques* 68 (2012), 37–59.
5. Bernard Rougier, "Le Jihad En Afghanistan Et L'émergence Du Salafisme-Jihadisme," in Bernard Rougier, eds., *Qu'est-Ce Que Le Salafisme?* (Paris: Presses Universtaires de France, 2007), 65–86; Jean-Pierre Filiu, "Définir Al-Qaida," *Critique internationale* 47 (2010), 111–133; Fawaz A. Gerges, *The Far Enemy: Why Jihad Went Global* (New York: Cambridge University Press, 2009); Manuel Ricardo Torres, J. Jordan, and Nicola Horsburgh, "Analysis and Evolution of the Global Jihadist Movement Propaganda," *Terrorism and Political Violence* 18, no. 3 (2006), 399–421; Marc Sageman, *Understanding Terror Networks* (Philadelphia: University of Pennsylvania Press, 2004); Aaron Y. Zelin, "The War between Isis and Al-Qaeda for Supremacy of the Global Jihadist Movement," The Washington Institute for Near East Policy, 2014. http://www.washingtoninstitute.org/uploads/Documents/pubs/ResearchNote_20_Zelin.pdf (accessed April 6, 2017) Daniel Byman, *Al Qaeda, the Islamic State, and the Global Jihadist Movement: What Everyone Needs to Know* (Oxford, UK: Oxford University Press, 2015).
6. Thomas Hegghammer, *Jihad in Saudi Arabia* (New York: Cambridge University Press, 2010); Stéphane Lacroix, *Les Islamistes Saoudiens, Une Insurrection Manquée* (Paris: PUF, 2010).
7. Max Abrahms, Nicholas Beauchamp, and Joseph Mroszczyk, "What Terrorists Leaders Want: A Content Analysis of Terrorist Propaganda Videos," *Studies in Conflict & Terrorism* 40, no. 11 (2017), 899–916; Charlie Winter, "Documenting the Virtual 'Caliphate'," The Quilliam Foundation, 2015. http://www.quilliaminternational.com/wp-content/uploads/2015/10/FINAL-documenting-the-virtual-caliphate.pdf (accessed April 6, 2017) Donald Holbrook, *The Al-Qaeda Doctrine: The Framing and Evolution of the Leadership's Public Discourse* (London, UK: Bloomsbury Publishing, 2014); Miron Lakomy, "Cracks in the Online 'Caliphate': How the Islamic State Is Losing Ground in the Battle for Cyberspace," *Perspectives on Terrorism* 11, no. 3 (2017), 40–53.
8. Daniel Milton, "Communication Breakdown: Unraveling the Islamic State's Media Efforts," 2016. https://www.ctc.usma.edu/v2/wp-content/uploads/2016/10/ISIL-Media2.pdf (accessed April 6, 2017) Craig Whiteside, "Lighting the Path: The Evolution of the Islamic State Media Enterprise (2003–2016)," 2016. https://icct.nl/publication/lighting-the-path-the-

evolution-of-the-islamic-state-media-enterprise-2003-2016/ (accessed April 6, 2017) Celine Marie I. Novenario, "Differentiating Al Qaeda and the Islamic State through Strategies Publicized in Jihadist Magazines," *Studies in Conflict & Terrorism* 39, no. 11 (2016), 953–967.

9. Manuel Ricardo Torres-Soriano, "The Dynamics of the Creation, Evolution, and Disappearance of Terrorist Internet Forums," *International Journal of Conflict and Violence* 7, no. 1 (2013), 164–178; Manuel Ricardo Torres-Soriano, "The Road to Media Jihad: The Propaganda Actions of Al Qaeda in the Islamic Maghreb," *Terrorism and Political Violence* 23, no. 1 (2010), 72–88; Manuel Ricardo Torres-Soriano, "The Caliphate Is Not a Tweet Away: The Social Media Experience of Al-Qaeda in the Islamic Maghreb," *Studies in Conflict & Terrorism* (à paraître); Torres, Jordan, and Horsburgh, "Analysis and Evolution of the Global Jihadist Movement Propaganda"; Nico Prucha, "Is and the Jihadist Information Highway—Projecting Influence and Religious Identity Via Telegram," *Perspectives on Terrorism* 10, no. 6 (2016), 48–58; Nico Prucha and Ali Fisher, "Tweeting for the Caliphate: Twitter as the New Frontier for Jihadist Propaganda," *CTC Sentinel*, 2013, https://www.ctc.usma.edu/posts/tweeting-for-the-caliphate-twitter-as-the-new-frontier-for-jihadist-propaganda (accessed April 14, 2017) Moign Khawaja, "How Jabhat Al-Nusra Uses Twitter to Spread Propaganda," 2017, http://www.voxpol.eu/how-jabhat-al-nusra-uses-twitter-to-spread-propaganda/ (accessed April 14, 2017) Jytte Klausen, "Tweeting the Jihad: Social Media Networks of Western Foreign Fighters in Syria and Iraq," *Studies in Conflict & Terrorism* 38, no. 1 (2015), 1–22.
10. Anne Aly, "Brothers, Believers, Brave Mujahideen: Focusing Attention on the Audience of Violent Jihadist Preachers," *Studies in Conflict & Terrorism* 40, no. 1 (2017), 62–76.
11. Charles Tilly, "Les Origines Du Répertoire D'action Collective Contemporaine En France Et En Grande-Bretagne.," *Vingtième Siècle. Revue d'histoire* 4 (1984), 89–108, at 99.Translated from French.
12. Alex P. Schmid and Janny de Graaf, *Violence as Communication: Insurgent Terrorism and the Western News Media* (London, UK: Sage, 1982); Ralph E. Dowling, "Terrorism and the Media: A Rhetorical Genre," *Journal of Communication* 36, no. 1 (1986), 12–24; John L. Martin, "The Media's Role in International Terrorism," *Terrorism: An International Journal* 8, no. 2 (1985), 127–146; Ronald D. Crelinsten, "Power and Meaning: Terrorism as a Struggle over Access to the Communication Structure," in *Contemporary Research on Terrorism*, ed. Paul Wilkinson and Alasdair M. Stewart (Aberdeen, UK: Aberdeen University Press, 1987).
13. Nadège Freour, "Le Répertoire D'action Collective Comme Répertoire D'offre D'engagement: Un Écairage Sur Les Contraintes Liées Aux Processus De Mobilisation Contemporains" (paper presented at the 8e Congrès de l'Association Française de Science Politique. Table Ronde n°1: Où en sont les théories de l'action collective?, 2005).
14. John D. McCarthy and Mayer N. Zald, "Resource Mobilization and Social Movements: A Partial Theory," *American Journal of Sociology* 82, no. 6 (1977), 1212–1241.
15. Alberto Melucci, "Mouvements Sociaux, Mouvements Post-Politiques," *Revue Internationale d'Action Communautaire/International Review of Community Development* 10, no. 50 (1983), 13–30; Alain Touraine, *Production De La Société* (Paris: Seuil, 1973); Alain Touraine, *La Voix Et Le Regard* (Paris: Seuil, 1978); Mayer N. Zald and John D. McCarthy, "Social Movement Industries: Competition and Cooperation among Movement Organizations," 1979, https://deepblue.lib.umich.edu/bitstream/handle/2027.42/50975/201.pdf?sequence =1 (accessed April 14, 2017)
16. Douglas D. Heckathorn, "Collective Action and Group Heterogeneity: Voluntary Provision Versus Selective Incentives," *American Sociological Review* 58, no. 3 (1993), 329–350; Pamela E. Oliver, Gerald Marwell, and Ruy Teixeira, "A Theory of the Critical Mass. I. Interdependence, Group Heterogeneity, and the Production of Collective Action," *American Journal of Sociology* 91, no. 3 (1985), 522–556; Luther Gerlach and Virginia Hine, *People, Power, Change: Movements of Social Transformation* (Indianapolis, IN: Bobbs-Merrill, 1970).

17. Douglas D. Heckathorn, "Collective Sanctions and Group Heterogeneity: Cohesion and Polarization in Normative Systems," in *Advances in Group Process Theory and Research*, ed. Ed Lawler (Greenwich, CT: JAI Press, 1992), 41–63.
18. Doug McAdam, *Political Process and the Development of Black Insurgency, 1930–1970* (Chicago, IL: University of Chicago Press, 1982).
19. Alberto Melucci, "Société En Changement Et Nouveaux Mouvements Sociaux," *Sociologie et sociétés* 10, no. 2 (1978), 37–54; Melucci, "Mouvements Sociaux, Mouvements Post-Politiques"; Touraine, *La Voix Et Le Regard*; Alain Touraine, S. Hegedus, and M. Wieviorka, *La Prophétie Antinucléaire* (Paris: Seuil, 1980).
20. Érik Neveu, *Sociologie Des Mouvements Sociaux* (Paris: La Découverte, 2015).
21. Nadine Gurr and Benjamin Cole, *The New Face of Terrorism* (New York: I.B.Tauris, 2002); Brian Michael Jenkins, "The New Age of Terrorism," in *Mcgraw-Hill Homeland Security Handbook*, ed. David Kamien (New York: McGraw-Hill Education, 2006), 117–130; Walter Laqueur, "Postmodern Terrorism," *Foreign Affairs* 75, no. 5 (1996), 24–36; Ashton B. Carter, John Deutch, and Philip Zelikow, "Catastrophic Terrorism," *Foreign Affairs* 77, no. 6 (1999), 80–94.
22. Isabelle Duyvesteyn, "How New Is the New Terrorism?," *Studies in Conflict & Terrorism* 27, no. 5 (2004), 439–454; Alexander Spencer, "Questioning the Concept of New Terrorism," *Peace Conflict & Development* 8 (2006), 1–33; David Tucker, "What Is New About the New Terrorism and How Dangerous Is It?," *Terrorism and Political Violence* 13, no. 3 (2001), 1–14.
23. Benjamin Ducol, "Comment Le Jihadisme Est-Il Devenu Numérique? Évolutions, Tendances Et Ripostes," *Sécurité et stratégie* 1, no. 20 (2015), 34–43; Bruce Hoffman, "The Leaderless Jihad's Leader," *Foreign Affairs* (2011). [En ligne], http://www.foreignaffairs.com/articles/67851/bruce-hoffman/the-leaderless-jihads-leader (accessed April 17, 2017) Brad McAllister, "Al Qaeda and the Innovative Firm: Demythologizing the Network," *Studies in Conflict & Terrorism* 27, no. 4 (2004), 297–319; Marc Sageman, *Leaderless Jihad: Terror Networks in the Twenty-First Century* (Philadelphia: University of Pennsylvania Press, 2008).
24. Tilly, "Les Origines Du Répertoire D'action Collective Contemporaine En France Et En Grande-Bretagne."
25. Torres, Jordan, and Horsburgh, "Analysis and Evolution of the Global Jihadist Movement Propaganda"; Joseph A. Carter, Shiraz Maher, and Peter R. Neumann, "#Greenbirds: Measuring Importance and Influence in Syrian Foreign Fighter Networks," ICSR Report, 2014, http://icsr.info/wp-content/uploads/2014/04/ICSR-Report-Greenbirds-Measuring-Importance-and-Infleunce-in-Syrian-Foreign-Fighter-Networks.pdf (accessed April 17, 2017) Jessica Stern and J. M. Berger, *Isis: The State of Terror* (New York: HarperCollins, 2015); Ducol, "Comment Le Jihadisme Est-Il Devenu Numérique? Évolutions, Tendances Et Ripostes."
26. Filiu, "Définir Al-Qaida."
27. Bruce Hoffman, *Inside Terrorism* (New York: Colombia University Press, 2006); Hoffman, "The Leaderless Jihad's Leader"; Sageman, *Leaderless Jihad*; Sageman, *Understanding Terror Networks*.
28. Donatella Della Porta et al., *Globalization from Below: Transnational Activists and Protest Networks* (Minneapolis: University of Minnesota Press, 2006).
29. Filiu, "Définir Al-Qaida"; Sageman, *Leaderless Jihad: Terror Networks in the Twenty-First Century*.
30. Filiu, "Définir Al-Qaida."
31. John Arquilla and David Ronfeldt, *Networks and Netwars: The Future of Terror, Crime, and Militancy* (Santa Monica, CA: RAND Corporation, 2001).
32. McAllister, "Al Qaeda and the Innovative Firm."
33. Ibid.; Arquilla and Ronfeldt, *Networks and Netwars*.
34. Sageman, *Leaderless Jihad*.
35. Hoffman, "The Leaderless Jihad's Leader."

36. Jason Burke, *The New Threat: The Past, Present, and Future of Islamic Militancy* (New York: The New Press, 2015); Ducol, "Comment Le Jihadisme Est-Il Devenu Numérique? Évolutions, Tendances Et Ripostes"; Torres, Jordan, and Horsburgh, "Analysis and Evolution of the Global Jihadist Movement Propaganda."
37. Barak Mendelsohn, *The Al-Qaeda Franchise: The Expansion of Al-Qaeda and Its Consequences* (New York: Oxford University Press, 2016).
38. Bill Ardolino, *Fallujah Awakens: Marines, Sheikhs, and the Battle against Al-Qaeda* (Annapolis, MD: Naval Institute Press, 2013); William McCants, *The Isis Apocalypse: The History, Strategy, and Doomsday Vision of the Islamic State* (New York: St. Martin's Press, 2015).
39. Ardolino, *Fallujah Awakens*; Stern and Berger, *Isis.*
40. McCants, *The Isis Apocalypse: The History, Strategy, and Doomsday Vision of the Islamic State*; Stern and Berger, *Isis: The State of Terror*; Clint Watts, "Isis and Al Qaeda Race to the Bottom," *Foreign Affairs* 2015.
41. McCants, *The Isis Apocalypse*; Novenario, "Differentiating Al Qaeda and the Islamic State through Strategies Publicized in Jihadist Magazines"; Watts, "Isis and Al Qaeda Race to the Bottom"; Clint Watts, "Zawahiri's Latest Message: Please Listen to Me Jihadis, Stop Bickering," *Geopoliticus* (2013), http://www.fpri.org/geopoliticus/2013/10/zawahiris-latest-message-please-listen-me-jihadis-stop-bickering (accessed April 18, 2017) Tore Refslund Hamming, "The Al Qaeda-Islamic State Rivalry: Competition Yes, but No Competitive Escalation," *Terrorism and Political Violence* (2017).
42. Javier Lesaca, "On Social Media , Isis Uses Modern Cultural Images to Spread Anti-Modern Values," *Brookings Institution* 2015, n.p.
43. Zelin, *The War between Isis and Al-Qaeda for Supremacy of the Global Jihadist Movement.*
44. Charlie Winter, "The Virtual 'Caliphate': Understanding Islamic State's Propaganda Strategy," The Quilliam Foundation, 2015. http://www.quilliamfoundation.org/wp/wp-content/uploads/publications/free/the-virtual-caliphate-understanding-islamic-states-propaganda-strategy.pdf (accessed April 18, 2017)
45. Wilayat al-Falluja, Wilayat Ṣalaḥ al-Din, Wilayat Baghdad, Wilayat Ninawa, Wilayat al-Anbar, Wilayat Dijla, Wilayat al-Janub, Wilayat Kirkuk, Wilayat Diyala and Wilayat Shamal Baghdad.
46. Wilayat al-Khayr, Wilayat al-Baraka, Wilayat Halab, Wilayat Dimashq, Wilayat Hama, Wilayat Homs and Wilayat al-Raqqa.
47. Wilayat al-Furat and Wilayat al-Jazira.
48. Wilayat Adan-Abyan, Wilayat al-Bayda, Wilayat Lahj, Wilayat San'aa, Wilayat Shabwa, Wilayat al-Liwa al-Akhdar and Wilayat Haḍramawt.
49. Wilayat Najd and Wilayat al-Hijaz.
50. Wilayat Sayna and Wilayat Masr
51. Wilayat Khurasan.
52. Rukmini Calimachi, "A News Agency with Scoops Directly from Isis, and a Veneer of Objectivity," *New York Times*, 14 January 2016.
53. Jenkins, "The New Age of Terrorism."
54. Ducol, "Comment Le Jihadisme Est-Il Devenu Numérique?"
55. Aaron Y. Zelin, "The State of Global Jihad Online," 2013. http://www.washingtoninstitute.org/policy-analysis/view/the-state-of-global-jihad-online (accessed April 18, 2017)
56. Benjamin Ducol, "Devenir Jihadiste À L'ère Numérique" (Thèse de doctorat, Université Laval, 2015).
57. Gilles Kepel and Jean-Pierre Milelli, *Al-Qaida Dans Le Texte* (Paris: Presses Universitaires de France, 2008).
58. Klausen, "Tweeting the Jihad."
59. Stern and Berger, *Isis.*
60. Howard Saul Becker, *Outsiders: Studies in the Sociology of Deviance* (New York: Free Press, 1963).

61. Kyle J. Greene, "Isis: Trends in Terrorist Media and Propaganda," 2015, http://digitalcommons.cedarville.edu/international_studies_capstones/3 (accessed April 18, 2017) Milton, *Communication Breakdown*; Torres-Soriano, "The Caliphate Is Not a Tweet Away: The Social Media Experience of Al-Qaeda in the Islamic Maghreb"; Torres, Jordan, and Horsburgh, "Analysis and Evolution of the Global Jihadist Movement Propaganda"; Winter, *The Virtual "Caliphate."*
62. Torres, Jordan, and Horsburgh, "Analysis and Evolution of the Global Jihadist Movement Propaganda"; Winter, *The Virtual "Caliphate."*
63. Carter, Maher, and Neumann, *#Greenbirds.*
64. Greg Miller and Souad Makhennet, "Inside the Surreal World of the Islamic State's Propaganda Machine," *The Washington Post* 2015; Milton, *Communication Breakdown: Unraveling the Islamic State's Media Efforts*; U.S. Government, "Conference Report on National Defense Authorization Act for Fiscal Year 2016" (Washington, DC: U.S Government Publishing Office, 2015), http://www.gpo.gov/fdsys/pkg/CRPT-114hrpt270/pdf/CRPT-114hrpt270.pdf (accessed May 8, 2017)
65. Ducol, "Comment Le Jihadisme Est-Il Devenu Numérique? Évolutions, Tendances Et Ripostes"; Prucha and Fisher, *Tweeting for the Caliphate: Twitter as the New Frontier for Jihadist Propaganda*; Gilbert Ramsay, *Jihadi Culture on the World Wide Web* (London, UK: Bloomsbury Publishing, 2013); Torres-Soriano, "The Road to Media Jihad"; Torres-Soriano, "The Dynamics of the Creation, Evolution, and Disappearance of Terrorist Internet Forums"; Yannick Veilleux-Lepage, "Paradigmatic Shifts in Jihadism in Cyberspace: The Emerging Role of Unaffiliated Sympathizers in Islamic State's Social Media Strategy," *Journal of Terrorism Research* 7, no. 1 (2016), 36–51.
66. Milton, *Communication Breakdown.*
67. Carter, Maher, and Neumann, *#Greenbirds*, 17–18.
68. Ducol, "Comment Le Jihadisme Est-Il Devenu Numérique? Évolutions, Tendances Et Ripostes"; Torres-Soriano, "The Dynamics of the Creation, Evolution, and Disappearance of Terrorist Internet Forums."
69. Nahed Eltantawy and Julie B. Wiest, "The Arab Spring Social Media in the Egyptian Revolution: Reconsidering Resource Mobilization Theory," *International Journal of Communication* 5 (2011), 1207–1224; Paolo Gerbaudo, *Tweets and the Streets: Social Media and Contemporary Activism* (London, UK: Pluto Press, 2012); Habibul Haque Khondker, "Role of the New Media in the Arab Spring," *Globalizations* 8, no. 5 (2011), 675–679.
70. Stern and Berger, *Isis.*
71. Ibid., 166.
72. Carter, Maher, and Neumann, *#Greenbirds*; Stern and Berger, *Isis.*
73. Ali Fisher, "Swarcast: How Jihadist Networks Maintain a Persistent Online Presence," *Perspectives on Terrorism* 9, no. 3 (2015), 3–20; Winter, *The Virtual "Caliphate": Understanding Islamic State's Propaganda Strategy*; Della Porta et al., *Globalization from Below: Transnational Activists and Protest Networks.*
74. Archetti, *Understanding Terrorism in the Age of Global Media.*
75. Gadi Wolfsfeld, Elad Segev, and Tamir Sheafer, "Social Media and the Arab Spring: Politics Comes First," *The International Journal of Press/Politics* 18, no. 2 (2013), 115–137.
76. Fisher, "Swarcast: How Jihadist Networks Maintain a Persistent Online Presence"; Winter, *The Virtual "Caliphate": Understanding Islamic State's Propaganda Strategy.*
77. Julia E. Wright and Michael Bachmann, "Inciting Criminal Violence: An Examination of Al Qaida's Persuasive Devices in the Digital World," *Journal of Terrorism Research* 6, no. 2 (2015), 70–82, at 77.
78. Michael Barthel et al., "The Evolving Role of News on Twitter and Facebook," 2015, http://www.journalism.org/2015/07/14/the-evolving-role-of-news-on-twitter-and-facebook/ (accessed May 8, 2017) Trevor Diehl, Brian E. Weeks, and Homero Gil de Zuniga, "Political Persuasion on Social Media: Tracing Direct and Indirect Effects of News Use and Social Interaction," *New Media & Society* (à paraître); Paolo Gerbaudo and Emiliano Treré, "In Search of the

'We' of Social Media Activism: Introduction to the Special Issue on Social Media and Protest Identities," *Information, Communication & Society* 18, no. 8 (2015), 865–871.
79. Garth S. Jowett and Victoria O'Donnell, *Propaganda & Persuasion* (6th ed.) (Los Angeles, CA: Sage, 2015).
80. Turkle, *Alone Together*.
81. David A. Snow et al., "Frame Alignment Processes, Micromobilization, and Movement Participation," *American Sociological Review* 51, no. 4 (1986), 464–481; David A. Snow and Robert D. Benford, "Ideology, Frame and Resonance," *International Social Movement Research* 1, no. 1 (1988), 197–217; David A. Snow and Robert D. Benford, "Master Frames and Cycles of Protest," in *Frontiers in Social Movement Theory*, ed. Aldon D. Morris and Carol McClurg Mueller (New Haven, CT: Yale University Press, 1992).
82. Robert D. Benford, "Frame Disputes within the Nuclear Disarmament Movement," *Social Forces* 71, no. 3 (1993), 677–701; Mayer N. Zald and John D. McCarthy, "Social Movement Industries: Competition and Cooperation among Movement Organizations," in *Research in Social Movements, Conflict and Change*, ed. Louis Kriesberg (Bingley, UK: JAI Press, 1980), 1–20.
83. Holbrook, *The Al-Qaeda Doctrine*.
84. Kepel and Milelli, *Al-Qaida Dans Le Texte*.
85. Patrick Charaudeau, "Le Discours Propagandiste. Essai De Typologisation," in *La Propagande: Image, Paroles Et Manipulations*, ed. Alexandre Dorna, Jean Quellien, and Stéphane Simonnet (Paris: L'Harmattan, 2008).
86. J. M. Berger, *Jihad 2.0: Social Media in the Next Evolution of Terrorist Recruitment* (Washington, DC: C-SPAN, 2015); Stern and Berger, *Isis*.
87. Ayman al-Zawahiri, Oh People Of Islam (As-Sahab Foundation for Media Production, 2016).
88. Charaudeau, "Le Discours Propagandiste. Essai De Typologisation."
89. Rukmini Callimachi, "A News Agency with Scoops Directly from Isis, and a Veneer of Objectivity," *New York Times*, 14 January 2016.
90. Prucha, "Is and the Jihadist Information Highway."
91. Snow and Benford, "Ideology, Frame and Resonance."
92. Bill Braniff and Assaf Moghadam, "Towards Global Jihadism: Al-Qaeda's Strategic, Ideological and Structural Adaptations since 9/11," *Perspectives on Terrorism* 5, no. 2 (2011), http://terrorismanalysts.com/pt/index.php/pot/article/view/braniff-towards-global-jihadism/289. (accessed May 8, 2017)
93. Gilles Kepel and Antoine Jardin, *Terreur Dans L'hexagone. Génèse Du Djihad Français* (Paris: Gallimard, 2015).
94. McAdam, *Political Process and the Development of Black Insurgency, 1930–1970*.
95. Hoffman, "The Leaderless Jihad's Leader."

Competition and Innovation in a Hostile Environment: How Jabhat Al-Nusra and Islamic State Moved to Twitter in 2013–2014

Gunnar J. Weimann

ABSTRACT

Social media offer unprecedented opportunities to terrorist groups to spread their message and target specific audiences for indoctrination and recruitment. In 2013 and 2014, social media, in particular Twitter, overtook Internet forums as preferred space for jihadist propaganda. This article looks into Arabic statements by Jabhat al-Nusra, Islamic State and jihadist forum administrators and online activists to argue that, beside the easier use of social media and disruption and infiltration of the forums, the conflict between the jihadist groups accelerated the migration to social media and the building of a presence on Twitter that provided relative resilience to suspensions.

In early 2013, most analysts still agreed that, while increasing *jihadist* activities were detected on Twitter, a microblogging site launched in 2006, *jihadist* Internet forums would retain their central function in terrorist conversation and information distribution.[1] Only one year later, Thomas Hegghammer felt that

> Today forums remain important, but they seem to have been overtaken in 2013 by Facebook and Twitter as the preferred platform for internal multi-user communication. The jihadi migration to Facebook and Twitter has yet to be properly explained, but the breakdown in trust on the forums may have been a contributing factor.[2]

By late 2014, *jihadist* forums had either disappeared or lost much of their former relevance. Twitter had become a preferred platform not only for chatter among supporters but also for official releases by terrorist groups.[3]

Without doubt, the reasons for this shift are manifold. They include arrests of forum administrators and the frequent disruption of *jihadist* forums. Disruption of forums, despite all efforts to restore the platforms in the shortest time possible, resulted in a relative decrease of popularity after coming back online and accelerated the migration of members to either other forums,[4] or ultimately to social media. In addition, the loss of trust on the part of terrorist organizations that supply the forums with material and, thus, their ability to serve as an authentic source for terrorist propaganda has been identified as a principal reason for the loss of relevance and the disappearance of forums.[5]

This article aims to shed light on another factor contributing to the loss of relevance of *jihadist* forums: the development of strategies by the so-called Islamic State (IS) and Jabhat al-Nusra to ensure a resilient presence on social media, in particular Twitter, which did not need authentication through *jihadist* forums. The two groups were not the first *jihadist* organizations to create official Twitter accounts,[6] and other *jihadist* groups such as Al Qaeda in the Islamic Maghreb (AQIM) recognized the potential value of establishing themselves on Twitter during the same period of time.[7] It is however argued that the competition between IS and Jabhat al-Nusra precipitated the migration from the forums to Twitter, as it forced the groups to build a resilient presence on the microblogging site despite increasing efforts by Twitter at disruption. In effect, the competition between IS and Jabhat al-Nusra stimulated innovation in terrorist communication in an increasingly hostile environment through the groups' need to gain ascendency over their opponents.

This study relies primarily on Arabic statements by the two groups and *jihadist* forum administrators to analyze the motivations of their actions. The analysis relies on social media posts, statements posted on social media and discussion forums, and documents released by the actors involved, which were collected during monitoring of official accounts in 2013 and 2014. The selection of the material was guided by the aim to trace the relationship between known actors, in particular IS, Jabhat al-Nusra, and prominent *jihadist* discussion forums. During the period of time under review, communication by these actors was still centralized to an extent that this methodology provided a comprehensive picture of their public statements. This notwithstanding, the approach has also limitations. Rather than telling a complete story, online statements provide punctual information on the declared motivations of the actors at a specific point in time. Entities representing particular actors disappear without explanation and others arise without defining exactly the relationship to former iterations. Rather than establishing a continuity of the actors involved, the sources allow identifying dynamics and trends.

The period under review was one of turmoil. In early April 2013, the leader of the Islamic State of Iraq (ISI), Abubakr al-Baghdadi, announced that Jabhat al-Nusra was nothing but an extension of the ISI in Syria. ISI and Jabhat al-Nusra would merge under the new name of Islamic State in Iraq and the Levant (ISIL). In an immediate reaction, Jabhat al-Nusra's leader Abu Muhammad al-Jawlani rejected the merger and declared his group to be an independent member of the Al Qaeda network responsible directly to Al Qaeda's nominal head Ayman al-Zawahiri. Al-Zawahiri ordered ISI to restrict its activities to Iraq and leave Syria to Jabhat al-Nusra, but by mid-2013, all mediation efforts by the Al Qaeda leadership had failed. The mediator appointed by al-Zawahiri was killed in an ISIL suicide attack; and ISIL rejected the orders given by al-Zawahiri.[8] In 2013, tensions between the factions increased gradually on the ground, as they tried to assert themselves in the face of their competitors. The same was happening on the Internet, which illustrates the importance attached to the online sphere by *jihadist* groups.

A *Jihadist* Online Infrastructure

Al Qaeda recognized early the possibilities that the Internet provided for disseminating propaganda messages, bypassing the state-controlled media in many Arab countries, such as Saudi Arabia. Al Qaeda leaders felt that they were suffering a "media siege," which was meant to prevent them from reaching out to the Muslim masses.[9] Exploiting the possibilities offered by the Internet required special skills and dedication to keep pace with new technologies and counterattacks on the group's online presence. This created opportunities for supporters with the necessary skill set to provide services to *jihadist* groups. Al Qaeda and other groups have valued these efforts and incorporated them in *jihadist* ideology under the label of "media *jihad*" (*al-jihad al-i'lami*), which means that the spiritual reward of these activities is equaled to participation in fighting. Following the death of Osama bin Laden in May 2011, for example, the al-Fajr Media Centre (*markaz al-fajr lil-i'lam*, "dawn media center") called the Internet a "battlefield for jihad" and appealed to all *jihadist* sympathizers to be "media mujahidin."[10]

In an effort to become independent from mass media, such as al-Jazeera, Al Qaeda and other groups created specific brands for propaganda releases, most prominently al-Sahab Media, which, among other productions, has been in charge of publishing messages by Al Qaeda's central leadership. Creating a name, logo, and corporate design served to distinguish official propaganda productions from surrounding media and Internet content and create an impression of trustworthiness. It, thus, helped to authenticate original content issued by the groups.

After static websites of Al Qaeda and other terrorist organizations had been exposed to repeated attacks, *jihadist* forums, containing disclaimers that shifted legal responsibility for content from administrators to users, gained ascendency. The main *jihadist* forums appear to have considered themselves as independent initiatives supporting the global *jihadist* movement, rather than supporters of a specific group. Their vocation has been to provide a stage for members of the global movement from different conflict zones.[11] Nevertheless, in case they were accepted by Al Qaeda's leadership as trusted distributors of their message, they were engaged in a relationship that demanded submission and acceptance of a hierarchy that ultimately depended on the Al Qaeda central leadership.[12]

Al Qaeda's instrument to control the forums was the al-Fajr Media Centre. Established in 2006, it provided the forums with original propaganda material from *jihadist* groups within the Al Qaeda network. For both *jihadist* groups and forums, adherence to the network controlled by al-Fajr Media was a sign of acceptance as part of the global *jihadist* movement and a "proof of authenticity" of the message.[13] With regard to the forums, al-Fajr Media played a coordinating role, serving, for example, as an instance to which forum administrators could appeal in case of dispute.[14] Al-Fajr Media also provided technical support to *jihadist* forums to remain online in the face of attacks.[15] The administrators of the Ansar al-Mujahidin Network, for example, had no doubt that al-Fajr Media was directly linked to the Al Qaeda leadership, probably in the person of Atiyatullah al-Libi, who was killed in a drone strike in North Waziristan in August 2011.[16]

In early 2013, three top-tier *jihadist* forums were active under the umbrella of al-Fajr Media: the Ansar al-Mujahidin Network (*shabakat ansar al-mujahidin*, "supporters of mujahidin network"), the Shumukh al-Islam Network (*shabakat shumukh al-Islam*, "loftiness of Islam network"), and the al-Fida' Islamic Network (*shabakat al-fida' al-Islamiyya*, "sacrifice Islamic network").

Social Media and *Jihadist* Online Communication

When social media platforms first emerged, *jihadist* groups preferred to use them by posting links that pointed back to the secure space of official websites or *jihadist* forums, which continued to serve as tools for authentication.[17] This certainly had to do with the existing hierarchical system of verification embodied by al-Fajr Media that was feeding the forums.[18] By contrast, social media increased the possibilities for their opponents, be it state agencies, online activists or ordinary people, to counter *jihadist* propaganda by posting alternative views, spreading disinformation or using blatant impersonation.

This notwithstanding, *jihadist* forums, whose self-imposed role was to mediate between terrorist groups and larger audiences, felt that they needed to reach out to social media. Since 2011, Ansar al-Mujahidin and Shumukh al-Islam, among others, actively encouraged supporters to develop social media profiles.[19] The Ansar al-Mujahidin English Forum created a Twitter account in October 2011, whereas the Arabic forum of Ansar al-Mujahidin created a Facebook page, also in 2011, which was fed automatically with contents from the forum.[20] These efforts served to reach out to social media users and lure them to their platforms.

Individual *jihadist* supporters also used social media to promote *jihadist* perceptions. They took advantage of the activities of nonviolent activists in Syria that in 2012 were documenting human rights abuses and war crimes by the Syrian regime of Bashar al-Asad:

> Social-media smart and professional jihadists adopted this treasure grove for their propaganda. By rebranding and reframing the content created by civil society activists, jihadi propaganda used these grievances to support a key jihadist self-perception; the obligation to respond by force to defend and protect the Sunnites in Syria.[21]

Following them, self-styled media outlets started creating social media accounts, in particular on Twitter, from where they linked to content available on *jihadist* forums, but also other social media platforms, primarily YouTube and Facebook. As a result, networks on Twitter sharing *jihadist* content began coexisting with *jihadist* forums.[22]

By 2013, a prominent *jihadist* online author, Abu Sa'd al-Amili, lamented a general decline in participation on *jihadist* forums. One of the reasons for this, in his view, was that *jihadists* were migrating to social media platforms such as Twitter and Facebook. Whereas the displacement was caused in part by the frequent disruption of the forums, he added, in the long run relying on social media was an error that endangered the central position of *jihadist* forums, "our protected strongholds." People needed to recognize that social media were no adequate alternative to the forums, for they were run by "our enemies." Inevitably there would come a day when "they shut their doors in our faces." Therefore, the forums should remain the "base and foundation" of *jihadists* online.[23]

Centralized Social Media Profiles

During the same period, Jabhat al-Nusra and ISIL recognized that they could not afford abandoning social media to their opponents or supporters, for fear that these activities, if left uncontrolled, could dilute the corporate identity of the group. In early 2013, Jabhat al-Nusra's official Twitter account was embedded in a large network of supporting accounts.[24] In the course of the year, Jabhat al-Nusra published a series of "media statements,"[25] signed by its central media outlet al-Manara al-Bayda' Media Company (*mu'assasat al-manara al-bayda' al-i'lamiyya*, "white minaret [of the Umayyad mosque in Damascus] media company"), in which it tried to regulate the activities of its supporters on Twitter. In order to avoid confusion between official accounts and supporters' accounts, the group asked supporters that created accounts using the name or logo of Jabhat al-Nusra or al-Manara al-Bayda' Media to change this and to state "in a stable, visible place" on their pages that these were supporting, not official, pages.[26] The group insisted that it had no official website, forum, Facebook account, or Wordpress page, after the initial ones had been suspended. The only official accounts of Jabhat al-Nusra were those on the three major *jihadist* forums at the time, the Shumukh al-Islam Network, the Ansar al-Mujahidin Network, and the al-Fida' Islamic Network, supported by Jabhat al-Nusra's Twitter account (@JbhtAnNusrah, then after suspension of the former @JabhtAnNusrah), "as a secondary source for Jabhat [al-Nusra]'s publications."[27] Initially, the split between Jabhat al-Nusra and ISIL, which occurred in April 2013, did not affect these positions.

In addition, on 7 July 2013, a new media outlet on Twitter was introduced: the Himam News Agency (@Hemm_Agency, *wikalat himam al-ikhbariyya*, "concerns news agency"). Himam News was described as an independent media company based in Syria, which aimed to report on "the life of the mujahidin in particular, living their victories, telling their heroic deeds and following their social life." It was "concerned with covering the living conditions of Muslims in general, report their opinions, picture their creativity and tell their stories."[28] The idea of creating a purportedly independent news agency reporting on the non-combatant activities of a specific *jihadist* group had a precedent in the Madad News Agency, which was created by Ansar al-Shari'a in Yemen in 2011–12, when it was able to cease control of territory in southern Yemen.[29]

Himam News immediately started posting short videos, uploaded to YouTube and advertised on its Twitter account, showing the provision of aid and services by Jabhat al-Nusra to the local population and interviews with local residents on the benefits of Jabhat al-Nusra's administration. In a tweet on its official Twitter account in January 2014, Jabhat al-Nusra declared that Himam News's correspondents were "deployed to most regions in Syria, covering the activities of Jabhat al-Nusra in the liberated areas."[30] Himam News was active until late August 2014, after which it disappeared.[31]

In the same period, following the April 2013 split, ISIL started creating its own media profile. In mid-August 2013, ISIL declared that, during a temporary interruption of the publication of its statements and media productions, which was due to "the known circumstances through which the Levant arena has gone," supporters on social media accounts had tried to fill the gap by posting news and comments with regard to ISIL.[32] Others, however, exploited the opportunity to spread, under its name, "fabricated news, exaggerations and opinions that do not express the programme and direction" of ISIL. Some of these used names, titles, and logos of ISIL or one of its media outlets, such as al-Furqan Media or al-I'tisam Media, to suggest an official link or by claiming that they were linked to some field commander in Syria. The statement insisted that the only official communication channels of the group were the al-I'tisam Media account on the Shumukh al-Islam Network and its official Twitter account.

The al-I'tisam Media Production Company (*mu'assasat al-i'tisam lil-intaj al-i'lami*, "adherence [to God's rope] media production company") had emerged in March 2013 with a first video production that still focused on terrorist activities in Iraq.[33] It was described as an entity of the "information ministry" (*wizarat al-i'lam*) of ISI. Since August 2013, al-I'tisam Media started issuing a series of videos, the "Windows onto the land of epic battles" (*nawafidh ala ard al-malahim*) series, which combined coverage of ISIL combats with social activities and services provided to the population in areas controlled by ISIL.[34] These videos were posted simultaneously on *jihadist* forums and the official Twitter account of al-I'tisam Media, which was suspended and had to be re-created several times in 2013. Whereas al-I'tisam Media functioned in ways similar to those of Himam News, it had been identified since the beginning as an official media outlet of ISI/ISIL. Maybe for this reason the brand of al-I'tisam Media was abandoned in 2015. By this time, its news agency function had been replaced by A'maq News, which, starting in late 2014, has functioned as an allegedly independent "news agency" covering IS activities.

Thus, the split in 2013 was followed by a period in which both groups tried to develop centralized media profiles that were adapted to social media use. Nevertheless, the forums still served as a backup and authentication tool in case of account suspension and impersonation attempts on Twitter. Followers of both groups were requested to identify their services clearly as supporting activities.

Diffusion

This situation changed in 2014. The tensions between ISIL and the rest of the Syrian armed opposition escalated into large-scale violence through an attempt by large segments of the opposition to drive ISIL out of Syria at the turn of 2014. Jabhat al-Nusra first tried to mediate, but was quickly drawn into the conflict. As a result of the intransigent positions of ISIL, Al Qaeda's central leadership officially excluded the group from the Al Qaeda network in late January 2014.[35] ISIL's defiant attitude seemed to be justified in the light of its military successes: in June ISIL forces conducted a large-scale offensive from Syria across the Iraqi border, taking control of large swathes of northern Iraq, including the second largest Iraqi city Mosul. Shortly afterward, ISIL announced that it had reestablished the caliphate, changed its name to Islamic State and declared that all other *jihadist* groups in areas being or coming under its control were thereby dissolved. It thus may not come as a surprise that, in late July, Jabhat al-Nusra vowed to deliver, in cooperation with other *jihadist* groups in Syria, the land and the people from extremists, in a clear reference to IS.[36]

In January 2014, ISIL started creating specific Twitter accounts for each of its "provinces" (*wilayat*, sing. *wilaya*), which reported on local events. Maybe this was triggered by a disruption of communications between regional ISIL factions and the centralized media outlets due to the hostilities. The "provincial" Twitter accounts quickly developed into a network with a corporate identity, in which, if one account was suspended, the others could be used to authenticate an account newly created to replace the suspended one. Included in this network of accounts were also those of the official media outlets, including al-Furqan Media and al-I'tisam Media. This resulted in a network with sufficient resilience to withstand occasional suspensions. As a result, ISIL/IS was not forced anymore to rely on the authentication through the forums.

Whereas in April 2014, Jabhat al-Nusra still denied that al-Manara al-Bayda' Media had an official Twitter account,[37] it changed its position shortly afterward, probably in reaction to the new strategy developed by IS. In July it introduced a Twitter account for the "network of correspondents of al-Manara al-Bayda'," whose aim was "continuous coverage of local Jabhat al-Nusra news from different regions."[38] Al-Manara al-Bayda' Media's "network of correspondents" functioned in ways similar to the ISIL network of "provinces," with Twitter accounts with regional responsibilities that served to authenticate one another in case of suspension.

The resilience of IS's network of accounts was put to the test by the start of proactive suspension of accounts promoting terrorism by Twitter. The platform started developing capacities to disrupt IS propaganda messaging on a massive scale in August 2014, after IS had published a video showing the assassination of U.S. American journalist and video reporter James Foley.[39] IS tried to recreate its network of accounts on other platforms, including VKontakte (vk.com), but was quickly evicted. The group had to change strategy again and decided to replace authentication through dedicated accounts by authentication through the creation of massive numbers of accounts that posted identical messages simultaneously. These accounts were bound together by hashtags, first referring to IS "provinces" or its central media outlets, then to titles of new releases. These hashtags ensured that, even if accounts were deleted quickly, it was possible to find other postings that were still active. This system remained workable until the 13 November 2015 attacks in Paris, after which the hashtags were massively spammed by IS opponents.[40]

During the same period, Jabhat al-Nusra's "network of correspondents" faced suspensions to a far lesser extent and could largely maintain its network of "correspondents" even after it renamed into Jabhat Fath al-Sham in July 2016, relinquishing publicly its relation to Al Qaeda. While the brand of al-Manara al-Bayda' Media was abandoned after the change, the "network of correspondents" remained active, until Jabhat Fath al-Sham merged with other *jihadist* groups to form Hay'at Tahrir al-Sham in early 2017. Changing corporate identity might have been another strategy to evade eviction.

The Reaction of the Forums

By the end of 2014, then, both IS and Jabhat al-Nusra had implemented strategies to maintain a sufficiently resilient presence on Twitter and distinguish their message from disinformation without the need for authentication through *jihadist* forums. A major motivation for this was certainly the need to be present in the space where their supporters communicated. In addition, it now became clear that the forums were not the independent entities that they purported to be, and the fact that they had to show loyalty to either camp weakened their position further. In what follows, the positions of two of the major forums, the Ansar al-Mujahidin Network and the Shumukh al-Islam

Network, are examined. Ansar al-Mujahidin remained firmly within the al-Fajr Media network, whereas Shumukh al-Islam sided with IS.

With regard to the mounting tensions in Syria, the administrators of Ansar al-Mujahidin warned, in September 2013, all "those who follow [Ansar al-Mujahidin] and all other writers and Muslims on Twitter that have commented on recent events" that they had to be careful not to side with one of the conflicting parties and to abstain from slandering the opposing party.[41] Supporters were asked to convey a positive image of the "*mujahidin*" and their supporters and avoid inciting Muslims, and in particular Muslim scholars, against them. They were enjoined to think highly of Muslims in general, and *jihadist* scholars in particular. In light of this advice, Ansar al-Mujahidin stated its commitment to remain neutral in the conflict between different *jihadist* groups or currents and to prevent its members from verbally attacking or insulting Muslims and *jihadist* scholars, while allowing constructive criticism. At the same time, Ansar al-Mujahidin emphasized that its abstention from publishing official releases of a particular group was not to be understood as an attack or an insult and did not put into question the validity of the struggle of this group. Finally, it stressed that the official position of the Network was published exclusively on its official accounts on "*jihadist* networks," that is forums, and on its official Twitter account.

The statement seems to be directed primarily to supporters of ISIL at the time, due to its emphasis on the respect due to *jihadist* scholars. Most prominent *jihadist* ideologues had supported Al Qaeda in the dispute and now faced strong reactions from social media users sympathetic of ISIL. The forum administrators admitted indirectly that they stopped publishing ISIL releases but tried to explain that this was not to be seen as criticism. One cannot escape the impression that this decision might have been imposed on the forum by the al-Fajr Media administration. At some point after this, the Arabic Ansar al-Mujahidin forum disappeared from the Internet.[42]

Shumukh al-Islam's story is very different. In a first reaction after the outbreak of violence between the ISIL and other armed opposition groups in Syria, the Shumukh al-Islam Network issued, on 5 January 2014, a statement in support of ISIL.[43] In its capacity as

> one of the frontlines [*thaghr*] of jihadi media, which provided its best men for the cause of continuing the word of truth, unifying the ranks of the mujahidin, containing the dissentions and calamities brought to us by the Crusader enemy and his supporters from among those who wear the garment of advice and concern for the religion,

the Shumukh al-Islam Network deplored the state of "our brothers in the Levant of caliphate, especially our brothers in the Islamic State in Iraq and the Levant [ISIL]," who for many years had been steadfast and perseverant, but now faced new ways employed by the enemies of Islam, who

> have found a new location in which to squirt out their venom and evil—Twitter—after the jihadi networks had restrained them, repelled their obstruction and counteracted them with all might. Some of them wear the garment of religion to lead [others] astray from God's path and issue fatwas on the killing of mujahidin and the lawfulness of [shedding] their blood.

The statement continued by pointing out that a war was being waged against the "mujahidin for God's cause" in Syria by "criminal gangs" equipped and trained by

Istanbul and Amman, after some armed factions were incited to fight against "our brothers in the Islamic State." They killed both "*ansar*" (i.e., Syrian members) and "*muhajirun*" (i.e., foreigners) and attacked the families of the "*muhajirun.*" In the light of this, the Shumukh al-Islam Network demanded that all truthful "*mujahid*" groups side with the ISIL in this proxy war, for this was not a war against Abubakr al-Baghdadi and his men but against anyone who strove to implement the *Sharia*. Any incitement against ISIL had to stop, and a *Sharia* tribunal was to be established to identify those responsible for the in-fighting. The authors stressed that self-defense and the repelling of aggression were legitimate under Islam.

Shumukh al-Islam's appeals for protecting ISIL against the aggression that it suffered continued until the administrators officially declared their support of ISIL in a statement published on 10 March 2014.[44] The authors insisted that the Shumukh al-Islam Network had existed for seven years,

> during which we have lost many of our cadres, while the others are awaiting [capture], are captives or exiles, all for the sole purpose of communicating the voice of the people of jihad to the umma;
>
> seven years of supporting the mujahidin and striving for unity of their ranks without creating fissions between them;
>
> seven years of advising and directing the supporters of jihad;
>
> seven years of clarity of vision and programme.

In the current circumstances, the statement continued, Shumukh al-Islam needed to take a position and, therefore, declared that it supported ISIL, against which all nations of unbelief, hypocrisy, and apostasy had conspired. Nevertheless, Shumukh al-Islam would not tolerate on its platform anyone slandering or defaming *jihadist* scholars or commanders, including Ayman al-Zawahiri. Such members would be expelled: "We cannot let Shumukh [al-Islam] become pasture for those who want to behave in evil manners and attack jihadi commanders and their representatives." In line with this, Shumukh al-Islam would provide advice and direction to Jabhat al-Nusra, which at the same time it accused of helping "apostates, rebels, thieves etc., who fight our brothers in the [Islamic] State." Shumukh al-Islam considered Jabhat al-Nusra "our brothers," whom they were obliged to guide back to the truth. All postings inciting further conflict would be prevented. Nevertheless, all members of Shumukh al-Islam, in particular its senior members, were called upon to strive for reconciliation between the "*mujahidin*" and to close the ranks. The statement finished with a renewed call for a *Sharia* tribunal to settle the conflict between Jabhat al-Nusra and ISIL.

In response to this statement, Jabhat al-Nusra announced that it would stop distributing its propaganda via the Shumukh al-Islam Network.[45] "Since the start of the dispute between Jabhat [al-Nusra] and the [Islamic] State and the interruption of the publication [of propaganda statements], while we all awaited the decision of Shaykh [Ayman] al-Zawahiri,"[46] and even after its publication, Shumukh al-Islam sided with the ISIL. Shumukh al-Islam was accused of not taking action against forum members openly insulting Jabhat al-Nusra. Recent publications by its "media arm," in a likely reference to Shumukh al-Islam's al-Ma'sada Media Company, showed that it had lost "every meaning of professionalism and trustworthiness, on which the lofty edifice of media jihad had been based for years."

In late April 2014, Shumukh al-Islam appealed to its supporters—"you should consider yourselves family of the al-Shumukh house"—to show commitment by contributing to remedy and contain the conflict.[47] Public forums and chatrooms should not be used to discuss the origin of the conflict. This should be left to *jihadist* leaders and advisers (*ahl al-hall wal-aqd*)[48] in private conversations. Equally, the conflict should not be transferred to arenas outside Syria. Shumukh al-Islam was committed to containing it and so should its members. Shumukh al-Islam pledged that, in addition to ISIL productions, it would continue publishing propaganda items from all groups accredited with al-Fajr Media (*jami' al-jihat al-mu'tamada lada al-Fajr*), as long as those materials did not openly oppose one of the parties in the conflict. It declared that it had launched a "media initiative" to bring the concerned parties—"the [Islamic] State, Jabhat [al-Nusra], al-Fajr [Media], al-Fida' [Network]"—back together. Shumukh al-Islam emphasized again that constructive criticism was wanted but verbal attacks and slander would not be tolerated. Any content that might increase hatred and tension would be deleted. Unacceptable behavior on Shumukh al-Islam included the use of links to the Network in content that was copied and pasted from it, presumably to social media, without prior permission. Official publications of *jihadist* groups were to be disseminated exclusively through official accounts, with the exception of those that were disseminated through official Twitter accounts. It was forbidden to copy insults and false information from Twitter and other social media into Shumukh al-Islam. Shumukh al-Islam should be a place of support only. Silence should be kept about the "*mujahidin*'s" disagreements or situation, the reality of which was unknown to outsiders (and, thus, to the community of online supporters of either camp).

What is striking in Shumukh al-Islam's attitude is its insistence on the length of its struggle and the sacrifice that it had made. This seems to suggest that its long-standing legitimacy as one of the major *jihadist* forums was at stake when it started supporting ISIL, likely in defiance of instructions given by al-Fajr Media. The reference to Twitter as a main arena in which the fight against ISIL was led reveals that the competition with social media was perceived as another threat to the position of the forum as central communication space.

Whereas Shumukh al-Islam supported ISIL, it tried to keep its position as an independent service provider to all *jihadist* groups, which is evidenced by its pledge not to allow the slandering of Ayman al-Zawahiri and to publish material from all groups linked to al-Fajr Media, as long as they did not contain inflammatory statements against one of the parties. Nevertheless, Shumukh al-Islam's condescending attitude toward Jabhat al-Nusra led the latter to disown it. The appeals for a tribunal to settle the conflict illustrate the forum's difficult position, in the light of ISIL's categorical refusal to submit to mediation. In the end, Shumukh al-Islam tried to contain the conflict by preventing users from discussing its causes on the forum and from applying it to areas outside Syria. To achieve this, it intended to control the contents that were copied from and to social media.

Another aspect is of importance: Shumukh al-Islam actively tried to involve its supporters to contribute to the struggle and get involved. Likely in response to its weakened relations with al-Fajr Media, Shumukh al-Islam seems to have sought to compensate the impending loss of relevance by attracting new actors that had appeared on social media.

Re-Configuration

In the meantime, supporters of the two camps were already re-grouping on social media. A comprehensive overview of these initiatives cannot be provided here due to limited space. Two examples will be discussed, one in support of Al Qaeda and one in support of IS.

In April 2014, the al-Tahaya Media Company (*mu'assasat al-tahaya lil-i'lam*, "rememberances media company") was established. In its founding statement,[49] the entity stated that "after the jihadi media reached a dangerous and rough stage that needs [taking] a stance of review, reconstruction and re-assessment after a state of chaos, and imposing a realistic policy by some [media] companies on the mujahidin and their supporters," the al-Tahaya Media Company was launched as "one spearhead of the mujahidin against the imams of unbelief and hypocrisy," which would "represent our commanders, scholars, mujahidin and prisoners." In particular, al-Tahaya Media defined as its tasks "the transcription and translation of material issued by the [two official Jabhat al-Nusra media outlets], the al-Basira and al-Manara al-Bayda' Companies" and "some works of truthful mujahidin everywhere." It specifically committed to "the policies of our brothers in the al-Fajr Media Centre."

Since its launch, al-Tahaya Media has issued hundreds of documents, including transcripts of video and audio speeches by Al Qaeda leaders and ideologues.[50] Its main aim seems to be to put these texts into circulation on social media and file sharing sites and, thereby, ensure that they remain available also outside *jihadist* forums and websites.[51] Its explicit reference to the al-Fajr Media Centre shows that this endeavor aimed to perpetuate the centralized hierarchical communication structure built by Al Qaeda.

By contrast, the creation of the Media Front for the Support of the Islamic State (*al-jabha al-i'lamiyya li-nusrat al-dawla al-Islamiyya*) was the culmination of a self-organization of activists, bringing together a number of self-proclaimed entities on social media that were supporting IS. In its founding manifesto, published in October 2014,[52] the authors announced that the "media soldiers in support of the State of Islam" created a "unified central leadership" comprising the "most important supporting jihadi media companies" to "support the blessed global caliphate project." As examples of the effectiveness of online propaganda, they referred to the "terror" sparked in America by the decapitation of James Foley, the effect of Twitter hashtag campaigns and the productions of IS's al-Hayat Media Centre, which specialized in propaganda, such as the English-language magazine *Dabiq*, directed to non-Arab audiences. The "legend of the lone wolf," the statement said, was over. IS supporters should join the "structure of your blessed front" (i.e., the Media Front). In particular, they appealed to technical experts, hackers, translators, media activists, graphic designers, video and audio producers, experts in Arabic language, scenario writers, *nashid* composers, and poets to join. People that did not have such capabilities could transcribe texts, upload files, and disseminate them on social media. All participating entities would conserve their original name. The statement contains a list of entities that joined the Media Front: al-Ghuraba' Media; al-Wafa' Media Production; al-Battar Media; al-Wagha Media; al-Ansar League; A'isha Media Centre; Minbar al-Ansar Room; Fada'ih al-Almaniyya Media Production; Dabiq Media; Mahsud Jihadi Media; al-Minhaj Media Production;

Nasa'im Audio Production; Adwa' al-Ribat Media Production; al-Raqqa Islamic Network; and al-Ansar Islamic Network.

Some of the entities composing the Media Front for the Support of the Islamic State subsequently became prominent media outlets on social media promoting IS. They developed close relationships with the organization.[53]

Analysis

The competition between Jabhat al-Nusra and ISIL after April 2013 accelerated a process that had been underway for some time, the migration of *jihadist* activity from discussion forums to social media. As a result, it helped to speed up the loss of relevance of *jihadist* forums, which had been undermined over the years by infiltration and disruption.

Individual supporters of *jihadism* had started using Twitter and other social media platforms long before, and their activity had reached an extent that put the *jihadist* groups at risk of losing control over their communication. The groups thus had to relinquish their initial reluctance and establish their own presence on social media, in particular Twitter. The matter acquired more urgency after the April 2013 split between Jabhat al-Nusra and ISIL, when neither could afford leaving the field to its competitor.

Already at this stage, the two groups chose slightly different approaches. Jabhat al-Nusra remained firmly within the al-Fajr Media system with its three major forums, using Twitter only as a "secondary" source for its official releases. It, nevertheless, supplemented its official media outlet, al-Manara al-Bayda' Media, with a new format adapted to social media, Himam News. By contrast, from the beginning, ISIL treated Twitter and the Shumukh al-Islam Network, the only top-tier forum openly siding with it, as equally valid sources for its propaganda. This might have been due to an initially weak position, as the growing conflict with Al Qaeda risked leading to the exclusion of ISIL, and consequently Shumukh al-Islam, from established distribution channels. ISIL, to a certain extent, copied Jabhat al-Nusra's approach of establishing a media outlet adapted to social media, al-I'tisam Media, even if the distribution of tasks between the former and ISIL's central media outlet, al-Furqan Media remained less clear. In this initial phase both groups adopted a strategy of strict branding to authenticate their messages on Twitter.

The reliance on branding of official accounts with possible verification through the forums served the requirement of authentication. It, however, offered only limited resilience and carried the risk of interruption of messaging during the time needed to announce a new account through the forums, thereby opening opportunities for the opponent. This likely motivated the development of a new strategy relying on a network of accounts that were used to introduce and verify new accounts without passing through the forums. ISIL "provincial" accounts, possibly created following a temporary breakdown of the centralized communication system of ISIL in early 2014, rapidly developed into a network with a clear corporate identity on Twitter, thereby forming an additional layer in which the official media outlet accounts were embedded. The fact that Jabhat al-Nusra adopted a similar system on Twitter indicates that it was deemed a successful strategy. In addition to providing additional breadth to the reporting, the new system afforded relative resilience against suspensions and independence from *jihadist* forums for verification and the related delay or interruption of messaging. Thus, for the first time, Jabhat al-Nusra and ISIL bypassed the forums, a fact that contributed greatly to the latter's loss of relevance.

Another factor is the apparent breakdown of the centralized distribution system controlled by Al Qaeda through the al-Fajr Media Centre. The reactions of the forums put in evidence the former central position of al-Fajr Media. On the one hand, the example of Ansar al-Mujahidin shows the continuing commitment to the al-Fajr Media network. Shumukh al-Islam's example, on the other hand, with the forum insisting on its long trajectory of *jihadist* activism, clearly displays fear of losing legitimacy in case of exclusion, presumably as a result of disobedience. To compensate, Shumukh al-Islam tried to mobilize its followers to work toward reconciliation. In addition, and contrary to ISIL, Shumukh al-Islam warned its supporters of the dangers of Twitter and, finally, tried to impose strict controls on the information exchanged between the forum and Twitter. All these attempts seem to have remained largely futile.

During the same period, efforts increased to structure supporters' activities on Twitter in support of the two camps. While the available sources do not allow establishing a personal link between the entities, by referring to al-Fajr Media in its founding statement, al-Tahaya Media put itself in the line of tradition of Al Qaeda's supervisory body and tried to preserve Al Qaeda's legacy on the Internet. By contrast, ISIL supporters created self-styled media entities on Twitter, which then formed an alliance of media activists that actively recruited skilled, like-minded individuals. It is more than likely that these networks of supporters on social media served as a recruitment pool for IS's media capabilities. This explains the enormous innovation capacity of IS with regard to media production and dissemination that gained it its ascendancy in the online sphere for the major part of 2015 and 2016.

When IS supporters were finally forced to seek alternative platforms to replace the increasingly contested space on Twitter, they did not fall back on *jihadist* forums. At the time of writing, Shumukh al-Islam continued active—despite frequent changes of its Uniform Resource Locator, probably as a result of disruption efforts—and posted IS propaganda in a timely manner. However, only registered users could access content posted on it; and no possibility to register new accounts was provided.[54] In addition, technology has evolved, and discussion forums that are difficult to access from smartphones and other mobile devices are far less attractive at present. Instead, the bulk of *jihadist* supporters and consequently also terrorist groups and their media outlets have moved to Telegram, a cloud-based encrypted messaging service that allows recreating the community that cannot thrive anymore on Twitter.[55] Jabhat al-Nusra was exposed to a lesser degree to suspensions[56] and, thus, was not forced to innovate.

Conclusion

For terrorist groups, public communication fulfills multiple purposes, including intimidating opponents, justifying violent acts, and attracting volunteers and funding. To achieve this, they need access to public space and, simultaneously, must ensure that their audiences can distinguish their messages from the surrounding noise and disinformation. The period under review illustrates the interplay between these two basic, but often contradicting, requirements of terrorist communication in a hostile online environment.

Terrorist groups must be present in places where their supporters are, if they want to exercise some degree of control over what is said about them, both by their supporters and opponents. Forums and Twitter both provide a public space to the extent that information posted on both types of platforms can be accessed openly and is indexed by search engines. Twitter, of course, offers far greater opportunities to engage directly with audiences beyond the closed *jihadist* community.

On forums, authentication is achieved through distribution channels providing exclusive access to original material from terrorist groups, on the one hand, and the control of the content through forum administrators, on the other. It has become apparent that the impression of independence of the forums needs qualification, as at least the major ones have been engaged in a hierarchical relationship with terrorist organizations, as exemplified by Al Qaeda's al-Fajr Media. Their legitimacy resided in the faithful implementation of the publishing policies defined by al-Fajr Media.

Such internal disciplinary mechanisms are absent on Twitter. Unable to control content directly, terrorist groups needed to be present on Twitter themselves, to counter their opponents as much as to discipline their supporters. They thus started to disseminate their content directly without the services of forum administrators. New authentication mechanisms needed to be designed, such as the use of networks of accounts to create resilience. Simultaneously, the competition between IS and Al Qaeda led to the creation of new media outlets and an escalation of content production.

Social media platforms not only challenged the established communication methods of terrorist groups but made it difficult for *jihadist* activists to influence the discourse in ways done by forum administrators in the past. The equivalent of forum administrators on Twitter, and now Telegram, is media entities established with the purpose to support a terrorist group. Contrary to forum administrators, these entities cannot exercise control over the content posted by other users and must try to influence their audiences with their own content output, which must be disseminated widely and clearly branded to achieve authentication.

Some entities, such as al-Tahaya Media, which presumably have direct access to a network controlled by a terrorist group, apply a top-down approach, aiming to maintain available online central texts and utterances of the group that they support. Others, as those organized in the Media Front for the Support of the Islamic State, grow bottom-up, creating alliances of seemingly independent entities to form a front in support of a certain group, presumably one that breaks with established communication patterns.

Whatever strategies are devised to maintain a presence in a hostile online environment, these do not result from a carefully designed plan but respond in flexible ways to current challenges. The answers found are subsequently formalized into a strategy that serves until the next wave of disruption necessitates further innovation.

The shift of Jabhat al-Nusra and IS from forums to Twitter goes to show that innovation in communication is a reaction to external pressure. The al-Fajr Media Centre was established to stabilize the system of discussion forums that had formed as a reaction to attacks on websites. Once established, however, for a long time, the al-Fajr Media system hindered innovation with regard to exploiting the new opportunities of the social media by Al Qaeda–linked groups. Eventually, it was the escalating conflict within the *jihadist* movement and, consequently, the breakdown of the al-Fajr Media system that spurred innovation and pushed the groups into the hostile environment of Twitter. Here, innovation was led by IS, which through its depiction of extreme violence and aggressive incitement of terrorism, quickly managed to concentrate countermeasures on itself.

Cut off from the established information distribution channels and facing increasing disruption efforts, IS reached out for new talent and within a short period of time used this innovative force to create the most powerful propaganda machinery known from any nonstate group in history.

Acknowledgments

I thank Noha Eid, Antonios Samouris, Manuel Torres Soriano, and the two anonymous reviewers for their useful comments on a draft of this article. All remaining errors of fact or judgment are mine.

Notes

1. Aaron Y. Zelin, "The State of Global Jihad Online: A Qualitative, Quantitative, and Cross-Lingual Analysis," New America Foundation, January 2013; Manuel Ricardo Torres-Soriano, "The Dynamics of the Creation, Evolution, and Disappearance of Terrorist Internet Forums," *International Journal of Conflict and Violence* 7, no. 1 (2013), 164–178.
2. Thomas Hegghammer, "Can You Trust Anyone on Jihadi Internet Forums?," in *Fight, Flight, Mimic: Identity Signalling in Armed Conflicts*, ed. Diego Gambetta (Oxford: Oxford University Press, forthcoming), draft available at http://hegghammer.com/_files/Interpersonal_trust.pdf.
3. Today, *jihadist* terrorist groups such as the so-called Islamic State (IS) and, maybe to a lesser extent, Al Qaeda do not have a sustained presence on Twitter. Accounts that are clearly marked as representing or supporting these organizations are quickly deleted. Maura Conway et al., *Disrupting Daesh: Measuring Takedown of Online Terrorist Material and Its Impacts* (No place: Vox-POL, 2017), http://www.voxpol.eu/download/vox-pol_publication/DCUJ5528-Disrupting-DAESH-1706-WEB-v2.pdf (accessed on 19 September 2018).
4. Zelin, "The State of Global Jihad Online," 10.
5. Torres-Soriano, "The Dynamics," 175.
6. For example, the al-Shabab al-Mujahidin Movement in Somalia created its first Twitter account in December 2011. Alexander Meleagrou-Hitchens, Shiraz Maher, and James Sheehan, "Lights, Camera, Jihad: Al-Shabaab's Western Media Strategy," The International Centre for the Study of Radicalisation and Political Violence (ISCR), 2012, 31, http://icsr.info/wp-content/uploads/2012/11/ICSR-Lights-Camera-Jihad-Report_Nov2012_ForWeb-2.pdf (accessed on 19 September 2018).
7. AQIM created its first Twitter account in March 2013. Manuel R. Torres-Soriano, "The Caliphate is Not a Tweet Away: The Social Media Experience of Al Qaeda in the Islamic Maghreb," *Studies in Conflict & Terrorism* 39, no. 11 (2016), 968–981.
8. Gunnar J. Weimann, "Between the Arab Revolutions and the Islamic State's Caliphate: Al-Qaeda Leaders' Online Propaganda 2012–2014," in *Terrorists' Use of the Internet:*

Assessment and Response, ed. Maura Conway, Lee Jarvis, Orla Lehane, Stuart Macdonald, and Lella Nouri (Amsterdam: iOS Press, 2017), 129–145.

9. Akil N. Awan and Mina al-Lami, "Al-Qa'ida's Virtual Crisis," *The RUSI Journal* 154, no. 1 (February 2009), 56–64, at 56.
10. "Internet is a battlefield for jihad, a place for missionary work, a field of confronting the enemies of God. It is upon any individual to consider himself as a media mujahid, dedicating himself, his wealth and his time for God." Al-Fajr Media Centre statement, 6 May 2011, quoted in Nico Prucha, "Online Territories of Terror—Utilizing the Internet for Jihadist Endeavors," *Orient* 52, no. 4 (2011), 43–47, at 46.
11. A precursor of this attitude is found in early *jihadist* magazines, such as the *al-Ansar* newsletter or Al Qaeda in the Arabian Peninsula (AQAP)'s *Sawt al-Jihad*, which contained sections reporting on *jihadist* activities in different conflict zones. Undoubtedly, *jihadist* online propaganda has been instrumental for fostering the global character of the *jihadist* movement.
12. This assessment is based on statements in private communications by administrators of the Ansar al-Mujahidin Network. Manuel R. Torres-Soriano, "The Hidden Face of Jihadist Internet Forum Management: The Case of Ansar Al Mujahideen," *Terrorism and Political Violence* 28 (2016), 735–749, at 741.
13. Brynjar Lia, "Jihadi Web Media Production: Characteristics, Trends, and Future Implications," Norwegian Defence Research Establishment (FFI), 2007, 12.
14. Torres-Soriano, "The Hidden Face," 743.
15. Ibid. See for example a December 2012 statement by the al-Fida' Islamic Network, announcing its return online and thanking the "technical committee" of al-Fajr Media for their support. "New Statement from al-Fidā' Arabic Forum: 'On the Occasion of the Return of al-Fidā', the Opening of Registration for One Day,'" *Jihadology*, 17 December 2012, http://jihadology.net/2012/12/17/new-statement-from-al-fida-arabic-forum-on-the-occasion-of-the-return-of-al-fida-the-opening-of-registration-for-one-day (accessed on 19 September 2018).
16. Torres-Soriano, "The Hidden Face," 740.
17. See, for example, Shaun Waterman, "Terrorists Discover uses for Twitter: Other Social Media Blocked or Limited," *The Washington Times*, 28 April 2011, http://www.washingtontimes.com/news/2011/apr/28/terrorists-discover-uses-for-twitter (accessed on 19 September 2018).
18. In a comment on ibid., Will McCants suggested that what held *jihadist* groups from using Twitter was the vulnerability of Twitter accounts, which could be easily suspended, and the highly effective system of *jihadist* forums that had evolved since 2005. Will McCants, "Why Don't Jihadi Orgs Tweet?" *Jihadica*, 30 April 2011, http://www.jihadica.com/why-dont-jihadi-orgs-tweet (accessed on 19 September 2018).
19. Nico Prucha, "IS and the Jihadist Information Highway—Projecting Influence and Religious Identity via Telegram," *Perspectives on Terrorism* 10, no. 6 (December 2016), 48–58, at 50.
20. Gabriel Weimann, "Terror and the Internet," *International Encyclopedia of the Socal & Behavioral Sciences*, 2nd edition, Volume 24, 227–236, at 231–232.
21. Nico Prucha, "Jihadi Twitter Activism—Introduction," *Jihadica*, 27 April 2013, http://www.jihadica.com/jihadi-twitter-activism-introduction (accessed on 19 September 2018).
22. Ibid.
23. Cole Bunzel, "Are the Jihadi Forums Flagging? An Ideologue's Lament," *Jihadica*, 20 March 2013, http://www.jihadica.com/are-the-jihadi-forums-flagging-an-ideologue%E2%80%99s-lament (accessed on 19 September 2018).
24. Nico Prucha and Ali Fisher, "Tweeting for the Caliphate: Twitter as the New Frontier for Jihadist Propaganda," *CTC Sentinel* 6, no. 6 (June 2013): 19–23; Ali Fisher, "Swarmcast: How Jihadist Networks Maintain a Persistent Online Presence," *Perspectives on Terrorism* 9, no. 3 (June 2015): 3–20.
25. Jabhat al-Nusra, *Bayan i'lami raqm (5): shukr wa-i'tidhar* [Media statement no. 5: thanks and apologies], al-Manara al-Bayda' Media Company, posted on 13 February 2013, https://justpaste.it/1ywj (accessed on 19 September 2018); Jabhat al-Nusra, *Bayan i'lami raqm (6):*

itlaq hisab Jabhat al-Nusra al-rasmi ala Twitter [Media statement no. 6: launch of Jabhat al-Nusra's official account on Twitter], al-Manara al-Bayda' Media Company, posted on 24 August 2013, https://justpaste.it/4iij (accessed on 19 September 2018); Jabhat al-Nusra, *Bayan i'lami raqm (7): tajdid hisab Jabhat al-Nusra al-rasmi ala Twitter wa-kalima lil-munasirin* [Media statement no. 7: renewal of Jabhat al-Nusra's official account on Twitter and a word to the supporters], al-Manara al-Bayda' Media Company, posted on 31 December 2013, https://justpaste.it/dyj8 (accessed on 19 September 2018).

26. Like supporters, members of Jabhat al-Nusra were also prohibited from speaking in the name of the group without authorization. In January 2015, Jabhat al-Nusra acknowledged the "important role played by social media platforms in the jihad arenas in general, and in the Levant arena in particular." However, the group's policies forbade its members to speak in its name. Infringement of these policies could result in trial and exclusion. In recent times, the statement continued, several members were expelled for this reason. Jabhat al-Nusra, *Bayan i'lami raqm (11)* [Media statement no. 11], al-Manara al-Bayda' Media Company, posted on 20 January 2015, https://justpaste.it/j002 (accessed on 19 September 2018).
27. Jabhat al-Nusra, *Bayan i'lami raqm (5): shukr wa-i'tidhar* [Media statement no. 5: thanks and apologies], al-Manara al-Bayda' Media Company, posted on 13 February 2013 at https://justpaste.it/1ywj (accessed on 19 September 2018).
28. Series of tweets on Himam News Agencies Twitter account (@Hemm_Agency), 7 July 2013.
29. AQAP created Ansar al-Shari'a in 2011 to operate and propagate in Yemen's tribal society. Abandoning the elitist quasi-jurisprudential rhetoric of Al Qaeda in favor of a more populist message, it created its own media outlets, including Madad News Agency, and produced propaganda aimed at Yemen's Sunni tribesmen. Christopher Swift, "Arc of Convergance: AQAP, Ansar al-Shari'a and the struggle for Yemen," *CTC Sentinel* 5, no. 6 (June 2012), 1–6.
30. Tweet on Jabhat al-Nusra's official Twitter account (@JabhtAnNusrah), 30 January 2014.
31. Its last known posting was "video report no. 94," posted on 27 August 2014.
32. Islamic State in Iraq and the Levant, *Tanwih muhimm* [Importance notice], posted on 17 August 2013, https://justpaste.it/3m0p (accessed on 19 September 2018). The group stressed this point again in an October 2013 statement. Islamic State in Iraq and the Levant, *Tanwih muhimm hawla wasa'il al-i'lam* [Important notice concerning the media], posted on 15 October 2013, https://justpaste.it/dcvp (accessed on 19 September 2018). By early 2014, at the latest, ISIL had managed to control the Twitter activities at least of its foreign fighters in areas under its control. Jytte Klausen, "Tweeting the *Jihad*: Social Media Networks of Western Foreign Fighters in Syria and Iraq," *Studies in Conflict & Terrorism* 38, no. 1 (2015), 1–22.
33. Al-I'tisam Media video *Dakk al-husun* [The destruction of forteresses], dated 21 February 2013, posted at Ansar al-Mujahidin Arabic forum (www.as-ansar.com/vb/showthread.php?p=502781) on 8 March 2013 (accessed on 19 September 2018).
34. The first installment of the series was published on 7 August 2013. The last known installment was no. 50, published on 3 March 2014. After this, al-I'tisam Media continued publishing videos, partially with extremely graphic content, until April 2015, after which it disappeared. Al-I'tisam Media's "Windows onto the land of epic battles" series was complemented by another series of videos, "Messages from the land of epic battles" (*rasa'il min ard al-malahim*), issued by ISI/ISIL's central media outlet al-Furqan Media also between August 2013 and March 2014.
35. Weimann, "Between the Arab Revolutions and the Islamic State's Caliphate," 133.
36. Jabhat al-Nusra, *Bayan i'lami raqm (10): hawla rad' al-mufsidin* [Media statement no. 10: on containing those who spread corruption], al-Manara al-Bayda' Media Company, posted on 21 July 2014, https://justpaste.it/gbni (accessed on 19 September 2018).
37. Jabhat al-Nusra, *Bayan i'lami raqm (8)* [Media statement no. 8], al-Manara al-Bayda' Media Company, posted on 4 April 2014, https://justpaste.it/ez7h (accessed on 19 September 2018).
38. Tweet on Jabhat al-Nusra's official Twitter account (@JabhtAnNusrah), 9 July 2014.

39. Lorenzo Franceschi-Bicchierai, "Twitter is Suspending Accounts that Post Images of Journalist's Beheading," *Mashable*, 20 August 2014, http://mashable.com/2014/08/20/twitter-suspends-accounts-james-foley-beheading-execution (accessed on 19 September 2018). See also Prucha, "IS and the Jihadist Information Highway," 51.
40. Europol, *Terrorism Situation and Trend Report* (TE-SAT), 2016, 16.
41. *Bayan nash wa tawdih* [Statement of advice and clarification], Ansar al-Mujahidin Network, posted on 26 September 2013 at https://justpaste.it/d7ah (accessed on 19 September 2018).
42. The English Ansar al-Mujahidin forum ceased activities in June 2015, posting a notice on its homepage, which stated that they henceforth aimed to build "the best possible media platform in support of our mujahideen brothers" in Syria. "AMEF Says It Has Shut Down In Order To Provide Media Services For Mujahideen In Syria," *MEMRI*, 18 June 2015, http://cjlab.memri.org/lab-projects/tracking-jihadi-terrorist-use-of-social-media/amef-says-it-has-shut-down-to-instead-work-on-providing-media-services-for-the-mujahideen-in-syria (accessed on 19 September 2018).
43. Shumukh al-Islam Network statement, posted on 5 January 2014, https://justpaste.it/e00s (accessed on 19 September 2018).
44. Shumukh al-Islam Network statement, posted on 10 March 2014, https://justpaste.it/ep1k (accessed on 19 September 2018).
45. Jabhat al-Nusra, *Bayan i'lami raqm (8)* [Media statement no. 8], al-Manara al-Bayda' Media Company, posted on 4 April 2014, https://justpaste.it/ez7h (accessed on 19 September 2018).
46. For several weeks following the dispute between al-Baghdadi and al-Jawlani in early April 2013, Jabhat al-Nusra suspended its continued release of official statements, apparently awaiting the decision by the Al Qaeda leader. Statement 297 appeared on 8 April 2013, with statement 298 being issued only on 14 June 2013.
47. Shumukh al-Islam statement, posted on 30 April 2014, https://justpaste.it/facf (accessed on 19 September 2018).
48. *Ahl al-hall wal-aqd* (lit. "those who loose and bind") is a traditional term referring to people of authority, in particular those who would be entitled to elect the caliph.
49. *Bayan intilaq mu'assasat al-tahaya lil-i'lam* [Statement on the launch of al-Tahaya Media Company], al-Tahaya Media Company, 7 April 2014, https://archive.org/details/tahaya_byan (accessed on 19 September 2018).
50. A collection of al-Tahaya documents uploaded to the Internet Archive in November 2015 contains 478 documents. See https://archive.org/details/tayaha.archive.
51. The most important library of *jihadist* literature, *Minbar al-Tawhid wal-Jihad*, ceased activity around the same time. This made accessing jihadist literature online more difficult.
52. *Bayan al-i'lan an intilaq al-jabha al-i'lamiyya li-nusrat al-dawla al-Islamiyya* [Statement announcing the launch of the Media Front for the Support of the Islamic State], 25 October 2014.
53. Europol, *Terrorism Situation and Trend Report* (TE-SAT) 2017, 30.
54. Also the al-Fida' Islamic Network continues online. It has remained committed to Al Qaeda and accepts new registrations.
55. Prucha, "IS and the Jihadist Information Highway," 51. In addition to networking and evading countermeasures, IS saw operational benefits in the move to Telegram, including encrypted communication and protection against cyber-attacks. Ahmad Shehabat et al., "Encrypted Jihad: Investigating the Role of Telegram App in Lone Wolf Attacks in the West," *Journal of Strategic Security* 10, no. 3 (2017), 26–53.
56. Based on a sample from early 2017, it was found that other *jihadist* groups are subject to much lower levels of disruption by Twitter compared to IS accounts. Maura Conway et al., *Disrupting Daesh*.

A Dialectical Approach to Online Propaganda: Australia's United Patriots Front, Right-Wing Politics, and Islamic State

Imogen Richards

ABSTRACT

This article examines how the United Patriots Front (UPF), an Australian far-right organization, has communicated its ideology with reference to right-wing politics in Australia, Western Europe, and the United States, and through allusions to Islamic State. The investigation uses critical discourse and documentary analysis and a framework derived from the theory of Pierre Bourdieu to analyze textual and audiovisual postings on UPF Facebook pages, YouTube channels, and Twitter accounts. Relevant to the discussion are Bourdieu's interdependent theories on "doxa" as a condition in which socially constructed phenomena appear self-evident, and "habitus" and "field," which explain how structures and agents, through their reflexive behavior, become dialectically situated.

In recent years there has been an intensification and growth of right-wing nationalism and far-right extremism in Australia and internationally. Where right-wing politics has historically been characterized by heterogeneous elements, determined by sociopolitical context, in contemporary environments it has entailed social conservatism, law and order politics, and the promotion of a survival-of-the-fittest ethic.[1] Individuals and organizations that espouse far-right ideological sentiments, including nationalism, xenophobia, anti-parliamentarianism, and an advocacy of militaristic governance, have justified their extreme political positions with reference to a number of geopolitical events. These include the ongoing Syrian civil war that broke out in 2011, the evolution of the transnational terrorist organization Islamic State (IS) in 2013, and IS's June 2014 declaration of their so-called Caliphate. Included too is political unrest in Africa and the Middle East, which collectively catalyzed what was described in 2015 as the "European migrant crisis." The United Nations Office of the High Commissioner for Refugees found when reporting on this "crisis" that in 2015, 65.3 million people were displaced; the highest number on record.[2]

In combination with IS-inspired and directed attacks, and deleterious international economic conditions that followed the 2008 Global Financial Crisis,[3] popular anxiety regarding intensified migration has been manipulated by leaders of far-right movements to garner support and sympathy for their causes. Reflecting the increasingly global twenty-first-century flows of people, goods, and services in part made possible by the

Internet, right-wing and far-right groups have embraced social media to propagandize, recruit, and coordinate operations. In response to this situation, this article explores how an Australian far-right organization, the United Patriots Front (UPF), has used social media to bolster its public appeal since its establishment in May 2015. The article uses critical discourse and documentary methods to analyze propaganda produced by high profile members of the UPF, through a lens of dialectical theory deriving from the work of sociologist Pierre Bourdieu. It examines how the organization, via its core membership, attempts to legitimize its political orientation through dialectical interactions with domestic and international politics, and with IS. The article is divided into four parts: the first part reviews relevant literature; part two supplies a background of the UPF; the third section outlines a research design including methods and theoretical framework; while the final section provides an empirical account of the UPF's social media activity.

Propaganda, the Social Media Environment, and Far-Right Activity Online

While "network" literature has for some time addressed strategic uses of the Internet by organizations and individuals with extremist ideologies, it has not typically explored the explicit role of propaganda, or adopted a comparative analytical approach to extremist media. Despite this, certain aspects of network theory are useful and relevant for understanding this article's analysis. Perhaps most important is Manuel Castells's theory that the Internet led to "a new mode of development, *informationalism*, of which networking is the critical attribute."[4] Also relevant is Douglas Kellner's adaptation of "actor-network" theory in which he proposes that individuals and organizations with non-mainstream ideals can overcome "the limitations of post-modern identity politics" via means of connectivity afforded by the Internet.[5] To conceptualize the function and effects of far-right propaganda in contemporary societies, this article reflects on theories of informationalism and connectivity, in combination with Jean Baudrillard's ideas. Specifically, the analysis draws from Baudrillard's assertion that in contemporary digital media, extreme and violent events can become "hyperreal"; that is, more "real" to the viewer than reality itself.[6] This is integral to the functioning of extremist propaganda, which is here understood in line with Bruce Smith's definition as a "more or less systematic effort to manipulate other people's beliefs, attitudes, or actions by means of symbols (words, gestures, banners, monuments, music, clothing, insignia, hairstyles, designs on coins and postage stamps and so forth) (https://www.britannica.com/topic/propaganda)."[7]

Regarding the impact of online propaganda, the analysis considers Walter Laqueur's assertion that the effect of hyperreality is compounded by users' engagement with the Internet, whereby they experience dislocation, immediacy, and subject conflation, within environments of time-space compression.[8] In line with Christian Fuchs's understanding of digital spaces, it interprets these conditions as being more pronounced in social media than in other online settings.[9] The unique effects of social media propaganda are empirically evidenced by the reality that social media content is accessible, it provides a low entry point for users, and the fact that it proliferates, mutates, and is remediated via interactions afforded by platforms, such as the Facebook, YouTube and Twitter functions of "likes," "shares," and "retweets."[10]

Given the comparative focus of this article, and its attention to social media environments, it is worth noting that, while the "informational" and "networked" social media activity of Islamist groups, (or "jihadist," as the nonreligious and violent politicization of Islam), such as Al Qaeda and IS has been explored by critics including Gabriel Weimann[11] and Jytte Klausen,[12] there has been a lack of similar consideration for how far-right social media operates. There has also been a lack of attention to online dialectics of communication that exist between far-right groups and other political entities such as IS, and the impact this has on these entities' usage of propagandized persuasion. Despite this, insight may be gained by reflecting on studies that compare the online activity of far-right groups and other entities from thematic and subcultural perspectives.

In several examples, Ryan Shaffer,[13] Daniela Pisoiu,[14] and Juris Pupcenoks and Ryan McCabe[15] explored evidence of thematic relationships between Islamist violence and right-wing extremism, and their strategic implications. In their respective studies, these authors explained that the themes of xenophobia and religious fanaticism common to far-right and Islamist groups, as evidenced by their online and offline actions, can fuel recursive violence and become mutually reinforcing. Others such as Lorraine Bowman-Grieve,[16] Jose Pedro Zuquete,[17] and Michael Suttmoeller and his co-authors[18] have highlighted the distinct subcultural and strategic characteristics of online far-right organizations, including their community support for one another, strategies of global collaboration, and the correlation between mediatized violence and far-right organizational longevity. J. M. Berger has also shown that while IS has been more active on Twitter than other extremist organizations, the platform has become an increasingly important means of disseminating internationally resonant messages by the infamous (and first dedicated online) White nationalist discussion forum, Stormfront.[19]

Within the Australian context, Amelia Johns's political–economic analysis of White nationalism has been particularly useful in explicating the importance of symbolism in far-right media; in particular the persuasive effects of political symbols such as the Australian flag and the beach; although her account does not consider how discursive or dialectical techniques are used coterminously by far-right organizations.[20] On the other hand, Geoff Dean and his co-authors' mixed-method account of discursive themes present in Australia's far-right social media—such as "western values" and "anti-establishmentarism"—while comprehensive, does not elaborate on how the communicative methods employed by these groups can function as propaganda and foster far-right sympathies.[21]

Differing from the above literature, this article focuses on propaganda produced by the UPF organization from a dialectical perspective, in relation to IS and the broader right-trending political field in which it operates. The analysis highlights that UPF propaganda entails discursive and audiovisual social media that is constituted in part by its interaction with other political entities. Specifically, it argues that UPF media is reflexive and mirrors the stated values of both far-right politicians, and in certain respects, the jihadist organization, IS. Before the theoretical framework for the analysis is explained, the following section of this article provides a brief background of the UPF.

The UPF

The UPF can be understood as "far-right" given its members' opposition to Islam, race-based reasoning, critique of egalitarianism, and militaristic posturing. Extremism within the organization is also illuminated by the criminal histories of the UPF's core membership, and by their respective affiliations with neo-Nazism, although they have claimed, perhaps unconvincingly, to reject neo-Nazi expression and values. It is necessary to note initially that the organization emerged in May 2015 when it split from Reclaim Australia (Reclaim). Reclaim opposes Halal certification, "Islamic extremism," and what the organization perceives as "minority groups who want to change the Australian cultural identity."[22] Social media personality Shermon Burgess, aka "The Great Aussie Patriot," founded the UPF, and in a YouTube video posted to Facebook in May 2015 described the organization as:

> More hardline nationalist compared to some other groups that are more democratic anti-Islam. Now the problem with democratic anti-Islam is a lot of these movements without even realizing it can be diluted, watered down and become politically correct themselves.[23]

Prior to the UPF, in April 2014, when Burgess was active in Reclaim and another far-right organization, the Australian Defense League (ADL), he released a song that referenced the 11 December 2005 New South Wales "Cronulla Riots," in which approximately 5,000 people gathered near a Sydney beach to stage violent protests (with placards displaying the phrases "ethnic cleansing" and "take Australia back"), against Lebanese and Egyptian migrants living in Australia, leading to a series of physical attacks. At a trial for those involved on 19 July 2006, 104 people were charged with 285 offenses, including rioting, assaulting police, threatening violence, and possession of a prohibited weapon.[24] In a September 2014 YouTube video, the leader of the ADL, Ralph Cerminara, threatened another Cronulla-style attack, declaring that Australian "mosques and prayer rooms are going to burn."[25] Evoking similar sentiments, Burgess's song "Border Patrol" featured the lyrics:

> We're sick of your Sharia, burn your fucking mosques, it's time to show you muzzrats we're the fucking boss, you thought you had it easy, but you surely lost, Cronulla was Australia's Muslim holocaust.[26]

Beyond Burgess's early social media notoriety, the UPF's most notorious acts include a 10 October 2015 rally led by Burgess in Bendigo against the proposed building of a mosque. It drew over 1,000 demonstrators from around the country and was held in Rosalind Park on the same day as the World Wide Rally for Humanity, an international anti-Islam protest coordinated by Jon Ritzheimer in Phoenix.[27] The rally was preceded by an incident in which three core members of the UPF, Blair Cottrell, Neil Erikson, and Chris Shortis, filmed and broadcast on Facebook the beheading of a dummy filled with fake blood outside of the Bendigo City Council, in protest of the mosque and what they perceived as the broader "Islamization of Australia."[28] Since its inception, the UPF central Facebook page has displayed the by-line: "Australia's political resistance against the spread of Islam and far-Left treason!"

In October 2015, Burgess posted videos to YouTube and Facebook announcing that he was leaving the UPF due to his outrage that members of the group had mocked his "tough man" image and the fact that his videos were broadcast from his mother's basement. At the time, the UPF had around 19,000 followers on Facebook; however, it was gaining momentum by campaigning off the back of protests staged by other far-right organizations including Reclaim and the ADL. As with other far-right movements internationally, such as the American Nazi Party,[29] the UPF was beset by infighting, with Erikson departing due, he claimed, to corrupting "neo-Nazi" elements infiltrating the UPF,[30] and Shortis side-lined for asserting in videos and interviews that Australia must remain a "white nation."[31]

Divisions within the UPF left Blair Cottrell and Tom Sewell as the two remaining founders, with Cottrell as ranking chairman. Subsequently, Perth man Dennis Huts joined Cottrell and Sewell and became a prominent UPF spokesperson. Although Cottrell posted several videos announcing the dissolution of the UPF and his own abdication of leadership, he continued to act as the primary administrator of the UPF Facebook page and make statements as leader. At the time of its deletion by Facebook at the apparent behest of Australian intelligence agencies on 9 May 2017,[32] the UPF page had over 120,000 "likes." On 10 April 2017 Cottrell had declared during an Australian Broadcasting Corporation (ABC) interview on their Four Corners television program:

> Facebook's been extremely effective for us; it's, ah, indispensable to the development of our organization ... without it, we would probably be a separatist cult where no one would be able to relate to us because no one would be able to actually hear us directly ... they would only hear about us through established media corporations.[33]

During the time of Cottrell's leadership, high profile UPF incidents included an occasion in April 2016 when the organization displayed banners with the message "stop the Mosques" at an Australia Football League game.[34] In November 2016, in collaboration with the far-right True Blue Crew organization, the UPF also held a pro–Donald Trump rally in celebration of the U.S. Federal election, where Cottrell asserted that Trump's win was a "victory for the West."[35] In September 2015, the UPF announced their establishment of a political party called Fortitude, and pledged to register in Australia's 2016 Federal Election, however; they failed to raise the requisite 500 electoral votes.[36] The Fortitude website explains:

> The UPF in the beginning took a strong and public stance against further Islamic immigration, further building of mosques etc. This sparked outrage from among the egalitarian social circles, the adherents to which can be found at any time in their dwellings: State Universities, local institutions of government, news and journalistic organs and anywhere else in Australia where there is money & [*sic*] influence but no real work.[37]

In addition to demonstrations and campaigning, the UPF engaged in borderline criminal activity, including harassing attendants at a community cultural organization and site where left-wing anti-fascist activists gather; Melbourne's 3CR radio station and the Melbourne Anarchist Club (MAC), respectively.[38] Other criminal connections include when Victoria Police found a copy of the bomb-making manual, the *Anarchist Cookbook,* and related materials, in the home of UPF member Phillip Galea, and charged him with possession of a prescribed chemical and prohibited weapon,[39] three days before a UPF anti-mosque rally was scheduled to be held in Melton on 22 November 2015. In April 2017, Galea was charged with "collecting or making documents to prepare for a terrorist act" and "doing acts in preparation for a terrorist act," with police alleging that he placed an order for explosive chemicals, researched bomb-making techniques, and discussed bombing the MAC between 2015 and 2016.[40] In February 2014, the ostensibly anti-Nazi ex-UPF member, Erikson, was convicted of stalking and harassing Rabbi Dovid Gutnick of Melbourne City Synagogue, threatening: "give me the money Jew or else I will get you"; among other faith-based insults.[41] In the years prior to the establishment of the UPF, Cottrell had been fined $3,000 for driving offenses and served time in prison for aggravated burglary, arson, possessing a controlled weapon, breaching court orders, and trafficking testosterone.[42] Finally, on 23 May 2017, Cottrell, Erikson, and Shortis appeared before the Melbourne Magistrates Court. They were charged with a number of offenses relating to publishing the aforementioned "beheading" video, including "the intention of inciting serious contempt for, or revulsion or severe ridicule" of Muslims.[43]

Since the removal of the UPF's official Facebook page, and twenty-three affiliated accounts, Cottrell has intensified his individual social media output on Facebook, Twitter, and YouTube. At the time of this article's writing, Cottrell's new Facebook page has 3,391 "likes" (although his pages are repeatedly removed), while he has 18,853 followers on Twitter. This output, along with that of other UPF leaders prominent at various points in the organization's history, is the subject of this article's investigation.

Research Design

Methodology

Primary data for this article were collected by two means: through an empirical method and by accessing a number of open sources. In the empirical method, the researcher accessed and compiled social media examples that related to the research interest in "IS" and "Right-wing Politics" produced and distributed by former and present UPF members, Blair Cottrell, Shermon Burgess, Neil Erikson, Chris Shortis, and Thomas Sewell, on accounts that these individuals owned, between May 2015 and June 2017. Material related to these themes was searched for across Twitter, YouTube, Instagram, and Facebook during this time period. Audiovisual and textual media posted on the UPF central Facebook page, "United Patriots Front," during this period was also accessed via Facebook prior to the removal of the page on 9 May 2017. Following this time, data were collected by accessing cached versions of the Facebook page on the search engines Yahoo!, Google, and Bing. Relevant material was accessed by searching for "site: Facebook 'United Patriots Front'" in combination with the keywords of "Le Pen," "Merkel," "Trump," "France," "UK," "Europe," "America," and "Islam." Screenshots of audiovisual and textual media relevant to the analysis were then uploaded and coded using the qualitative research data collection and analysis software NVivo, for the key themes of "UPF & Western Europe," "UPF & the U.S.," and "UPF & IS."

In the second part of the data collection, supplementary material was gathered from a number of open-access sources and added to the initial dataset. These sources include the blog of the anti-fascist activist who goes by the pseudonym Andy Fleming (aka

"Slackbastard"), research findings published in the book, *Depends What You Mean By Extremist* (2017) by Melbourne author John Safran, and examples from news media sources, including primarily material distributed by the ABC. After these data were coded according to the themes previously stated, the complete textual and audiovisual data set was re-coded using an axial approach for cross-sectional criteria related to Bourdieu's theory. These criteria are explained in the theoretical framework section below and include: "Right-trending Political Field," "Far-right Habitus," and "Islamophobic Doxa." Although the theoretical definitions and descriptors applied to UPF data may not perfectly characterize the social media examples examined, the approach was underwritten with an interpretivist methodology less concerned with quantifying a scientific basis for comparison than with exploring how Bourdieu's dialectical theory might help illuminate some under-explored aspects of far-right propaganda.[44]

In the analysis, coded textual and audiovisual UPF propaganda artifacts were interpreted using critical discourse and documentary analysis. The analysis drew from Norman Fairclough's interpretation of critical inquiry as "relational," "dialectical," and "transdisciplinary."[45] In line with the comparative focus of this article, the methodology is concerned with the nature of social relations, rather than with distinct individuals or entities. It is dialectical in the sense that "no one object or element (such as discourse) can be analyzed other than in terms of its dialectical relations with others."[46] It is transdisciplinary given that the interplay between the empirical data set of media, its contextual political environment, and the philosophical framework of dialectics, is itself a subject and source of interest to the analysis. The analysis is therefore concerned with the relationships that exists between frames of orientation, the semantic interactions between the entities examined, and the domestic and international political environment in which UPF propaganda operates. The following section outlines the explicit sociological interpretation of Bourdieu's dialectics relevant herein, before it is applied in the analytical sections.

Theoretical framework: Doxa, Habitus, and Field

To understand how UPF propaganda operates within domestic and international political settings, this article interprets the material examined through a framework that derives from the work of Pierre Bourdieu. Of particular relevance are Bourdieu's interdependent theories of doxa, habitus, and field. Where "doxa" represents a condition in which socially constructed phenomena appear self-evident, the "habitus" and "field" explain how structures and agents, through their reflexive behavior, become dialectically situated. Applying these concepts, the analysis explores the extent to which a UPF habitus, as enacted through its key agents, operates in a dialectical relationship with an internationally expanding field of right-wing politics. It then considers how an additional dialectic exists between UPF propaganda and ideologies associated with IS. Collectively, these interactions are interpreted as related to a condition of "doxa," in which proliferating Islamophobia, in connection with right-wing politics, is increasingly normalized, expected, and tolerated.

In line with Bourdieu's description of the concept, "habitus" in this article refers to the psychological dispositions of individuals, which derive from their education, upbringing, and subjective life experiences, and serve as motivators for their future actions.[47] Although the habitus is created by the interplay between subjective free will and objective structural constraints, and is therefore not generalizable across groups of people, a "shared" habitus, which is nuanced within different actors, may evolve in certain situations.[48] Importantly, this is not the same as a "collective consciousness" which, in the Durkheimian sense, connotes "a system of collective beliefs and practices that have special authority."[49] Rather, the habitus, whether it be shared or individual, is in a constant process of re-negotiation, as determined by dialectical interactions with other agents and with the field in which it operates. Drawing from Bourdieu's description of habitus as "a structuring structure, which organizes around practices and the perception of practices,"[50] the concept is here applied to explain the right-wing and far-right political orientation that becomes manifest in the propaganda practices of the UPF. It is explored through reference to the discursive and audiovisual social media produced by key former and present UPF members.[51]

Also drawing from Bourdieu's theory, this article interprets the "field" as the arena in which agents compete for political, social, and economic capital, via their expression of habitus. The concept is summarized by Bourdieu as: "a system of deviations on different levels and nothing, either in the institutions or in the agents, the acts or discourses they produce, has meaning except relationally, by virtue of the interplay of oppositions and distinctions."[52] By virtue of its interdependency with the expressions of habitus, the field is likewise constituted by a series of dialectical interactions between structures and agents. Distributions of capital within the field are also inextricable with the means by which the habitus is formed, rendering actions and events, and agency and structure, endlessly relational.

Diverging from Hegel's interpretation of dialectics, which saw interactions between entities produce a series of events in which opposing entities would destroy and replace one another in a series of "moments" (i.e., thesis–antithesis–synthesis),[53] Bourdieu contended that through their dialectical interactions, opposing entities mutate and merge in ways that form new paradigmatic situations.[54] It is with reference to this self-perpetuating process of response, mutation, and mimicry that this article conceptualizes and articulates the concepts of "reflexivity" and "mirroring" to explain dialectical components of UPF social media. As mentioned, the analysis considers how UPF propaganda is reflexive of and mirrors the acts and discourses produced by political actors in a field of right-trending politics, and on the part of IS. This situation is interpreted as strategically significant, given that the UPF and other far-right groups erroneously conflate IS with Islam, and use the organization as a foil to justify their xenophobic, far-right tendencies. Further to this, the analysis argues that such dialectical interactions occur within a broader political–philosophical "doxa" of tolerated, normalized, and expected Islamophobia. As explained by Bourdieu in *Outline of a Theory of Practice*, the doxa itself represents "an adherence to relations of order which, because they structure inseparably both the real world and the thought world, are accepted as self-evident."[55]

The next section of this article considers how the habitus and social media practices of influential, high-profile, past and present members of the UPF operate within a field of internationally prevalent right-wing politics. It considers that, although right-wing movements around the world are intrinsically concerned with political and socioeconomic conditions unique to their host nations, these differences are overlooked in UPF propaganda, to the effect that a relatively homogenous doxa is reinforced, predicated on Islamophobia. A field analysis is initially undertaken in preparation for the subsequent discussion, which considers how UPF social media evokes an international array of right-wing, anti-immigration, and anti-Islam sentiments, in order to legitimize its extreme political orientation.

The International Political Field

Of significant import to a study of the contemporary right-wing political field, and the reinforcement of an Islamophobic doxa within this field, are international anti-immigration debates that occurred during the time period this article examines, including the rhetoric of U.S. President Donald Trump preceding and following his election to office on 8 November 2016. Notorious in Trump's campaign was his call for "a total and complete shutdown of Muslims entering the United States until our country's representatives can figure out what the hell is going on."[56] Also relevant was his Reagan-esque pledge to "Make America great again" by building a wall between Mexico and the United States, and instantiation of protectionist economic policies in the form of reduced international diplomatic collaboration and severe tariffs on foreign direct investment. Indicating his nationalistic militarism, Trump also promised increased U.S. spending on defense, and admonished North American Treaty Organization partners for not having increased their own respective defense budgets.

Trump's rise to power reflects an international trend of electoral success of right-wing parties. While thus far few ultra-right-wing parties have assumed power in Western Europe, there are noteworthy exceptions. These include the anti-immigration Swiss People's Party, which received the largest share of the vote in the country's Parliamentary elections in October 2015, in what was described as "the best performance by a party in at least a century."[57] They also include the Progress Party in Norway, which won in 2013 with 16.3 percent,[58] the National Alliance in Latvia, which won in 2014 with 16.6 percent,[59] the Finns Party in Finland who rose to power with 17.7 percent in 2015,[60] and the victory of the Belgian New Flemish Alliance in 2014 with 20.3 percent.[61]

Beyond elected governments, internationally occurring sympathy toward an expanding field of right-wing nationalism is evidenced by growing public support for far-right political entities. Such entities include the Greek Golden Dawn party, which came third in Greece's September 2015 election, and whose spokesman Ilias Kasidiaris bears a swastika tattoo and denies the official history of the Holocaust.[62] Under the infamous leadership of Geert Wilders, the burgeoning Party for Freedom in the Netherlands spearheaded a call for the country to leave the European Union, while Wilders asserted: "Islam is not a religion, it's an ideology, the ideology of a retarded culture."[63] Also far-right, and remarked upon almost as frequently as Trump in Western media, is Marine le Pen's far-right National Front Party, which was defeated in a high-profile race in France on 23 April and 7 May 2017.[64]

Although le Pen and other political figures have historically denounced "imperialists" and communicated anti-American sentiments, they have recently expressed solidarity with the Trump administration in the U.S. At a January 2017 gathering of far-right leaders in Koblenz, attended by Wilders, Le Pen, Frauke Petry of the Alternative for Germany (AFD), and Matteo Salvini of Italy's Northern League, Wilders announced their collectivized support for Trump's policy platform with the Twitter hashtag #WeWillMakeOurCountriesGreatAgain.[65]

UPF Social Media

Within an expanding field of right-wing politics, over Facebook, Twitter, and YouTube, UPF members have expressed a far-right habitus by evoking the rhetoric and ideologies of European and U.S. politicians. Specifically, UPF members draw from these international movements not only to articulate their anti-Islam, anti-immigration principles, but also to legitimize their extreme political position. Through a series of dialectical interactions, within a field of right-trending populism, the far-right orientation of high-profile UPF members becomes enacted and re-inscribed through social media practices, in turn reinforcing for their audience, the "self-evident" nature of the Islamophobic political field in which their media operates.

In addition to supporting Trump at the aforementioned Melbourne rally, for instance, UPF members have endorsed Trump's right-wing ideals via reflexive mimicry, and by engaging with U.S. political themes. Of all UPF individuals examined in this article, overt mimicry is perhaps most apparent in the social media activity of Neil Erikson. On 3 January and 24 May 2017, for example, Erikson displayed Facebook profile pictures bearing the slogan: "Trump: Make America Great Again" and featuring him wearing Trump merchandise including campaign hats. Previously, on 27 October 2016, Erikson uploaded a black and white Donald Trump Facebook cover photo.[66]

Demonstrating UPF members' thematic endorsement of Trump's campaigns, the organization's central Facebook page hosted news media headlines and articles that referred to domestic U.S. politics. On 24 March 2016, for instance, the UPF Facebook administrator posted news from the Moscow-owned Russia Today (RT), with the slogan: "Trump shuts down Merkel in recent meeting—'immigration is a privilege, not a right.'"[67] On 25 May 2017 over Facebook and Twitter, Cottrell re-posted an image taken of himself at the previously discussed Victorian court hearing by Australia's Rupert Murdoch–owned MSN Channel 9 News, bearing the caption: "The Trump Smile: When you're surrounded by cameras, lies and stupidity, but you know you're going to win so it's all good."[68] Elsewhere, Cottrell has recited Trump's emphasis on global media, corporate elites, and an alleged proliferation of "fake news."[69] As "The Great Aussie Patriot," Shermon Burgess also infamously demonstrated support for U.S. law and order policies. Evoking the country's right-wing rhetoric, Burgess declared early in the UPF's history that the organization would run for Senate, with the comment: "Shit yeah, Aussie's [sic] will have the right to bare [sic] arms again if UPF gets into a position where we can make this law change."[70]

Another high-profile political figure who has been inspirational to the UPF, and cited extensively in the organization's propaganda, is Marine le Pen. On 23 February 2017, for example, the UPF Facebook administrator posted a link to an article by right-wing Australian shock-jock Andrew Bolt criticizing Foreign Minister Julie Bishop's decision to wear a headscarf in Iran, with the caption: "Marine le Pen, you are welcome in Australia anytime, in fact you can replace Julie Bishop if you like."[71] Later, on 9 March 2017, the administrator shared a news article with the title: "Marine le Pen savages Angela Merkel to her face in EU Parliament," "to which they added the comment, 'excellent'".[72] Demonstrating the organization's related anti-Parliamentarism, on 23 February 2017 Cottrell commented via his Twitter handle: "in Parliamentary politics, the women have more balls than the men" and tagged @marinelepen.[73] Furthermore, indicating a conflation of solidarity for le Pen with far-right anti-Semitism, on 8 May 2017, former UPF leader Shermon Burgess uploaded a video to YouTube entitled "Emmanuel Macron is a Rothschild globalist" with the description: "The French people went full retard and just voted for their own cultural genocide. Emmanuel Macro [sic] is a Rothschild agent who works for the corporate banking elite."[74]

Beyond endorsing specific political parties, UPF members have also demonstrated an organizational awareness of their subjective positioning within the broader field of right-trending politics and social media. From a Bourdieuian perspective, this may be considered to reflect the notion that a shared habitus itself is not solely deterministic; it operates within a field in which there are certain common understandings of the "rules of the game."[75] In a YouTube video entitled "Explaining Propaganda," for example, Cottrell outlines that propaganda itself is neither inherently "good nor bad," but that it is "essential, indispensable in fact, in any system of government, in any political party, in any business."[76] In "Weaponized Words," another video on the same channel, Cottrell qualifies his justification for right-wing propaganda tactics, imploring supporters to "follow the patriot movements … we are one hundred percent truth and reality, and for this reason, we must prevail over all the fucking bullshit in the world."[77]

The organization's observance of a transnational expanding right-trending populism is also reinforced by UPF members' acknowledgment of prevalent right-wing political sentiments. On 30 May 2017, for example, Cottrell (in addition to Burgess and Erikson elsewhere), published a capture of a Murdoch-owned SkyNews tweet in which Australian Senator Malcolm Roberts was quoted saying: "we believe Islam is a way of structuring a society, in many ways that's the same as socialism and communism."[78] In an example of the UPF's engagement with Eurocentric nationalism, Cottrell posted a video to both Facebook and YouTube expressing sympathy with victims in the aftermath of the November 2015 Al Qaeda massacre at the French satirical magazine *Charlie Hebdo*. In the video, he declared:

> We're here at the French consulate in Melbourne … we're here for France, because we are France. We all come from Europe in one way or another, which makes Europe our mother, and when you hurt our mother, you hurt us too. We all feel it, because we are all linked in spirit. We are Europe. The son of France, the son of Europa.[79]

As Melbourne author John Safran recalled, the French consulate posted a photograph of Cottrell at the scene to their Web page, before it was removed an hour later.[80]

On this point it is useful to note that broad-based political commentary expressed by UPF members indicates their dialectical interaction with a field of far-right ideologies, beyond literal mimicry and thematic reference. Several UPF members have also engaged in reflexive identity politics comparable to those of other international far-right organizations. From a Bourdieuian perspective, identity politics within the habitus of UPF members serve as both "classificatory principles as well as being the organizing principles of action."[81] While there are numerous examples of this, it is in particular worth briefly explicating the UPF's dialectical interaction with the politics of a high-profile group that, like the UPF, has recently gained political traction—the "Identitarians."

The Identitarians are a far-right, pan-European collective that originated as "Generation Identitaire" in France, and now maintains contingents under similar names in Germany, Austria, and the Netherlands. A prominent Identitarian figure is the 27-year-old Viennese Martin Sellner, who advocates building "camps" around Europe to house "legitimate refugees," in order to ensure the preservation of traditional European "cultural identities."[82] Indicating the Identitiarians' social media savvy, Sellner created a smart phone application modeled on the GPS tracking services of dating applications, which enables "patriots" who pledge allegiance to the organization to identify one another.[83]

Tangible connections between the UPF and the Identitarians are demonstrated by Cottrell's numerous YouTube video references to "cultural identity," his claims that Australians have lost their "identity," and his general conflation of race-based politics and civilizational thinking with nationalism and cultural pride. Additionally, the symbol of the UPF, and its political party Fortitude, is starkly reminiscent of the Identitarians' symbol. With yellow and black markings in the shape of a triangle surrounded by a circle, they collectively recall the Lambda, which was once painted on the shields of the Spartan Army, and is often interpreted to represent the Battle of Thermopylae.[84]

Indicating the classificatory nature of the shared habitus, and its historical origins, both the Identitarians and the UPF engage with anti-Semitism. Sellner was previously affiliated with extremist Austrian figures, who in 2010 and 2011 were subject to arrests and search warrants.[85] An early example of the UPF's neo-Nazi connections is a YouTube video posted mid-2015 in which the producers profess "solidarity" with the Greek neo-fascist movement Golden Dawn.[86] Other examples include Shermon Burgess's post on 24 May 2017, entitled "Poland. The True Beacon of Light for White European Survival,"[87] in which he spoke at length about how Israel is "here to destroy white Europe," while advocating Poland's Euroscepticism, its burgeoning far-right voting bloc, and related demonstrations. These include May and November 2015 rallies that saw 200,000 and 75,000 people, respectively, march in Warsaw against immigration, a large contingent of whom were brandishing iron crosses and shouting profanities with reference to the Quran.

At this point, it is worth briefly recalling how the individual habitus of UPF members reflects a broader habitus that extends beyond the organization, or what Bourdieu described as a "conscience collective,"[88] and in line with his theory, is transposable: it can act across religious and political settings. In other words, the UPF members' habitus resonates with an organizational political philosophy that is also shared by members of like groups. From a Bourdieuian perspective, this represents a mutable and "immediate adherence to the tastes and distastes, sympathies and aversions, fantasies and phobias" that, to a greater extent than explicit and considered reasoning, "forges unconscious unity" between societal organizations.[89] In the case of the UPF and comparable groups internationally, the mutability of a right-wing habitus predicated on phobia and aversion is specifically reflected in these groups' transition from politics based on anti-Semitism to those based on Islamophobia. To ascertain the nature of this transition with respect to the UPF, it is useful to briefly reflect on distinctly anti-Semitic and neo-Nazi ideals that are discernible in the leaders' historical social media behavior.

Neo-Nazism

Chief among evidence of the UPF's early collective habitus of neo-Nazism are its interpersonal associations. As the antifascist activist, Andy Fleming, aka "Slackbastard," has revealed, Erikson was variously photographed meeting infamous Canadian Holocaust denier Paul Fromm, at a musical performance by the neo-Nazi Hammerskins organization in Melbourne in October 2011; at the Geert Wilders meeting at the La Mirage Receptions in Somerton, Victoria in February 2013 during which several neo-Nazi figures were present; and at an anti-Muslim rally with well-known Australian White supremacists outside the Victoria State Library in September 2012.[90] Indicating the prevalence of such sentiments within the organization, a post on Cottrell's Instagram page displays founders and leaders of the group, Sewell and Cottrell, in the company of three other men, celebrating Adolf Hitler's birthday at a German Restaurant in Melbourne, while making a pinched thumb and forefinger sign;[91] a gesture that Cottrell is making in his current Twitter photo, and which the group publicly acknowledged has become recently associated with White supremacy.

In another example of the UPF's early neo-Nazi sympathies, and as a Bourdieuian habitus of "embodied history, internalized as second nature and so forgotten as history,"[92] Thomas Sewell publicly advocated unity between "patriots" and "neo-Nazis" before the video was removed after an hour from the UPF Facebook page by administrators. As mentioned, Burgess, who professes to be anti-Nazi, has also endorsed the Holocaust in connection with anti-Islamic violence. Since his departure from the UPF, Burgess continues to publish YouTube videos about "The Real Holocaust" of Anglo-Saxon populations, and the corruption of the "Zionist" banking system, while publicly subscribing to YouTube channels, including: "White is Beautiful."[93] In a more militant tone, Shortis has preached anti-Islamic sentiments in online videos while brandishing firearms. He has been likened to Norwegian White supremacist and far-right terrorist Anders Breivik, and since leaving the UPF has joined the White separatist Australia First Party.[94] This party is spearheaded by Jim Saleam, who was incarcerated for 3 years for coordinating a shotgun attack on the home of Sydney's African National Congress (ANC) representative in 1989.[95]

Insofar as Cottrell himself can be connected to neo-Nazi ideologies, it is useful to reflect again on evidence compiled by Fleming. Most compelling are a series of Facebook posts where Cottrell commented on a photo of Adolf Hitler: "there should be a picture of this man in every classroom and every school and his book [*Mein Kampf*] should be issued to every student annually."[96] As Fleming's screenshots reveal, Cottrell has made a number of anti-Semitic remarks over social media, including that: "the modern woman is corrupted, not inherently evil. Jews are parasites, women are just one of their hosts" and, interestingly, "the Jews are as small physically as they are degenerate in character … enjoy your bullying of the lesser nation of Palestine while you can, because the white races are coming for you."[97] Although it falls outside of the time period this article examines, in another relevant example, the former leader of the UPF, Shermon Burgess, expressed his overt endorsement of Nazi values with a Twitter posting on 2 July 2017 in which he states: "3 WORDS—Hitler Was Right!"[98]

Indicating the classificatory nature of the habitus, and its socially stratifying orientation, UPF social media postings variously demonstrate that leaders have further endorsed neo-Nazi sentiments on an organizational basis. A noteworthy example of this is a video entitled "My Aryan," produced by Dennis Huts, the leader of the UPF Perth branch. As John Safran relates in *Depends What You Mean By Extremist*, in the video, Huts states of his two daughters: "I love their whiteness … their blond hair. One of them's got green eyes. I love that about them! I love their racial features … "[99]

Australian Politics

To understand the domestic field of right-trending politics in which UPF propaganda operates, it is useful to address how the Bourdieuian field's "hierarchy of power relations,"[100] expressed through Australia's parliamentary system, encourages a normalization and doxa of Islamophobic politics. Moreover, it is also relevant to note that this field is contiguous with international right-wing political environments. The Australian Liberty Alliance (ALA), for instance, was launched by Geert Wilders in October 2015 at a secret Perth location. Its policies include banning face coverings, removing Australia from the UN Refugee Convention, and introducing a ten-year moratorium on visa applications by people from Muslim countries.[101] After the Liberal Party's poor performance in the 2016 Federal elections, Liberal and Nationals Members for Parliament (MPs) have been observed as leaving in large numbers to join the ALA.[102]

As mentioned, the Australia First Party (AFP) is directed by convicted offender Dr. Jim Saleam, who was incarcerated for inciting violence on an ANC member. Indicating the extension of far-right extremism in Australia to mainstream political and intellectual arenas, it is worth noting that he earned a Ph.D. from the University of Sydney for his study of the rise of right-wing nationalist populism in Australia, and infamously announced: "the racist label doesn't bother me."[103] Core policies of the AFP include reinstating the White Australia policy and ending migration to Australia for everyone except for White Europeans.

Another well-known example of Australia's right-wing political figures that normalize and reinforce political inequality is the longest-serving member of the New South Wales Parliament, the eighty-two-year-old conservative Christian Democratic Party MP, Reverend Fred Nile. Nile has variously claimed that homosexuality is a "mental disorder" and declared his wish for a ten-year ban on Muslim immigration to allow for an increased quota of Christian migrants from the Middle East. Although (indicating the relevant international connection), Nile was invited to speak at Trump's inauguration, he was denied a U.S. visa due to an "unspecified security threat."[104]

Fringe groups sympathetic to the UPF in Australia include Rise Up Australia, led by Danny Nalliah, a Sri Lankan-Australian Evangelical pastor for "Catch the Fire" ministries, who opposes multiculturalism despite his lineage and has spoken at rallies with

Cottrell. Another example perhaps most well-known internationally is Pauline Hanson's One Nation Party (ONP). Hanson rose to political fame in 1996, at which time she was serving as a Liberal MP, with an infamous letter published in the *Queensland Times*. In the letter she stated:

> How can we expect this race to help themselves when governments shower them with money, facilities and opportunities that only these people can obtain no matter how minute the Indigenous [sic] blood is that flows through their veins and that is what is causing racism.[105]

As a result of her letter, Hanson was disendorsed by John Howard, the future prime minister and then leader of the Liberal Party. She was already listed on Ballot papers as a Liberal candidate, however, and was elected to Federal Parliament in 1996. In her maiden speech on 10 September, she famously declared: "I believe we are in danger of being swamped by Asians."[106] After a series of setbacks including waning popular support for the party and a period of imprisonment for electoral fraud, Hanson and the ONP ran twenty-seven candidates and won four seats in the Senate in the 2016 Federal election, and enjoyed considerable success in her home seat of Queensland. Demonstrating the transposable nature of the doxa to which Hanson appealed, she shifted not from anti-Semitism (as she did not publicly profess anti-Semitic values), but rather from the anti-Indigenous and anti-Asian rhetoric and values she espoused in previous periods, to an explicit endorsement of Islamophobia. Her new campaign was founded on the proposed banning of Muslim immigration and building of new mosques. In the campaign, she called for a "Royal Commission" into Islam; an investigative apparatus that in Australia has been deployed to address national issues including aboriginal deaths in custody, institutional responses to child sexual abuse, and family violence.[107]

While spokesmen for Rise Up Australia, the ALA, and AFP have appeared at public events with the UPF, the organization has most extensively supported Pauline Hanson on social media. On 25 February 2017, for instance, the UPF Facebook page hosted a Yahoo news item: "'I have a problem with his religion, not his skin colour': Hanson says of departing CEO,"[108] while on 2 February 2017, Cottrell posted on Twitter, "Shoutout to @realDonaldTrump! Pauline Hanson gets an inauguration invite from the President himself and Turnbull gets a kick in the arse."[109] Subsequently, in March 2017, the UPF promoted an Apple.news piece that read: "One Nation leader Pauline Hanson says Australians are calling for a leader like Russian President Vladimir Putin who 'will stand up and fight for this country.'"[110] Later in March, the UPF Facebook page hosted a *Daily Mail* news item entitled: "Pauline Hanson fighting for British immigrants facing deportation."[111]

Although there is insufficient scope to quantify Australia's broad-based right-wing populism, and its correlation to Islamophobic doxa as a blindness to social inequality,[112] a number of additional examples illustrate this point. Mainstream, right-wing politicians who have been endorsed in UPF social media include Federal Coalition MP George Christensen, who has spoken at Reclaim rallies about what he perceives to be the connection between Islam and terrorism, and, like Trump, has infamously evoked the rhetoric of ex–U.S. President Ronald Reagan.[113] Another example is ex-Coalition MP Cory Bernardi, who left to form his own Conservatives party, and once compared homosexuality to bestiality, described advocating the right to have an abortion as being "pro-death," and declared Islam to be a "totalitarian, political and religious ideology."[114] On 6 November 2016 he was endorsed by the UPF on Facebook with the posting and by-line: "Senator Bernardi from Adelaide, always defiant."[115] Tasmanian Independent Senator Jacquie Lambie, who defended Trump's Muslim Ban in an ABC debate on its Q&A program, was also quoted in a UPF Facebook posting: "Australia is founded on the separation of church and state and I'll use the words of Jacqui Lambie: 'not on my bloody watch.'"[116] On 24 March 2017, the UPF Facebook page hosted a Yahoo news excerpt that displayed Australian Nationals MP Bob Katter (active in Parliament since 1993) captured on a spectator's "selfie" camera, stating: "I don't want Muslims coming here."[117]

Islamic State

This article contends that in addition to the dialectics that exist between UPF propaganda and right-wing politics, there is a dialectical relationship between UPF social media and IS ideologies. This section of the analysis draws from Nicholas Fogle's explanation of dialectics as a "self-perpetuating loop, wherein the outputs are fed back into the system as inputs" and "may be labelled as reflexive, self-referential, self-organizing, or simply dialectical."[118] In combination with the interplay between the habitus of UPF members, their social media practices, and broader right-wing politics, reflexivity and mirroring between UPF social media and IS reinforces and intensifies a doxa of normalized anti-Islam politics.

The UPF's endorsement of Islamophobia is patent in its social media that has, since 2015, reflexively exploited IS-related attacks that have occurred in Western countries. Members of the organization have highlighted and drawn from these events to promote the UPF's anti-Islam, anti-immigration platform, and to connect with a panoply of international reactionary movements. For example, in addition to the 2015 Charlie Hebdo example previously discussed, Cottrell, Sewell, and Shermon posted scare-mongering articles and commentary on Facebook and Twitter about the "Sydney Siege" by gunman Man Haron Monis on 15 December 2014,[119] the 2 October 2015 shooting of Victoria police worker Curtis Cheng, and the 6 June 2017 "Brighton Siege" in Victoria, in which Yacqub Khayre shot a hotel clerk, Kai Hao, and took three women hostage.[120] With respect to international events, a characteristic UPF response to IS-related events was Cottrell's Twitter post following the 4 June 2017 London Bridge Borough Market: "sometimes the most simplistic solution is the best and only one. Stop. Letting. Them. In."[121]

Moreover, in addition to social media that is reactionary to IS events, broad-based conflations of anti-Islamic sentiment with the risk posed by IS are evident in UPF media characterized by the Bourdieuian themes of anti-intellectualism, power, and societal stratification. On 15 March 2017, for instance, the UPF central Facebook page hosted an article related to a seizure in Spain of 10,000 assault rifles, grenades, and anti-aircraft guns, with the by-line: "while the ethnic European population is being disarmed by Left-Wing anti-gun laws, the Islamic communities are importing tens of thousands of assault rifles and other munitions!"[122] On 24 March 2017, the Facebook page hosted an RT news article that stated "Turkish President Recep Erdogan has urged all Turks living in Europe to have at least five children, saying they are the future of the continent and that it would be the best response to the 'injustices' imposed on expatriates there." The by-line to this article written by the UPF moderator asserted: "there is a conscientious effort being made by Muslim leaders to out-breed Europeans or people of European decent [sic]—and you're expected not to notice." Comments to the posting included ramblings about threats from terrorism, and, in a demonstration of IS-UPF dialectics in relation to "race"-based, religious-civilizational thinking, the dangers associated with "eugenic" belief systems, including specifically IS's stated desire to violently defend the ancestral heritage and lineage of Muslim people, at the expense of non-Muslim peoples' heritage and lineage.[123]

Given the radical anti-Islam posturing of UPF members, and their implicit and explicit conflation of the Islamic religion with IS terrorism, it is pertinent that UPF propaganda has thematically and symbolically mirrored the propaganda output of IS. From the perspective of this analysis, the nature of this relationship reflects Bourdieu's problematization of traditional dialectical theory in which categorical opposites are understood to reflect, destroy, and replace one another.[124] It alternately accords with Bourdieu and Norman Fairclough's nonlinear approach to social phenomena, whereby complex interactions between relational structures produce endlessly reflexive outcomes. One overt example of this was the mock beheading of the dummy at Bendigo City Council, which occurred in the aftermath of the Cheng shooting. Another occurred when Erikson appeared at the May 2017 court hearing dressed in Salaafi Islamic attire.[125] Indicating the flow-on effects of such actions, the leader of the ONP, Pauline Hanson, wore a Burqa to the Australian Parliament in August 2017.

With regard to the UPF, although stunts such as Erikson's are sensational and high-profile, covert examples of thematic and symbolic mirroring of IS by the UPF are most significant to the nature of their dialectical relationship, given that these examples reinforce implicit ideologies predicated on Islamophobia, by virtue of the fact that they are often unrecognized. One example of this is UPF members' various invocations of terror. In one case, Cottrell commented via his now-defunct Facebook account: "women have manipulated me using sex and emotion, demoralization, and I have manipulated them using violence and terror. We use what we have to get what we want."[126] Furthermore, the by-line of Tom Sewell's current Twitter account, in which he proudly declares his "fascism," is "Force and Terror."[127] Demonstrating the UPF's endorsement of violence that is reminiscent of groups such as IS, Cottrell has also historically made threatening Facebook comments. Regarding the extra-marital dating site Ashley Madison, for example, he wrote: "I just saw a fucking TV ad for women encouraging adultery … that putrid Marxist propaganda is ruthless. In my humble opinion adultery should be punishable by death just like the good old days."[128]

Beyond terror and capital punishment, an overarching theme common to the UPF and IS is their respective embrace of eschatological thinking. In the first instance, the doomsday ethic of IS is patent in its propaganda of all types, including the organization's Al Hayat and Al Furqan video productions, and their magazine *Dabiq*, which is named after the proposed Syrian site of the apocalypse. In comparison, the eschatology of the UPF is again more implicit than explicit. This is reflected in UPF figures' tangible affiliations with evangelical religious figures such as Fred Nile and Danny Nalliah (given that they espouse related ideologies and appear at public speaking events together), and an organizational ideology predicated on the extremist belief, in Safran's words, that a "Messianic age … is inching closer."[129]

One video on Cottrell's YouTube page with distinct apocalyptic themes is entitled "Nationalism, Mental Illness and 'Our People'" and includes fervent reference to the notion of a collective identity, a shared "great mission," and the "spirit" of national salvation.[130] In another civilizational-themed video, entitled "Why do we take in refugees," Cottrell quotes Napoleon, and outlines a nefarious motivation for why governments might seek to welcome asylum seekers.[131] He argues that increased refugee intake will prompt chaos, which will in turn lead to public support for the inauguration of a globalist governance regime. He contends that refugees will act as "ethnic gangs slaughtering people," they will produce a "crisis … so bad that you can't walk down a street because you won't be able to walk down the street without the fear of rape or explosions," and that this will coincide with "so much inflation that people will starve." Citing "terror attacks in Paris" and "mass rapes in Germany," he asserts of those he denotes the "progressive kids" and "trendies," "when the crisis hits, you're going to die."[132]

Extremist religiosity reminiscent of IS among founding UPF members is most apparent in social media postings by co-founder Chris Shortis. His Twitter handle is currently "@christgun" and his by-line: "my name is Chris and Jesus Christ is my LORD, God's only begotten Son. Australia" starkly recalls the flags and sayings of extremist monotheism, in some ways like the flag and propaganda of IS.[133] Furthermore, on a series of Facebook postings in which he brandishes firearms, Shortis describes himself as a "biblical crusader," explicitly recalling IS propaganda that analogizes Western societies with the tenth- and eleventh-century Christian Crusades.[134] Moreover, although Cottrell himself professes to be atheist, following the hearing in March 2017, he posted images of a man adorned in a white robe with a red cross standing over his interview with press outside the Melbourne Magistrates' court. In one Twitter image where Cottrell is surrounded by journalists, he commented in stark evocation of Crusade-themed IS media: "had this gentleman watching over me yesterday. Some of us 'talk' about another crusade—but this guy is 100% ready to go."[135]

In other cases, both reflexivity and mirroring is apparent in UPF propaganda characterized by dialectical interactions with IS. A pictographic example is Cottrell's Twitter and Facebook postings in May 2017 of U.S. comedian Kathy Griffin posing with a fake decapitated head of Donald Trump, alongside the caption: "the doll we made represented no one in particular. But this left-wing nutter can freely behead an effigy of Donald Trump and actually gets positive press as a result? Twisted Islamo-Communism."[136] A rhetorical example, enacted in response to what the UPF perceived as a physical threat from Islamic populations living in Australia, was a well-known Facebook posting: "sometimes it is necessary to take up swords and stand against the enemy who would kill our children, our elderly, and us."[137]

A final important characteristic of the dialectic between the UPF and IS, in addition to other forms of extremism, relates to certain points of political confluence. One example is a video released on 23 November 2015 in which Shortis asserted that he and Abu Bakr al-Baghdadi, the leader of IS, would agree on their interpretation of Islam. A number of commentators have, in fact, highlighted that the UPF and IS effectively have analogous interpretations of the role of Muslims living in countries such as Australia. An Islamic-Australian girl, Rahila Haidary, who was used in a UPF video for propaganda purposes in a manner that she did not consent to, for instance, remarked in an interview: "if the terrorists read the Koran and interpret it in the wrong way, they become terrorists. That's also what these people are doing. … I actually can't differentiate between them."[138] A well-known solicitor with the Muslim Legal Network in Australia, Lydia Shelly, likewise stated in an ABC Hack Live talk show that by virtue of their radical and xenophobic tendencies, Islamists and those from the far right are "two sides of the same coin."[139] Moreover, although there is insufficient space in this article to further explore aspects of the dialectic between IS and the UPF, such as their appeal to existential nihilism, it is pertinent to note that such interactions reflect an often-observed convergence of extremisms at the far ends of political spectrums.[140]

Conclusion

Using the UPF as a case study, this article has demonstrated that an international intensification of far-right extremism, as expressed on social media, can be understood by examining these entities' media practices through a lens of dialectical theory. Critical discourse and documentary analysis were applied within a framework of Pierre Bourdieu's theory, to demonstrate that UPF social media practices function as part of a dialectic constituted by reflexivity and mirroring with groups such as IS, and with right-trending international politics. Specifically, the analysis revealed that members of the UPF express a habitus of far-right politics, through their stated solidarity with domestic and international groups within a field of right-trending politics, predicated on xenophobia, nationalism, and militarism. It then revealed that, despite the UPF's conflation of IS with the religion of Islam, and its stated rejection of Islam and migrant populations on this basis, key organizational members in fact implicitly and explicitly endorse ideologies they have in common with IS. These include their usage of "terror" as a political weapon, extreme religiosity, and eschatological thinking. With reference to Bourdieuian theory, the analysis explained that these social media practices take place within a doxa of normalized, expected, and tolerated Islamophobia.

As mentioned early in this article, the theoretical significance of a dialectical approach for exploring the social media propaganda of extremist groups is twofold: it provides a means for comparing and understanding the mutually constitutive nature of extremist groups' online communications, while at the same time methodologically taking account of the reflexive and dialectical way in which social media content proliferates. Where it has been widely observed that owing to the affordances of the platforms themselves, social media content is intrinsically relational[141]—as "retweets," "likes," and "shares" are themselves examples of the remediation and repurposing of social media content—the dialectical nature of the relationships between such media, as characterized by opposition, contestation, and similarity, is often overlooked. In the case of social media disseminated by extremist groups this is particularly significant, given that the grievances and ideologies that render various extremist narratives attractive to vulnerable people are often situationally and philosophically related. While there is insufficient scope in this article to complete a rigorous profile of extremist groups, or draw from extensive data sets, it has outlined the broad strokes of a new research agenda focused on addressing extremist groups from a comparative perspective. The current political need to understand the various spectrums of extremism, and the need for further research in this area, is outlined below.

First, with the current "refugee crisis", and sustained wars taking place in Africa and the Middle East, Muslim people may be subject to intensified deprivation, physical displacement, and increasingly globalized experiences of marginalization. Second, the historical precedent of far-right Islamophobic groups in violent anti-Semitism is too often under-examined; it is all too easy to forget that the precursor to World War II was an understated but nevertheless apparent pan-European hostility toward Judaism. As the June 2017 attack on a mosque by a right-wing extremist in London's Finsbury Park demonstrated, the tangible threat of violence derived from Islamophobia is patent. Finally, by interacting with and reinforcing the false dichotomizing ideology of IS, groups such as the UPF expedite IS's stated mission to "eliminate the grayzone" of co-existence between Islam and the West.[142] It is in the Western and Eastern world's strategic interest to address the narratives of the far-right, lest they catalyze what will, for all intents and purposes, be described as a "clash of civilizations."[143]

Acknowledgments

The author thanks those who read drafts of this article and Andy Fleming for sharing his insight and information about Australian far-right organizations.

Notes

1. By extension, far-right extremism has featured "anti-democratic dispositions and attempts that are traditionally positioned at the extreme 'right' of the left-right spectre." Uwe Backes and Eckhard Jesse, "Politischer Extremismus in der Bundesrepublik Deutschland," *Bundeszentrale für politische Bildung* (1993), 474, quoted in Cas Mudde, *The Ideology of the Extreme Right* (Manchester: Manchester University Press, 2000), 10. Cas Mudde, "The Paradox of the Anti-Party Party Insights from the Extreme Right," *Party Politics* 2, no. 2 (1996), 265–276.
2. "'Unprecedented' 65 Million People Displaced by War and Persecution in 2015—UN," United Nations Office of the High Commissioner for Refugees, 20 June 2016, http://www.un.org/apps/news/story.asp?NewsID =54269 (accessed 1 June 2017).
3. See the findings of Oxfam's 2017 report. Oxfam, "Just 8 Men Own Same Wealth as Half the World," 16 January 2017, https://www.oxfam.org/en/pressroom/pressreleases/2017-01-16/just-8-men-own-same-wealth-half-world (accessed 1 June 2017).
4. Manuel Castells, *The Rise of the Network Society*. Vol. 1 of *The Information Age: Economy, Society, and Culture* (Oxford: Blackwell, 1996), 162.
5. Douglas Kellner, *Media Culture: Cultural Studies, Identity and Politics Between the Modern and the Post-Modern* (London: Routledge, 2003), 307.
6. Jean Baudrillard, *Simulacra and Simulation* (Ann Arbor: University of Michigan Press, 1994); Anthony Giddens, *The Consequences of Modernity* (Victoria: Wiley & Sons, 2013).
7. Randal Marlin, *Propaganda and the Ethics of Persuasion—Second Edition* (Ontario: Broadview Press, 2013), 9.

8. Walter Laqueur, *The New Terrorism: Fanaticism and the Arms of Mass Destruction* (Oxford: Oxford University Press, 2000).
9. Christian Fuchs, *Social Media: A Critical Introduction* (London: Sage, 2017).
10. Fuchs, *Social Media.*
11. Gabriel Weimann, *Terrorism in Cyberspace: The Next Generation* (New York: Columbia University Press, 2015).
12. Jytte Klausen, "Tweeting the Jihad: Social Media Networks of Western Foreign Fighters in Syria and Iraq," *Studies in Conflict & Terrorism* 38, no. 1 (2015), 1–22.
13. Ryan Shaffer, "Jihad and Counter-Jihad in Europe: Islamic Radicals, Right-wing Extremists, and Counter-Terrorism Responses," *Terrorism and Political Violence* 28, no. 2 (2016), 383–394.
14. Daniela Pisoiu, "Subcultural Theory Applied to Jihadi and Right-Wing Radicalization in Germany," *Terrorism and Political Violence* 27, no. 1 (2015), 9–28.
15. Juris Pupcenoks and Ryan McCabe, "The Rise of the Fringe: Right Wing Populists, Islamists and Politics in the UK," *Journal of Muslim Minority Affairs* 22, no. 2 (2013), 171–184.
16. Lorraine Bowman-Grieve, "Exploring 'Stormfront': A Virtual Community of the Radical Right," *Studies in Conflict and Terrorism* 32, no. 11 (2009), 989–1007.
17. Jose Zuquete, "The New Frontlines of Right-Wing Nationalism," *Journal of Political Ideologies* 20, no. 1 (2015), 69–85.
18. Michael Suttmoeller, Steven Chermak and Joshua Freilich, "Is More Violent Better? The Impact of Group Participation in Violence on Group Longevity for Far-Right Extremist Groups," *Studies in Conflict and Terrorism*, 7 April, 1-23.
19. J. M. Berger, "Nazis vs. ISIS on Twitter: A Comparative Study of White Nationalist and ISIS Online Social Media Networks," George Washington University: Program on Extremism, September 2016, https://cchs.gwu.edu/sites/cchs.gwu.edu/files/downloads/Nazis%20v.%20ISIS%20Final_0.pdf (accessed 1 June 2017).
20. Amelia Johns, "Flagging White Nationalism 'After Cronulla': From the Beach to the Net," *Journal of Intercultural Studies* 38, no. 3 (2017), 349–364.
21. Geoff Dean, Peter Bell, and Zarina Vakhitova, "Right-Wing Extremism in Australia: The Rise of the New Radical Right," *Journal of Policing, Intelligence and Counter Terrorism* 11, no. 2 (2016), 121–142.
22. "Reclaim Australia Clashes with Opposing Groups at Rallies around the Country over Extremism and Tolerance," *ABC News*, 5 April 2015, http://www.abc.net.au/news/2015-04-04/reclaim-australia-extremism-rallies-face-tolerance-groups/6370672 (accessed 1 June 2017).
23. "These Are the People Behind Anti-Muslim Protests in Australia," *ABC News*, 12 December 2015, http://www.abc.net.au/7.30/content/2015/s4330308.htm (accessed 1 June 2017).
24. Yoni Bashan Lia Harris, "Fight For the Right To Hold Cronulla Riot Rally to Mark 10th Anniversary," *News.com.au,* 5 December 2015, http://www.news.com.au/national/nsw-act/fight-for-the-right-to-hold-cronulla-riot-rally-to-mark-10th-anniversary/news-story/159676ff007570a790590185a4ba493d (accessed 1 June 2017).
25. "Australian Man Warns of Another Cronulla Riot after Being Bashed for Filming Muslim Women," *News Corp Australia Network*, 9 September 2014, http://www.news.com.au/national/australian-man-warns-of-another-cronulla-riot-after-being-bashed-for-filming-muslim-women/news-story/47c184d5ca77c654688eac1a8d9b4675 (accessed 1 June 2017).
26. "These Are the People Behind Anti-Muslim Protests in Australia," *ABC News*, 12 December 2015, http://www.abc.net.au/7.30/content/2015/s4330308.htm (accessed 1 June 2017).
27. "United Patriots Front," Anti-Fascist Action Sydney, 26 May 2016, https://antifascistactionsydney.wordpress.com/category/united-patriotic-front/ (accessed 1 June 2017).

28. Blair Cottrell, "Possible Jail Time for Facebook Post," YouTube, https://www.youtube.com/watch?v=y93tXzTI-sE (accessed 1 June 2017).
29. Lorraine Bowman-Grieve, "Exploring 'Stormfront': A Virtual Community of the Radical Right," *Studies in Conflict & Terrorism* 32, no. 11 (2009), 989–1007.
30. Ozconspiracy.com and The Great Aussie Patriot, "Top Ten Reasons Why UPF are Cants," Facebook, https://www.facebook.com/1590707441239960/videos/1594220477555323/?pnref=story (accessed 1 May 2017).
31. See Chris Shortis in videos on the United Nationalists of Australia's YouTube account, https://www.youtube.com/channel/UCv6C8Y_ALELhRkqVk-msLSg (accessed 1 May 2017).
32. This according to Cottrell, as stated on a Twitter posting and Facebook video, https://www.facebook.com/Blaircottrell89/videos/1969454510001334/ and https://twitter.com/blaircottrell89/status/876576066562805760 (accessed 10 June 2017).
33. Coen Ayers, "Blair Cottrell on Facebook and the UPF," YouTube, https://www.youtube.com/watch?v=-wg4E1oFxWs (accessed 1 May 2017).
34. "United Patriots Front Displays 'Stop the Mosques' Banner on Kwinana Freeway," *PerthNow,* 19 May 2016, http://www.perthnow.com.au/news/western-australia/united-patriots-front-displays-stop-the-mosques-banner-on-kwinana-freeway/news-story/5ff11338bc498f3785779fc92bd90711 (accessed 1 June 2017).
35. Calla Wahlquist, "Melbourne Pro-Trump Rally Outnumbered by Police and Counter-Protesters," *The Guardian,* 20 November 2016, https://www.theguardian.com/australia-news/2016/nov/20/police-brace-for-duelling-pro-and-anti-trump-rallies-in-melbourne (accessed 1 June 2017).
36. Gus Goswell, "United Patriots Front Misses Deadline to Register Political Party Ahead of Federal Election," *ABC News,* 2 June 2016, http://www.abc.net.au/news/2016-06-02/united-patriots-front-misses-federal-election-deadline/7470350 (accessed 1 June 2017).
37. http://www.fortitude-australia.com/about-us/ (accessed 1 June 2017).
38. @ndy, "Australian Pride March/Flagwit Rally, Melbourne: June 25, 2017," Slackbastard, 18 June 2017, http://slackbastard.anarchobase.com (accessed 1 June 2017).
39. Anthony Galloway and Wes Hosking, "Police Find Anarchist Cookbook in Melbourne Home of United Patriots Front Member," *News.com.au*, 20 November 2015, http://www.news.com.au/national/courts-law/police-find-anarchist-cookbook-in-melbourne-home-of-united-patriots-front-member/news-story/55c1241623727bd0ff5c26a3b77787d7 (accessed 1 June 2017).
40. Galea is the first "far-right" figure to be charged with a terrorism-related offense in Australia. Australian Associated Press, "Alleged Extremist Phillip Galea Faces Court on Charges of Preparing for Terrorist Act," *The Guardian*, 19 April 2017, https://www.theguardian.com/australia-news/2017/apr/19/phillip-galea-faces-court-on-charges-of-preparing-for-terrorist-act (accessed 4 January 2018).
41. @ndy, "Give me the money Jew or else I will get you," Slackbastard, 16 February 2014, http://slackbastard.anarchobase.com/?p=35596 (accessed 1 June 2017).
42. Geir O'Rourke and Angus Thompson, "United Patriots Front Leader Blair Cottrell Details Violent Criminal Past in Video," *Herald Sun*, 11 June 2016, http://www.heraldsun.com.au/news/victoria/united-patriots-front-leader-blair-cottrell-details-violent-criminal-past-in-video/news-story/d107bccff2d3b305788e17d881ccec27 (accessed 1 June 2017).
43. Adam Holmes, "Three Charged After 'Mock Beheading' in Bendigo," *Bendigo Advertiser,* 27 September 2016, http://www.bendigoadvertiser.com.au/story/4192804/three-charged-after-mock-beheading-in-bendigo/ (accessed 1 June 2017).
44. Norman Fairclough, *Critical Discourse Analysis* (London: Routledge, 2013).
45. Ibid., 4.
46. Ibid.
47. Pierre Bourdieu, *Outline of a Theory of Practice*, trans. Richard Nice (Cambridge: Cambridge University Press, 1977).
48. Pierre Bourdieu, *The Logic of Practice*, trans. Richard Nice (Stanford, CA: Stanford University Press, 1990).

49. Steven Lukes, "Durkheim's 'Individualism and the Intellectuals,'" *Political Studies* 17, no. 1, 14–30, at 14.
50. Pierre Bourdieu, *Distinction: A Social Critique of the Judgment of Taste*, trans. Richard Nice (Cambridge, MA: Harvard University Press, 1984), 170.
51. Following the writing of this article, the UPF, as a cohesive organization, has to an extent dissolved, while its members have moved into other far-right groups.
52. Pierre Bourdieu, *Language and Symbolic Power*. Ed. J. Thompson, Trans. Gino Raymond and Matthew Adamson (Cambridge, MA: Harvard University Press, 1982), 185.
53. Nikolaus Fogle, *The Spatial Logic of Social Struggle: A Bourdieuian Topology* (Lanham, MD: Lexington Books, 2011), 74.
54. Bourdieu, *Outline of a Theory of Practice*.
55. Ibid., 471.
56. Jenna Johnson, "Trump Calls for 'Total and Complete Shutdown of Muslims Entering the United States,'" *The Washington Post*, 7 December 2015, https://www.washingtonpost.com/news/post-politics/wp/2015/12/07/donald-trump-calls-for-total-and-complete-shutdown-of-muslims-entering-the-united-states/?utm_term=.bae86acbc14b (accessed 1 June 2017).
57. Reuters, "Anti-immigration Party Wins Swiss Election in 'Slide to the Right,'" *The Telegraph*, 19 October 2015, http://www.telegraph.co.uk/news/worldnews/europe/switzerland/11939953/Anti-immigration-party-wins-Swiss-election-in-slide-to-the-Right.html (accessed 10 June 2017).
58. "Norway's Progress Party Strides Forward in Latest Polls," *The Local*, 1 June 2017, https://www.thelocal.no/20170601/norways-progress-party-strides-forward-in-latest-polls (1 June 2017).
59. Human Rights First, "Far-Right Parties in European Elections," April 2015, http://www.humanrightsfirst.org/sites/default/files/HRF-European-Extremism.pdf (accessed 1 June 2017).
60. Jussie Rosendahl and Toumas Forsell, "Finnish Coalition at Risk After Nationalists Pick Hardline Leader," *Reuters*, 10 June 2017, https://www.reuters.com/article/us-finland-government-finnsparty-idUSKBN19109T (accessed 1 June 2017).
61. Philip Blenkisop and Robert-Jan Bartunek, "Flemish Separatists are Big Winners in Belgian Election," *Reuters*, 25 May 2014, http://www.reuters.com/article/us-belgium-election-idUSBREA4O0DT20140525 (accessed 1 June 2017). In Eastern Europe, nationalist parties are in power in the two Former Yugoslav republics of Macedonia and Serbia, while governments in Slovakia, Estonia, and Bulgaria have stated that they want to accept no refugees at all. Although these entities may not ubiquitously be referred to as "far-right" in ideology, they have all broadly campaigned on the bases of Euroscepticism, and anti-immigration policies from either outside their national borders or outside the boundaries of Schengen.
62. Jon Henley and Lizzy Davies, "Greece's Far-Right Golden Dawn Party Maintains Share of Vote," *The Guardian*, 19 June 2012, https://www.theguardian.com/world/2012/jun/18/greece-far-right-golden-dawn (accessed 1 June 2017).
63. "In Quotes: Geert Wilders," *BBC News*, 4 October 2010, http://www.bbc.com/news/world-europe-11469579 (accessed 1 June 2017).
64. Two other examples are the growing popularity of the Sweden Democrats and Austria's Freedom Party. Lega Nord in Italy, which holds ties to Russia's Vladimir Putin administration and right-wing nationalist groups across Europe is also currently polling fourth, and the Danish People's party, which openly called for Denmark's withdrawal from the EU Schengen agreement in the lead-up to the 2015 general election, is now the country's second largest political party.
65. Michelle Fitzpatrick, "Europe's Far-Right Leaders Have a New Slogan—#WeWillMakeOurCountriesGreatAgain," *Business Insider*, 21 January 2017, http://www.businessinsider.com/afp-le-pen-headlines-european-counter-summit-in-germany-2017-1?IR=T (accessed 1 June 2017).

66. Neil Erikson, Facebook page, https://www.facebook.com/profile.php?id =100010754987073 (accessed 1 May 2017).
67. United Patriots Front, "Trump shuts down Merkel in recent meeting—'immigration is a privilege, not a right,'" Facebook. Formerly available at https://www.facebook.com/unitedpatriotsfront/posts/438398543161270 (accessed 1 February 2017).
68. Blair Cottrell, "The Trump Smile: When You're Surrounded by Cameras, Lies and Stupidity, But You Know You're Going to Win So It's All Good," Facebook, https://www.facebook.com/Blaircottrell89/videos/1956102624669856/ (accessed 1 June 2017).
69. See Blair Cottrell's Twitter updates, https://twitter.com/blaircottrell89.
70. Bianca Hall, "Far-Right Group UPF Plans to Run for Senate and Campaign on Right to 'Bare Arms,'" *The Age*, 11 September 2015, http://www.theage.com.au/victoria/farright-group-upf-plans-to-run-for-senate-and-campaign-on-right-to-bare-arms-20150911-gjk73n.html (accessed 10 June 2017).
71. United Patriots Front, "Marine le Pen, You Are Welcome in Australia Anytime, In Fact You Can Replace Julie Bishop If You Like," Facebook. Formerly available at https://www.facebook.com/unitedpatriotsfront/photos/a.107033656297762.1073741828.106736366327491/426993350968456/?type =3 (accessed 10 April 2017).
72. United Patriots Front, "Marine le Pen Savages Angela Merkel to Her Face in EU Parliament," Facebook. Formerly available at https://www.facebook.com/unitedpatriotsfront/?rc=p (accessed 1 April 2017).
73. Blair Cottrell, "In Parliamentary Politics, the Women Have More Balls Than The Men. @marinelepen," Twitter, https://twitter.com/blaircottrell89/status/834586014463037440 (accessed 1 June 2017).
74. Shermon Burgess, "Emmanuel Macron is a Rothschild Globalist," YouTube, https://www.youtube.com/watch?v=72V00VDUICs (accessed 1 May 2017).
75. Bourdieu, *Outline of a Theory of Practice.*
76. Blair Cottrell, "Explaining Propaganda," YouTube, https://www.youtube.com/watch?v=OYDSG36qhm4 (accessed 1 May 2017).
77. Blair Cottrell, "Weaponized Words," YouTube, https://www.youtube.com/watch?v=WF6yKKPvRc4 (accessed 1 May 2017).
78. Blair Cottrell, "Islamo-Communism, The New World-Wide Threat to Freedom?" Twitter, https://twitter.com/blaircottrell89/status/869416466256338944 (accessed 1 June 2017).
79. John Safran, *Depends What You Mean by Extremist* (Victoria: Penguin, 2017), 139.
80. Ibid.
81. Pierre Bourdieu, *In Other Words: Essays Towards a Reflexive Sociology.* Trans. Matthew Adamson (Stanford, CA: Stanford University Press, 1990), 12.
82. Evan Williams and Joel Tozer, "Dateline Europe Special: Young Hip and Far Right," *SBS*, 25 April 2017, http://www.sbs.com.au/news/dateline/story/dateline-europe-special-young-hip-and-far-right (accessed 1 June 2017).
83. Ibid.
84. While nationalist far-right groups tend to use the yellow and black insignia, anti-globalization far-left groups have adopted the Lambda symbol in black and red.
85. Ibid.
86. Patrick Hatch, "Far-Right Anti-Islam Group to Rally at Victorian Parliament House," *The Age*, 12 July 2015, http://www.theage.com.au/victoria/farright-antiislam-group-to-rally-at-victorian-parliament-house-20150712-giajz9.html (accessed 1 June 2017).
87. Shermon Burgess, "Poland. The True Beacon of Light for White European Survival," YouTube, https://www.youtube.com/watch?v=Yp-RRhKEBq0 (accessed 1 June 2017).
88. Bourdieu, *The Logic of Practice.*
89. Bourdieu, *Distinction*, 77, 83.
90. "Antifa Notes (February 17, 2016): Neil Erikson ~ versus ~ Nationalist Alternative, United Patriots Front Etc.," Slackbastard, 17 February 2016, http://slackbastard.anarchobase.com/?tag=neil-erikson (accessed 1 June 2017).

91. @ndy, "Melbourne neo-Nazis celebrate Adolf Hitler's Birthday & ANZAC Day 2017," Slackbastard, 26 April 2017, http://slackbastard.anarchobase.com/?p=41151 (accessed 1 June 2017).
92. Bourdieu, *The Logic of Practice*, 56.
93. Shermon Burgess, YouTube, https://www.youtube.com/user/BringingBackTheMan (accessed 1 June 2017).
94. Luke McMahon, "Gun-Toting ASnti-Muslim 'Crusader' at Lead of United Patriots Front," *The Sydney Morning Herald*, 7 November 2015, http://www.smh.com.au/national/guntoting-antimuslim-crusader-at-lead-of-united-patriots-front-20151105-gkrk80.html (accessed 10 June 2017).
95. Hatch, "Far-right Anti-Islam Group to Rally at Victorian Parliament House."
96. Jeff Sparrow, "A Fascist by Any Other Name," *Eureka Street*, 16 November 2015, https://www.eurekastreet.com.au/article.aspx?aeid=45700#.WUdku8ZL1Bw (accessed 1 June 2017).
97. Brendan Foster, "Right-Wing Group the Wanted Hitler in Classrooms to Launch Political Party," *WA Today*, 25 November 2015, http://www.watoday.com.au/wa-news/rightwing-group-that-wanted-hitler-in-classrooms-to-launch-political-party-20151125-gl7gmg.html (accessed 1 June 2017). Beyond his social media footprint, Cottrell has variously remarked on the difference between "highborn Jews" and "lowborn Jews" and expressed a variety of eugenic ideals that overtly recall the biological positivism of neo-Nazi Germany. In a series of videos on YouTube, Cottrell also referenced anti-Jewish conspiracy literature including *The Protocols of the Elders of Zion*, and stated that certain literature had "opened his eyes." Safran, *Depends What You Mean by Extremist*, 152; @ndy, "Quotations From Chairman Blair Cottrell," Slackbastard, 27 July 2015, http://slackbastard.anarchobase.com/?p=38730 (accessed 1 June 2017); @ndy, "Antifa Notes (February 21, 2016): Whitelaw Towers, United Patriots Front, Etc.," Slackbastard, 21 February 2016, http://slackbastard.anarchobase.com/?p=39617 (accessed 1 June 2017).
98. Shermon Burgess, "3 WORDS—Hitler Was Right!," Twitter, https://twitter.com/shermon_burgess/status/881497808854949888 (accessed 4 January 2018).
99. Safran, *Depends What You Mean by Extremist*, 143.
100. Bourdieu, *Language and Symbolic Power*.
101. "Australian Liberty Alliance: Home," http://australianlibertyalliance.org.au (accessed 1 June 2017).
102. Kathy McCabe, "Angry Anderson Joins Anti-Islam Party to Chase a Senate Seat at the Federal Election," *News.com.au*, 6 May 2016, http://www.news.com.au/entertainment/angry-anderson-joins-antiislam-party-to-chase-a-senate-seat-at-the-federal-election/news-story/cf23fd04d6e709c99d5feaeacb818f11 (accessed 1 June 2017).
103. Oliver Murray, "Far-Right-Wing Parties After Your Vote on Election Day," *News.com.au*, 26 April 2016, http://www.news.com.au/finance/work/leaders/farrightwing-parties-after-your-vote-on-election-day/news-story/dea024a911e4e5bf2d8d6bb6fbd1f0b0 (accessed 1 June 2017).
104. James Robertson, "Fred Nile Denied Visa for Donald Trump Inauguration, Deemed a 'Security Threat,'" *The Sydney Morning Herald*, 25 January 2017, http://www.smh.com.au/nsw/rev-fred-nile-denied-visa-for-donald-trump-inauguration-deemed-a-security-threat-20170125-gtycau.html (accessed 1 June 2017).
105. Uma Patel, "Pauline Hanson: One Nation Party's Resurgence After 20 Years of Controversy," *ABC News*, 11 July 2016, http://www.abc.net.au/news/2016-07-10/timeline-rise-of-pauline-hanson-one-nation/7583230 (accessed 1 June 2017).
106. Ibid.
107. Ibid. Highlighting the Party's policy connection to groups such as the UPF, the ONP furthermore advocated for the installation of closed-circuit television surveillance cameras in all Muslim mosques and schools in Australia; a political philosophy that activists such as Fleming have highlighted, extends beyond condemnation of groups such as IS, to an explicit promotion of criminalizing Muslim life in Australia.

108. United Patriots Front, "'I have a problem with his religion, not his skin colour': Hanson says of departing CEO," Facebook. Formerly available at https://www.facebook.com/unitedpatriotsfront/posts/428375617496896 (accessed 1 April 2017).
109. Blair Cottrell, "Shoutout to @realDonaldTrump! Pauline Hanson Gets an Inauguration Invite From the President Himself and Turnbull Gets a Kick in the Arse," Twitter, https://twitter.com/blaircottrell89/status/827018459896705024 (accessed 1 June 2017).
110. United Patriots Front, "One Nation Leader Pauline Hanson Says Australians Are Calling For a Leader Like Russian President Vladimir Putin Who 'Will Stand Up and Fight for this Country,'" Facebook. Previously available at https://www.facebook.com/unitedpatriotsfront/posts/431877477146710 (accessed 1 April 2017).
111. United Patriots Front, "Pauline Hanson Fighting for British Immigrants Facing Deportation," Facebook. Formerly available at https://www.facebook.com/unitedpatriotsfront/posts/431658630501928 (accessed 1 April 2017).
112. Bourdieu, *Distinction.*
113. New Matilda, "We Read George Christensen's Reclaim Speech, So You Didn't Have To," *NewMatilda.com*, 19 July 2015, https://newmatilda.com/2015/07/19/we-read-george-christensens-reclaim-speech-so-you-didnt-have/ (accessed 1 June 2017).
114. Ashlynne McGhee, "Cory Bernardi: Where Does the Senator Stand on Key Issues?" *ABC News*, 6 February 2017, http://www.abc.net.au/news/2017-02-06/cory-bernardi-profile-who-is-he-and-where-does-he-stand/8244040 (accessed 1 June 2017).
115. United Patriots Front, "Senator Bernardi from Adelaide, Always Defiant," Facebook. Formerly available at https://www.facebook.com/unitedpatriotsfront/posts/371025866565205 (accessed 1 June 2017).
116. Wayne Flower, "Protests as United Patriots Front Members Appear in Court," *Herald Sun*, 23 May 2017, http://www.heraldsun.com.au/news/law-order/protests-as-united-patriots-front-members-appear-in-court/news-story/55a851c54527cd341cb6b1c73cad2b0a (accessed 1 June 2017).
117. United Patriots Front, "I don't want Muslims coming here," Facebook. Formerly available at https://www.facebook.com/unitedpatriotsfront/posts/?ref=page_internal (accessed 1 June 2017).
118. Nicholas Fogle, *The Spatial Logic of Social Struggle: A Bourdieuian Topology* (Lanham, MD: Lexington Books, 2011), p. 73.
119. This was, in fact, the event that triggered the formation of Reclaim Australia; a group from which the UPF emerged.
120. Blair Cottrell, "The Last Terror Attack in Brighton was a PAROLE Issue According to @TurnbullMalcolm—Its Got Nothing To Do With Islam & It's Teachings," Twitter, https://twitter.com/blaircottrell89/status/871971689764012032 (accessed 10 June 2017).
121. Blair Cottrell, "Sometimes the Most Simplistic Solution Is the Best and Only One. Stop. Letting. Them. In.," Twitter, https://twitter.com/blaircottrell89/status/871277275706138624 (accessed 8 June 2017).
122. United Patriots Front, "While the Ethnic European Population is Being Disarmed by Left-Wing Anti-Gun Laws, the Islamic Communities are Importing Tens of Thousands of Assault Rifles and Other Munitions," Facebook. Formerly available at https://www.facebook.com/unitedpatriotsfront/posts/437326263268498 (accessed 1 June 2017).
123. United Patriots Front, "Turkish President Recep Erdogan has urged all Turks living in Europe to have at least five children, saying they are the future of the continent and that it would be the best response to the 'injustices' imposed on expatriates there," Facebook. Formerly available at https://www.facebook.com/unitedpatriotsfront/posts/438383513162773 (accessed 1 June 2017).
124. Fogle, *The Spatial Logic of Social Struggle*, 74.
125. Flower, "Protests as United Patriots Front Members Appear in Court."
126. Michael Bachelard and Luke McMahon, "Blair Cottrell, Rising Anti-Islam Movement Leader, Wanted Hitler in the Classroom," *The Sydney Morning Herald*, 17 October 2015,

http://www.smh.com.au/national/blair-cottrell-leader-of-aussie-patriots-upf-wanted-hitler-in-the-classroom-20151016-gkbbvz.html (accessed 1 June 2017).

127. Tom Sewell, Twitter page, https://twitter.com/tom_sewell93?lang=en (accessed 1 June 2017).
128. @ndy, "Quotations From Chairman Blair Cottrell."
129. Safran, *Depends What You Mean By Extremist*, 187.
130. Sunshinepolicy, "Blair Cottrell—Nationalism, Mental Illness and 'Our People,'" YouTube, https://www.youtube.com/watch?v=zVTeE4JhtbM (accessed 1 June 2017).
131. SwedenIsCucked BlackLiesMatter, "Why Do We Take in Refugees?" YouTube, https://www.youtube.com/watch?v=T2PCx6kpxIk (accessed 1 June 2017).
132. SwedenIsCucked BlackLiesMatter, "Why Do We Take in Refugees?"
133. Chris Shortis, Twitter page, https://twitter.com/christgun?lang=en (accessed 1 June 2017).
134. Luke McMahon, "Gun-Toting Anti-Muslim 'Crusader' at Lead of United Patriots Front."
135. Blair Cottrell, "Had This Gentleman Watching Over Me Yesterday. Some Of Us 'Talk' About Another Crusade—But This Guy is 100% Ready To Go," Twitter, https://twitter.com/blaircottrell89/status/867201898968866816 (accessed 1 June 2017). Safran also revealed that in interview he announced that Judaism and Islam served as an ideological "blueprint" for the UPF "because they all have a single and uncompromising ideology," Safran, *Depends What You Mean By Extremist*, 214.
136. Blair Cottrell, "More Ammo For Our Legal Defence," Facebook, https://www.facebook.com/Blaircottrell89/posts/1959397157673736 (accessed 1 June 2017).
137. Martha Azzi, "Right-Wing Extremists Placed on Terrorism Watch Lists Over Fears They Are Plotting Violent Attacks in Australia," *DailyMail*, 23 July 2016, http://www.dailymail.co.uk/news/article-3703660/Right-wing-extremists-placed-terrorism-watch-lists-fears-plotting-violent-attacks-Australia.html (accessed 1 June 2017).
138. Royce Kermelovs, "Australian Far Right Group 'Used Me For Propaganda,'" *BBC News*, 29 November 2015, http://www.bbc.com/news/world-australia-34918311 (accessed 1 June 2017).
139. IBT, "Hack Live Aussie Patriots," YouTube, https://www.youtube.com/watch?v=tGwHXPFRRRo (accessed 1 June 2017).
140. Albert Breton, *Political Extremism and Rationality* (Cambridge: Cambridge University Press, 2002).
141. Fuchs, *Social Media*.
142. Al-Hayat, "From Hypocrisy to Apostasy: The Extinction of the Grayzone," *Dabiq*, 12 February 2014, http://media.clarionproject.org/files/islamic-state/islamic-state-Dabiq-magazine-issue-7-from-hypocrisy-to-apostasy.pdf (accessed 1 January 2015).
143. Samuel Huntington, *The Clash of Civilizations and the Remaking of the World Order* (Delhi: Penguin Books India, 1997).

Grading the Quality of ISIS Videos: A Metric for Assessing the Technical Sophistication of Digital Video Propaganda

Mark D. Robinson and Cori E. Dauber

ABSTRACT

This article offers a method for systematically grading the quality of Islamic State of Iraq and Syria (ISIS) videos based on technical production criteria. Using this method revealed moments when ISIS production capacity was severely debilitated (Fall 2015) and when they began to rebuild (Spring 2016), which the article details. Uses for this method include evaluating propaganda video output across time and across groups, and the ability to assess kinetic actions against propaganda organizations. This capacity will be critical as Islamic State media production teams will be pushed out of its territory as the State collapses.

The process by which groups go about radicalizing individuals is complex and not yet completely understood. But it is clear that terrorist groups invest enormous resources producing visual and audio media in the hopes these media products will contribute to radicalization and recruitment. Even an untrained eye can tell vast differences in quality exist between the propaganda products produced by different groups or between the same groups at different times. More sophisticated evaluations make possible more sophisticated judgments and thus more sophisticated conclusions. This article provides a method for systematized qualitative judgments of extremist propaganda videos.

There has been substantial work done on the still imagery produced by Islamic State of Iraq and Syria (ISIS) and Islamic State (IS).[1] The emphasis in the literature on still imagery seems somewhat odd, however, given that moving images are so prevalent in the ISIS and IS corpus of work, and given that moving images, if they are well done, will almost inevitably have a more powerful impact than stills under most circumstances.[2] Yet available studies of ISIS and IS video output have focused on the amount of video production and determining typologies within which these products could be placed,[3] or its dissemination channels.[4] All of this is important work, but it still seems to leave a somewhat obvious gap. Given that the videos are the materials most likely to be the content with the highest impact on viewers, there is a need to understand the qualitative aspect of these products. Changes in content over time are already known, as are changes in which categories are dominant.[5] But without a way to assess quality, a critical piece of the picture is missing.

The application of this method is used to make the determination that ISIS video production was of extremely high quality, and remained high after the IS, or "Caliphate," was declared. After the coalition bombing campaign began in earnest, the quality of the group's video production declined precipitously. However, the research revealed quality rebounded not long after that. The article considers the implications for the application of this method going forward, as IS's media teams no doubt scatter with the collapse of the State.

The authors have worked for a number of years analyzing the propaganda videos of *jihadist* groups: one has an extensive background in media production as both analyst and maker, while the other is trained in rhetoric and argument studies with a focus on the visual. Combining these analytical approaches enables a focus on the ways in which compositional elements of video (editing, lighting, graphics, audio, camera angles, etc.) contribute to their rhetorical and persuasive power. While there is intrinsic value to such analysis, this form of qualitative work is inherently subjective. The goal, therefore, has been to design a method injecting systemization, and ultimately even inter-coder reliability, into this work.

In working to refine this method, a specific use for this type of analysis of video became clear: it can function as a form of "digital BDA," or bomb damage assessment, enabling the evaluation of video propaganda to be one form of evaluation of the progress of kinetic military campaigns. This article will first explain the method developed for analyzing the compositional elements of *jihadist* video,[6] then explain what the use of this system makes clear about IS media production over the last several years, and, finally, demonstrate the argument using three examples.

The system is based on a basic analytical grid: along the Y-axis are plotted a range of categories about which a qualitative judgment about a video may be made. These categories, from lighting to editing, audio, effects, use of software, graphics, and so forth, together constitute the assessment criteria for any particular video, and they have been grouped together as clusters labeled as *Messaging* and *Production Elements* as seen in Table 1.

The X-axis plots a graduated range of the qualitative judgments that can be made about each of these categories, and that allows a ranking of a specific category in a relatively clear, specific, and communicable way. These increase in quality starting with *Consumer*, moving to *Guerrilla*, then to *Prosumer*, from there to *Corporate-Pro*, then *Professional-Advertisement* and, finally, *Professional-Hollywood* as laid out in Table 2. To be clear, while these terms may have meanings in the vernacular or in other disciplines, they have well-understood meanings within media production that anyone in that field would be familiar with, and it is those meanings we draw on here.

Consumer represents what any household user of the technology would be expected to achieve in a naïve, untrained way. From there the grid goes to *Guerilla*. A Guerilla maker transcends the limitations of their equipment to be better, for example, than the camera they are using.

Professional-Consumer, or "Prosumer," the next highest level, refers to both a level of equipment and a level of maker. This is a transitional category: what is of higher quality than this is clear and what is lower than this is clear. Makers at this level exhibit training, a rich knowledge of what can be expected, what can be made, and how to make it.

Table 1. Y axis.

Messaging
Target and appeal
Delivery technique: Compression, metadata quality pixilation (implications)
Story: Content
Organization scene/sequence
Editing: Enhance story
Graphics messaging
Resolution
Marketing
Message: Target
Delivery
Implications: Narrative themes
Symbology
Semantics
Media elements: Use/Type
Production elements
2-D graphic implementation
FX (Aftereffects)
3-D graphic implementation
FX (Cinema or Maya, MOTION)
Audio-Craft
Acquisition microphone: craft/skills
Foley
Audio: Mix/engineering
Camera technique (movement, angles, etc.)
Camera type
Cinematography
Composition: Image (l/3rds)
Image quality (Flattened or intention) continuity
Diegetic representation
Set: Quality and location
Editing CRAFT (Mechanics, Timing)
Graphics: Introduction quality
Intersection points vulnerability, valence
Lighting type/technique
Logo, brand (quality, inference)
Mechanics (Sophistication of technique and craft)
Intention: location Mise en Scene (what composes)
Equipment knowledge (grain, depth of field, etc.)
Standards –> local/Regional/National/International
Synchronous audio vs. VO
Timing
Visual/artistic sophistication
Auteur level and sophistication of mark
Actors: identity, continuity, character

Table 2. X axis.

Production Value – Quality
Percentage of Production Completion towards an Industry, commercial Hollywood Production Value
0% ———————————— 50% ———————————— 100%
Consumer Guerilla Professional-Consumer Corporate-Professional Professional-Advertisement Professional-Hollywood

A "level of intent to the work" is present, meaning that the audience can see informed decisions being made. Intention and vision in both craft and technology are evident, demonstrating the clear execution of planning. Intent is present in the message as well, making clear that makers at this level are saying, doing, and creating purposefully. In other words, at this level a maker clearly considers the message they wish to deliver, and plans for how to deliver that message visually and acoustically through craft.

By contrast, Guerilla makers demonstrate intent, but how they execute that intent remains conditional upon circumstances; it is not necessarily a purposeful, pre-meditated act. They have a mission, but are not always sure how to bring that mission to fruition. Prosumers produce work using more professional equipment, including cameras with specialized lenses, drones, jibs, and dollies, but even the finest Prosumer work does not necessarily have the spit and polish of professional craft.

After Prosumer comes *Corporate-Pro*. This level includes works characterized as the bottom of the professional market, often equated in quality to intra-industry videos, such as corporate training videos. The maker expresses a clear level of intent, and care in craft, but risk-averse decisions and oversimplified memes and storylines typify the work.

The final two degrees of quality are both considered Professional: *Professional-Advertisement*, and the highest level, *Professional-Hollywood*. A high level of craft, professional quality equipment, and a story that is clearly targeted toward a particular audience typifies the Professional-Advertisement category. Often short and to the point, the work employs sophisticated techniques, animation (including 3-D animations with clear and bold intent), and is certainly not risk-averse. (Think, as an example, of an Adidas ad.)

Professional-Hollywood describes the highest level of craft, equipment, story refinement, message, intent, and completeness, and adheres to a standard established through historic precedent. Few mistakes are made, continuity is paramount, all stages of production are equally focused on, and thus the final product, the amalgamation of those steps, approaches seamlessness in suspension of reality and transcendence of the screen. Unless conditions change radically it is unlikely this level of quality will be seen in any terrorist-produced material (except when it has been directly ripped from Hollywood product, which the authors have documented); however, this upper limit provides a useful marker for quality, well known and universally recognized, and therefore against which other products can be measured.

The immediate goal of this project was to systematize the ability to make quality judgments about *jihadist* videos; to that end the grid was refined by running multiple IS videos through over a prolonged period of time.[7] This initial test of the method required a minimum of two videos selected at random from each month of 2015 through 2017 (concluding with June of 2017, when the study concluded) for a total pull of sixty-six videos: twenty-eight from 2015, twenty-four from 2016, and fourteen from 2017. All videos were initially pulled from a database that is organized by month, *Jihadology.net*, but to ensure that quality judgments were not artifacts of the way videos were posted to that site, random videos from the data set were then crosschecked against additional sources, such as *justpasteit.com* or *Archive.org*.[8]

Early 2014 Through Late Summer/Early Fall 2015: Centralization

Initially, the research revealed a relatively uniform and fairly high degree of quality. In fact, there was sufficient uniformity across production method and visual aesthetic to evidence a clear conclusion that logos were not merely being slapped on the final work of multiple makers working completely independently: instead, it appears that there was actually a centralized production process and vision.[9] A detailed report appearing in the *Washington Post* describes a tightly controlled production process during this period:

> Only sanctioned crewmembers were allowed to carry cameras, and even they were to follow strict guidelines on the handling of their material. Once finished with a day's shooting, the crews were to load their recordings onto laptops, transfer the footage to memory sticks, then (sic) deliver those to designated drop sites.[10]

Organizationally, *wilayats* (provinces, for our purposes provincial media production centers) did exist and were producing some content at this time:

> The Ministry of Media of the IS is the central hub for all creation and distribution of official IS content, to include videos, statements, photos, etc. It is made up of four different components: al-Furqan, al-Hayat, al-I'tisam, and Ajnad Foundation. … Note that each of the wilayah (provinces) within the IS has its own regional media bureau, all of which can produce and distribute their own content. For example, the media bureau in Nineveh created a photomontage that showcased the creation of a local IS police force. However, it is most likely the case that these regional media bureaus do not have complete autonomy and are required to receive approval from the Ministry of Media for some of their releases.[11]

In his study of IS media output for the snapshot week of 18–24 April 2015, for example, Aaron Y. Zelin found materials pushed out under the "labels" of twenty-four of the thirty-three *wilayats* IS claimed to control during that period.[12] The question is less whether a distributor attached a logo to the video that identifies it as being from Al Hayat or from a specific regional outlet, and more whether quality markers suggest the video looks like every other video produced from the center, or whether something radical impacted their production capacity.

Phase 2, Roughly September 2015: Decentralization and Quality Collapse

Sometime in the fall of 2015, IS appears to have halted the centralized control over video production. Instead, the multiple *wilayats* were now tasked not simply with pushing out videos, but with the primary responsibility for their production as well. (Obviously videos were appearing with the logos of particular *wilayats*, the question is whether or not they were produced somewhere in the geographic location associated with those logos and who had primary responsibility for that production process.) Video production, presumably assigned to multiple teams in multiple *wilayats*, manifested an abrupt and sharp decrease in quality.

There is no way to know what caused this change. It may have been planned, it may have been a response to an airstrike that destroyed production facilities or equipment, or killed key personnel, or the change may have been a preemptive response, an attempt to get ahead of the air campaign. Whatever the *cause*, the *effect* was clear. As personnel dispersed, overall quality weakened.[13]

Phase 3, December 2015 to July/August 2016: Decentralization and Recovery

Later in 2015, on an extremely uneven basis, the quality in some of the *wilayats* began to recover, to return to pre-decentralization levels, and by May 2016 it is fair to say a more consistent return to higher production values became visible. The members of the original core team appeared to disperse to the outer *wilayats*, where they had no choice but to train the people with whom they were now working.[14] A pattern emerged that often appears in the work of new media professionals: their first works are inevitably weak, and as they learn by doing, they hit plateaus, and thus, by leaps, their work begins to improve. By *forcing IS media production to disperse but not destroying it completely, coalition strikes not only multiplied IS production capacity, but also built resilience into that capacity and demonstrated to them that they could replicate it again at will.*

While *wilayats*' production quality has changed on an individual basis, it remains the case that their overall visual aesthetic has not. From the start, when production first split off, for example, the opening graphics packages of all the *wilayats* were strikingly similar. (They are now identical, except for the actual names of the *wilayats*, which strongly suggests that at least the graphics are being produced at a central location.)[15] The causes for similarity in aesthetic could include: control was still exercised from the center or the same person or people had trained all the people running these production centers or, prior to decentralization, the people now running these production centers simply had worked together for long enough to come to share the same aesthetic sensibility. Any of those explanations might be valid, and without evidence external to the videos, the actual cause is non-determinable. Initially, however, IS benefited from having multiple production centers capable of producing narratives tailored to local events and interests.[16]

Now, of course, current IS propaganda output reflects the tremendous military strain placed on IS. This is true both in terms of the quantity of materials produced, which has sharply fallen, and in terms of the number of *wilayats* producing those materials, which has also sharply contracted. Additionally, the nature of that output has recently shown a complete reversal, so that "in early 2017, the Islamic State produced 74 percent *less* utopia-themed propaganda, and 100 percent *more* warfare-themed propaganda, than it did in the summer of 2015."[17] But because they have already had to take their core personnel and have them go through the experience of working with and training relative novices in what were, apparently, technology-austere environments once, they have no reason to think doing so again would present much challenge.

In order to make the case for this argument, and to demonstrate how the grid functions, three videos representing the three phases have been selected.

Case Study One: Mujatweets Episode #7: 21 July 2014

For the first phase, "Centralization," the authors have chosen Mujatweets Episode #7. It's relatively short, many people have seen it, and it has been written about by a number of scholars before.[18] The grid for the *Mujatweets* video makes clear the quality, across a wide range of measures, in a quick visual display, many of the grading bars pushed far to the right.

It has been posted, reposted, and removed by and from multiple accounts repeatedly over the years, but it appears on *Jihadology.net* (a relatively reliable indicator for when it would have first appeared) on 21 July 2014, after the declaration of the "Caliphate"

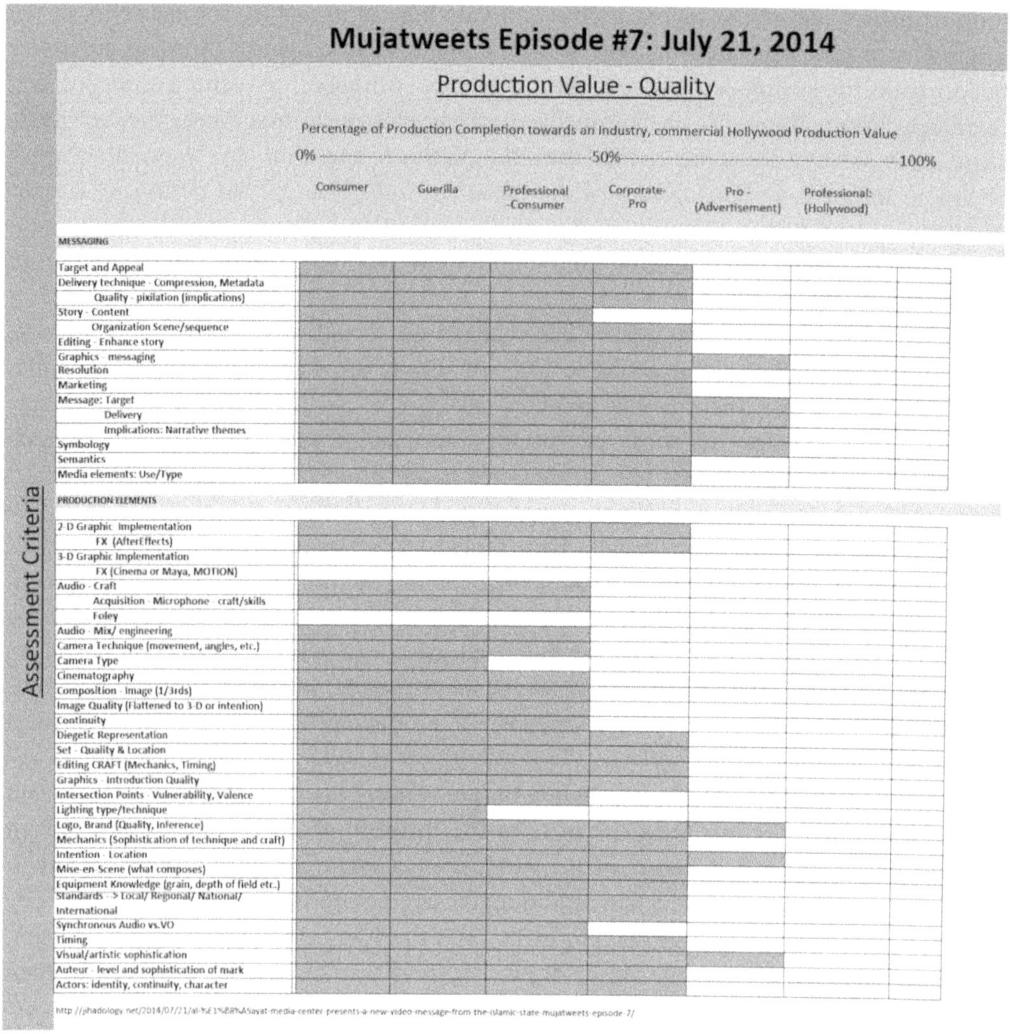

Figure 1. Mujatweets metrics.

and the IS, but only days after, suggesting that production must have been largely complete under the auspices of ISIS.[19]

A black screen with sound of marketplace chatter dissolves into a close-up of a young boy. All frames are branded "Al Hayat" in the upper right corner. The hand-held camera, evoking the first-person perspective pans to show a young man in Western clothes signing "number one" (which within *jihadist* symbology is a referent to the divine) as the frame dissolves into a blue screen with the animated text, in English, "mujatweets." The text jitters and fades back to an over-the-shoulder shot of the same young man as he enters the bustling marketplace. As he moves off into the crowd, the frame fills again with the same graphic, which repeats as a technique throughout, every 5–10 seconds. The colors are saturated, clearly manipulated in post-production. The camera moves though the marketplace following fighters and a man with a bullhorn making a call to the market goers appears and the call continues as a voice-over as the camera moves through the market. Fighters drive through the market with their guns prominently displayed. The camera and exposure are manipulated so as to prevent identifying the fighters, who are nonetheless received by young boys with heroic adulation. The final frames are a bookend dissolve to a black screen with the animated text and the same graphic, "mujatweets."

This video was scored on forty-two separate indicators, and on only two did it score lower than Corporate-Professional (both at Guerrilla.) On eight, close to one-quarter, it graded at Professional-Advertisement; on a full twenty-two it graded as Corporate-Professional. On ten it graded as Prosumer. Thus there is a reason this video can be considered as an example of "peak ISIS."

Case Study Two: "Progress of the Battle in al-Shindākhīyyāt Area – Wilāyat Ḥamāh," 7 October 2015[20]

The fact that the quality of video production has dramatically fallen off is made immediately clear by the grid for *Progress of the Battle*, where, compared to the first case study, the bars have shifted dramatically to the left. A black screen fades into crisp white Arabic text, which fades to the HAMAH logo, which dissolves into artillery discharging. Large Arabic 3-D text zooms in from off-scene as a transparent overlay. Simultaneously, a *nasheed* plays throughout. The following scenes are cut followed by cut of individual fighters, each pulling a trigger cord, followed by artillery fire consuming each scene in dust from the shock of the weapon's discharge. At approximately 50 seconds, the scene dissolves to an excruciatingly long shot where vehicles are traveling on a road; first an apparently irrelevant vehicle passes, then the target vehicle follows, hitting an improvised explosive device (IED) in the middle of the frame. The sound and image are heard reversing and then the explosion plays again, and again. Following scenes are poorly composed fighting scenes of anti-aircraft artillery being fired from a collection of sundry pick-up trucks. One cuts to the next as the guns shoot at an imagined horizon. The next cut focuses on a helicopter above, and an explosion is shown in the distance. The explosion has no clear reference to the helicopter and is provided more as a "what-if" than an actuality. This is followed again by the same vehicles firing off into the distance, intercut with explosions in the far distance of which little can be discerned. The next hard cut focuses on a fighter in a repurposed room that appears to be bunkered. The camera, focused first on the speaker, pulls back to reveal other fighters on the floor listening intently. The camerawork reveals a clear lack of practice, but some vague trace of training is evident in a limited number of frames. Fade to black.

From the end of the opening graphics (at 0:14) until 2:15, the video includes a repetitive series of shots, the first where one man after another pulls the lanyard of an artillery piece, is followed by one man after another firing large caliber weapons that have been attached in a variety of ways to the backs of pick-up trucks. The most visually interesting thing about these sequences is that they are filmed in such a way as to show clouds of dust created from the concussive force of the explosions, and slow motion magnifies the impact of the dust. The repetitive use of similar footage combined with a similar time effect like slow motion conveys a naiveté both in technique and storyline. This convenient editing style typifies younger makers who lack the experience to express

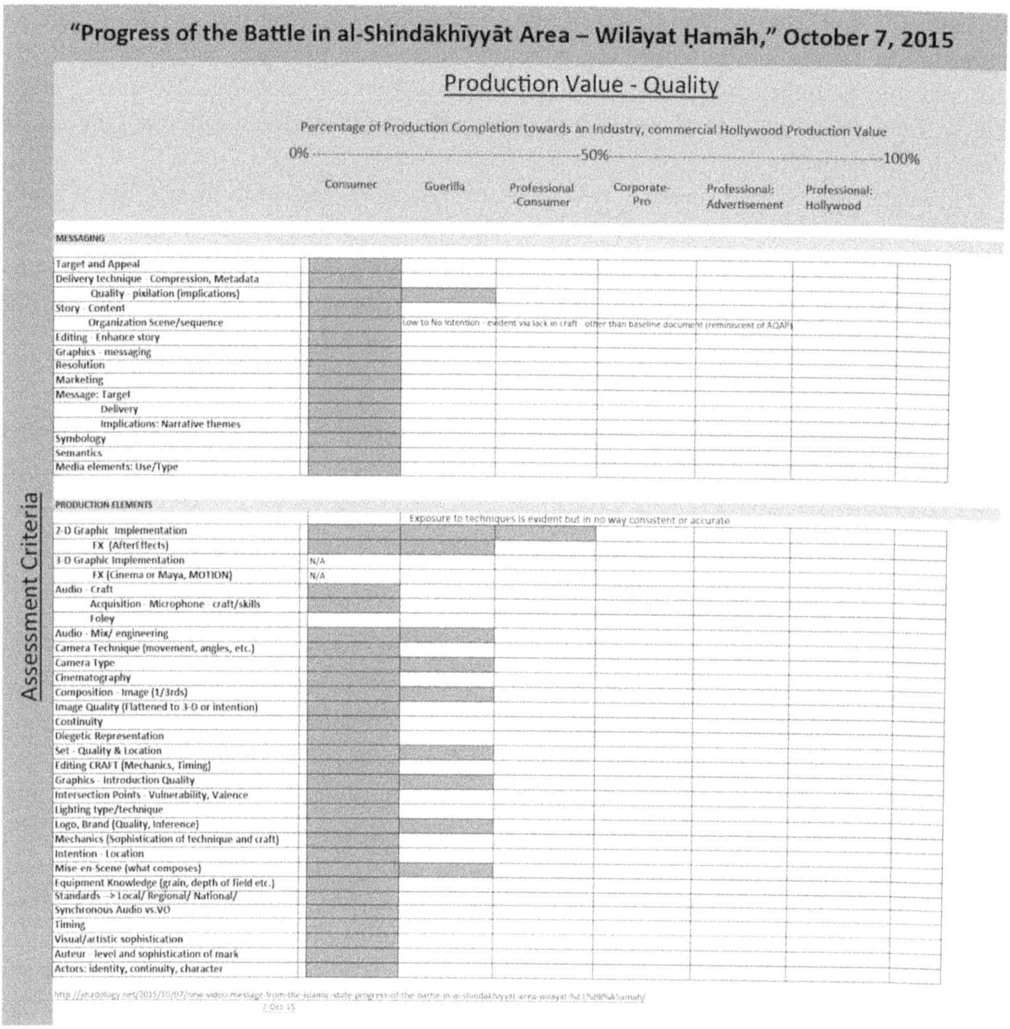

Figure 2. Progress of the battle metrics.

their message in more sophisticated ways. The shots themselves are generic, but have apparently been selected based on this effect, where the dust can be taken as evidence for the force or size of the blast.

There are several shots of an IED destroying a vehicle, and they perfectly represent the low quality of this video. The vehicle appears very far off in the distance, and the footage, gray and grainy, runs for quite a long time before the explosion is seen. A trained editor would have cut this scene in half. But again, the explosive dust cloud is very large. Clearly the makers meant for this to be the focal point, as the shot plays in slow motion and reverses, then plays again from the instant of the explosion to the peak of the dust cloud.

At 2:15 the video concludes with a young man speaking to an assembled group (in Arabic) for thirty seconds, a telling portion of the video. They clearly focused on what he said, his message, but had no other way to present this information than to film him speaking to this group of men, more a shot of convenience—or a consequence of the inherent risks of shooting out of doors in an active conflict zone. The footage includes nothing visually interesting or well produced. The scene is in a dark space, filmed with uninteresting camera angles, in ambient light. The only reason to do it this way is if you simply lacked the resources to do it any other way. They do not have a sound booth, so they cannot record his voice and use it as a narrative voice over for the rest of the video. They lack the equipment or skill to film him outside in a well-composed, well-lit shot. This is what they can do, so this is what they have done.

This second video grades as Consumer on thirty-three ratings and Guerilla on nine. On only one, the implementation of graphics, does it grade as Prosumer.

Case Study Three: "Despite the Bombings of the Crusaders Wilāyat Nīnawā," 31 January 2016[21]

Here, the grid visual clearly demonstrates production quality that is rebounding back toward that of the first case study, as bars are beginning to move back toward the right, but the recovery is not yet complete. Black screen fades in to crisp white Arabic text, fades to yellow pixels that coalesce to form a 3-D globe, and seamlessly to a ground-level view as the camera continues to travel over virtual ground made up of yellow pixels. A vehicle explodes on the horizon, and the yellow dots scatter and re-coalesce in the form of a logo for NINAWA. The logo fades to reveal a split screen view. On the left is an "after" scene of devastation. The scene on the right offers a "before;" footage of a city and the people going about their daily business. The images are edited in a fast paced forceful manner and fade to Arabic text. The screen goes black and then fades to a shot from the ground looking up at an aircraft, with red cross hairs superimposed over it. The aircraft rapidly fades to shots of impersonal destruction, sourced from the coalition. The de-humanized footage portrays destruction. Fade to black and a *nasheed* plays. The following scenes are of bombing aftermaths, shot with a hand-held camera and featuring lifeless bodies. The final scene from this section fades to a featured, elder, speaker. While the elder speaks in voice-over, the scenes show both the destruction and the repair of critical infrastructure such as bridges. Additional aerial infrared footage of a bomb exploding fades to more footage, panning, showing destroyed infrastructure. Scenes cut in of a first-person camera following children as they are rushed into surgery, adults whose wounds are being attended to, back to more footage of infrastructure damage.

At 4:31 the scene fades to black and emerges to reveal a complicated overlay animation of the flags of the world over text, and the images of Western and coalition leaders, and allies. 4:57 reveals a high-definition shot of a repairman with heavy construction machinery in the background and people repairing holes in the asphalt road. As he continues to be heard as voice-over, the viewer sees multiple construction projects under way. After a fade to black from the "repair" scenes, the audience hears a *nasheed* while seeing a functional bridge in a state of good repair, fading to an establishing shot of a bustling downtown. Next, the camera reveals a tight shot of a bridge with pedestrians and cars, followed by a mass outdoor prayer scene with busy markets and people. The editor uses a white flash as a cut before showing close-up scenes of the marketplace including abundant fresh food then fades to a single man engaged in a monologue. While he speaks, inter-spliced images of an overhead drone play to cuts of the busy

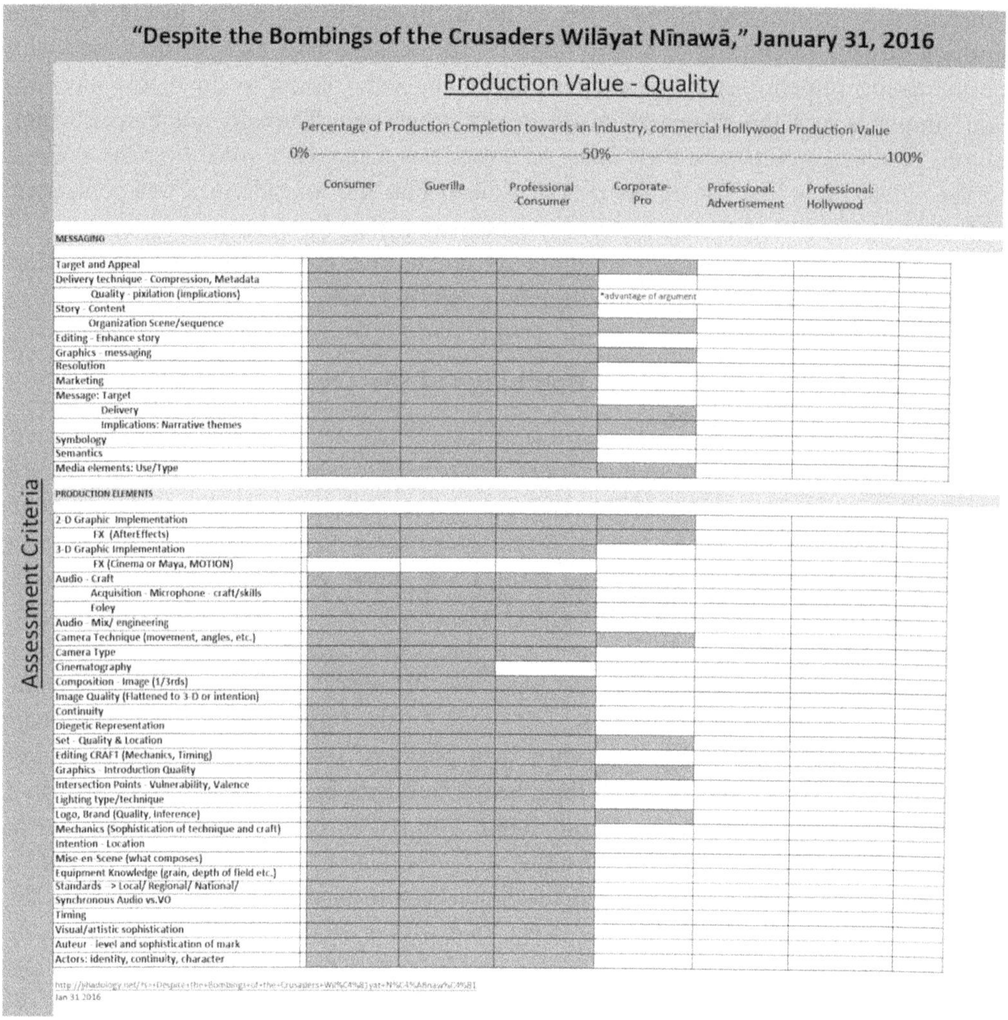

Figure 3. Despite the bombings metrics.

marketplace, and city traffic. At 7:40 there is a fade to black and what appears to be a U.S. military promo advertisement plays. A clear voice-over that plays throughout the scenes of the advertisement has been manipulated from multiple sources, displayed in split screen format, and inter-spliced in such a manner as to incriminate the coalition to the viewer. Fade to black.

The third video reflects an obvious jump in quality that will be clear to any viewer from the very beginning, when the opening graphic begins. Those graphics are clearly identical in style and iconography to the ones used in the second video, but are done in full color full motion graphics. After the graphics, the difference remains sharp, simply because this video is visually interesting (you are not watching the same sequence over and over again with slight variations.) In fact, the basic argument, a visually straight forward message, conveys meaning even to a viewer who lacks the language skills to follow what is being said by the various subjects during the "man-in-the-street" interviews peppered throughout.

Thus, this is a narrative about the fact that the Islamic State is being relentlessly bombed. Indeed, the opening images, which are shown through the use of special effects, line up before and after scenes side by side: bustling scenes of civilian life on one side, grim scenes of rubble emptied of even their color on the other—and, since the intended audience speaks Arabic, the "before" is on the right, the "after" on the left. Quickly the narrative shifts to footage of a coalition aircraft, helpfully centered as in various video games, rubble, grievously wounded citizens, and even footage pulled from U.S. military sites abruptly edited in, so the viewer watches the bombings from the perspective of the American pilots while listening to their voices. The Americans, of course, sound emotionless—clinical, detached, something that an Arabic speaker unable to understand precisely what they were saying would still be able to pick up on.

The results of the bombings are devastating, as demonstrated by many shots of rubble and destruction. But it *does not matter*. The citizens of the IS are undaunted (thus, the interviews.) As with the second video, what may appear at first glance as innocuous footage of single speakers is actually where this video conveys some of the most telling information. The first interview subject, after prolonged shots of rubble reduced to a colorless palette, presents us suddenly with saturated color. The shot itself, furthermore, presents a very carefully composed image, with great attention to the "rule of thirds."[22]

The next interview, shown after a great deal more narrative sequence, contrasts sharply with the speaker filmed at the end of the second video. This subject was filmed using a tripod and pan as well as multiple cameras. That means there was a substantial amount of equipment that had to be dragged out to the location of the shoot—which means there was a substantial amount of equipment *available* to be dragged to the shoot. It also means that someone had to think and plan how they wanted those shots to look in advance. Additionally, in this "interview" the man's voice provides a voice over for additional visual material ("B-roll") shown while the viewer listens to him speaking. In other words, the form changes to a voice-over as he continues to speak while the camera appears to pan behind him, a far more advanced use of audio (and editing) than anything in the second video. Both these "man-in-the-street" interviews are planned, composed shots. They are not accidental, they are not shots of convenience: these subjects were carefully positioned in specific spots for the benefit of the videographer—and thus the audience.

But again, the narrative functions to emphasize that the IS, no matter how substantial the attacks on it, will simply rebuild, as demonstrated by footage of road repair crews out fixing the damage to streets, highways, and bridges. The brutality of the attacks on the State are represented by scenes of the badly wounded, of course including very small children, being rushed to treatment in the hospital. And these scenes work rhetorically with the very ambiguity of the images of bombed out buildings. Because they are bombed out, the viewer has no way to determine what they were before they were destroyed: schools? Homes? Factories or shops? Some other place where innocent civilians were gathered? That is the clear implication of pairing the images of now-skeletal buildings with the scenes at the hospital.

The narrative hinges on the resilience of the citizens of the IS, and thus the viewer observes scenes of work crews fixing large holes in roadways and bridges. The video ends with scenes of life clearly returned to normal, traffic speeding along undamaged roadways and bridges, bustling markets, and so forth. This includes footage shot out the back of a truck speeding over a bridge (which the viewer is meant to assume was just repaired; in reality the viewer has no way to know if that specific location was ever bombed). The technique presents an extremely sophisticated method to visually demonstrate that the roads are back in business. It may not seem like much, but someone had to first think that this would work. A naïve videographer given a camera and told to shoot from a moving vehicle will not do this: they will at best shoot out a window. Shooting this way is still Prosumer (the camera is not, for example, locked down, something a professional would have done) but this is not a shot of happenstance or of convenience, it had to be planned. It makes clear use of the vanishing point, a significant issue that requires some kind of training.

The video ends with a scene of a bustling market, again obviously intended to demonstrate that the IS survives and will continue to thrive despite the bombing campaign. The well-composed scene respects the rule of thirds, and demonstrates the use of carefully planned camera angles, as both the market and another interview subject are shot from a balcony (where, again, equipment had to be pre-positioned.)

In the final seconds, the video reunites the viewer with the bridge—a bridge we *have now crossed.* These analytical details suggest that the makers of this video are, in effect, punching above their weight class. They are improving rapidly, but have limits, yet are still measurably better than the team that produced the second video.

And indeed this video is assessed as Corporate-Professional on twelve registers, Prosumer on thirty-two, and on only one did it score below Prosumer, at Guerrilla.[23]

Findings and Discussion

Once the grid for an individual video was completed, each of forty-six factors in the Y-axis has a possible score of as high as 6, for a total possible score (6×46) of 276. The total value of any individual video's score divided by the perfect possible score of 276 yields a quality judgment that can be expressed as a percent of perfect possible video assessment. Plotting the quality of videos over time yields a graphic comparison such that particulars about production capabilities might be measured across time as seen here:

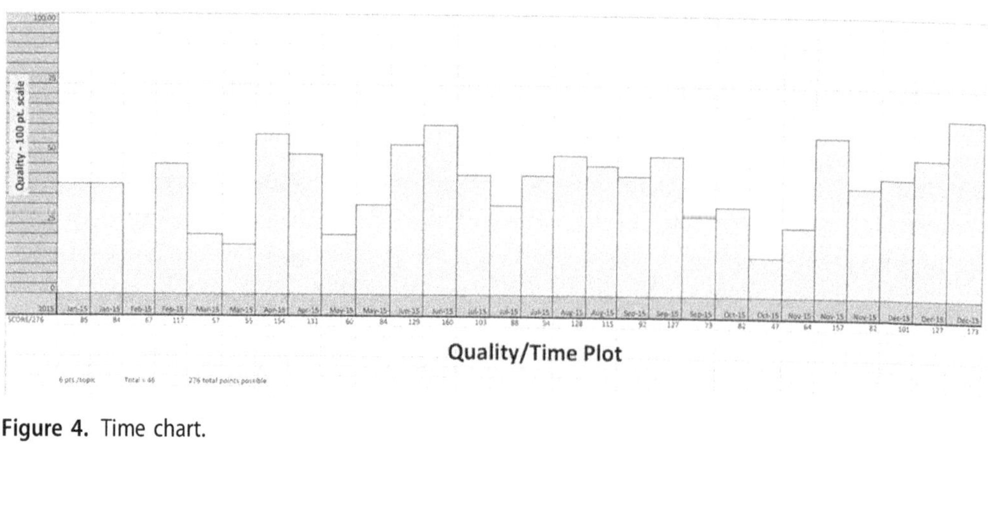

Figure 4. Time chart.

Initially the focus was primarily on the grid itself, but as a greater quantity of videos were run through contemporaneously, a clear pattern began to emerge. Thus the authors believe that inserting quality evaluations into the conversation is necessary to get a complete picture of what is happening with the propaganda output of any particular group.

Recent studies cited here make clear, for example, that IS video production, just in terms of raw volume of output, has decreased dramatically, and furthermore that there has been a noticeable shift in terms of how much effort is devoted to which categories of output. Yet looking at the videos they are producing it nonetheless seems to be the case that were this study to be begun now, the videos available would uniformly grade higher. The fact that the *quality* of their video production has recovered, and indeed continues to improve, must be a factor taken into consideration when assessing IS propaganda going forward.

Conclusion

Why does the ability to grade the relative quality of *jihadist* videos matter? After all, the argument has been persuasively made that it is unlikely anyone self-radicalizes simply from contact with material encountered on the Web.[24] While the authors agree it is surely an uncommon phenomenon, it is equally unlikely many people are radicalized *without* the use of Web-based materials, and particularly videos. Empirical data on this is scarce, of course, because research subjects are so inaccessible.[25]

We believe there are several possibilities for this analytical approach going forward. Testing inter-coder reliability for the grid is the next step. But while demonstrating inter-coder reliability would certainly be beneficial, it is not necessary in order to demonstrate the benefit of what has been presented here.

First, this approach permits assessments about the quality of videos to be turned into usable metrics regarding the progress of kinetic actions against the groups producing the videos. "BDA"— Bomb Damage Assessment or sometimes Battle Damage Assessment—is the sometimes arcane series of processes used to determine the degree to which a specific military strike has succeeded or failed. Refining methods for BDA is of particular interest, for example, to air forces, because they need to know if a target has actually been hit, and how effective a strike has been, in order to plan the next series of attacks.[26] On any given important date—and it is not necessary to know what makes that date relevant, what the "X" event is—videos produced before and after that date can be assessed to see if there is a measurable change in quality. There are reasons why kinetic activity might not impact video production, but our method allows an answer to the question, did a kinetic campaign have an impact in a measurable way?

Second, it is worth noting that this approach permits an evaluation of propaganda output not only across time, but also across groups. Analysts have noted that one "leading indicator" of a group's forging a relationship with IS has been a marked improvement in the quality of the propaganda they have released.[27] Trying to find a way to identify individual makers of propaganda materials, in using the grid as a way to develop the basis for "artistic fingerprints," has been a long-term goal for this research project. In theory, if one gathers a large enough data set, these fingerprints can be found, just as cinephiles can watch films and identify characteristics that are tell tale of particular directors or cinematographers. If over time a particular *wilayat* produces materials based on great videography but poor editing, and there is a sudden shift, that, for example, would suggest a sudden change in personnel.

The effort to develop this capacity will be critical going forward. Just as individual foreign fighters will be pushed out as the IS collapses, so will these media production teams. *Even if the teams themselves do not survive*, IS's media production personnel possess the adaptability to survive institutionally, taking key personnel out to the margins and using them to reconstitute capacity. So entire *teams* do not have to survive, *individual team members* who are trained have to survive: they are now not only trained in production, but in how to bring novices up to a reasonable degree of proficiency. Developing these "fingerprints" opens the potential to do more than just make note of improvement in overall quality in a given group's propaganda. The grid could conceivably come close to identifying—at least with a high degree of probability—the presence of someone who worked within a *wilayat* team prior to the collapse of IS.

It should be noted that the authors do understand that this method, as presented, will require a certain background in the communication discipline, for now. That does not, as we see it, lessen its value. Nevertheless, the goal for this project is to continue to systematize the method to the point that it would take only a minimal amount of training before someone without that background would be able to effectively utilize it.

Notes

1. See for example Carol Winkler, "Visual Images: Distinguishing Daesh's Internal and External Communication Strategies," in *Countering Daesh Propaganda: Action Oriented Research for Practical Policy Outcomes* (Atlanta: The Carter Center, February, 2016), 15–19, https://www.cartercenter.org/resources/pdfs/peace/conflict_resolution/countering-isis/counteringdaeshpropaganda-feb2016.pdf; Mia Bloom, John Horgan, and Charlie Winter, "Depictions of Children and Youth in the Islamic State's Martyrdom Propaganda, 2015–2016," *CTC Sentinel* 9, no. 2 (2016): 1–34. https://ctc.usma.edu/depictions-of-children-and-youth-in-the-islamic-states-martyrdom-propaganda-2015-2016/.
2. This is a function of physiology, of the way the eye and the brain work together. Moving images attract our attention and produce arousal in ways that still images cannot. See Robert F. Simons, Benjamin H. Detenber, Bruce N. Cuthbert, David D. Schwartz, and Jason E. Reiss, "Attention to Television: Alpha Power and Its Relation to Image Motion and Emotional Content," *Media Psychology* 5, no. 3 (2003): 283–301.
3. See for example Aaron Y. Zelin, "Picture or it Didn't Happen: A Snapshot of the Islamic State's Official Media Output," *Perspectives on Terrorism* 9, no. 4 (2015): 85–97, http://www.terrorismanalysts.com/pt/index.php/pot/article/view/445/876. In this piece Zelin says he is discussing "Quality" of video output, but what he means by quality we would consider typology (i.e., whether a particular video ought be characterized as combat or governance).
4. See for example Lorenzo Vidino and Seamus Hughes, *ISIS in America: From Retweets to Raqqa* (Washington, DC: The George Washington University Program on Extremism, December, 2015). isis_in_america-full_report.pdf.
5. Charlie Winter has documented shifts, as the physical space IS controls has contracted, in the percentages of product devoted to combat-themed material increase and the percentages devoted to governance and "Utopia" decrease. Charlie Winter, "The ISIS Propaganda Decline." ICSR Insight, International Centre for the Study of Radicalization, Kings College, London, 23 May 2017, http://icsr.info/2017/03/icsr-insight-isis-propaganda-decline/

6. This research project is focused on *jihadist* materials, but there is no reason this approach could not ultimately be used for any extremist product. While there is, of course, a growing body of research on the propaganda magazines produced both by Islamic State and by Al Qaeda, there is not nearly as much material studying the videos (from a form, as opposed to a content, basis.) See as examples Celine Marie I. Novenario, "Differentiating Al Qaeda and the Islamic State Through Strategies Publicized in *Jihadist* Magazines," *Studies in Conflict and Terrorism* 39, no. 11 (2016): 953–967, https://doi.org/10.1080/1057610X.2016.1151679; Haroro J. Ingram, "An Analysis of *Inspire* and *Dabiq*: Lessons From AQAP and Islamic State's Propaganda War," *Studies in Conflict and Terrorism* 40, no. 5 (2017): 357–375, https://doi.org/10.1080/1057610X.2016.1212551; Brandon Colas, "What Does *Dabiq* Do? ISIS Hermeneutics and Organizational Fractures Within *Dabiq* Magazine," *Studies in Conflict and Terrorism*," 40, no. 3 (2017): 173–190, https://doi.org/10.1080/1057610X.2016.1184062. This is despite the fact that there are thousands of videos, that video is as least as powerful a medium as still images, but probably more powerful, and despite the fact that there are so many ways to disseminate video.
7. There are, of course, excellent studies dividing IS output into distinct categories. See for example Charlie Winter, *Documenting the Virtual "Caliphate"* (London: Quilliam, October, 2015), http://www.quilliaminternational.com/wp-content/uploads/2015/10/FINAL-documenting-the-virtual-caliphate.pdf. Those distinctions, however, are not relevant for this work. While different categories may present different production challenges: Filming an outdoor combat scene in natural light will simply offer different options than filming a single speaker under controlled conditions indoors: One would use the same metrics to evaluate their quality. For a breakdown of which *wilayats* were emphasizing which types of video products, see Daniel Milton, *Communication Breakdown: Unraveling the Islamic State's Media Efforts* (New York: United States Military Academy Combating Terrorism Center, October, 2016), 37–40, https://www.ctc.usma.edu/v2/wp-content/uploads/2016/10/ISMedia_Online.pdf.
8. For consistency's sake, all the videos used throughout this study had been posted to the website maintained by Aaron Zelin, http://jihadology.net/. There are disadvantages to doing so, most obviously the need to be careful that what is being studied is the way *jihadist* groups post material and not an artifact of the way Zelin posts material. To guard against this, the authors cross-checked several videos from the data set chosen at random against the exact same videos as they appeared on Zelin's original source, for example *Archive.org* or *Justpasteit.com*, and the quality was the same (which makes sense, as there are only a limited number of differences based on a limited number of changes he could be making. For example he might by compressing the videos differently when he posts them). For purposes of this analysis it is worth the need to do this additional check given the security that comes from the stability of *Jihadology.net*: while videos do come down from that site, it's a rare occurrence, while videos appear and disappear from other sites with dizzying speed.
9. Indeed, there is evidence that the dissemination of material via social media was far more controlled and centralized than was understood at the time. Jytte Klausen, "Tweeting the Jihad: Social Media Networks of Western Foreign Fighters in Syria and Iraq," *Studies in Conflict and Terrorism* 38, no. 1 (2015): 1–22. doi:10.1080/1057610X.2014.974948.
10. The article appeared in late November, but was based on interviews with sources whose knowledge would not have been up to date, defectors held in prisons in countries in the region for example. See Greg Miller and Souad Mekhennet, "Inside the Surreal World of the Islamic State's Propaganda Machine," *Washington Post*, 20 November 2015, https://www.washingtonpost.com/world/national-security/inside-the-islamic-states-propaganda-machine/2015/11/20/051e997a-8ce6-11e5-acff-673ae92ddd2b_story.html?utm_term=.b50d8ad20ab9. For additional support regarding the centralized nature of Islamic State media, see Milton, *Communication Breakdown*, 16.
11. Daniel Milton, "Communicating Fear and Vision: The Media Organization of IS," in *The Group That Calls Itself A State: Understanding the Evolution and Challenges of the Islamic*

State, ed. Muhammad al-Ubaydi, Nelly Lahoud, Daniel Milton, and Bryan Price (West Point, NY: The Combating Terrorism Center, December, 2014), 48–49. https://www.ctc.usma.edu/v2/wp-content/uploads/2014/12/CTC-The-Group-That-Calls-Itself-A-State-December20141.pdf.

12. Zelin, "Picture Or It Didn't Happen."
13. Given what is known of IS's use of its media operations in the past, it is extremely unlikely that they would have completely decentralized everything (although that is certainly not necessary to our argument). See Craig Whiteside, "Lighting the Path: The Evolution of the Islamic State Media Enterprise (2003–2016)," *International Counter-Terrorism Centre—The Hague Research Paper*, no. 11, 15 November 2016, https://icct.nl/wp-content/uploads/2016/11/ICCT-Whiteside-Lighting-the-Path-the-Evolution-of-the-Islamic-State-Media-Enterprise-2003-2016-Nov2016.pdf.

    Apparently, until his death in August 2016, the official IS spokesman, Abu Muhammad al-Adnani, did exercise final control over what footage was released. See Rukmini Callimachi, "How A Secretive Branch of ISIS Built A Global Network of Killers," *The New York Times*, 3 August 2016, https://www.nytimes.com/2016/08/04/world/middleeast/isis-german-recruit-interview.html. But that is centralized control over what footage went out, it says nothing about where production facilities were located or who was staffing them, and therefore *what footage was available to choose from*, which is our argument.
14. AQI (Al Queda in Iraq) and ISI (Islamic State in Iraq), the Islamic State's predecessor organizations, had clear protocols in place for the training of personnel working in photography, interestingly enough, "using a list

    of 16 specific instructions, including the best time of day to shoot, the number of cameras to use for different operations, and the best angles to film." Milton, *Communication Breakdown,* 9.
15. It should also be noted that Charlie Winter observed the same thing happen at an earlier point in time across the network of IS affiliates. See Miller and Mekhennet, "Islamic State's Propaganda Machine," *Washington Post.* That would not be unprecedented: R. Green speculated that, "The quality of videos made in Sinai: Including some made prior to the official establishment of the Sinai Province: Suggest that raw footage may have been sent to be edited and polished by central media organs in Syria or Iraq." "ISIS In Sinai Increases Propaganda, Military Pressure on Egypt." Middle East Media Research Institute: Inquiry and Analysis Series No. 1201, November 8, 2015, https://www.memri.org/reports/isis-sinai-increases-military-propaganda-pressure-egypt.
16. See Daveed Gartenstein-Ross, Daniel Barr, and Bridget Moreng, "The Islamic State's Global Propaganda Strategy." ICCT Research Paper, International Centre for Counter-Terrorism-The Hague, March 2016. https://www.icct.nl/wp-content/uploads/2016/03/ICCT-Gartenstein-Ross-IS-Global-Propaganda-Strategy-March2016.pdf. While this study details specific differences between several of the *wilayat*'s overall approaches to propaganda, it does not discuss video production or compositional elements of videos, although the authors note that one benefit of joining the IS, for regional groups, is assistance in producing better propaganda materials. One reason IS provides this assistance "to new wilayats is because it seeks to maintain continuity and consistency in the propaganda produced with the IS logo" (67).
17. Winter, "ISIS Propaganda Decline."
18. See Cori E. Dauber and Mark Robinson, "Guest Post: ISIS and the Hollywood Visual Style," *Jihadology.net*, 6 July 2015, http://jihadology.net/2015/07/06/guest-post-isis-and-the-hollywood-visual-style/. (It is the very first video discussed.)
19. "Al-Hayat Media Center presents a new video message from the Islamic State: 'Mujatweets Episode #7,'" *Jihadology.net*, Posted by Aaron Y. Zelin, 21 July 2014, http://jihadology.net/2014/07/21/al-%E1%B8%A5ayat-media-center-presents-a-new-video-message-from-the-islamic-state-mujatweets-episode-7/.

20. "New Video Message from the Islamic State: 'Progress of the Battle in al-Shindakhiyyat Area—Wilayah Hamah,'" *Jihadology.net*, Posted by Aaron Y. Zelin, 7 October 2015, http://jihadology.net/2015/10/07/new-video-message-from-the-islamic-state-progress-of-the-battle-in-al-shindakhiyyat-area-wilayat-%E1%B8%A5amah/.
21. "New Video Message from The Islamic State: 'Stability of the Muslims Despite the Bombings of the Crusaders—Wilayat Ninawa,' "*Jihadology.net*, 31 January 2016, Posted by Aaron Y. Zelin, http://jihadology.net/2016/01/31/new-video-message-from-the-islamic-state-stability-of-the-muslims-despite-the-bombings-of-the-crusaders-wilayat-ninawa/.
22. This is a well-established rule for composing shots, whether filming fictional, documentary, or news footage. Imagine a grid placed on the image such that it is divided into three equidistant sections in the Y direction and three equidistant sections in the X direction. The resulting grid has four points of intersection where the X and Y lines meet. These are the four focal points of the image, and in order to create movement for the viewer's eye, the primary focus of the scene should fall on one of those points of intersection. If you are interviewing a subject, then, they should not be centered but instead positioned so that the eye of the interviewee falls on one of the top two points of intersection. Thus the subject will be asymmetrically balanced in the frame. This resulting optical balance is proven to make the viewer more comfortable with the subject. This is a psychological phenomenon, and thus an optical tool.
23. While there are scenes of combat in these three selections, they are not particularly violent. Many of the videos looked at included scenes of great violence, but many did not. Multiple studies have proven empirically that the ultra-violent images that received the greatest attention in the Western media were an exceedingly small percentage of IS output. Charlie Winter, "Fishing and Ultraviolence," *BBC.com*, 6 October 2015, http://www.bbc.co.uk/news/resources/idt-88492697-b674-4c69-8426-3edd17b7daed or Zelin, "Picture Or It Didn't." Lydia Wilson notes that the persistent focus on the ultra-violent videos, "obscured to a Western audience the revolutionary message of idealism and joy that attracts many young people to the cause, which in turn blocks our understanding of and our ability to combat the appeal." "Understanding the Appeal of ISIS," *New England Journal of Public Policy* 29, no. 1 (2017): 5, https://scholarworks.umb.edu/cgi/viewcontent.cgi?referer=https://www.google.com/&httpsredir =1&article =1704&context=nejpp.
24. Shiraz Maher, "Inside the Isis Social Network," *New Statesman*, 2 June 2017, http://www.newstatesman.com/world/2017/06/inside-isis-social-network.
25. On the other hand, the University of Maryland reports that the Internet "contributed to the radicalization of 83%" of those who attempted to travel for purposes of joining a foreign terrorist organization by 2015, though it is not clear what they mean by "contributed." "Overview: Profiles of Individual Radicalization in the United States-Foreign Fighters (PIRUS-FF)." START: National Consortium for the Study of Terrorism and Responses to Terrorism, University of Maryland, College Park, Md., April 2016, 4, https://www.start.umd.edu/pubs/START_PIRUS-FF_InfographicSeries_April2016.pdf.
26. For an easy to understand description of BDA see John T. Rauch Jr., *Assessing Airpower's Effects: Capabilities and Limitations of Real-Time Battle Damage Assessment* (Thesis Submitted to the Faculty of the School of Advanced Airpower Studies, Air University, Maxwell Air Base, June, 2002), ADA420587.pdf
27. Note the case of Boko Haram. See Gartenstein-Ross, Barr, and Moreng, "Islamic State's Global Propaganda Strategy," 67.

Women's Radicalization to Religious Terrorism: An Examination of ISIS Cases in the United States

Lauren R. Shapiro and Marie-Helen Maras

ABSTRACT

American women joining Islamic State of Iraq and Syria (ISIS) have increased and their roles evolved beyond auxiliary and domestic provisions, demonstrating both agency and tenacity for pursuing, recruiting, supporting, and spreading extreme Islamist ideals and terrorism. Social learning theory was applied to information gained from open-source court cases as a way of examining how thirty-one U.S. women acquired, maintained, and acted pursuant to radicalization to religious terrorism for ISIS. Internet functionalities, reasons, roles, and support types for radicalization and illegal activities for ISIS were examined using self-, dyad-, and group-classifications. A gendered interventive program based on social learning theory's extinguishing of radicalized ideology and behavior was outlined.

Radicalization is a widely studied yet contested concept that is sometimes, but mistakenly, used interchangeably with terrorism.[1] Although lacking a universal definition, radicalization is defined in this article as a gradual process whereby individuals are socialized into extreme beliefs that are articulated in nonviolent and/or violent acts.[2] Society is particularly concerned with radicalization to terrorism, whereby individuals adopt extreme beliefs that justify the use of violence to promote political, national, religious, or ideological goals of the terrorist organization they are inspired by or join, through coercion, intimidation, or inculcation of fear in people and their government, regardless of their own roles.[3] Hoffman purported that in comparison to secular terrorist groups, those who are radicalized to religious terrorism (i.e., endorsing violent acts to achieve goals based on radical interpretations of their faith) are the most dangerous due to the lethality and violence of their actions.[4]

Historically and presently, individuals subscribing to extreme interpretations of different faiths (e.g., Christianity, Hinduism, Buddhism, Judaism, Islamism) have engaged in religious terrorism. A recent report indicated that the proportion of terrorist attacks from religious extremists in the United States has increased from 9 percent in the 2000s to 53 percent in the 2010s.[5] Attacks from 1992 to 2017 by Islamist terrorists accounted for more deaths and injuries than nationalist, right-wing, left-wing, and other/unknown terrorist groups combined (52 percent vs. 48 percent), even when the Oklahoma City

Color versions of one or more of the figures in the article can be found online at www.tandfonline.com/uter.

and 11 September 2001 bombings were removed.[6] Technology, particularly the smartphone and Internet with its various functionalities, has provided the Islamic State of Iraq and Syria (ISIS; a.k.a. Islamic State of Iraq and Levant [ISIL] or Islamic State [IS]) with a global platform to facilitate the radicalization process using propaganda to appeal to both men and women for support, sympathy, and recruits to further its goal of Islamic state-building.[7] Although ISIS expects men to fulfill their roles as fighters and martyrs, women have gendered, domestic roles as wives and mothers to the next generation for the caliphate.[8] Women's proclivity online and their agency in expanding assigned roles to include auxiliary and operational functions, combined with the public's difficulty in perceiving them as perpetrators, makes them as big, if not a bigger threat to American security.

The current study examined radicalization of women in the United States to religious terrorism; specifically, the focus was on women who engaged in operational and/or support activities for ISIS by fostering the religious and cultural ideology of a radical interpretation of Islam. Despite Western women[9] comprising a lower proportion of migrants to ISIS (10–15 percent) than men,[10] their involvement in the group has been increasing since 2015 while men's migration has been tapering off.[11] Moreover, women in general are reputed to be steadfast in their radical religious ideals and pursuit of their extreme beliefs, despite loss of their male counterparts from arrests and death, by financing and facilitating operations; influencing and advancing the group's cause; and using propaganda to recruit and educate new members, particularly their own children.[12] The main goal of this article was to employ social learning theory as a framework by which to examine how women in the United States acquire, maintain, and act pursuant to radicalization to religious terrorism for ISIS.[13]

Radicalization: Social learning theory and Internet functionalities

The trajectory toward radicalization to religious terrorism differs for each person, although there are common underlying "ideological, psychological, and community-based factors" contributing to one's susceptibility to ISIS propaganda.[14] According to Akins and Winfree, "All crime is learned, a claim that includes illegal acts committed by terrorists, no matter the underlying ideology, religious (or pseudo-religious) underpinnings, or location in the world."[15] Radicalization to religious terrorism, as defined in this study, includes both cognitive and behavioral components that correspond to the legal criminal requirements of *mens rea* (intention) and *actus rea* (action) for terrorism. This concept of radicalization is consistent with the notion that social processes contribute to changes in the acceptance of ideology and illegal behavior of religious terrorism.[16] Akers's social learning theory (SLT)[17] was employed in this study as a means of understanding the social-cognitive mechanisms underlying U.S. women's radicalization to religious terrorism, and illicit engagement in terrorism and terrorist-related activities for ISIS.[18] Unlike stage or step theories explaining radicalization,[19] the four factors in SLT contributing to the acquisition and maintenance of societal-deemed "deviant" behaviors are ongoing processes.[20] As such, this approach provides insight into how the extremist ideologies and associated behaviors can be extinguished through deradicalization.[21]

A central tenet of SLT, *differential association*, holds that social interactions and identification with the primary groups' members structure the setting within which beliefs and behaviors occur. People learn ideas and activities, regardless if these are extremist or non-extremist in nature, as a product of their social interactions.[22] Applying this component of SLT to radicalization to religious terrorism, the social community is key to constructing an environment, whether physical or online, conducive to this process. Women are active agents in their own radicalization, regardless of whether these extremist beliefs are linked subsequently with violent or nonviolent actions.[23] ISIS takes advantage of the fact that many of the Muslim converts (born and raised in another or no religion) and reverts (born Muslim, striving to reengage) exposed to its propaganda have little knowledge of and/or limited experience with mainstream Islam.[24] Women who are interested or curious about Islam may seek out this information from others in their communities.[25] However, many of the opportunities for public face-to-face real-world locations that Western men may have to congregate, such as at the mosques and Islamic bookstores, are not available to them.[26] According to Pearson, Western women are often banned physically and culturally to "these highly gendered spaces."[27] Even when mosques do not exclude women, they are prevented from discussing religion with the men due to physical segregation, and are given only limited access to Islamic literature.[28]

In contrast, the Internet seems to offer women an inclusive virtual social environment for religious exploration in an always-accessible format that allows rapid development of differential association for the users.[29] As specified in SLT, the rate of radicalization to religious terrorism fluctuates with the intensity, frequency, and endurance of the interactions between the recruit and those who possess and share pro-ISIS attitudes and values.[30] The advantage for ISIS is that it has whole networks of supporting enablers for their operation whose sole purpose is to communicate via websites, publications, blogs, apps (e.g., Fir al-Bashaer) and other social media, particularly Facebook, which has over two billion monthly users[31] and Twitter, which has over 69 million monthly users.[32] Using a grassroots approach through decentralized peer-to-peer radicalization, recruiters are able to encourage and advise, organize hashtag campaigns, and enlist followers to retweet so ISIS messages trend on Twitter.[33] In this way, ISIS creates group dynamics online that mimic the sharing and caring shown in real social milieu, thereby allowing women to enjoy a sisterhood of friendship and support within a gendered community.[34] Women with only a rudimentary understanding of Islam who use the Internet to learn more information are the most vulnerable to extremist ideology, mainly because they lack the knowledge and skills needed to evaluate the messages critically.[35] To ensure radicalization, ISIS discourages recruits from asking outsiders about Islam, thereby preventing them from being introduced to potentially conflicting information.[36]

The online social network[37] provides ISIS with an inexpensive means for finding female sympathizers, connecting with them frequently over long periods of time to discuss, educate, and recruit them to radicalized Islam.[38] ISIS was able to wage electronic *jihad*[39] because by 2013, most Americans (91 percent) owned cell phones[40] and by 2015, a large subsection of young adults used their phones to access social media (86 percent) and the Internet (88 percent), especially YouTube (82 percent) and Facebook (77 percent).[41] ISIS also increased recruitment success by capitalizing on American adolescents' desire to interact online daily with their friends (59 percent) and their penchant for making new friends online (60 percent), who they sometimes even met subsequently in person (20 percent).[42] In particular, adolescent girls use social media to meet new friends, most commonly on Instagram and Facebook (78 percent), and text messaging is their preferred means of daily communication with friends (62 percent).

A second component of SLT involves adopting *neutralizing definitions* toward extreme beliefs condoning violence, despite these acts being illegal.[43] SLT identifies communication and socialization with members of the extremist group as essential to the process of transformative learning during radicalization of violent behaviors and the extremist attitudes, values, and ideology supporting these behaviors.[44] Social affiliation facilitates the women's acceptance of violence against an enemy, which ISIS dehumanizes by applying the degrading terms of infidels or apostates, excommunicating them, and killing them.[45] The women are able to minimalize the negative emotions society ascribes to terrorist acts and rationalize that although terrorism in general is immoral according to societal rules and laws, committing these acts are justifiable in some circumstances, such as religious wars. The women are also swayed by the positive messages associated with ISIS, such as happy families enjoying life in the caliphate that are posted on Facebook and Twitter[46] and Mujatweets, which are brief videos posted on YouTube that depict ISIS as a generous organization and positive presence in its territories.[47]

The Internet aids in women's search for peers with whom to interact and explore these extreme beliefs and it serves as "the decade's radical mosque."[48] Internet technology in America makes ISIS's centralized goals of propaganda marketing; fund-raising for travel, training, and operations through fraud; and opportunities for planning, organizing, and obtaining weapons and other materials, easily accessible.[49] ISIS uses graphic violent images to distort reality and gain attention, notoriety, and sympathy for their cause.[50] To ensure their propaganda will be found online by anyone curious, interested, or predisposed, multiple languages are used in ISIS electronic books and magazines, chat rooms, blogs, videos (YouTube, LiveVideo, PalTalk), Twitter, Facebook, and other social media accounts.[51] Adolescents are comfortable communicating and strengthening their relationships with friends through various online modes: video chat (59 percent) and texting through instant messaging (79 percent), social media (72 percent), e-mail (64 percent), and messaging apps, like What's App (42 percent). Similarly, half of the young adults who own smart phones access the Internet and use apps, including What's App (36 percent) and Snapchat (41 percent).[52]

ISIS recruiters send out tweets, post on Facebook, and visit chat rooms and cyber cafés to interact with potential adherents and prospective terrorists.[53] Through discussions with ISIS sympathizers and supporters, the women intensify their anger toward "nonbelievers" who allegedly suppress them; justify the use of violent terrorist acts, such as murder; and mobilize resources to arrange, direct, and subsequently conduct illicit activities.[54] The women's attitudes, values, and beliefs are strongly influenced by group membership and dynamics that forces them to subordinate their own ideas for that of the group through the process of groupthink.[55] The collective perspective expressed in the online ISIS community is by default "more extreme than that of any individual alone" and "members conform to majority views."[56] Interest and sympathy with the group, particularly by girls and young women in Muslim diaspora communities who adhere to religious traditions and feel alienated from their Western peers, may turn their thoughts into actions.[57] For example, cognitive changes in ideology are externalized through corresponding changes in the women's clothing, such as wearing the *burqa* and *niqab*, and behaviors, including distancing themselves from others, particularly friends or family who reject their new extreme beliefs in favor of those who accept them.[58]

Differential reinforcement (also known as operant conditioning), the third factor in SLT, refers to the process whereby the desired extremist beliefs and behaviors are acquired through a system of past and anticipatory reinforcers by internal or external sources in the environment.[59] The likelihood that the women will voice neutralizing beliefs and engage in terrorism and terrorist-related activities is modulated by the frequency and type of reinforcer. An immediate and continuous reinforcement schedule (i.e., each and every time the act occurs) is used to facilitate the acquisition of new, desirable behaviors and is typically followed by variable ratio reinforcement, such as applying reinforcers after a set number of times desired behavior occurs, to maintain the newly acquired behaviors. During acquisition and maintenance phases, a person increases the number of desired behaviors exhibited when positive consequences or rewards are applied or unpleasant consequences are removed and decreases undesirable behaviors when unpleasant consequences or punishments are applied.[60] Online ISIS members, sympathizers, and supporters control recruits through continuous application of social and physical reinforcers that rapidly normalize extremist actions and thoughts.[61] Positive reinforcement can be measured on social media platforms by the number of likes, retweets, friends requests, followers, and other interactions that posts receive.[62] Negative reinforcement occurs when a women who has been shunned by the community is reintegrated into the group. Likewise, punishment on social media include posting hateful, shaming, and degrading comments on a message or picture that is inconsistent with ISIS propaganda. It could also consist of tweeting or posting names or details about women who received lashings by the al-Khanssaa Brigade for their failure to comply with rules under *Sharia* Law, such as transgressions involving Western modesty and fashion notions in public.[63]

The last factor in SLT involves learning through *imitation of modeled behaviors* that are reinforced, often with minimal comprehension of how the behaviors fit within the group's grand scheme.[64] The women will be more likely to emulate opinions and behaviors by a model who is rewarded than punished, a type of learning called *vicarious reinforcement*.[65] According to SLT, women's exposure to ISIS models who espouse terrorist beliefs and engage in terrorism and terrorist-related behaviors and their perception of these models as desirable and similar to them are key to their decision to imitate them.[66] Some women have models available in their physical environment, but there is an abundance of online models on various social platforms and apps accessible from computers, tablets, and cellphones. Many of the ISIS recruiters boast on various social media platforms about successful attacks on Westerners, urging the men to continue the fight and shaming those who have not yet joined.[67] The most typical ways women could imitate other women would be by physically traveling to the caliphate, which is highly praised, or by retweeting a message or image online supporting ISIS.[68]

Women's attraction to ISIS

The appeal of ISIS to newly converted and reverted Islamic girls and women from Western countries has fascinated researchers, Western society, and the media. Online propaganda espoused by ISIS through "social media, rap videos, counter culture magazines" (*Dabiq*) have achieved "hip and trendy" status particularly among the youth in Europe and North America,[69] encouraged discussion of extreme Islamic ideology in virtual communities,[70] and promised female recruits "empowerment, deliverance, participation, and piety."[71] ISIS is adept at using the Internet as a facilitator and catalyst for radicalization of women (and men) in the United States and abroad,[72] promising a sense of belonging and a utopian life to those who travel to Syria to join them.[73] ISIS started recruiting women out of necessity rather than a desire to be inclusive,[74] specifically to perform state-building roles for the caliphate—mainly domestic and support (e.g., financial, training, propaganda)—to legitimatize the terrorist group and their creation of an "Islamic State" within ISIS-controlled territories.[75] Evidence of ISIS's success includes their ability to overtake major cities in Syria/Iraq from the start of the Syrian conflict in 2011, to establish their caliphate in 2014, to govern the current residents and newly arrived foreign recruits, to maintain control of the region until the end of 2017, and, most remarkably, to continue recruiting new members despite the loss of the caliphate and high death rate of its residents during airstrikes.[76]

Existing literature shows that women's reasons for joining terrorist groups, supporting terrorism, and engaging in terrorism inspired by a group's ideology vary[77] and interestingly, often differ from the terrorist group's reason for recruiting them.[78] Men and women may join ISIS and/or otherwise support them for similar reasons, including adventure, sympathy, dedication to the terrorists' cause, escape from religious harassment, socioeconomic advancement, mental health or personal problems, ethno-national goals, and belief that it is their fundamental duty to build the Islamic state.[79] Applying a gendered approach to understanding women's agency in joining ISIS, Sjoberg and Gentry indicated that women compared daily social and political struggles in their lives versus what ISIS offered them.[80] For example, Kneip found the main reason for women migrating to join ISIS was "female emancipation"; that is, they sought independence from parental control and freedom from Western oppression in the forms of deciding to travel and choose a mate, gaining honor and respect from the ISIS community, and obtaining power over others.[81] Although women may travel with male migrants or as a family to join ISIS, those who travel as single women (sometimes in pairs or groups, against wishes of or unbeknown to family) were classified by Hoyle, Bradford, and Fernett as having three motives: *grievances* (e.g., perceived mistreatment of Muslims), *solutions* (i.e., state-building, sense of belonging, identity), and *personal* (e.g., revenge, redemption, relationships, respect).[82] Women also seek equality with men[83] by emerging as agents of fundamentalist Islam and demonstrating their commitment to ISIS to the same degree as men.[84]

Push/pull factors have been suggested by researchers to explain what predisposes certain individuals to be receptive to radicalization of extremist beliefs and subsequently to propel them toward engaging in terrorism or terrorism-related acts.[85] *Push* factors for radicalization may include: sociopolitical alienation; religious identity; and anger, hostility, and/or frustration over perceived discrimination, socioeconomic inequality, and foreign policy.[86] Political, religious, and/or ideological goals to which terrorists subscribe are often antecedents to their behavior.[87] *Pull* factors explain why individuals are vulnerable to radicalization and attracted to the extremist ideology.[88] Saltman and Smith identified the *push factors* for Western women who joined ISIS as social and/or cultural isolation, perception that the Muslim community was being persecuted, and resentment over the lack of action by the international community concerning this persecution.[89] They also identified strategic and tactical *pull factors* as the building of an "Islamic utopia," the availability of roles in the "building" of the Islamic state or "Caliphate Brand," romanticizing life in the Islamic state, pursuit of sense of belonging and identity, and desire to fulfill perceived religious duty.[90]

Women's roles and types of support for ISIS

Researchers examining the roles women play in religious terrorist organizations have generated different typologies, some of which are dependent upon the women's location in Western- versus Muslim-governed areas. Griset and Mehan described four roles that represent increasing involvement within the group: *sympathizers*, who serve men's financial and domestic needs; *spies*, who provide strategic support; *warriors*, who engage in operations to impose violence; and *dominant forces*, who inspire, plan, and guide the group.[91] Using a similar framework, Cragin and Daly reported that women's roles in terrorist groups included *logisticians* (participating in basic and major terrorist operations), *recruiters*, *suicide bombers*, *operational leaders and fighters*, and *political vanguards* who influence decision making within the terrorist group.[92] Dissatisfied with the lack of an empirical foundation in these aforementioned typologies, Vogel, Porter, and Kebbell evaluated women's roles in political and revolutionary conflict groups using a thematic framework: *active* (which included attempting and engaging in terrorist attacks and leadership activities); *caring* (including traditional female roles; e.g., mothers and wives); *support* (covering logistics); and *ideological* (i.e., activities that promote the terrorist group's ideology).[93]

Alexander classified the predominant contributions of U.S. women in ISIS as: *plotters*, who create, attempt and/or execute terrorist attacks; *supporters*, who obtain material support, spread propaganda, and/or otherwise promote terrorists' agenda; and *travelers*, who travel to the terrorists' locations (Islamic territories under *Sharia* law or *hijrah*) to engage in supportive or operational activities[94] and thus fulfill their religious duty.[95] Applying their own typology to Western women who had migrated to ISIS-controlled territory, Saltman and Frenett grouped roles women played into *state-builders*, including domestic, educational, and medical roles; *recruiters*, actively promoting propaganda, educating about Islam, and enticing recruits; and *potential militants*.[96] Roles by women in ISIS in Spencer's typology included: *domestic* (mother and wife); *operational* (Al-Khansaa brigade and online recruiter); and *state building* (skilled worker, student).[97] Based on her sample of seventy-two women, she found the roles they performed were mainly operational, particularly recruiter (43 percent), and domestic (30 percent).

The roles women play contribute to the type of support that they provide to their terrorist organization. General information regarding female terrorists operating outside the United States has revealed a variety of patterns of involvement and levels of agency,[98] which may likely also be true for those inside the United States.[99] Women have joined various existing terrorist groups (Shining Path, Fuerzas Armadas Revolucionarias de Colombia [Revolutionary Armed Forces of Colombia], Ku Klux Klan, Animal Liberation Front, Earth Liberation Front, Al Qaeda, and ISIS, to name a few), serving in ideological (e.g., exchanging information, recruitment) and instrumental support roles (e.g., doing administrative tasks, such as bookkeeping, and fund-raising).[100] In some cases women, albeit to a lesser extent, have contributed operational support through leadership (e.g., Red Army Faction and the Red Brigades) or terrorist execution, such as suicide bombers (e.g., Tamil Tigers), sometimes even through creation of their own groups (e.g., Black Widows).[101]

Initially, women who joined ISIS were blocked from providing *operational* support, such as fighting except in exceptional circumstances as occurred in Libya in 2016;[102] but their roles have evolved, at least within ISIS-controlled territory as part of the all-female al-Khanssaa Brigade they have been allowed to gather intelligence, enforce women's compliance with Islamic morality, and search other women at checkpoints.[103] However, regardless of location, women predominantly render *instrumental* or tangible support that serves the objectives of ISIS, including inciting violence and mobilizing sympathizers and supporters to join the group and/or take action, such as sending money and guns.[104] Involuntary instrumental support as sexual slaves for ISIS fighters,[105] sanctioned by the religious leaders of the group,[106] is provided by kidnapped children and adult women considered unbelievers or "infidels."[107] Women also engage in *social-cognitive* support by promoting and disseminating ISIS propaganda, shaming men for not being actively involved, and praising men who provided operational and instrumental support.[108]

The usefulness of the aforementioned typologies for roles in an empirical examination of Western women who have joined ISIS is limited for three reasons. First, some of the roles described are only relevant to those living in the caliphate, such as state-builder, operational leader, or suicide bomber. Second, different typologies inconsistently grouped the same role with different activities (e.g., state-builders referred to domestic activities in one typology but referred to learning skills in another). Third, the typologies do not provide an adequate breakdown of the women's roles within ISIS into unique or mutually exclusive categories as distinct from the types of support the women provide. For example, the role of sympathizer was associated with instrumental support, that of financing and cooking activities, or the roles of raising funds and distributing propaganda were both categorized as material support. This is particularly problematic because it does not adequately differentiate the roles and corresponding activities performed by the women, limiting its applicability.[109]

Current investigation

The aim of the current investigation was to examine radicalization of U.S. women to religious terrorism for ISIS through the lens of SLT. The study made use of the government investigations of ISIS supporters in the United States by examining the court documents submitted into evidence during prosecution, which are available through open-source websites. The data were coded for: social milieu during the radicalization process as alone or with others; the reasons why women in the United States committed or attempted to commit terrorist acts and other terrorism-related activities for ISIS; the

Table 1. Demographics for U.S. sample of thirty-one women accused of terrorist crimes for ISIS.

Variable	*n*		*n*
Age		**Religion**	
Under 21	9	Islam-born	21
21–30	7	Islam-convert	10
31–40	8		
41–55	7	**Birthplace**	
		United States	15
Residential location		Somalia	7
Northeast	5	Bosnia	3
Midwest	15	Pakistan	1
South	8	Turkey	1
West	3	Afghanistan	1
		Bangladesh	1
Marital/family status		Sudan	1
Single/no children	11	Unknown	1
Single/children	4		
Relationship/no children	1	**Education level***	
Relationship/children	2	Less than high school	5
Married/no children	3	GED/high school	3
Married/children	10	College/graduate	9
		Unknown	14

Note. *Less than high school referred to girls who were homeschooled or currently in high school. College/graduate referred to women who had some college and those with college and graduate degrees.

types of roles women had within ISIS; the types of support these women provided to ISIS; and the Internet functionalities used by these women to gain and further their radicalized beliefs and actions. Ultimately, the study sought to fill in existing gaps in the empirical research on understanding female supporters of ISIS in the United States and to determine whether SLT could be used both as a vehicle to understand radicalization and a mechanism for deradicalization of extremist beliefs and acts.

Consistent with the goal of the study, hypotheses corresponding to the four tenets of SLT were tested. Hypothesis 1 proposed that ISIS created a social community through a mixture of online and offline members to promote their extremist beliefs and recruit the U.S. women to their cause. Hypothesis 2 proposed that ISIS encouraged the recruited women to develop neutralizing definitions through exposure to violence and to a narrative supporting the use of violence as justifiable for the cause through online and offline propaganda. Hypothesis 3 proposed that ISIS subjected recruited women to a system of continuously reinforced values and beliefs in real-life and online that rewarded them for their acts of support/compliance and punished them for failures to the mission. Hypothesis 4 proposed that ISIS provided female models performing roles and espousing extremist ideology, rewarding them both online and in real-life, to encourage imitation of the observed ideas and behaviors by the recruited women.

Method

Sample

The sample consisted of thirty-one women ($M = 31$ years, $SD = 11.12$ years).[110] All cases that met the following criteria were included: (1) female, (2) labeled as "homegrown," defined as born, raised, and/or legally living in the United States, including those with naturalized citizen and permanent resident status, and (3) evidence supported that they conspired to, attempted to, or committed one or more acts from 2009 to 2017 that were inspired by, assisted in furthering the ideology or goals of, or in the name of al-Shabaab (and developed into support for ISIS) and ISIS terrorists recognized by the U.S. government as terrorism-related.[111]

Demographics of age, residential region, marital and family status, religion, birthplace, and educational level for these women are shown in Table 1.[112] Nine of the thirty-one women identified were under 21 years of age. The government did not press formal charges against the four adolescent minors under age 18 years (13 percent of the sample) for attempting to travel to ISIS territory. The juveniles, only one of whom was born in the United States—the other three were not (two in Somalia, one in Sudan)—were Muslims living with their parents in the Midwestern region of the United States and attending high school. Five of the late adolescent girls (16 percent of the sample) ages 18 to 20 years old were formally charged; two had cases against them in absentia, two plead guilty and received prison terms, and one received community service and probation for her cooperation in a related case. All of them were practicing Muslims (two through conversion), but only three were born in the United States. The other two were born in Somalia. Three of them earned high school degrees and two had some college, and although two of the five were in relationships, only one had children.

The remainder of the sample included seven young adults ages 21 to 30 (23 percent of the sample) and fifteen middle-aged adults (48 percent of the sample) ages 31 to 55 years (eight were in their thirties, five were in their forties, and two were in their fifties). Of the seven young women, one was dead, one has a case in absentia, three plead guilty, and two are awaiting indictment. Four of the young women were born in the United States (57 percent), all were practicing Muslims (three through conversion), many were living in the Midwest region (43 percent; Southern, 29 percent; Western, 14 percent; Northeastern, 14 percent) of the United States, and all were married with children. One of the middle-aged adult women was dead, five plead or were found guilty, and eight plead not guilty and/or had cases pending, and one was given probation. Many of the middle-aged adult women lived in the Midwestern region (40 percent; Southern, 27 percent; Western, 20 percent; Northeastern, 13 percent) of the United States and had been born in a foreign country (60 percent, mainly Somalia and Bosnia), but all were practicing Muslims (five converts). Five of the eight married women (53 percent) and four of the seven single women had children (57 percent). The data were predominantly incomplete regarding the highest education of these women.

Procedure and coding

The data consisted of court documents, official press releases, and reports available on open-access websites for the Federal Bureau of Investigation, Counter Extremism Project, George Washington University Program on Extremism, and the Investigative Project on Terrorism.[113] The benefits of using all four databases was to ensure that all possible cases could be included; many of the women were listed on multiple sites, allowing for verification of information and ensuring it would be as complete as possible. Court documents consisted of criminal complaints, courtroom minutes, affidavits, exhibits detention hearing transcripts, continuing trial order and transcripts, indictment, motions, criminal discovery, general allegations, plea agreements, and detention orders. These documents provided demographic data (age, ethnicity, current location, birthplace), information about the motives, and actions of the women (e.g., social media use, travel, fund-raising).[114] Two coders reviewed the data for demographics of each woman and any discrepancies were discussed and resolved.

Radicalization process classification. To understand the radicalization process and subsequent social influences that contributed to women's acts in support of terrorism, the sample was grouped into one of three classifications—self, dyad, or group. The *self*-class described women who started and stayed alone during the radicalization process and activity. The *dyad*-class described women who either started alone and joined one other person or started with one other person and stayed with him/her during the radicalization process and activity. The *group*-class described the women who started as dyad and joined a group or started with a group and continued with it during the radicalization process and activity.

Socialization and support network. Women's perceived support from family and friends in their social worlds could contribute to the promotion or devaluation of extremist ISIS ideas and actions. Information in the data regarding whether family members (parents, siblings, spouse/partner, children, extended members) and/or friends of the women, both online and offline, *approved* of ISIS and/or encouraged her *involvement*, perhaps because they were also involved in ISIS activities or sympathized with the group. In addition, the use of the Internet to begin the radicalization process and its use thereafter in activities was also examined.

Internet functionality. The legal documents were examined for specific references to social media use, general Internet use, or no use specified for online communication used by the women during the radicalization and activity process. Theoretically, the Internet serves the dual purpose of being a mechanism to aid in the radicalization process and to abet the recruit in performing activities in service of the cause. Two methods were identified for the interactions between recruits and other sympathizers and/or those in the terrorist group. *Long-lasting/permanent messages* were made using Facebook, e-mail, Messenger, YouTube, Twitter, Tumblr, blogs, chat rooms, and Internet/text that was typically admitted as physical evidence in the case. *Temporary/encrypted messages* were made using Instagram, What's App Messenger, Kik, Surespot, and Skype, but due to their nature, would only be included as part of testimonial evidence.

Reasons for radicalization. The data were examined for six possible reasons for the women's radicalization, based on previous research findings.[115] Radicalization may occur because the woman may *identify* with the terrorist/group's religious, political, or extremist ideas. Another reason for radicalization stems from the woman's *need for belonging or to fill a void*. A woman's desire to *correct a real or perceived injustice* and/or *to get revenge* in the United States or abroad could also lead to radicalization. Radicalization may also result when the woman *sympathizes* with the group's situation and believes in its causes. Women may also radicalize as part of being in a *relationship* or desiring a relationship with a terrorist or sympathizer. Finally, a woman can become radicalized because she is *vulnerable* due to being mentally ill, cognitively challenged, young and impressionable, brainwashed, or bullied. The coding did not require that only one reason be identified and as such every reason indicated in the documents was identified.

Roles. A typology categorizing six possible roles that the women fulfilled was created and was used to examine the data. A *planner* attempted to provide or provided tactical strategies for at least one or more terrorist attacks or training. A *financial provider/adviser* attempted to provide or provided funds, connected the group to funding agents, or advised the group on how to get funding for one or more terrorist attacks or training. A *supplier* attempted to provide or provided supplies, (e.g., food, weapons) for training and/or at least one or more terrorist attacks. A *terrorist enactor* attempted or succeeded in carrying out at least one or more terrorist acts against a person/people in the United States and/or abroad.[116] A *spouse/companion and breeder* attempted to travel or traveled to ISIS territories/occupied land to be a spouse/companion for the male terrorist and to provide children for the caliphate. An *educator* promoted the cause by attempting to indoctrinate or gain support from new members, including their family, friends, and children, into the group. In recognition that the roles women held could be concurrent, all roles were identified.

Types of support. The data were examined for three types of support that the women could provide. *Instrumental support* was signified when the woman attempted to provide or provided tangible items and/or services (e.g., self, materials, funds, fighters) to ISIS, followers, or sympathizers. *Social cognitive support* was signified when the woman attempted to engage or engaged in dialogue with the group members, followers, or sympathizers to exchange knowledge and ideas, advice, feedback, and access to information. *Operational support* was signified when the woman attempted to organize and execute or executed an attack in furtherance of the terrorist goals. As the women could engage in multiple types of support types, all indicated were identified.

Reliability in the coding for features within each typology described above met the minimum 90 percent agreement during training. Scoring was completed by two coders and a master coder scored 20 percent of each coder's work. Percent agreement (number of agreements divided by the number of agreements and disagreement) between each coder and the master coder averaged 94 percent, ranging from 83 percent to 100 percent. Any discrepancies between coders were discussed and resolved.

Results

The purpose of the study was to use SLT as a framework for understanding the radicalization process of women in the United States to the religious terrorism of ISIS. The radicalization process classification for self, dyad, and group was used to examine each typology.

Socialization and support network

Many of the women began radicalization with at least one other person (65 percent), indicated that friends or family approved and were involved (90 percent), and used the Internet to begin (77 percent) and throughout (68 percent) their radicalization process. The radicalization process classification for the sample resulted in nine women being assigned to the *self*-class, ten to the *dyad*-class, and twelve to the *group*-class. Table 2 displays the socialization and support systems and Internet use by radicalization process

Table 2. Mean percentage of approval, involvement, and Internet use during radicalization by radicalization process class.

	Self	Dyad	Group
Approval			
Family	00	60	100
Friends	89	60	75
Involvement			
Family	00	60	83
Friends	100	70	75
Internet			
Start	78	100	58
Continued	78	90	83

classification. The data reflected different patterns of approval and support for the women's extreme beliefs and involvement with ISIS. One trend was strong approval and support given online by friends to the women in the self-class and offline by family and, to a lesser extent, friends to women in the group-class. The other pattern was moderate approval and support given by family and friends both offline and online to the women in the dyad-class. ISIS involvement for half of the dyad-class women began offline with their partners (50 percent), whereas the rest began with online partners they found (40 percent) or who found them (10 percent).

Internet functionality

The data were examined to determine the women's use of long-lasting/permanent messages and temporary/encrypted messages, both overall and by their radicalization process class. Figure 1 shows the mean percentage of women who used the eight types of long-lasting/permanent messages. The top three most commonly used were general Internet and texting (48 percent), Facebook (42 percent), and Twitter (35 percent). In contrast, the mean percentage of women using temporary/encrypted messages according to the official documents records was minimal (e.g., 13 percent used Skype, 7 percent used What's App), but this was likely not an accurate reflection of actual usage. The court documents rarely reported use of the temporary/encrypted messages in the women's testimony, barring some mentions of Skype or What's App. For 10 percent of the women, there was no information available for either long-lasting or temporary messages.

Different pattern use of long-lasting/permanent messages was indicated for women in the three radicalization classes. The self-class women used the widest variety of messaging systems, particularly Facebook (55 percent), Twitter (44 percent), e-mail (44 percent), and general Internet/texting (44 percent). The dyad-class women relied predominantly on two messaging systems—Facebook (60 percent) and general Internet/texting (70 percent), whereas the group-class women used mainly general Internet/texting (50 percent), and to a lesser extent, YouTube (33 percent) and chat rooms (33 percent).

Reasons for radicalization

Table 3 displays information regarding the reasons women were radicalized by the type of radicalization process class. Not surprisingly, relationship was the primary reason for

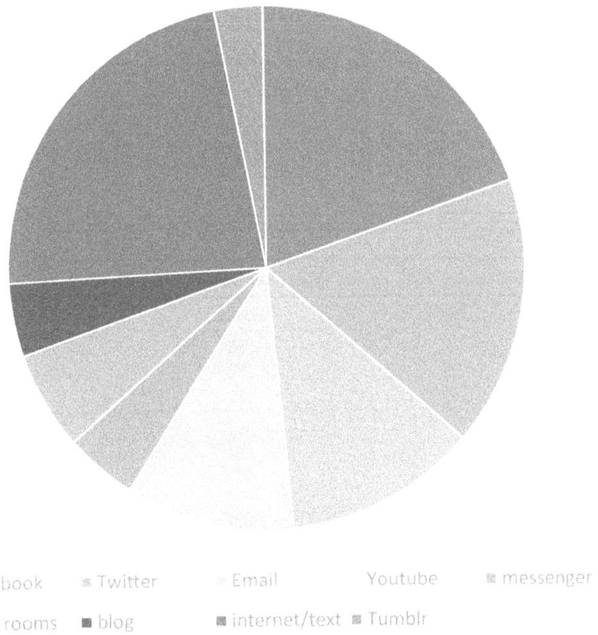

Figure 1. Mean percentage of women using nine types of long-lasting/permanent messages.

Table 3. Mean percentage of reasons by radicalization process class.

Reasons	Self	Dyad	Group	Mean
Identify	78	40	42	51
Need to belong	22	00	00	06
Correct injustice	00	10	00	03
Sympathize	67	50	33	48
Relationship	44	80	100	74
Vulnerable	33	10	33	26

dyad-class women and group-class women, whereas sympathy and identification were most often mentioned for self-class women. The number of reasons indicated in the data varied by radicalization process class. Women in the group-class had three (42 percent) or four (33 percent) reasons, whereas women in the self-class had two (44 percent) or three (33 percent) reasons and those in the dyad-class mainly had one reason (50 percent).

Roles

Table 4 displays information regarding the roles women played for ISIS by the type of radicalization process class. The predominant roles played by women in the self-class were traveler and educator. The women in the group-class were most likely to engage in the traveler role, whereas the middle-aged women served as financial providers. Women in the dyad-class were equally likely to be planners, terrorist enactors, and travelers. Although many women were travelers (48 percent) for ISIS, the number of roles they performed differed by radicalization class. Women radicalized in the dyad-class (60 percent) or group-class (75 percent) performed one role, whereas those radicalized in the self-class were equally likely to have one, two, or three roles.

Table 4. Mean percentage of roles by radicalization process class.

Roles	Self	Dyad	Group	Mean
Planner	22	40	00	19
Financial provider	22	20	50	29
Supplier	22	20	25	23
Terrorist enactor	22	40	00	19
Traveler	67	40	50	52
Educator	56	00	25	19

Table 5. Mean percentage of support type by radicalization process class.

Support type	Self	Dyad	Group	Mean
Instrumental	78	70	100	83
Social-cognitive	67	50	67	58
Operational	22	40	00	19

Types of support

Table 5 displays information regarding the types of support women played for ISIS by thetype of radicalization process class. The women in all three classes provided instrumental and social-cognitive, where operational support was only provided by the women in the self- and dyad-classes. The women in the group-class were more likely to provide two support types than one (67 percent vs. 33 percent), whereas women in the self- and dyad-classes was almost equally likely to provide one (56 percent) or two support types (44 percent).

Discussion

The rise in the number of Western women being radicalized to Islamist terrorism across the United States and worldwide is alarming to the public, but more importantly, it is a security issue as many of the recruits remain unidentified.[117] Religious terrorists are particularly dangerous as they seek to destroy, rather than correct, the existing system from which they feel alienated.[118] ISIS embraces the use of deadly force in their Holy War against a wide range of enemies of Allah.[119] Although the radicalization process to religious terrorism involves a combination of offline and online interactions,[120] Pearson warns that women who are culturally restricted to learn about Islam from public spaces will seek this information on the Internet.[121] The flexibility and constant accessibility of the Internet, through computers and related technologies, has enabled ISIS recruiters to succeed in radicalizing Western women, near and far, as it provides opportunities for them to communicate relatively undetected and without filters.[122] The Internet has become ISIS's most important personal tool for recruiting women, communicating with sympathizers and group members, and spreading propaganda to elicit funds, induce fearmongering, and encourage followers to fulfill the group's needs.[123]

Akers's SLT was applied to thirty-one cases of U.S. women radicalized to ISIS as a means of understanding both their adoption of ideology of extremist Islam beliefs during radicalization and subsequent acts supporting this terrorist organization. The women, as "small cells, groups of friends or even individuals," interacted with ISIS "via social media and personal contacts."[124] To capture this aspect in radicalization that subsequently led them to join and provide support for the larger social network of ISIS supporters, sympathizers, and members, the women were classified as self, dyad, or group and their classification was used for the analyses of their Internet functionalities, reasons, roles, and support.

Social network is encompassed under *differential association* in SLT and is one of the key elements for the women's initial and continued connection to the group and desire to learn about their extremist ideology during the radicalization process.[125] Consistent with H1, the results indicated that ISIS created a social community through a mixture of online and offline members, supporters, and sympathizers who promoted their extremist beliefs and recruited these women to their cause. Relationships were the predominant gendered reason indicated for radicalizing the women, especially for in the dyad- and group-classes and probably were the "glue" keeping them together.[126] The women in the dyad-class were primarily radicalized with or by spouses (60 percent), offline friends (20 percent), and online men offering them marriage (20 percent), but their ideological development was likely supplemented through online connections given their high use of the Internet. In contrast, every woman in the group-class had undergone radicalization with offline friends (33 percent), family (25 percent), or both friends and family (42 percent).

The development and maintenance of violent extremist beliefs that led the women to engage in supportive ISIS acts were facilitated through their interactions with a community of similarly minded people, many of whom they knew in the real world.[127] This notion was evident for the women in the dyad- and group-classes, all of whom had either family or offline friends and half had both family and friends who sympathized and were themselves involved with ISIS. One woman from the dyad-class was likely radicalized at the Pakistan campus of Al Huda Institute, the sister school to the one in Mississauga where four unnamed Canadians ages 16 to early 20 s attended prior to traveling to ISIS-held territories. Another example was a convert from this group, who was likely radicalized by her friend with extremist ideology resulted in his creation of the Al Qaeda magazine, *Inspire*; she, in turn, radicalized her roommate, a revert who was also included in this group.

The gendered factors for women in the self-class for connecting to the ISIS social network were identity (33 percent), sympathizing with perceived injustices linked to exclusion, marginalization, and discrimination (22 percent), or both (44 percent).[128] Obvious signs of radicalization shown by the women were consistent with someone forging a new identity through religious exploration, including adoption of pious clothing, religious conversion, and attempts to convert family members, change in friends, rejecting Westernized un-Islamic hobbies, online searches for information and postings on social media, and seeking out Islamic public spaces.[129] For example, two of the women in the self-class withdrew from their hometown mosques that did not support *Salafi-jihadist* movement espoused by ISIS and transferred to ones that did. Six of the women in the self-class were born in the United States, but converted to Islam in their search for identity. Unlike the other two groups, none of these women had family approval or sympathy for ISIS or their involvement. They rejected their family and offline friends, who disapproved of their extremist beliefs in favor of an online support system of friends and suitors who sympathized (56 percent) or were themselves involved (67 percent) with ISIS.[130] Sympathy was also motivated the women, as exemplified by the adolescent in the dyad-class contacted by a former classmate to help stop the alleged rape of Somalian women and children by Ethiopians through financing travel for *jihadist* fighters.

The women in the sample also used social media to construct their identity and express their concern and outrage for Muslim victims worldwide. Freiburger and Crane suggested that social bonds forged "over the Internet may be especially strong and influential for stigmatized groups," resulting in them resorting quickly to the next step of carrying out support or operational actions in the real world."[131] Facebook and Twitter were important in providing these women with access to a virtual community that befriended them, taught them the extremist narrative justifying the need for violence, and provided explanations for their discontent.[132] Women generally use social media for interpersonal communication and to maintain their relationships.[133] By decentralizing the task to unofficial recruiters, ISIS can build close relationships in a short amount of time through constant and frequent online interaction. An example of this intense interchange occurred with three adolescents in the group-class, who vocalized their extreme ideology on Twitter and Tumblr and exchanged thousands of messages with ISIS facilitators.[134] Many of the recruits were not necessarily religious or had little knowledge about main-stream Islam initially, making it easier for ISIS to convince them that the presented extremist ideology was the only correct one and to discourage them from seeking out other views that may provide them with conflicting interpretations.[135]

The second component of SLT involves definitions that promote and support violence as the preferred option to obtain the goal, while minimizing negative emotions associated with terrorist acts. Support was shown for H2 in that ISIS encouraged these recruited women to develop neutralizing definitions through exposure to violence and to a narrative supporting the use of violence as justifiable for the cause through offline and online propaganda. For example, court documents indicated that the women in the sample had magazines, DVDs, and books created by terrorists/*jihadists* advocating guerilla warfare and insurgency, including how to engage in violent attacks and glorifying the death of their enemy in the name of Allah.[136] This type of propaganda gives the illusion that the deviant ideology depicted is in fact the norm and acceptance of it contributes to the mutual interdependence among group members.[137]

The women also had online footprints by e-mailing, texting, and engaging in social media platforms like Facebook and Twitter. Online propaganda justifying murder and beheadings as "*halal* [permissible under Islamic law]" facilitate its acceptance among ISIS recruits, sympathizers, and followers, and paradoxically normalize this concept by juxtaposing the violent messages with innocuous scenes of sunsets and children playing.[138] The adoption of pro-terrorist, violent ideas is a gradual process, likely the result of multiple interactions in the women's online community. The documents revealed that the women watched violent beheadings and suicide bombers imploding on YouTube and Facebook; learned how to construct bombs from the Internet; read, responded to, and posted pro-ISIS messages on Facebook and Twitter; disseminated violent *jihad* propaganda; and joined discussion forums in chat rooms regarding the aggression against and victimization of Muslims around the world. Acceptance of the neutralizing definitions for ISIS was voiced by the women who desired to have their male loved ones get training to become fighters and to die martyrs. The women also used the Internet to obtain operational and tactical information, training manuals, websites for fund-raising, and seemingly legitimate news constructed to garner their support.[139]

During radicalization, the women sought out others online who had similar views and confirm their beliefs, normalizing and solidifying their extreme ideology under the guise of unity of Islam.[140] ISIS disguises its narrative in private spaces on the Internet, such as chat rooms, to give the illusion of objectivity to participants, such that the ideas they are discussing are evolving, but, in reality, they are simply echoing the group's rhetoric.[141] Not surprisingly the women's online vocalizations through multiple accounts were more radical and provoking than anything they stated in public. In some cases, the women tweeted approval and endorsement for a violent ISIS-inspired shooting incident in the United States or tweeted contact information of federal employees to be killed, yet their offline quiet natures prompted their families to deny that the women were dangerous or intended harm.

Differential reinforcement is the third component and refers to the process whereby the behaviors associated with support of terrorist acts and beliefs are reinforced by internal or external sources, normalizing them and increasing their likelihood of reoccurrence.[142] Consistent with H3, ISIS-recruited women were subjected to a system of continuously reinforced values and beliefs in real-life and online that rewarded them for their acts of support/compliance and punished them for failures. Women who joined the caliphate were promised two rewards—the congenial connection to other Muslims who share their beliefs in how to live and practice their religion here on earth and "a place in paradise."[143] According to Peresin, the prize for *hijra* to the ISIS-controlled territory is the romantic opportunity to be the bride of a strong heroic fighter and "a free house, equipped with top-of-the-line appliances and all expenses paid."[144] The online recruiters emphasized the beauty of the sisterhood to the adolescents and young women in the sample, making it a strong lure and incentive for them. The role of traveler was also important to the unmarried girls and women in the self- and group-classes, although few successfully made it overseas. Even married women with children willingly accompanied their husbands on the journey. For example, a married woman from the dyad-class traveled to ISIS territory with her husband and brother to live in the caliphate, where she successfully had and raised a child and worked in a hospital.

Women who engaged in instrumental support for ISIS, raising funds and supplies, were lauded within their American communities. Female terrorist enactors were recognized and praised by both the men and women of ISIS, either online or in the magazine, *Dabiq*, and used as an example to shame the men into action. Online educators receive their rewards in the form of becoming instant celebrities and influencing others based on the number of likes, followers, friends, and retweets they have on their social media platform, both of which are perceived by adolescents and young adults to be an important achievement.[145] Severe punishments were doled out to women by ISIS, such as disfiguring them by having acid thrown in their face by men or lashings by the women's brigade for those who fail to follow *Shariah* rules (e.g., not wearing a *niqab*). The media broadcast a terrifying story about an Austrian adolescent who attempted to escape being forced to become a sexual slave and then beaten to death.[146] One of the women in the group-class, who turned state's evidence by testifying against her friends, required protection and was shunned by both her family and the pro-ISIS community.[147]

The fourth component of SLT refers to social learning processes of observation and imitation of acts associated with terrorism. The data supported H4 that the recruited women observed and imitated the offline and online extremist ideology and behaviors of rewarded ISIS female role models. The educators for ISIS had three main tasks: find followers through the provision of the "true" interpretation of Islam, encourage supporters to provide money and supplies, and convince women to perform *hijra* to ISIS-controlled areas to become wives and mothers of *jihadists* to build a utopian caliphate for believers.[148] Consistent with the social media research, all of the adolescents (under 21) communicated vis-à-vis Twitter and Facebook, exposing them to propaganda promoting a happy domestic lifestyle of ISIS brides under *Shariah* law.[149] For example, an online Scottish recruiter, who joined ISIS at age 19, served as a model by meeting and befriending a 20-year-old in the self-class on Twitter, who then left home to perform *hijra*, traveling to ISIS-held territory, marrying a fighter, and becoming a recruiter by posting propaganda on Twitter.

Overall, the women in the sample regardless of radicalization route primarily provided instrumental support (81 percent) and served in the role of traveler (52 percent). The women supplied ISIS with money, weapons, and people. Travel to the caliphate was an important aspect of this type of support, particularly when they offered themselves as potential wives and mothers (69 percent). Two adolescent sisters and their adolescent friend[150] attempted to travel in 2014 to ISIS-held territory, perhaps copying the highly publicized attempted travel of another adolescent from the sample and her brothers, or perhaps even imitating successful non-American travelers, such as the 16-year-old British twins or 15- and 17-year-old Austrian friends.[151] They, in turn, may then have served as inspiration models for the attempted travel in 2015 by three Canadian adolescent girls and successful travel by three British adolescent girls.[152]

The other roles women in the sample imitated differed by radicalization class. The educator role, such as posting opinions and support for ISIS and anti-Western sentiment, was adopted primarily by women ranging in age from 20 to 38 years in the self-class (56 percent). For example, one woman from this group reposted violent videos and photos, such as a weapon-wielding boy, on Twitter. Women in the group-class were financial providers, having successfully launched fund-raising campaigns in their communities combined either with e-mail and Facebook or with chat rooms and texting. Six of the women charged with collecting money for al-Shabaab likely learned fund-raising from their collaborators (three were part of a group of twelve and the other three were part of a group of five).

Women in the dyad-class (40 percent) and in the self-class (22 percent) provided operational support and served as planners (26 percent) and terrorist enactors (32 percent). The six women who planned and committed or attempted to commit these violent terrorist acts used guns, bombs, and grenades against innocent people and government forces. For example, a woman in the self-class gained "fame" as the first American woman killed overseas; she was shot alongside her male counterparts after throwing a grenade at Syrian government forces in 2013. She, in turn, may have served as a role model for a woman in the dyad-class, who was killed alongside her husband in a shootout with police in 2015. Of the women in the dyad-class, one was charged with aiding and abetting her husband's attempt to blow up the prison where he was incarcerated and two were charged with plotting to detonate a bomb in the United States.

Conclusions

The study determined that women's radicalization process could be conceptually separated into three distinct classes of self, dyad, and group. The most commonly used online tool for interacting with ISIS members, sympathizers, and supporters by the women was Internet/texting, whereas secondary use of the other Internet functionalities depended on radicalization class: Facebook and Twitter were used by self-class women; Facebook by dyad-class women; and YouTube and chatrooms by group-class women. The main reason for radicalization of women in the dyad- and group-classes was relationship, but women in the self-class were radicalized due to sympathy and identification. Self-class women were travelers and educators, group-class adolescents were travelers and adult women were financial providers, and dyad-class women were travelers, planners, and terrorist enactors. Women provided mainly instrumental support and secondarily social-cognitive support, with operational support rare and only given by a few women in the self- and dyad-classes.

SLT principles provided an explanation for how the women acquired and maintained the Islamist terrorist ideology and performed terrorist-related actions. Just as SLT holds that all behavior is learned, it also contends that behavior can be unlearned. This social, cognitive, and behavioral approach provides a multidisciplinary perspective to countering religious terrorism that can be applied at the preventative level to inoculate at-risk/potential recruits from accepting extremist propaganda and at the intervention level to heal and re-socialize those who defected prior to or returned after the collapse of the caliphate.[153] Most importantly, just as women were agents in their radicalization, actively seeking extremist ideology and carrying out roles for ISIS, they must correspondingly be agents in the deradicalization process. Specifically, it is important to partner with the local Muslim community consistent with their culture, whose *imams*, leaders, and members can become a meaningful part of the social network the women need, as well as serve as models for the ideology and behavior consistent with mainstream Islam. Female practitioners should be employed to help the women in both the prevention and deradicalization intervention levels by teaching critical thinking for Internet-related information, developing social networks within the local community, providing peer-to-peer counseling and guidance, and offering and accepting alternative perspectives.[154]

The program will need to create an open-minded social environment that allows the women with extremist views to express their ideas and examine their neutralizing definitions of violence as the only solution to creating *Ummah* (collective community of Muslims) by listening to different points of view from a variety of people, particularly those in the same age range, religion, and culture, as well as the leaders and members of their community. By exposing them to a balance of beliefs and encouraging them to seek information from multiple online and offline sources that can then be brought into the discussions, they can develop the requisite critical thinking skills needed to appraise the credibility of the source and the legitimacy and quality of the information. Rather than prevent the women from using online examples to bolster their justification of extremist Islamic ideology, examples of the psychological, emotional, and physical damage caused by acts condoned by ISIS should be included in the discussion. That is, the victims' stories must be represented, such as the impact on the individuals, their families, and their communities when women and children are kidnapped, raped, and enslaved or men are killed simply because they were not Muslim or were Muslims who did not accept ISIS ideology. As Westerners' treatment of Muslims is a concern and a driving force for radicalization, it is important that non-Muslim community members be invited into the discussion. This will also allow Muslims and non-Muslims to learn about each other, understand the fears and concerns each has about the other, identify intolerance expressed through bullying and the effects it has on individuals and the group, and help them to find common ground on the path to becoming an integrated American community. The women should also be exposed to mainstream models in the real world and online—both within and outside of their own religion and culture, given praise for using critical thinking to examine their beliefs, and positively reinforced for enacting acts observed by these models that contribute to a nonviolent solution to building tolerant communities.

There were three limitations of this study. First, the study relied on secondary data of court documents gathered by the government to provide evidentiary support for prosecuting these defendants. It was not possible to interview or otherwise obtain information directly from the women accused or involved in terrorism due to their acts being of national security. The alternative option was to create a dataset based primarily on media news reports and articles, however, these sources contain their own biases. Hence, the decision was made to use multiple datasets constructed from government documents. Second, the data itself was limited in that the government was not systematic or thorough in every case regarding information collected and admitted into evidence for the Internet functionalities used by the women in furthering of their alleged crimes. Despite concerted efforts to configure as much relevant detail as possible about the women's network, reasons, and activities, not all information was publicly available. For example, it was not possible to determine the extent that the Internet, especially social media platforms, and apps were used in the radicalization process and criminal acts. New information may have emerged in cases after this article was written and thus will not have been included in the analyses. Third, it was not possible due to the small sample size to perform comparative statistical analysis nor was it deemed necessary for this study. Official court documents provide an opportunity for researchers to examine the "etiology of terrorism," especially "the actors and their motivation and justification behind their actions."[155]

Future researchers can examine the efficacy of using SLT in understanding both men and women's radicalization to terrorism for left-wing and right-wing groups. Of importance, however, regardless of which group women are motivated to join, their roles in "creating a hatred-filled, revenge-seeking and military-trained next generation" should not be underestimated.[156] As a way of helping researchers in understanding the dynamic of how social media enables radicalization, the government prosecuting terrorists should collect this information systematically. In particular, interviews with terrorists should include questions specifically asking them which social media they used and which influenced them during radicalization.

Acknowledgments

The authors received an OAR Faculty Scholarship grant (90692-03 01) from John Jay College of Criminal Justice in June 2016.

Notes

1. Anne Aly and Jason-Leigh Striegher, "Examining the Role of Religion in Radicalization to Violent Islamist Extremism," *Studies in Conflict & Terrorism* 35, no. 2 (2012): 849–862; Mark Sedgwick, "The Concept of Radicalization as a Source of Confusion," *Terrorism and Political Violence* 22, no. 4 (2010): 479–494.
2. John Horgan, *The Psychology of Terrorism* (London: Routledge, 2005); Laura Sjoberg, Grace D. Cooke, and Stacy Reiter Neal, "Introduction. Women, Gender, and Terrorism," in *Women, Gender, and Terrorism*, ed. Caron E. Gentry and Laura Sjoberg (Athens: The University of Georgia Press; Studies in Security and International Affairs, 2011), 1–28; Jamie Bartlett and Carl Miller, "The Edge of Violence: Toward Telling the Difference between Violent and Non-Violent Radicalization," *Terrorism and Political Violence* 22, no. 1 (2012): 1–21.
3. Marie-Helen Maras, *Counterterrorism* (Burlington, MA: Jones and Bartlett, 2012), 260.
4. Bruce Hoffman, *"Holy Terror": The Implications of Terrorism Motivated by a Religious Imperative* (Santa Monica, CA: RAND Corporation, 1993); Bruce Hoffman, *The Contrasting Ethical Foundations of Terrorism in the 1980s* (Santa Monica, CA: RAND Corporation, 1988); Bruce Hoffman, "'Holy Terror': The Implications of Terrorism Motivated by a Religious Imperative," *Studies in Conflict and Terrorism* 18 (1995): 271–284.
5. Erin Miller, *Ideological Motivations of Terrorism in the United States, 1970–2016, Background Report* (National Consortium for the Study of Terrorism and Responses to Terrorism/START, November 2017).
6. Alex Nowrasteh, *Terrorism Deaths and Injuries by Ideology: Excluding the Outlier Attacks* (CATO Institute, August 2017).
7. Anne Aly, Stuart Macdonald, Lee Jarvis, and Thomas M. Chen, "Introduction to the Special Issue: Terrorist Online Propaganda and radicalization," *Studies in Conflict & Terrorism* 40, no. 1 (2017): 1–9; Erin Marie Saltman and Charlie Winter, *Islamic State: The Changing Face of Modern Jihadism* (London: Quilliam Foundation, 2014); Robin Thompson, "Radicalization and the Use of Social Media," *Journal of Strategic Security* 4, no. 4 (2011): 167–190; Catherine A. Theorhary and John Rollins, *Terrorist Use of the Internet: Information Operations in Cyberspace* (Congress Research Service Report for Congress, 2011).
8. Audrey Alexander, *Cruel Intentions: Female Jihadists in America* (Washington, DC: Program on Extremism, 2016), Accessed at: https://cchs.gwu.edu/sites/cchs.gwu.edu/files/downloads/ Female%20Jihadists%20in%20America.pdf (January 6, 2018).
9. Western women are those born and raised in Western countries and who speak English as their primary language, consistent with Erin Marie Saltman and Ross Frenett, "Female Radicalization to ISIS and the Role of Women in CVE," in *A Man's World? Exploring the Roles of Women in Countering Terrorism and Violent Extremism*, ed. Naureen Chowdhury Fink, Sara Zeiger, and Rafia Bhulai (Hedayah and the Global Center on Cooperative Security, 2016), 142–163.

10. Migrants from Europe far exceed those from the United States, according to Brian Michael Jenkins, "The Origins of America's Jihadists" (Santa Monica, CA: RAND Corporation, 2017), https://www.rand.org/pubs/perspectives/PE251.html (accessed 2 January 2018).
11. Alexander, *Cruel Intentions*; Jessica Katz, "Where Do the Women Fit In? A Theoretical Analysis of Western Women's Participation and Role in the Islamic State," *Final Report: Combating Terrorist and Foreign Fighter Travel* (Homeland Security Committee Task Force, 2015); Erin Marie Saltman and Ross Frenett, "Female Radicalization to ISIS and the Role of Women in CVE," 142–163.
12. Amanda N. Spencer, "The Hidden Face of Terrorism: An Analysis of Women in the Islamic State," *Journal of Strategic Security* 9, no. 3 (2016): 74–98; Katharina Von Knop, "The Female Jihad: Al Queda's Women," *Studies in Conflict & Terrorism*, 30, no. 5 (2007): 397–414.
13. J. Keith Akins and L. Thomas Winfree, Jr., "Social Learning Theory and becoming a Terrorist: New Challenges for a General Theory," *The Handbook of the Criminology of Terrorism*, ed. Gary LaFree and Joshua D. Freilich (New York: John Wiley & Sons, Inc., 2016), 133–149; Heather Ann Cone, *Differential Reinforcement in the Online Radicalization of Western Muslim Women Converts* (Walden University, ProQuest Dissertations Publishing, 2016).
14. George Selim, "Approaches for Countering Violent Extremism at Home and Abroad," *Annals of the American Academy of Political and Social Science* 688 (2016), 95.
15. J. Keith Akins and L. Thomas Winfree, Jr., "Social Learning Theory and becoming a Terrorist," 137.
16. John Horgan, *Walking Away from Terrorism: Accounts of Disengagement from Radical and Extremist Groups* (New York: Routledge, 2009); Peter R. Neumann, "The Trouble with Radicalization," *International Affairs* 89, no. 4 (2013), 873–893.
17. Ronald Akers, *Social Learning and Social Structure: A General Theory of Crime and Deviance* (Boston, MA: Northeastern University Press, 1998).
18. Akins and Winfree, Jr., "Social Learning Theory and becoming a Terrorist"; Tina Freiberg and Jeffrey S. Crane, "A Systematic Examination of Terrorist Use of the Internet," *International Journal of Cyber Criminology* 2, no. 1 (2008): 309–319; Heather Ann Cone, *Differential Reinforcement in the Online Radicalization of Western Muslim Women Converts*, Walden University, ProQuest Dissertations Publishing, 2016. 10240546; Marc S. Hamm, *Terrorism as Crime: From Oklahoma City to Al-Qaeda and Beyond* (New York: NYU Press, 2007); Ronald L. Akers and Adam L. Silverman, "Toward a Social Learning Model of Violence and Terrorism," in *Violence: From theory to research*, ed. Margaret A. Zahn, Henry H. Brownstein, and Shelly. L. Jackson (Cincinnati, OH: Lexis-Nexis-Anderson Publishing, 2004), 19–36; L. Thomas Winfree and J. Keith Akins, "Expanding the Boundaries of Social Learning Theory: The Case of Suicide Bombers in Gaza," *International Journal of Crime, Criminal Justice, and Law* 3, no. 1 (2008): 145–158.
19. Clark McCauley and Sophia Moskalenko, "Mechanisms of Political Radicalization: pathways to Terrorism," *Terrorism and Political Violence* 20, no. 3 (2008), 415–433; Clark McCauley and Sophia Moskalenko, "Toward a Profile of Lone Wolf Terrorists: What Moves an Individual from Radical Opinion to Radical Action," *Terrorism and Political Violence* 26, no. 1 (2014), 69–85; Mohammed Hafez and Creighton Mullins, "The Radicalization Puzzle: A Theoretical Synthesis of Empirical Approaches to Homegrown Extremism," *Studies in Conflict & Terrorism* 38, no. 11 (2015): 958–975.
20. Akers, *Social Learning and Social Structure.*
21. Martha Crenshaw, "'Till Martyrdom Do Us Part' Gender and the ISIS Phenomenon," *Political Psychology* 21, no. 2 (2000): 405–420; Rex A. Hudson, "The Sociology and Psychology of Terrorism: Who becomes a Terrorist and Why?" (Washington, DC: Library of Congress, Federal Research Division, 1999); Rona M. Fields, "Child Terror Victims and Adult Terrorists," *Journal of Psychohistory* 7, no. 1 (1979): 71–76; Akers and Silverman, "Toward a Social Learning Model of Violence and Terrorism."; Alex S. Wilmer and Claire-Jehanne Dubouloz, "Transformative Radicalization: Applying Learning Theory to Islamist

Radicalization," *Studies in Conflict & Terrorism* 34 (2011): 418–438; Mark S. Hamm, *Terrorism as Crime: From Oklahoma City to Al-Qaeda and beyond* (New York: NYU Press (2007); Winfree and Akins, Expanding the Boundaries of Social Learning Theory: The Case of Suicide Bombers in Gaza."

22. Ronald L. Akers and Adam L. Silverman, "Toward a Social Learning Model of Violence and Terrorism," in *Violence: From Theory to Research*, ed. Margaret A. Zahn, Henry H. Brownstein, and Shelly. L. Jackson (Cincinnati, OH: Lexis-Nexis-Anderson Publishing, 2004), 19–36.
23. Laura Sjoberg, "Conclusion: The Study of Women, Gender, and Terrorism," in *Women, Gender, and Terrorism*, ed. Caron E. Gentry and Laura Sjoberg (Athens: The University of Georgia Press), 227–239.
24. Elizabeth Pearson and Emily Winterbotham, "Women, Gender, and Daesh Radicalization: A Milieu Approach," *RUSI Journal* 162, no. 3 (2017): 60–72.
25. Marc Sageman, *Understanding Terror Networks* (Philadelphia: University of Pennsylvania Press, 2004).
26. Tanja Dramac Jiries, "Rise of Radicalization in the Global Village: Online Radicalization vs. In-person Radicalization—Is There a Difference?" *Journal of Deradicalization* 6 (2016), 206–230; Peter R. Neumann and Brooke Rogers with contributions from Rogelio Alonso and Luis Martinez, *Recruitment and Mobilization for the Islamist Militant Movement in Europe*. Kings' College London, University of London, 2007.
27. Elizabeth Pearson, "The Case of Roshonara Choudhry: Implications for Theory on Online Radicalization, ISIS Women, and the Gendered Jihad," *Policy & Internet* 8, no. 1 (2015), 5–33, at 16.
28. Ibid.; Pearson and Winterbotham, "Women, Gender, and Daesh Radicalization," 60–72.
29. Akers, *Social Learning and Social Structure*; Freiberg and Crane, "A Systematic Examination of Terrorist Use of the Internet," 313.
30. Heather Ann Cone, *Differential Reinforcement in the Online Radicalization of Western Muslim Women Converts*, Walden University, ProQuest Dissertations Publishing, 2016. 10240546
31. "Facebook, Number of Monthly Active Users Worldwide 2008–2017," https://statista.com/statistics/264810/number-of-monthly-active-facebook-users-worldwide (accessed 10 January 2018).
32. "Twitter, Number of Monthly Active US Users 2010–2017," https://www.statista.com/statistics/274564/monthly-active-twitter-users-in-the-united-states (accessed 10 January 2018).
33. Maras, *Counterterrorism*; UK House of Commons, Report of the Official Account of the Bombings in London on 7th July 2005, HC 1087 (11 May 2006). London: The Stationery Office, http://www.official-documents.gov.uk/document/hc0506/hc10/1087/1087.pdf; Jytte Klausen, "Tweeting the Jihad: Social Media Networks of the Western Foreign Fighters in Syria and Iraq," *Studies in Conflict & Terrorism* 38, no. 1 (2015), 1–22; Anti-Defamation League, "Hashtag Terror: How ISIS Manipulates Social Media," 21 August 2014, http://www.adl.org/eduation/resources/reports/isis-islamic-state-social-media.
34. Carolyn Hoyle, Alexandra Bradford, and Ross Frenett, *Becoming Mulan? Female Western Migrants to ISIS*, Institute for Strategic Dialogue (2015); Erin Marie Saltman and Melanie Smith, "'Till Martyrdom Do Us Part': Gender and the ISIS Phenomenon," Institute for Strategic Dialogue, http://www.isdglobal.org/wp-content/uploads/2016/02/Till_Martyrdom_Do_Us_Part_Gender_and_the_ISIS_Phenomenon.pdf; Alessandra L. González, Joshua D. Freilich, and Steven M. Chermak, "How Women Engage Homegrown Terrorism," *Feminist Criminology* 9, no. 4 (2014): 344–366.
35. Elisa Lee and Laura Leets, "Persuasive Storytelling by Hate Groups Online Examining Its Effects on Adolescents," *American Behavioral Scientist* 45, no. 6 (2002): 927–957; Marc Sageman, *Leaderless Jihad: Terror Networks in the Twenty-First Century* (Philadelphia: University of Pennsylvania Press).
36. J. Keith Akins and L. Thomas Winfree, Jr., "Social Learning Theory and becoming a Terrorist: New Challenges for a General Theory," *The Handbook of the Criminology of*

Terrorism, ed. Gary LaFree and Joshua D. Freilich (New York, New York: John Wiley & Sons, Inc., 2016), 133–149.

37. Sageman, *Understanding Terror Networks*; Sageman, *Leaderless Jihad*.
38. Raffaello Pantucci, "Typology of Lone Wolves: Preliminary Analysis of Lone Islamist Terrorists," *International Centre for the Study of Radicalisation and Political Violence* (2011), http://icsr.info/wp-content/uploads/2012/10/1302002992ICSRPaper_ATypologyofLoneWolves_Pantucci.pdf; Phyllis B. Gerstenfeld, Diana R. Grant, Chau-Pu Chiang, "Hate Online: A Content Analysis of Extremist Internet Sites," *Analyses of Social Issues and Public Policy* 3, no. 1 (2003): 39–40; Anti-Defamation League, "Jihad Online: Islamic Terrorists and the Internet" (2002), 3. http://www.adl.org/internet/jihad_online.pdf
39. Gabriel Weimann, *New Terrorism and New Media* (Washington, DC: Common Lab of the Woodrow Wilson International Center for Scholars, 2014).
40. Pew Research Center, "Cell Internet Use 2013," http://www.pewinternet.org/2013/09/16/cell-internet-use-2013 (accessed 10 January 2018); Pew Research Center, Mobile Messaging and Social Media 2015, http://www.pewinternet.org/2013/09/16/cell-internet-use-2013/ (accessed 1 January 2018).
41. Monica Anderson, "5 Facts About Online Video, For YouTube's 10th Birthday" (2018), http://www.pewresearch.org/fact-tank/2015/02/12/5-facts-about-online-video-for-youtubes-10th-birthday (accessed 10 January 2018).
42. Amanda Lenhart, "Teens, Technology and Friendships," Pew Research Center (2015), http://www.pewinternet.org/2015/08/06/teens-technology-and-friendships (accessed 10 January 2018).
43. Akins and Winfree, Jr., "Social Learning Theory and becoming a Terrorist."
44. Wilmer and Dubouloz, "Transformative Radicalization"; Brian Michael Jenkins, "The Origins of America's Jihadists," RAND Corporation (2017), https://www.rand.org/pubs/perspectives/PE251.html (accessed 2 January 2018).
45. Tanja Dramac Jiries, "Rise of Radicalization in the Global Village: Online Radicalization vs. In-Person Radicalization—Is There a Difference?" *Journal of Deradicalization* 6 (2016): 206–230.
46. Nabeelah Jaffer, "The Secret World of Isis Brides: 'U dnt hav 2 pay 4 ANYTHING if u r wife of a martyr,'" *The Guardian*, 24 June 2015, https://www.theguardian.com/world/2015/jun/24/isis-brides-secret-world-jihad-western-women-syria
47. Anti-Defamation League, "Hashtag Terror: How ISIS Manipulates Social Media," 21 August 2014, https://www.adl.org/education/resources/reports/isis-islamic-state-social-media
48. Charlie Winter, *The Virtual "Caliphate": Understanding Islamic State's Propaganda Strategy* (London: Quilliam, 2015), 7; Gabriel Weimann, "New Terrorism and New Media," The Wilson Center, Research Series 2 (2014): 1–16.
49. Shima D. Keene, "Terrorism and the Internet: A Double-Edged Sword," *Journal of Money Laundering Control* 14, no. 4 (2011): 359–370; Todd M. Hinnen, "The Cyber-Front in the War on Terrorism: Curbing Terrorist Use of the Internet," *The Columbia Science and Technology Law Review* 5, no. 5 (2004), 1–42.
50. Erin Marie Saltman and Charlie Winter, *Islamic State: The Changing Face of Modern Jihadism* (London: Quilliam Foundation, 2014); Maura Conway, "Special Section: Terrorism and Contemporary Mediascapes," *Critical Studies on Terrorism* 5, no. 3 (2012), 445–453.
51. Dean C. Alexander, "The Radicalization of Extremists/Terrorists: Why it Affects You," *Security* 47, no. 7 (2010): 42–43; Joseph H. Felter, "The Internet: A Portal to Violent Extremism." Statement Before the Committee on Homeland Security and Governmental Affairs, United States Senate, First Session, 110th Congress, 2007, 4, http://www.investigativeproject.org/documents/testimony/224.pdf; Steven Emerson, *Jihad Incorporated: A Guide to Militant Islam* (New York: Prometheus, 2006), 470.
52. Pew Research Center," Cell Internet Use 2013," http://www.pewinternet.org/2013/09/16/cell-internet-use-2013 (accessed 10 January 2018); Pew Research Center, "Mobile Messaging and Social Media 2015," http://www.pewinternet.org/2013/09/16/cell-internet-

use-2013/ (accessed 1 January 2018); Facttank, "Record Shares of Americans Now Own Smartphones, have Home Broadband, http://www.pewresearch.org/fact-tank/2017/01/12/evolution-of-technology (accessed 10 January 2018).
53. Phyllis B. Gerstenfeld, Diana R. Grant, and Chau-Pu Chiang,"Hate Online: A Content Analysis of Extremist Internet Sites," *Analyses of Social Issues and Public Policy* 3, no. 1 (2003): 39–40.
54. Raffaello Pantucci, "A Typology of Lone Wolves: Preliminary Analysis of Lone Islamist Terrorists," *International Centre for the Study of Radicalisation and Political Violence* (2011), http://icsr.info/wp-content/uploads/2012/10/1302002992ICSRPaper_ATypologyofLoneWolves_Pantucci.pdf; Phyllis B. Gerstenfeld, Diana R. Grant, Chau-Pu Chiang, "Hate Online: A Content Analysis of Extremist Internet Sites," *Analyses of Social Issues and Public Policy* 3, no. 1 (2003), 39–40; Anti-Defamation League, "Jihad Online: Islamic Terrorists and the Internet" (2002), 3, http://www.adl.org/internet/jihad_online.pdf
55. Kira Harris, Eyal Gringart, and Deirdre Drake, *Understanding the Role of Social Groups in Radicalization* (Edith Cowan University Research Online, 2014). doi:10.4225/75/57a83235c833d
56. Pearson, "The Case of Roshonara Choudhry," 21.
57. Farahnaz Ispahani, "Women and Islamist Extremism: Gender Rights under the Shadow of Jihad," *The Review of Faith & International Affairs* 14, no. 2 (2016): 101–104; Sasha Havlicek, *The Islamic State's War on Women and Girls* (Institute for Strategic Dialogue, 2015).
58. Alexander Meleagrou-Hitchens and Nick Kaderbhai, "Research Perspectives on Online Radicalization, A Literature Review, 2006–2016," VOX-Pol Network of Excellence, 2017.
59. Burrhus Frederic Skinner, *Science and Human Behavior* (New York: Free Press, 1953); Burrhus Frederic Skinner, *Beyond Freedom and Dignity* (New York: Knopf, 1971); Ronald L. Akers, "Rational Choice, Deterrence, and Social Learning Theory in Criminology: The Path Not Taken," *Journal of Criminal Law and Criminology* 81, no. 3 (1990): 653–676.
60. A. Charles Catania, ed., *Contemporary Research in Operant Behavior* (Glenview, IL: Scott Foresman and Company, 1968); Howard Rachlin, *Introduction to Modern Behaviorism* (San Francisco, CA: Freeman, 1970); and William H. Redd, Albert L. Porterfield, and Barbara L. Anderson, *Behavior Modification* (New York: Random House, 1979).
61. Catania, *Contemporary Research in Operant Behavior*; Howard Rachlin, *Introduction to Modern Behaviorism* (San Francisco, CA: Freeman, 1970); and William H. Redd, Albert L. Porterfield, and Barbara L. Anderson, *Behavior Modification* (New York: Random House, 1979); Akins and Winfree, Jr., "Social Learning Theory and becoming a Terrorist."
62. Heather Ann Cone, *Differential Reinforcement in the Online Radicalization of Western Muslim Women Converts* (Walden University, ProQuest Dissertations Publishing, 2016).
63. Hoyle, Bradford, and Frenett, *Becoming Mulan?*
64. Albert Bandura, *Social Foundations of Thought and Action: A Social Cognitive Theory* (Englewood Cliffs, NJ: Prentice Hall, 1986).
65. Akers, *Social Learning and Social Structure.*
66. Martha Crenshaw, "Current Research on Terrorism: The Academic Perspective," *Studies in Conflict & Terrorism* 15, no. 1 (1992), 1–11; Robert J. Kelly and Robert W. Rieber, "Psychosocial Impacts of Terrorism and Organized Crime: The Counterfinality of the Practico-Inert," *Journal of Social Distress and the Homeless* 4, no. 4 (1995): 265–286.
67. Jytte Klausen, "Tweeting the Jihad: Social Media Networks of Western Foreign Fighters in Syria and Iraq," *Studies in Conflict & Terrorism* 38, no. 1 (2015), 1–22.
68. Freiberg and Jeffrey S. Crane, "A Systematic Examination of Terrorist Use of the Internet"; Maeghin Alarid, "Recruitment and Radicalization: The Role of Social Media and New Technology," in *Impunity: Countering Illicit Power in War and Transition*, ed. Michelle Hughes and Michael Miklaucic (National Defense University, Centre for Technology and National Security Policy, 2016).
69. Laura Huey, "This is Not Your Mother's Terrorism: Social Media, Online Radicalization and the Practice of Political Jamming," *Journal of Terrorism Research* 6, no. 2 (2015): 1–16;

Caroline Joan S. Picart, "'Jihad Cool/Jiahd Chic': The Roles of Internet and Imagined Relations in the Self-Radicalization of Colleen LaRose (Jihad Jane)," *Societies* 5 (2015): 354–383.

70. Aly, Macdonald, Jarvis, and Chen, "Introduction to the Special Issue," 2.
71. Haras Rafiq and Nakita Malik, *Caliphettes: Women and the Appeal of Islamic State* (Quilliam Foundation, 2015), 38; Laura Huey, *No Sandwiches Here: Representations of Women in Dabiq and Inspire Magazines* (Canadian Network for Research on Terrorism, Security and Society, Working Paper Series No. 15-4, 2015).
72. Alexander Meleagrou-Hitchens, Audrey Alexander, and Nick Kaderbhai, "Literature Review: The Impact of Digital Communications Technology on Radicalization and Recruitment," *International Affairs* 93, no. 5 (2017); Karla J. Cunningham, "Countering Female Terrorism," *Studies in Conflict and Terrorism* 30, no. 2 (2007): 113–129.
73. Louisa Tarras-Wahlberg, "Seven Promises of ISIS to its Female Recruits," International Center for the Study of Violent Extremism, Research Reports, 9 January 2017, http://www.iscve.org/research-reports/seven-promises-of-isis-to-its-female-recruits/ (accessed 3 January 2018).
74. Mia Bloom, "Bombshells: Women and Terrorism," *Gender Issues* 28 (2011): 1-21; Kim Cragin and Sara A. Daly, *Women as Terrorists: Mothers, Recruiters, and Martyrs* (Santa Barbara, California: ABC-CLIO, 2009); Maura Conway and Lisa McInerney, "'What's Love Got to Do with it'? Framing 'JihadiJane' in the US Press," *Media, War and Conflict* 5, no. 1 (2012): 6–21; David Makin and Season Hoard, "Understanding the Gender Gap in Domestic Terrorism Through Criminal Participation," *Criminal Justice Policy Review* 25, no. 5 (March 2013): 531–552.
75. Karla J. Cunningham, "Countering Female Terrorism," *Studies in Conflict and Terrorism* 30, no. 2 (2007): 113–129; Louisa Tarras-Wahlberg, "Promises of Paradise? A Study on Official ISIS-Propaganda Targeting Women," 2016, http://fhs.diva-portal.org/smash/get/diva2:942997/FULLTEXT01.pdf (accessed 3 January 2018).
76. CNN, "ISIS Fast Facts," http://www.cnn.com/2014/08/08/world/isis-fast-facts/index.html (accessed 4 January 2018); Richard A. Clarke and Emilian Papadopoulos, "Terrorism in Perspective: A Review for the New American President," *ANNALS of the American Academy* 668 (2016): 8–18.
77. Maras, *Counterterrorism.*
78. von Knop, "The Female Jihad," 406; also see Katherine M. Kelley, *"Picking a Side," the Western Muhajirat of ISIS: What the Women Want, What ISIS Wants with Them, and What Western Governments can do about It.* Proquest 10159100.
79. Erin Marie Saltman and Melanie Smith, "'Till Martyrdom Do Us Part'"; Peresin and Cervone, "The Western Muhajirat of ISIS," 495–509; Deborah Galvin, "The Female Terrorist: A Socio-Psychological Perspective," *Behavioral Science and the Law* 1 (1983): 19–32; Laura Sjobert and Reed Wood, "People not Pawns: Women's Participation in Violent Extremism across MENA," *USAID Research Brief* 1 (2015).
80. Laura Sjoberg and Caron E. Gentry, *Mothers, Monsters, Whores: Women's Violence in Global Politics* (London: Zed Books, 2007).
81. Katharina Kneip, "Female Jihad—Women in ISIS," *IAPSS Political Science Journal* 29 (2016): 88–106; von Knop, "The Female Jihad," 406.
82. Hoyle, Bradford, and Frenett, *Becoming Mulan?*; Kubra Gultekin, "Women Engagement in Terrorism: What Motivates Females to Join in Terrorist Organizations?" in *Understanding Terrorism: Analysis of Sociological and Psychological Aspects*, Vol. 22, ed. Suleyman Ozeren, Ismail Dincer Gunes, and Diab M. Al-Badayneh (NATO Science for Peace and Security Series–E: Human and Societal Dynamics, 2007), 167–175; Bloom, "Bombshells"; Emmanuel Karagiannis, "European Converts to Islam: Mechanisms of Radicalization," *Politics, Religion & Ideology* 13, no. 1 (2012): 99–113; Eileen M. MacDonald, *Shoot the Women First* (New York: Random House, 1992).
83. Anat Berko, Edna Erez, and Julie L. Globokar, "Gender, Crime and Terrorism: The Case of Arab/Palestinian Women in Israel," *The British Journal of Criminology* 50, no. 4 (2010): 670–689.

84. Sasha Havlicek, *The Islamic State's War on Women and Girls* (Institute for Strategic Dialogue, 2015).
85. Robert Agnew, "A General Strain Theory of Terrorism," *Theoretical Criminology* 14, no. 2 (2010): 132–133.
86. Alex S. Wilner and C.-J. Dubouloz, "Homegrown Terrorism and Transformative Learning: An Interdisciplinary Approach to Understanding Radicalization," *Global Change, Peace & Security* 22, no. 1 (2010): 33–51.
87. Rex A. Hudson, *The Sociology and Psychology of Terrorism: Who becomes a Terrorist and Why?* (Washington, DC: Library of Congress, Federal Research Division, 1999); Boaz Gaynor, "Terror as a Strategy of Psychological Warfare," *International Institute for Counter-Terrorism*, 15 July 2002, https://www.ict.org.il/Article/827/Terror%20as%20a%20Strategy%20of%20Psychological%20Warfare (accessed 7 January 2018).
88. Saltman and Smith, "'Till Martyrdom Do Us Part' Gender and the ISIS Phenomenon"; Elizabeth Pearson and Emily Winterbotham, "Women, Gender, and Daesh Radicalization: A Milieu Approach," *RUSI Journal* 162, no. 3 (2017): 60–72.
89. Erin Marie Saltman and Melanie Smith, "'Till Martyrdom Do Us Part.'"
90. Ibid.
91. Pamala L. Griset and Sue Mehan, *Terrorism in Perspective* (Thousand Oaks, CA: Sage, 2003).
92. Cragin and Daly, *Women as Terrorists*. This book, however, covered various forms of terrorism and different terrorist groups from all over the world—beyond religious terrorism (such as that perpetrated by ISIS).
93. Lauren Vogel, Louise Porter, and Mark Kebbell, "The Roles of Women in Contemporary Political and Revolutionary Conflict: A Thematic Model," *Studies in Conflict & Terrorism* 37, no. 1 (2014): 91–114.
94. Audrey Alexander, *Cruel Intentions: Female Jihadists in America* (Washington, DC: Program on Extremism, 2016), Accessed at: https://cchs.gwu.edu/sites/cchs.gwu.edu/files/downloads/ Female%20Jihadists%20in%20America.pdf (January 6, 2018).
95. Louisa Tarras-Wahlberg, "Seven Promises of ISIS to its Female Recruits" (International Center for the Study of Violent Extremism, Research Reports, 9 January 2017); Naureen Chowdhury Fink, Rafia Barakat, and Liat Shetret, "The Roles of Women in Terrorism, Conflict, and Violent Extremism: Lessons for the United Nations and International Actors," Policy Brief (Center on Global Counterterrorism Cooperation, 2013); Rex A. Hudson, *The Sociology and Psychology of Terrorism.*
96. Erin Marie Saltman and Ross Frenett, "Female Radicalization to ISIS and the Role of Women in CVE," in *A Man's World? Exploring the Roles of Women in Countering Terrorism and Violent Extremism*, ed. Naureen Chowdhury Fink, Sara Zeiger, and Rafia Bhulai (Hedayah and the Global Center on Cooperative Security, 2016), 142–163.
97. Spencer, "The Hidden Face of Terrorism," 74–98.
98. Mia Bloom, "Bombshells: Women and Terrorism," *Gender Issues* 28 (2011), 1–21; Laura Sjoberg and Caron E. Gentry, "Looking Closely at Women in Violent Extremism," *Georgetown Journal of International Affairs* 17, no. 2 (2016): 23–30.
99. Audrey Alexander, *Cruel Intentions: Female Jihadists in America* (Washington, DC: Program on Extremism, 2016), Accessed at: https://cchs.gwu.edu/sites/cchs.gwu.edu/files/downloads/ Female%20Jihadists%20in%20America.pdf (January 6, 2018).
100. Hoyle, Bradford, and Frenett, *Becoming Mulan?*; Cindy D. Ness, "In the Name of the Cause: Women's Work in Secular and Religious Terrorism," *Studies in Conflict and Terrorism* 28, no. 5 (2006): 353–373.
101. Bloom, "Bombshells"; von Knop, "The Female Jihad"; Karla J Cunningham, "Cross-Regional Trends in Female Terrorism," *Studies in Conflict & Terrorism* 26, no. 3 (2003): 171–195; Cragin and Daly, *Women as Terrorists*; Maras, *Counterterrorism*.
102. Peresin and Cervone, "The Western Muhajirat of ISIS"; Bloom, "Bombshells"; Von Knop, "The Female Jihad"; Karla J Cunningham, "Cross-Regional Trends in Female Terrorism,"

Studies in Conflict & Terrorism 26, no. 3 (2003): 171–195; Kim Cragin and Sara A. Daly, *Women as Terrorists: Mothers, Recruiters, and Martyrs*; Maras, *Counterterrorism*.

103. Lorenzo Vidino, Francesco Marone, and Eva Entenmann, *Fear Thy Neighbor: Radicaliation and Jihadist Attacks in the West* (Milano, Italy: Ledizioni LediPublishing, 2017), https://icct.nl/publication/fear-thy-neighbor-radicalization-and-jihadist-attacks-in-the-west/ (accessed 8 January 2018).
104. Jyette Klausen, "Tweeting the Jihad: Social Media Networks of Western Foreign Fighters in Syria and Iraq," *Studies in Conflict and Terrorism* 38 (2015): 1–22; von Knop, "The Female Jihad"; Farahnaz Ispahani, "Women and Islamist Extremism: Gender Rights under the Shadow of Jihad," *The Review of Faith & International Affairs* 14, no. 2 (2016): 101–104; Hoyle, Bradford, and Frenett, *Becoming Mulan?*; Bloom, "Bombshells."
105. Alexander, *Cruel Intentions*, p. 2; Rukmini Callimachi, "ISIS Enshrines a Theology of Rape," *New York Times*, 13 August 2015, https://www.nytimes.com/2015/08/14/world/middleeast/isis-enshrines-a-theology-of-rape.html (accessed 10 January 2018); Cragin and Daly, *Women as Terrorists*; David Barnett, "Women Who are Captured by Isis and Kept as Slaves Endure more than just Sexual Violence," *The Independent*, 29 November 2016, http://www.independent.co.uk/news/world/middle-east/isis-sex-slaves-lamiya-aji-bashar-nadia-murad-sinjar-yazidi-genocide-sexual-violence-rape-sakharov-a7445151.html (accessed 10 January 2018).
106. Rukmini Callimachi, "ISIS Enshrines a Theology of Rape," *New York Times*, 13 August 2015, https://www.nytimes.com/2015/08/14/world/middleeast/isis-enshrines-a-theology-of-rape.html (accessed 10 January 2018).
107. The slaves are predominantly Yazidi, but have also been Sunni Arabs or Christians and purportedly disgraced female ISIS members as punishment for crimes, such as trying to escape the caliphate. See Thomas Burrows, "Teenage Islamist 'Poster Girl' Who Fled Austria to Join ISIS was used as a Sex Slave for New Fighters before She was Beaten to Death as She Tried to Escape, Former Prisoner Reveals," *DailyMail*, 31 December 2015, http://www.dailymail.co.uk/news/article-3378986/Teenage-Islamist-poster-girl-fled-Austria-join-ISIS-used-sex-slave-new-fighters-beaten-death-tried-escape-former-prisoner-reveals.html.
108. Kim Cragin and Sara A. Daly, *Women as Terrorists: Mothers, Recruiters, and Martyrs* (Santa Barbara, CA: ABC-CLIO, 2009).
109. Fink, Barakat, and Shetret, "The Roles of Women in Terrorism, Conflict, and Violent Extremism."
110. Only thirteen of the women included in the sample were investigated and prosecuted as individuals. In eighteen cases, the women were grouped as part of alleged conspiracy with one or multiple women and/or men. Not all of the cases led to formal charges, despite their actions being consistent with terrorist crimes, due to their age and/or cooperation with law enforcement, such as turning state's evidence in exchange for probation.
111. The cases used were tried by federal prosecutors using the standard in 18 U.S.C. § 2331. Criminal act of domestic terrorism in accordance with 18 U.S. Code § 2331 on Terrorism, including acts resulting in kills or injures as per § 2332 (Criminal penalties), and/or commits associated terrorist related acts listed in 18 U.S.C. §2339 (Harboring or concealing terrorists), 2339A (Providing material support to terrorists), 2339B (Providing material support or resources to designated foreign terrorist organizations), 2339C (Prohibitions against the financing of terrorism), and 2339D (Receiving military-type training from a foreign terrorist organization).
112. One additional demographic, current employment, was examined but it was incomplete for most of the dataset.
113. Federal Bureau of Investigation, "Arvada Woman Sentenced for Conspiracy to Provide Material Support to a Designated Foreign Terrorist Organization," 23 January 2015; *United States v. Muhammad Oda Dakhlalla*, Factual Basis (2016); *United States v. Jaelyn Delshaun Young and Muhammad Oda Dakhlalla*, Criminal Complaint and Affidavit (2015); *United States v. Keonna Thomas*, Criminal Complaint and Affidavit (2015); *United States v. Shannon Maureen Conley*, Criminal Complaint and Affidavit (2014); Federal Bureau of

Investigation, "Orange County Woman Sentenced to Five Years in Federal Prison for Providing Material Support to Terrorists by Sending Money to Pakistan to be Used in Attacks Against U.S. Forces Overseas," 29 March 2013; *USA v. Oytun Ayse Mihalik*, Government's Response to Defendant's Sentencing Memorandum (2013); *USA v. Saynab Abdirashid Hussein*, Government's Response to Defendant's Position Regarding Sentencing (2014); *United States v. Heather Elizabeth Coffman*, Criminal Complaint and Affidavit (2014); *United States v. Hodzic, et al.*, Indictment (2015); *United States v. Mohammed Hamzah Khan*, Criminal Complaint and Affidavit (2014); *United States v. Mohammed Hamzah Khan*, Plea Agreement (2015); *United States v. Safya Roe Yassin*, Criminal Complaint and Affidavit (2016); *United States v. Yusra Ismail*, Criminal Complaint and Affidavit (2014); *USA v. Saynab Abdirashid Hussein*, Saynab Hussein's Position Regarding Sentencing (2013); *United States v. Noelle Velentzas and Asia Siddiqui*, Criminal Complaint and Affidavit (2015). Please note that Farhia Hassan, Fardowsa Jama Mohamed, and Barira Hassan Abdullahi, are not included in this investigation. Farhia Hassan was arrested at her residence in the Netherlands; Fardowsa Jama Mohamed is a fugitive in Kenya and the subject of a pending arrest warrant; and Barira Hassan Abdullahi is a fugitive in Somalia and also the subject of a pending arrest warrant. See *USA v. Muna Osman Jama*, et al., Superseding Indictment (2014); see also Department of Justice Press Release, "Three Defendants Arrested on Charges of Material Support to a Foreign Terrorist Organization," 23 July 2014, https://www.fbi.gov/contact-us/field-offices/washingtondc/news/press-releases/three-defendants-arrested-on-charges-of-providing-material-support-to-a-foreign-terrorist-organization (accessed 11 January 2018).

114. In cases of missing information (e.g., demographics, Internet functionality), credible news media sources were also examined. However, to ensure corroboration of facts and a simple index of reliability, only when the same information was provided through multiple sources was the information added to the dataset.
115. The authors proposed an additional category, *thrill seeking*, that is, as a way for the woman to feel alive, have fun, or be excited, suggested by the literature, but we did not find that it described any of the women in the sample.
116. The location, the United States or abroad, was noted.
117. Lorenzo Vidino and Seamus Hughes, *Isis in America: From Retweets to Raqqa* (Washington, DC: Program on Extremism, 2015).
118. Bruce Hoffman, "'Holy Terror.'"
119. Ibid., 271–284, Audrey K. Cronin, "Behind the Curve: Globalization and International Terrorists," *International Security* 27, no. 3 (2002–2003): 30–58.
120. Alexander, "The Radicalization of Extremists/Terrorists," 42–43.
121. Pearson, "The Case of Roshonara Choudhry"; Pearson and Winterbotham, "Women, Gender, and Daesh Radicalization."
122. Maras, *Counterterrorism*; Freiberg and Jeffrey S. Crane, "A Systematic Examination of Terrorist Use of the Internet"; Paul Gill, Emily Corner, Maura Conway, Amy Thornton, Mia Bloom, and John Horgan, "Terrorist Use of the Internet by the Numbers: Quantifying Behaviors, Patterns, and Processes," *Criminology & Public Policy* 16, no. 1 (2017): 99–117.
123. Maras, *Counterterrorism*.
124. Akins and Winfree, Jr., "Social Learning Theory and becoming a Terrorist,"138.
125. Ibid., 133–149.
126. Pearson and Winterbotham, "Women, Gender, and Daesh Radicalization," 60–72.
127. Alexander, "The Radicalization of Extremists/Terrorists," 42–43..
128. Pearson and Winterbotham, "Women, Gender, and Daesh Radicalization," 60–72.
129. Ibid.; Jytte Klausen, "Tweeting the Jihad: Social Media Networks of the Western Foreign Fighters in Syria and Iraq," *Studies in Conflict & Terrorism* 38, no, 1 (2015): 1–22.
130. Sageman, *Understanding Terror Networks*.
131. Freiberg and Crane, "A Systematic Examination of Terrorist Use of the Internet," 313.
132. Akins and Winfree, Jr., "Social Learning Theory and becoming a Terrorist."

133. Barak Stanley, "Uses and Gratification of Temporary Social Media: A Comparison of Snapchat and Facebook" (Masters Thesis, California State University at Fullerton).
134. Alexander, *Cruel Intentions.*
135. Akers, *Social Learning and Social Structure*; Freiberg and Crane, "A Systematic Examination of Terrorist Use of the Internet," 309–319; Pearson, "The Case of Roshonara Choudhry"; Winter, "The Virtual 'Caliphate'"; Robyn Torok, "Developing an Explanatory Model for the Process of Online Radicalization and Terrorism," *Security Informatics* 2, no. 6 (2013): 2–6.
136. Freiberg and Crane, "A Systematic Examination of Terrorist Use of the Internet," 309–319.
137. Ibid.; Alfred Rovai, "Building Sense of Community at a Distance," *International Review of Research in Open and Distance Learning*, 3, no. 1 (2002): 1–16.
138. Alexander, *Cruel Intentions.*
139. Maeghin Alarid, "Recruitment and Radicalization: The Role of Social Media and New Technology," in *Impunity: Countering Illicit Power in War and Transition*, ed. Michelle Hughes and Michael Miklaucic (National Defense University, Centre for Technology and National Security Policy, 2016); Maura Conway, "Terrorist Use of the Internet and Fighting Back," *Information & Security* 19 (2006): 9–30; Robyn Torok, "Developing an Explanatory Model for the Process of Online Radicalization and Terrorism," *Security Informatics* 2, no. 6 (2013): 2–6.
140. Torok, "Developing an Explanatory Model for the Process of Online Radicalization and Terrorism"; Paul Gill, Emily Corner, Maura Conway, Amy Thornton, Mia Bloom, and John Horgan, "Terrorist Use of the Internet by the Numbers: Quantifying Behaviors, Patterns, and Processes," *Criminology & Public Policy* 16, no. 1 (2017): 99–117.
141. Daniel Koehler, "The Radical Online: Individual Radicalization Processes and the Role of the Internet," *Journal for Deradicalization* 1 (2014/2015): 116–134.
142. Ronald L. Akers and Adam L. Silverman, "Toward a Social Learning Model of Violence and Terrorism," in *Violence: From Theory to Research*, ed. Margaret A. Zahn, Henry H. Brownstein, and Shelly. L. Jackson (Cincinnati, OH: Anderson Publishing, 2004), 19–36.
143. Anita Peresin, "Fatal Attraction: Western Muslimas and ISIS," *Perspectives on Terrorism* 9, no. 3 (2015): 24.
144. Mia Bloom, "How ISIS is using Marriage as a Trap," *The Huffington Post*, http://www.huffingtonpost.com/mia-bloom/isis-marriage-trap_b_6773576.html (accessed 3 January 2018), as cited in Peresin, "Fatal Attraction," 25.
145. Alice E. Marwick and Danah Boyd, "I Tweet Honestly, I Tweet Passionately: Twitter users, Context Collapse, and the Imagined Audience," *New Media & Society* 13, no. 1 (2010): 114–133.
146. Lizzie Dearden, "ISIS Austrian Poster Girl Samra Kesinovic 'used as Sex Slave' before Being Murdered for Trying to Escape," *Independent*, 31 December 2015, http://www.independent.co.uk/news/world/middle-east/isis-austrian-poster-girl-samra-kesinovic-used-as-sex-slave-before-being-murdered-for-trying-to-a6791736.html (accessed 10 January 2018).
147. Alexander, *Cruel Intentions.*
148. Peresin, "Fatal Attraction," 24; Saltman and Smith, "'Till Martyrdom Do Us Part.'"
149. Spencer, "The Hidden Face of Terrorism," 74–98.
150. Ben Brumfield, "Officials: 3 Denver Girls Played Hooky from School and Tried to Join ISIS," *CNN*, 22 October 2014, http://www.cnn.com/2014/10/22/us/colorado-teens-syria-odyssey/index.html (accessed 7 January 2018).
151. Nazia Parveen, "Small Part of Manchester that has been Home to 16 Jihadis," *The Guardian*, 25 February 2017, https://www.theguardian.com/uk-news/2017/feb/25/small-part-of-manchester-that-has-been-home-to-16-jihadis (accessed 7 January 2018); "Austrian Girl Who Joined ISIS in Syria was 'used as a Sexual Present' before being Beaten to Death," 1 January 2016, http://www.news.com.au/world/middle-east/austrian-girl-who-joined-isis-in-syria-was-used-as-a-sexual-present-before-being-beaten-to-death/news-story/ca34c5000472f8e07 65d424273e13da5 (accessed 7 January 2018).

152. Lizzie Dearden, "Isis' British Brides: What We know about the Girls and Women Still in Syria after the Death of Kadiza Sultana," *The Independent*, 12 August 2016, http://www.independent.co.uk/news/uk/home-news/isis-british-brides-kadiza-sultana-girls-women-syria-married-death-killed-aqsa-mahmood-islamic-state-a7187751.html (accessed 7 January 2018); BBC News, "Syria Girls: UK Trio 'Picked up by IS Men'—Smuggler," 25 February 2015, http://www.bbc.com/news/uk-31633002 (accessed 7 January 2018).
153. Sasha Havlicek, "The Islamic State's War on Women and Girls" (Institute for Strategic Dialogue, Verbal testimony to the Congress Committee on Foreign Affairs, 2015).
154. Ibid.; Naureen Chowdhury Fink, Sara Zeiger, and Rafia Bhulai, *A Man's World? Exploring the Roles of Women in Countering Terrorism and Violent Extremism* (Hedayah and the Global Center on Cooperative Security, 2016).
155. Amanda M. Sharp Parker, *The Applicability of Criminology to Terrorism Studies: An Exploratory Study of ISIS Supporters in the United States* (Dissertation, University of South Florida, 2016), 1–2.
156. Katharina Kneip, "Female Jihad—Women in ISIS," *POLITIKON, IAPSS Political Science Journal* 29 (2016): 99.

ORCID

Lauren R. Shapiro http://orcid.org/0000-0002-4895-8432

ᘐ OPEN ACCESS

"The Lions of Tomorrow": A News Value Analysis of Child Images in *Jihadi* Magazines

Amy-Louise Watkin and Seán Looney

ABSTRACT
This article reports and discusses the results of a study that investigated photographic images of children in five online terrorist magazines to understand the roles of children in these groups. The analysis encompasses issues of *Inspire, Dabiq, Jihad Recollections* (*JR*), *Azan*, and *Gaidi Mtanni* (*GM*) from 2009 to 2016. The total number of images was ninety-four. A news value framework was applied that systematically investigated what values the images held that resulted in them being "newsworthy" enough to be published. This article discusses the key findings, which were that *Dabiq* distinguished different roles for boys and girls, portrayed fierce and prestigious boy child perpetrators, and children flourishing under the caliphate; *Inspire* and *Azan* focused on portraying children as victims of Western-backed warfare; *GM* portrayed children supporting the cause peacefully; and *JR* contained no re-occurring findings.

There is a vast and growing scholarly literature focused on terrorist organizations' online magazines.[1] Most analyses are solely concerned with the magazines' textual content[2] and only very few with the images contained in the magazines, whether via combined analysis of text and images[3] or focused solely on the images.[4] Research into images of children in these publications is particularly scarce. This article aims to fill this gap in the literature by investigating images of children across five online terrorist magazine publications.

Several researchers have highlighted the potential that these understudied images may contain. First, Lemieux et al. noted in their textual analysis of *Inspire* that terrorist magazine images need to be researched in further detail with a systematic methodology.[5] Second, Droogan and Peattie, who also undertook a textual analysis of *Inspire*, wrote that the images are potentially as equally powerful as the text and as such, further research is required.[6] Finally, Benotman and Malik identified that similar work is required for online magazines as that which they had already undertaken on social media sites: how children are portrayed, the messages that these portrayals convey, and their target audience(s).[7]

Color versions of one or more of the figures in the article can be found online at www.tandfonline.com/uter.

Psychological studies have revealed that images can be very influential. For example, Stenberg found that people tend to have a better memory for images than text, which is known as the picture superiority effect.[8] Wanta and Roark found that the recall of newspaper articles increased for articles that included images, especially images that elicited emotion.[9] Similarly, Zillman, Knobloch, and Yu found that participants chose to read articles that featured victimization images instead of articles that featured no image or an innocuous image and that text in the articles with the accompanying victimization images was remembered better than text in the other articles.[10] Overall, a wide range of studies have shown that images tend to produce both "powerful" and "lasting emotional" responses.[11] These psychological studies emphasize the potential impact and influence of images in terrorist propaganda.

Further to this, Rhodes[12] makes an interesting point: "Nowhere is childhood more clearly constructed or adult perceptions more visible than in photographs of children."

Photographs of children are generally taken by adults and reveal the construction that adults believe to be appropriate for "typical" children and childhood.[13] Typical images of childhood in the West show that children are taken care of by their guardians (e.g., being clean and well dressed),[14] which matches with the Western perception of childhood. Therefore, we hypothesize that the images in the five terrorist organizations' magazines will reflect the perceptions and thinking of each specific terrorist organization, regarding children, in a similar manner.

This article develops an important but not yet systematically studied area in terrorism studies. It focuses on two representations that previous research has just begun to grapple with for the purpose of furthering understanding of the role that children play within these terrorist groups generally and their propaganda specifically: (1) children as perpetrators of violence, which we term "child perpetrators," and (2) children as victims of Western-backed warfare, which we term "child victims." Previous studies have only researched these representations in one magazine: *Dabiq*, and social media research has primarily focused on Islamic State (IS)'s depiction of children. This article broadens the scope of analysis by studying five magazines across four terrorist organizations: *Dabiq* (IS), *Inspire* (Al Qaeda), *Azan* (Taliban), *Gaidi Mtanni* (*GM*) (al-Shabaab), and *Jihad Recollections* (*JR*) (Al Qaeda). This article also analyzes the different gender portrayals in these images and changes in image type across time. Although all five magazines contain photographs of children, *Dabiq* and *Inspire* have the highest number, and more prominent, developed trends than the other three publications.

Literature review

The extant literature on child images in online terrorist propaganda is primarily focused on social media content. Bloom, Horgan, and Winter[15] and Benotman and Malik[16] both created databases of child images from IS online propaganda as circulated on social media sites. Bloom et al. collected eighty-nine images of child "martyrs" from Twitter and Telegram between January 2015 and January 2016 and compared this with a control database of 114 images of adult "martyrs." They found that not only did the number of child images increase on a monthly basis over the time period studied, but that the child images bore remarkable similarities to the adult images, concluding that child "martyrs" appeared to be treated the same as adult "martyrs." Additionally, they noted that IS's use of children is normalized by representing them as simply "heroes" instead of "young heroes." Bloom et al. argued that this ultimately comes down to a psychological warfare technique to emphasize strength and create fear among IS's enemies. Benotman and Malik, on the other hand, collected 254 images from sites such as Twitter, archive.org, and justpaste.it between August 2015 and February 2016. They proposed that five main themes emerged: participation in violence, normalization to violence, state building, utopia, and foreign policy grievances. Benotman and Malik noted that the majority of the propaganda included children as the perpetrators of violence or children witnessing and becoming normalized to violence, with the next most prominent theme being state building. Again, they argued that these techniques aim to instill fear in their enemies and legitimize IS's state-building project.

Christien[17] is the only researcher (at time of writing) to have analyzed child images in a *jihadist* online magazine. Christien studied the representation of youth in IS's *Dabiq* by analyzing the text and images contained in the first eight issues (from 2014 to 2015). Christien analyzed whether Giroux and Males's theory of the myth of childhood innocence appeared in *Dabiq* and found that "childhood innocence" was the most dominant representation of children and youth; found in almost half of the data set. Other prominent themes found were references to children as weak and victims of the West; as material commodities, with girls described as slaves; and as perpetrators of violence. Christien theorized that children are portrayed in these ways, first, to elicit anger and frustration within IS's target audience, and second, to portray their social and institutional rules and legitimize their long-term goal of building a powerful state. Christien noted that the representation of children as perpetrators of violence began to increase in issues 7 and 8 of *Dabiq* and suggested that research into whether this continued and increased was an area for future study.

According to Rhodes,[18] as adults, we tend to view children as the next generation of adults, and invest in them accordingly our hopes for the future. Although historically not always the case in Western nations, we have now reached a point in which we generally perceive children to be (and hope for them to be) carefree innocents spared of adult responsibilities, worries, and stresses,[19] with an overwhelming view that children require protection.[20] Faulkner[21] argues that there are few issues in Western society that provoke outrage in the same manner as that of the threat to childhood innocence, including but not limited to: abuse, neglect, violence, and sexualization. This view is in stark contrast with the current view and use of children by terrorist organizations.

Current literature has revealed that children are being used by terrorist organizations, particularly IS, like never before.[22] In the past, the use of children as perpetrators of violence in war and terrorism has only been seen in cases of desperation[23] and organizations have been shy in advertising this.[24] However, IS in particular understand the importance of planning ahead in order to achieve their ambition of building a state that will last.[25] The recruitment, indoctrination, and training of the next generation are how they plan to sustain their state.[26] Terrorists understand that children are more impressionable[27] and indoctrinating individuals into their worldview from a young age minimizes the chances of their fighters becoming converted to any other way of life, thus creating a stronger generation of fighters.[28] Advertising child perpetrators in their propaganda conveys that their violence has become a family affair[29] and consequently achieves a shock factor that guarantees their consistent appearance in Western media. This consequently results in counterterrorism strategies becoming trickier for the West and sends the message that they are prepared to fight for as long as it takes.[30] On the other hand, their images of children as innocent victims of Western-backed warfare aim to fulfill a different agenda. As mentioned in Christien's study, the main aims of these images are to generate anger and frustration in viewers.[31] They hope that the feelings of anger and frustration generated lead to further action by their supporters, and persuade people to join as new recruits. Additionally, they may be aiming to use these images as proof of their claims that the West is "evil," and to condone the attacks that their organization undertakes in the West.

The literature search into children in terrorist organizations highlighted that the roles that children play in terrorist organizations are gendered, although one limitation to this literature is that there is a disproportionately narrow focus on IS. Nevertheless, the general consensus appears to be that boys are given military training, which includes but is not limited to learning how to use weapons, martial arts, and studying the Quran.[32] After this training is complete, boys are expected to fight alongside their adult counterparts on the battlefield.[33] Boys are even expected to undertake executions as this will desensitize them to violence and eradicate remorse from a young age, allowing them to become brutal adult fighters.[34] Other noted tasks that boys are given are suicide missions, manning checkpoints, and undertaking security patrols.[35] Girls on the other hand, play a very different role and are often referred to as the "flowers and pearls of the Caliphate."[36] IS in particular keep girls as concubines for their fighters, which reportedly consists of girls being subjected to rape and forced marriage, from as young as eight years old.[37] Furthermore, girls must be veiled at all times and remain in their houses.[38]

Terrorist organizations are increasing their use of children in their online propaganda in more ways than one. Several researchers have put forward theories of why this could be. Singer theorizes that these organizations are playing on Western views of childhood innocence, and mentions a quote from the Taliban, "Children are innocent, so they are the best tools against dark forces."[39] Anderson[40] and Pinheiro[41] argue that terrorists understand that first, children are less likely to arouse suspicion, and second, due to Western perceptions of children, the West will find it difficult to know how to respond to these images. This may be the case; however, it is clear that further analysis needs to be undertaken to develop more sophisticated understandings of these images.

Method

The first online magazines in this dataset were published in 2009 and the last in 2016. The issues included are shown in Table 1. A database was created to collect all ninety-

Table 1. Magazine issues included in study.

Magazine	Issues	Time range
Dabiq	1–15	July 2014–July 2016
Inspire	1–15	January 2010–May 2016
Azan	1–6	May 2013–August 2014
GM	1–7	April 2012–February 2015
JR	1–4	April 2009–September 2009

four child images published in this time. The researchers searched through each magazine issue to identify the images and extracted them into a database. The only criteria during this process were that each image must include one or more children. This research used the UN Convention on the Rights of the Child's definition of a child,[42] which is an individual under 18 years old.[43]

There were two stages to coding the resultant dataset. The first determined whether the child perpetrator and child victim themes found in the first eight issues of *Dabiq* by Christien could be confirmed, and second, were also present in the other four magazines. Within the child victim theme we further coded the images as either vulnerable child or dead/injured child. We defined a child as vulnerable when they appeared to be scared or sad. Dead and injured children were coded together as both depicted events where violence had occurred. We noticed another theme within the magazines—that of happy children. This refers to images in which children were depicted at play, happy, and in good care of the organizations. We termed this category "Fulfilled children."[44] During this coding stage, we became aware that the child's gender was an important factor (Tables 2, 3 and 4). However, there were some images where both genders were present in an image and we refer to these images as "Mixed." Finally, we noted that children were either presented solely or as a group (Tables 5 and 6). Therefore, the entire dataset was coded at this stage according to the following categories: child perpetrators; child victims; fulfilled children; males; females; mixed; solo; and group.

In the second coding stage, we applied Bednarek and Caple's[45] news value framework to all the images. This systematically investigates what values the images hold that result

Table 2. Gender composition of children in images.

	Inspire (24 images)	*Dabiq* (49 images)	*GM* (10 images)	*Azan* (7 images)	*JR* (4 images)
Male	75% ($n=18$)	69.3% ($n=35$)	30% ($n=3$)	42.8% ($n=3$)	75% ($n=3$)
Female	20.8% ($n=5$)	16.3% ($n=8$)	10% ($n=1$)	14.2% ($n=1$)	0
Mixed	4.16% ($n=1$)	8.16% ($n=4$)	60% ($n=6$)	42.8% ($n=3$)	25% ($n=1$)
Unknown	0	4.08% ($n=2$)	0	0	0

Table 3. Gender composition of child perpetrators images.

	Inspire (24 images)	*Dabiq* (49 images)	*GM* (10 images)	*Azan* (7 images)	*JR* (4 images)
Child perpetrator (male)	4.1% ($n=1$)	34% ($n=17$)	10% ($n=1$)	0	0
Child perpetrator (female)	0	0	0	0	0
Child perpetrator (Mixed)	0	0	0	0	0
Total	4.1% ($n=1$)	34% ($n=17$)	10% ($n=1$)	0	0

Table 4. Gender compositions in fulfilled children images.

	Inspire (24 images)	*Dabiq* (49 images)	*GM* (10 images)	*Azan* (7 images)	*JR* (4 images)
Fulfilled children (Male)	4.1% ($n=1$)	14% ($n=7$)	10% ($n=1$)	0	50% ($n=2$)
Fulfilled children (Female)	4.1% ($n=1$)	8% ($n=4$)	0	0	0
Fulfilled children (Mixed)	0	2% ($n=1$)	30% ($n=3$)	0	0
Total	8.2% ($n=2$)	24% ($n=12$)	40% ($n=4$)	0	50% ($n=2$)

Table 5. Group and solo depictions of children within images.

	Inspire (24 images)	*Dabiq* (49 images)	*GM* (10 images)	*Azan* (7 images)	*JR* (4 images)
Solo Photos	71% ($n=17$)	53% ($n=26$)	20% ($n=2$)	28% ($n=2$)	25% ($n=1$)
Group Photos	29% ($n=7$)	47% ($n=23$)	80% ($n=8$)	72% ($n=5$)	75% ($n=3$)

Table 6. Group and solo depictions of child perpetrators within images.

	Inspire (24 images)	*Dabiq* (49 images)	*GM* (10 images)	*Azan* (7 images)	*JR* (4 images)
Child perpetrator (solo)	4.1% ($n = 1$)	10% ($n = 5$)	0	0	0
Child perpetrator (group)	0	24% ($n = 12$)	10% ($n = 1$)	0	0
Total	4.1% ($n = 1$)	34% ($n = 17$)	10% ($n = 1$)	0	0

in them being classed as more "newsworthy" than others.[46] The analysis of news values in this framework includes the "qualities" and "elements" that make the image newsworthy enough to be included in the publication.[47]

News values have previously been studied from cognitive perspectives[48] and are defined by Richardson[49] as "the (imagined) preferences of the expected audience." Bednarek and Caple's[50] news value framework, in contrast, is primarily discursive; that is, it considers the linguistic and visual means via which news values are realized in media (news) texts. This discourse analysis takes two considerations into account regarding how images construct news values.[51] First, the contextualization of the participants in the image: where they are photographed and who with, and how much or little is shown in the image.[52] Second, technical considerations, for example, shutter speed, focal length, aperture, and angle. Furthermore, there is no one-to-one relationship between devices and the news values; they can construct more than one news value.[53]

The news values that Bednarek and Caple examine are prominence, negativity, superlativeness, novelty, impact, personalization, and aesthetics.[54] Bednarek and Caple define prominence as the "*high status of individuals, organizations or nations*" in the event photographed. Therefore in this study, prominence was coded using indicators of high status among the children in the images, such as receiving training/education. Negativity is defined as "*the negative aspects of an event*" and, therefore, in this study was coded through indicators of negative occurrences experienced by the children in the images; being vulnerable, injured, or killed. This news value overlaps with our first-stage coding, specifically the labels "vulnerable" and "dead/injured." Superlativeness is defined as "*the maximized or intensified aspects of an event,*" and was thus coded when the activities were portrayed as large, extreme or intense such as large groupings of children. Novelty is defined as *the "unexpected aspects of an event,"* which was coded as anything that was thought to be unusual or surprising in the child images. Impact is the "*effects or consequences of an event,*" which was coded as the aftermath of acts committed on or by children. Personalization is defined as "*the personal or human interest aspects of an event,*" which was coded through the display of children's emotions in the images. Aesthetics is defined as "*the ways in which images are balanced through their compositional configurations,*" and was coded whenever there was noticeable photography techniques used in the images of children. It is important to note that multiple coding of these values were used; for example, superlativeness and personalization would be the display of extreme emotions. This makes it possible to have totals in the analysis that equal greater than 100 percent. Table 7 displays Bendarek and Caple's definitions of news values and their adapted realization in the present study.

Bednarek and Caple's news value framework was chosen, first, because the magazines are used in part to disseminate news of the respective *jihad* groups, their designs being quite similar to Western newspapers/magazines. Second, the framework aims to reveal the specific values that the terrorist organization *qua* the photographer aims to convey

Table 7. News values and realization in present study.

News value	Bednarek and Caple's definitions (2012, 104)	Realization in the images in present study
Prominence	*The high status of the individuals, organizations, or nations involved in the event*	High status was indicated through roles in the organization such as: child perpetrators, children receiving education/training, and children protesting enemies of *jihadi* groups (e.g., governments). The high status of children was also indicated through *jihadi* members protecting and taking care of children.
Negativity	*Negative aspects of an event*	Dead children, vulnerable children, injured children, children being attacked, children in impoverished conditions, and torn clothing on child victims.
Superlativeness	*The maximized or intensified aspects of an event*	Injured/vulnerable/dead children photographed together. Large groupings of child perpetrators and protesters. The presence of extreme emotions in children and mourning parents.
Novelty	*The unexpected aspects of an event*	Images that contrasted with the dominant trends/themes in their respective magazines.
Personalization	*The personal or human interest aspects of an event*	The emotions displayed by the children in the images. Clear shots of faces of children. Images where aesthetics draw attention to children's faces and emotions.
Impact	*The effects or consequences of an event*	The aftermath of acts committed on or by children. Dead bodies, injured children, people mourning, children sat in ruins.
Aesthetics	*The ways in which images are balanced through their compositional configurations*	Filters, effects, motion, use of color, aesthetic use of distance/angle to elicit a particular response.

to the target audience (i.e., followers and potential recruits), and how these values are interpreted by this audience, and consequently, how the audience is influenced by these values.[55] This should allow us to gain deeper insight into how terrorists are trying to influence their Western readers and potentially allow us to attempt to create effective counter-images.

The final analysis (see section "Trends Across Time") that was undertaken post-stage 1 and 2 coding was to identify and calculate changes and/or continuity in use of the observed themes over time and was only carried out for *Dabiq* and *Inspire* because the three other magazines did not have enough images or developed enough themes to do so.

Results

First stage of coding: Content analysis of child images

Gender

Overall there are a far higher number of images containing male children than female children in the dataset. *Inspire* and *Dabiq* in particular feature a large amount of images of males with *Dabiq* containing a 1:5 ratio of girls to boys.

Group photos and solo photos

Overall there is a near even split between images of children portrayed alone and images of children grouped together or with others. *Inspire* contains a larger proportion of images depicting children alone than grouped together while *Dabiq* contains a near 50/50 split.

Child perpetrators

In all magazines bar *Dabiq,* child perpetrators are a rarity (17/19). Both *Inspire* and *GM* contain one apiece while *Azan* and *JR* have none. They are uniformly male across the magazines. There is a theme of solo child perpetrators to be depicted gun in hand, in proximity to a murdered enemy while groups of child perpetrators are not shown violently; they are either stood to attention or praying.

Fulfilled children

This category amounts for twenty of the ninety-four-image dataset (21.5 percent). It is found most often in *Dabiq* where IS attempts to promote the good life awaiting children within the caliphate, where children are held smiling in the arms of the fathers and girls live the lives of idyllic innocents.

Child victims

The largest category of images found in the dataset concerns child victims, specifically, child victims of Western violence or aggression.

Overall, *Inspire* has the highest number of these images as shown in Table 8; of the twenty-four images of children present within the magazine 87.5 percent concern the portrayal of children as victims of Western, or Western-backed, violence. Within *Inspire,* children were more likely to be portrayed as vulnerable (12/24) rather than dead (9/24); there were more images of children stood among the rubble of buildings than under it.

While the victims depicted are predominantly male (34/50), *Dabiq* and *Inspire* do not shy away from showing dead girls with four images of dead girls between them. However *Inspire* depicts girls as vulnerable (2/21) whereas *Dabiq* does not, opting instead to depict them solely as fulfilled children. Two images are classified as

Table 8. Gender composition of dead or injured and vulnerable children images.

	Inspire (24 images)	*Dabiq* (49 images)	*GM* (10 images)	*Azan* (7 images)	*JR* (4 images)
Dead or injured child (male)	20% ($n = 5$)	8% ($n = 4$)	0	84% ($n = 6$)	0
Dead or injured child (female)	8% ($n = 2$)	4% ($n = 2$)	0	0	0
Dead or injured child (mixed)	8% ($n = 2$)	4% ($n = 2$)	10% ($n = 1$)	0	25% ($n = 1$)
Dead or injured child (unknown)	0	4% ($n = 2$)	0	0	0
Vulnerable child (male)	42% ($n = 10$)	12% ($n = 6$)	20% ($n = 2$)	0	25% ($n = 1$)
Vulnerable child (female)	8% ($n = 2$)	0	0	14% ($n = 1$)	0
Vulnerable child (mixed)	0	2% ($n = 1$)	0	0	0
Total	87.5% ($n = 21$)	34% ($n = 17$)	30% ($n = 3$)	100% ($n = 7$)	50% ($n = 2$)

"Unknown" in terms of gender due to the bloody nature of the image obscuring the gender of the child from the viewer.

Diachronic analysis: "Trends across time"

As we coded the images we noticed how depictions of children have changed over time in *Inspire* and *Dabiq*. Figure 1 shows the changes that have occurred in *Inspire* over the course of their publications and Figure 2 shows the same for *Dabiq*.

Inspire starts off by featuring six images of dead or injured children in Issue 1 and the trend remains fairly consistent. It decreases slightly in issues 2–8 but in issues 10, 12, and 13 they return to three to five images of dead or injured children per issue. There are very few images of fulfilled children or child perpetrators overall. There is one image of a child perpetrator and in the other two the theme of using children to humanize adults return. One in particular features a smiling Osama bin Laden holding a smiling child. Despite having twenty-four images of children, *Inspire* has not been consistent with depicting children; it has five issues with no children at all. The two highest counts of these images can be seen in two issues in particular; issue 1 and issue 13 and they are predominantly negative. The articles these images feature in often concern "the sins of the West." They include an interview with Abu Basir, an article called "The West should ban the Niqab covering its Real Face" and "Letter to the American People."

Interestingly *Dabiq* depictions have changed over its existence. While initially they kept in line with the practices of *Inspire* they have gradually phased out negative depictions of children for depictions showcasing child perpetrators and fulfilled children. After issue 9 there are only four negative images spread over six issues, compared to eleven images of child perpetrators and six fulfilled child images. Child perpetrators and fulfilled daughters dominate images post issue 10. Three of the negative depictions concern the treatment of children in the West, namely a child being raised by two mothers, and the treatment of Syrian refugees. Also in contrast with *Inspire*, *Dabiq* contains at least one image of a child in thirteen of its fifteen issues. There is a predominant theme

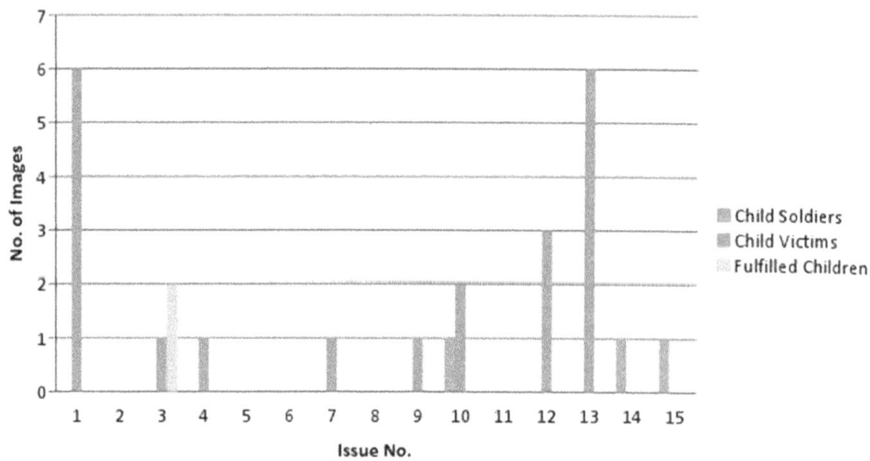

Figure 1. Number of images that contain child perpetrators, victims, and fulfilled children in *Inspire*.

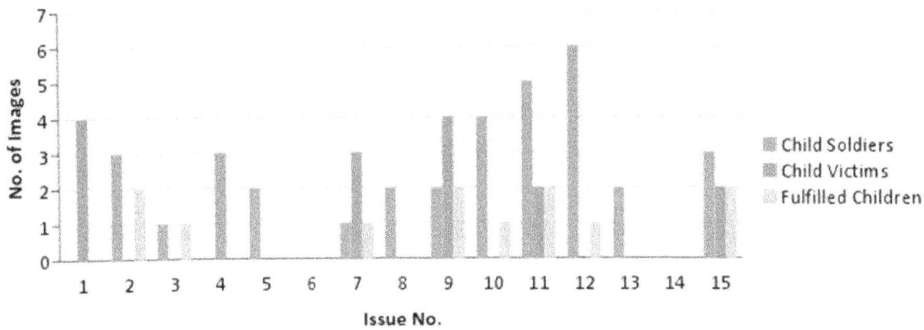

Figure 2. Number of images that contain child perpetrators, victims, and fulfilled children in *Dabiq*.

emerging for personalization; 83.7 percent of images seek to personalize the child to the viewer.

Second stage of coding: News values in child images

The second stage of coding involved the application of Bednarek and Caple's news value framework to all the images. Table 9 shows the frequency of use (in raw and percentage figures) of each news value in the dataset. No uses of the "Novelty" news value were observed in the dataset. Therefore, the news value has not been included in Table 9.

In terms of key patterns (Table 9), Prominence (42/94), Negativity (51/94), and Personalization (81/94) are the most frequently observed news values. The majority of imagery containing the Prominence news value is found in *Dabiq* (29/42), whereas the majority of imagery containing the Negativity news value is split between *Dabiq* (17/51) and *Inspire* (21/51). The Personalization news value is found regularly in *Inspire* (18/24), *Dabiq* (41/49), *Gaidi Mtanni* (6/10), *and Azan* (5/7), but largely absent in *Jihadi Recollections* (1/4). The Impact news value is highly present within *Inspire* (20/24) and *Azan* (7/7) but relatively scarce in *Dabiq* (20/49) and *Gaidi Mtanni* (3/10).

The following section reports the results of applying the news values framework to the subcategories found in the first stage of coding; specifically to the child perpetrator, fulfilled children, and child victims categories.

Child perpetrator

Images of child perpetrators are mainly found in *Dabiq*, and are depicted using three news values: prominence, personalization and aesthetics.

As shown in Table 10, all the images of child perpetrators use the prominence news value to highlight the high status given to child perpetrators and emphasize the importance of the military arm of Islamic State of Iraq and Syria (ISIS), Al Qaeda in the Arabian Peninsula, and Al-Shabaab. *Dabiq* display prominence in how each and every child perpetrator is dressed immaculately in military uniform, whereas, the single instance of child perpetrators in *Inspire* and *Gaidi Mtanni* are dressed in nonmilitary plain clothes. Half of child perpetrator images contained weapons emphasizing the high status and important responsibility that child perpetrators bear. This, along with the use

Table 9. All news values across all magazines.

	Inspire (24 images)	*Dabiq* (49 images)	*GM* (10 images)	*Azan* (7 images)	*JR* (4 images)
Prominence	12.5% (*n* = 3)	59.18% (*n* = 29)	60% (*n* = 6)	0% (*n* = 0)	50% (*n* = 2)
Negativity	87.5% (*n* = 21)	34.69% (*n* = 17)	40% (*n* = 4)	100% (*n* = 7)	50% (*n* = 2)
Superlativeness	25% (*n* = 6)	42.85% (*n* = 21)	70% (*n* = 7)	71.42% (*n* = 5)	100% (*n* = 4)
Personalization	75% (*n* = 18)	83.67% (*n* = 41)	60% (*n* = 6)	71.42% (*n* = 5)	25% (*n* = 1)
Impact	83.3% (*n* = 20)	40.81% (*n* = 20)	30% (*n* = 3)	100% (*n* = 7)	50% (*n* = 2)
Aesthetics	75% (*n* = 18)	53.06% (*n* = 26)	0% (*n* = 0)	57.14% (*n* = 4)	0% (*n* = 0)

Table 10. Prominence in child perpetrator imagery.

	Inspire (24 images)	*Dabiq* (49 images)	*GM* (10 images)	*Azan* (7 images)	*JR* (4 images)
Solo Photos	4.1% (*n* = 1)	10% (*n* = 5)	0	0	0
Group Photos	0	24% (*n* = 12)	10% (*n* = 1)	0	0
Total	4.1% (*n* = 1)	34% (*n* = 17)	10% (*n* = 1)		

Table 11. Personalization in "child perpetrators" imagery.

	Inspire (24 images)	*Dabiq* (49 images)	*GM* (10 images)	*Azan* (7 images)	*JR* (4 images)
Solo photo	4.1% (*n* = 1)	6% (*n* = 3)	0	0	0
Group photo	0	22% (*n* = 11)	10% (*n* = 1)	0	0
Total	4.1% (*n* = 1)	28% (*n* = 14)	10% (*n* = 1)	0	0

Table 12. Prominence in fulfilled children imagery.

	Inspire (24 images)	*Dabiq* (49 images)	*GM* (10 images)	*Azan* (7 images)	*JR* (4 images)
Fulfilled imagery of children (male)	4.1% (*n* = 1)	14% (*n* = 7)	0	0	25% (*n* = 1)
Fulfilled imagery of children (female)	4.1% (*n* = 1)	6% (*n* = 3)	0	0	0
Fulfilled imagery of children (mixed)	0	0	30% (*n* = 3)	0	0
Total	8.2% (*n* = 2)	20% (*n* = 10)	30% (*n* = 3)	0	25% (*n* = 1)

of personalization and aesthetics, underpins depictions of child perpetrators within the dataset.

Table 11 shows the majority (16/19) of the imagery of child perpetrators in the dataset makes use of the personalization news value by drawing attention to the faces of the perpetrators. A common theme throughout is their portrayal as stone-faced, emotionless killers or as uniformed zealots deep in prayer. Only in one instance is the child perpetrator depicted masked.

Eleven of the nineteen child perpetrator images make use of the aesthetics news value. The primary technique used in *Dabiq* is the aesthetic use of focus (9/49). The backgrounds of images containing child perpetrators are kept out of focus in order to draw the eye toward the faces of the perpetrator(s) in the foreground. In this way the use of focus is complementary to the use of the personalization news value. The use of bright colors (3/19) is mainly in the background too, child perpetrators are posed against white backdrops or, in one case, blue skies.

Fulfilled imagery of children

The prominence news value is (Table 12) in a majority of the images of fulfilled children (16/20). Prominence is found most often in *Dabiq* where IS attempts to promote

Table 13. Personalization in "fulfilled children."

	Inspire (24 images)	*Dabiq* (49 images)	*GM* (10 images)	*Azan* (7 images)	*JR* (4 images)
Fulfilled imagery children (male)	4.1% ($n = 1$)	14% ($n = 7$)	10% ($n = 1$)	0	0
Fulfilled imagery of children (female)	4.1% ($n = 1$)	8% ($n = 4$)	0	0	0
Fulfilled imagery of children (mixed)	0	2% ($n = 1$)	0	0	0
	8.2% ($n = 2$)	24% ($n = 12$)	10% ($n = 1$)	0	0

the good life awaiting children within the caliphate (10/20). Across the magazines prominence is utilized in depictions of children being educated (5/20) by the organization, being held in the arms of their presumed fathers (5/20), and in the case of *GM* in mass protests (3/20).

Personalization is heavily used in depicting fulfilled children as shown in Table 13. *Dabiq* utilizes it in every one of its twelve images. The focus of these images is drawn to the smiling faces of young children in the arms of their parents, at play, and the inquisitive faces of young boys being taught in school. *Jihadi* fighters are humanized by the presence of smiling children in their arms in *Dabiq* but this also occurs in an instance in *Inspire* where Osama bin Laden is pictured holding a young girl with both parties smiling.

Similar to their use of the aesthetics news value when depicting child perpetrators, *Dabiq* makes use of soft focus (4/12) on the background in order to draw the viewer's eye to the face of the child in question; however, this technique is also used to personalize the adults that often accompany these children as smiling father figures. Similarly again to child perpetrators, there is a use of bright colors in backgrounds but unlike child perpetrators there are also instances of children dressed in bright clothing.

Child victims

The largest category of images found in the dataset concerns child victims, specifically, child victims of Western violence or aggression. A variety of news values are employed here namely negativity (50/50), personalization (36/50), impact (49/50), superlativeness (28/50), and aesthetics (30/50).

The Negativity news value is found in every Child Victim image and is thus identical to the Child Victims table coded in the first stage of coding.

Despite having over twice the number of child images of *Inspire*, only 34 percent of *Dabiq's* images contained these images of children. Dead or injured children in *Dabiq* are, like in *Inspire*, often portrayed alone. This makes up the largest portion of images that use the negativity news value. Also, *Dabiq* were more likely than *Inspire* to show gory blood-filled images of child victims. Less than half of the small number of images in *GM* contained these images, all of *Azan*'s images and half of *JR*.

The negativity news value is supported through use of other news values, mainly those of impact (Table 14), personalization (Table 15), superlativeness (Table 16), and aesthetics (Table 17).

It is not a coincidence that, barring one image in *Inspire*, Table 18 (for the presence of negativity news values) lines up exactly with Table 14. The photographs of child victims are shot in the context of the impact of Western-backed warfare. In *Dabiq* dead

Table 14. Impact in "child victims" imagery.

	Inspire (24 images)	*Dabiq* (49 images)	*GM* (10 images)	*Azan* (7 images)	*JR* (4 images)
Dead or injured child (male)	20% (*n* = 5)	10% (*n* = 5)	0	84% (*n* = 6)	0
Dead or injured child (female)	8% (*n* = 2)	4% (*n* = 2)	0	0	0
Dead or injured child (mixed)	8% (*n* = 2)	2% (*n* = 1)	10% (*n* = 1)	0	25% (*n* = 1)
Dead or injured child (unknown)	0	4% (*n* = 2)	0	0	0
Vulnerable child (male)	37.5% (*n* = 9)	12% (*n* = 6)	20% (*n* = 2)	0	25% (*n* = 1)
Vulnerable child (female)	8% (*n* = 2)	0	0	14% (*n* = 1)	0
Vulnerable child (mixed)	0	2% (*n* = 1)	0	0	0
Total	83% (*n* = 20)	34% (*n* = 17)	30% (*n* = 3)	100% (*n* = 7)	50% (*n* = 2)

Table 15. Personalization in "child victim" imagery.

	Inspire (24 images)	*Dabiq* (49 images)	*GM* (10 images)	*Azan* (7 images)	*JR* (4 images)
Dead or injured child (male)	20% (*n* = 5)	10% (n = 5)	0	71% (*n* = 5)	0
Dead or injured child (female)	8% (*n* = 2)	2% (*n* = 1)	0	0	0
Dead or injured child (mixed)	8% (*n* = 2)	2% (*n* = 1)	10% (*n* = 1)	0	0
Dead or injured child (unknown)	0	0	0	0	0
Vulnerable child (male)	25% (*n* = 6)	4% (*n* = 2)	10% (*n* = 1)	0	0
Vulnerable child (female)	8% (*n* = 2)	0	0	14% (*n* = 1)	0
Vulnerable child (mixed)	0	2% (*n* = 1)	10% (*n* = 1)	0	0
Total	70% (*n* = 17)	20% (*n* = 10)	30% (*n* = 3)	85% (*n* = 6)	0

Table 16. Superlativeness in "child victim" imagery.

	Inspire (24 images)	*Dabiq* (49 images)	*GM* (10 images)	*Azan* (7 images)	*JR* (4 images)
Dead or injured child (male)	20% (*n* = 5)	0	0	84% (*n* = 6)	0
Dead or injured child (female)	8% (*n* = 2)	0	0	0	0
Dead or injured child (mixed)	8% (*n* = 2)	4% (*n* = 2)	10% (*n* = 1)	0	25% (*n* = 1)
Dead or injured child (unknown)	0	0	0	0	0
Vulnerable child (male)	20% (*n* = 5)	4% (*n* = 2)	0	0	0
Vulnerable child (female)	4% (*n* = 1)	0	0	0	25% (*n* = 1)
Vulnerable child (mixed)	0	0	0	0	0
Total	62.5% (*n* = 15)	8% (*n* = 4)	10% (*n* = 1)	84% (*n* = 6)	50% (*n* = 2)

Table 17. Aesthetics in "child victim" imagery.

	Inspire (24 images)	*Dabiq* (49 images)	*GM* (10 images)	*Azan* (7 images)	*JR* (4 images)
Filter	37.5% (*n* = 9)	10% (*n* = 5)	0	57% (*n* = 4)	0
Focus	0	28% (*n* = 14)	0	0	0
Graphics	45% (*n* = 11)	0	0	0	0
Bright colors	45% (*n* = 11)	8% (*n* = 4)	0	14% (*n* = 1)	0
Dark colors	8% (n = 2)	6% (n = 3)	0	42% (*n* = 3)	0
High angles	16% (*n* = 4)	4% (*n* = 2)	40% (*n* = 40)	71% (*n* = 5)	0
Low angles	0	4% (*n* = 2)	0	0	0

and injured children are portrayed in bloody rags. In *Inspire* vulnerable children sit in bombed ruins and cities and dead children are mourned by their friends and families.

Personalization is a dominant news value in all the magazines when depicting child victims. In particular it is used often in *Inspire*, *Dabiq*, and *GM*. *Inspire* personalizes vulnerable, injured, and dead children by either placing them alone at the center of the frame or by having other figures within the frame looking at them. It is used in the

Table 18. Gender and negativity in child victim imagery.

	Inspire (24 images)	*Dabiq* (49 images)	*GM* (10 images)	*Azan* (7 images)	*JR* (4 images)
Dead or injured child (male)	20% ($n=5$)	8% ($n=4$)	0	84% ($n=6$)	0
Dead or injured child (female)	8% ($n=2$)	4% ($n=2$)	0	0	0
Dead or injured child (mixed)	8% ($n=2$)	4% ($n=2$)	10% ($n=1$)	0	25% ($n=1$)
Dead or injured child (unknown)	0	4% ($n=2$)	0	0	0
Vulnerable child (male)	42% ($n=10$)	12% ($n=6$)	20% ($n=2$)	0	25% ($n=1$)
Vulnerable child (female)	8% ($n=2$)	0	0	14% ($n=1$)	0
Vulnerable child (mixed)	0	2% ($n=1$)	0	0	0
Total	87.5% ($n=21$)	34% ($n=17$)	30% ($n=3$)	100% ($n=7$)	50% ($n=2$)

images to engender an emotional response from the viewer. The emotions that *Inspire* focuses on are sadness, anger, and pain.

Superlativeness is defined as the maximized or intensified aspects of an event. When applied to the child victims' dataset there are several incidences of superlativeness. In *Inspire* and *Azan* there is a tendency to group injured and dead children together in order to intensify the negative aspects of the event. Likewise the emotions of vulnerable children and mourning parents are generally intensified; vulnerable children cry while mourning parents wail or appear to be shouting furiously.

Aesthetics are present in *Azan*, *Inspire*, and *Dabiq* while being absent from *GM* and *JR*. In terms of aesthetic effects there are several key trends. *Inspire* makes use of filters and graphics primarily (11/24). These graphics tend to be overlaid text written in either English or Arabic. Aesthetic use of focus is the primary technique in *Dabiq* (14/49) and is often used to draw the reader's eye to the face of the pictured child. Due to the low density of images overall in *Azan* the use of aesthetics is localized in one article that deals with the death of children at the hands of the West. Each image contains either a group of dead children or a dead child held in the hands of a grieving adult; each image is darkened by a filter. Within the used framework high camera angles are said to be used to denote negativity while high angles are said to promote prominence. Low angles are largely absent from the dataset and high angles are used just as much in negative images as in prominent. The majority of images in *Dabiq* (71.4 percent) are shot from a straight angle. This goes against the expected use of low and high camera angles to denote prominence and negativity. High camera angles appear in twelve images while low camera angles appear in the remaining two. Likewise, in *Inspire*, AQAP are not making use of high and low camera angles as much as was expected. The majority of images are shot in a straight on angle (75 percent) while 25 percent are shot using a high angle.

Discussion

This study collected the ninety-four images that contained a child or children in the five magazines between 2009 and 2016. The first coding stage identified whether the child perpetrator and child victim themes found in Christien's *Dabiq* study were present in the other magazines. This stage further identified the fulfilled children category, that gender was an important theme, and whether or not the children were presented solely or as a group. The second coding stage applied Bednarek and Caple's news value framework to the images. The final stage applied a diachronic analysis in order to identify the changes and/or continuity in use of the observed themes over the course of the issues for *Dabiq* and *Inspire*. This section will integrate and discuss the results of all three stages: content analysis, diachronic analysis, and the news value analysis.

It can be seen from the analysis that first, overall there are a considerably higher number of images containing boys than girls throughout the five publications. It could be argued that this makes sense given that the literature identified that men play primary roles in the organizations and women play more supportive secondary roles.[56] Second, children are shown almost equally on their own as they are in groups across the magazines. This is likely because each representation can further emphasize the organization's message, for example, when attempting to display strength they can photograph large groups, or when attempting to display vulnerability, they can photograph a lone child. Finally, both *Dabiq* and *Inspire* contain a significantly larger number of child images than *Azan*, *GM*, and *JR*. This is either simply due to the fact that these publications have a larger number of issues, or because these two organizations see a greater benefit in utilizing children in their propaganda than *Azan*, *GM*, and *JR*. Finally, the analysis revealed the three main roles that children play in these publications: child perpetrators, fulfilled children, and child victims, all of which are affected by gender in some form.

Child perpetrators

Dabiq was the only publication that included a compelling number of child perpetrators, which confirms the literature that states that IS are using children in ways unlike ever before.[57] They displayed child perpetrators through utilizing the prominent, personalization, and aesthetic news values. The child perpetrators were always male and shown as possessing high status in the group through prominence; this is indicated by wearing an immaculate military uniform, carrying weapons, and standing in proximity to murdered enemies. Additionally, prominence is also shown through undertaking other important activities such as praying. The show of high status is likely to entice readers who perhaps wish to gain that status and a sense of belonging for themselves and/or their children. In contrast, children who were not committed IS child perpetrators were displayed as being poor and hungry which signifies low status with the threatening purpose that this is the destined unpleasant and unvalued life for children who do not join them.

The personalization and aesthetic news value were used simultaneously; the aesthetic use of focus was used to draw attention to the faces of child perpetrators and personalization was used to display emotions, or rather, the lack of emotion. The child perpetrators in the images can be described as being stone-faced and emotionless, which is likely intended as a psychological warfare technique to display the brutality they have managed to instill and the children's abilities to kill. Further, as mentioned in the literature, these images could be used to prove that IS are training their strongest fighters yet and want to show their enemies that they have the ability to fight for a very long time.

An interesting observation was that only one image contained a masked child perpetrator. Although we did not compare child images with adult images, our anecdotal observation was that adults are often masked in images in these publications. Therefore, we theorize that children are not masked because they are relying on the contrast of fierceness and brutality with youthful faces to achieve their psychological warfare technique.

It is possible that the other publications did not want to portray children in this way for a variety of reasons. One example may be that they believe exploiting children will portray them negatively and thus reduce support from followers. This is possible in *GM*, which included images of children protesting peacefully. Conversely, *Inspire, JR*, and *Azan* focused on using children as victims, suggesting that they are more concerned with creating guilt and anger at the West than psychological warfare and training their next generation.

Fulfilled children and gender

Fulfilled children are what we have termed images that depict children at play, children that are happy, and children that are well-taken care of by the organization. Again, this is found mostly in *Dabiq* and uses the prominence, personalization, and aesthetic news values. Unlike child perpetrators, this trend found that the images included both boys and girls; however, there were differences between the genders. Children are displayed using the prominence news value to highlight that children are highly valued and the caliphate is an ideal place for children to flourish. Both genders are shown as being clean and well-dressed; however, boys are shown as receiving an education and training for an important role, such as fighting on the battlefield. Girls on the other hand, are shown as being held and protected by strong-looking adult males (most likely their fathers). Mothers are completely absent from the child images in these publications which is unlike images of the typical nuclear family often depicted in the West. We theorize that girls are portrayed in the arms of their fathers to convince their supporters that life is safer for them in the organization than in the West and that they will be respected and well-protected in the Caliphate.

Personalization and aesthetics are used again simultaneously; however, in this category, focus is used to draw attention to the smiley, happy faces of children playing, receiving an education, and being held in the arms of their fathers. This also occurs in regard to the fathers holding the girls, which is thought to humanize IS members as kind and loving individuals. These images also make use of bright colors both in terms of background and clothes. This use of color is thought to highlight the fulfilled emotions displayed in these images and emphasize that the Caliphate is a pleasant place to live.

Overall, we conclude that portraying girls as behaved, well-dressed, smiling, and protected, paints a picture that females in the organization are "idyllic innocents." In opposition, *Dabiq* includes an image of a Western girl, holding a protest sign declaring that she has two mothers. In contrast, this image displays that they believe that girls raised in the West engage in rebellious forbidden behavior.

Child victims

Child victims are the largest category of images in the dataset and include images of children as victims of Western violence and aggression. This trend contained males and females but did not make any distinctions between them. The news values included are negativity, personalization, impact, superlativeness, and aesthetics.

Inspire has the largest number of child victim images; however, *Dabiq* does contain a small number also, and all of *Azan*'s small dataset contains negativity. Negativity is used in these images through showing children as vulnerable, injured, and dead. Negativity was used simultaneously with impact and superlativeness to emphasize the gore, sizes of groups, and reactions of victims and mourning parents, particularly in *Dabiq*, to achieve maximum impact. *Dabiq* only has two images of dead female children and zero vulnerable female children, which confirm the earlier theory that they wish to portray their territory as a safe place for females. *Azan* mostly displayed images of dead or injured children, whereas *Inspire* showed more vulnerable images that were less gory. This may have been intentional as they might believe that gory images of dead children would be too much for their readers to handle and subsequently push them away from looking at these images. *Inspire* was also more likely to display lone children than groups, which is thought to highlight the vulnerable nature of the child victims.

Personalization and aesthetics are used again simultaneously; however, this time they are used in *Inspire*, *Dabiq*, and *GM* by placing the child victims at the center of the frame or by having other figures within the frame draw attention to them by looking at them. Again, there is a focus on the faces of the children. The purpose of this is likely to be that this is the body part that is most likely to instill a sense of shame, anger, frustration and guilt in readers because this is the part of the body that elicits emotions. The main emotions displayed in these images were sadness, anger, and pain. Additionally, *Azan* used aesthetics to darken their child victim images to emphasis the negativity and sadness of these images. We therefore support Christien's theory that these images are intended to create anger and frustration in their Western followers.[58]

Trends across time

Trends across time were only analyzed for *Dabiq* and *Inspire* because the other three publications did not have enough images or developed themes to do so. *Inspire*'s technique of portraying children as victims of the West remains throughout all of their issues despite five of the issues not containing any images of children. In contrast, *Dabiq* changes from mainly child victim images containing negative and personalization values to child perpetrator and fulfilled child images from around issue 8 onward, containing mainly negative and prominence values. *Dabiq* also contains at least one child image in thirteen out of its fifteen issues. This change in *Dabiq* indicates that IS saw a need for change to ensure their longevity and ensure their goal of achieving a state, and chose to do so by using their next generation of fighters and wives/mothers. However, it is important to note that these trends may have been affected by the content for child victim images in *Inspire* being more opportunistic than the child perpetrator content in *Dabiq* because they appear to rely on their child victim images from attacks undertaken by their enemies.

Conclusion and recommendations for further research

The aim of this article was to analyze the images of children across five online terrorist magazines in order to better understand the roles and representations of children in these organizations. *Dabiq* contained the most images and its main finding was a change in focus from child victims of Western-backed warfare to their use of fierce, prestigious child perpetrators, and a focus on how children can flourish under the caliphate. *Dabiq* was also the only publication to exploit both genders in their images, using images of girls to help portray the Caliphate as a pleasant place to live. They most likely chose these images and strategies to fulfill their aim of longevity and state-building. *Inspire* also had a large number of images; however, the main trend was focused on images of child victims that aimed to evoke anger, shame, frustration, and guilt in their readers for the Western-backed warfare in the Middle East. Despite having a very small number of images, *Azan* also focused on portraying children as victims and used aesthetics to emphasize sadness. Although *GM* had a very small number of images, they tended to show the children in their organization supporting their cause in a more peaceful manner than the other organizations. *JR* contained a very small number of images and did not appear to comprise any re-occurring trends.

The most obvious consideration is continued analysis of these publications as new issues are published. Additionally, it would be useful to continue the research in the IS's more recent publication *Rumiyah* and Jabhat al Nusra's *Al Risalah*. While *Dabiq* is focused on promoting the IS caliphate through shows of strength, *Rumiyah* has thus far been focused on inspiring lone actors to attack in the West. It would be interesting to see if the editors of *Rumiyah* utilize images of children in the same way as *Dabiq* or if they subscribe to *Inspire*'s methods. It would also be valuable to compare this dataset with other datasets such as images of adult perpetrators and adult victims in the magazines in order to investigate potential differences.

There is also the possibility of applying this news value framework to other propagandistic material produced by these violent *jihadist* groups. The magazine style publications covered in this study form only part of the volume of material ISIS, Al Qaeda, Al-Shabaab, and other groups produce. This framework could equally be applied to datasets of *jihadist* images and videos. It would be interesting to observe if the trends observed in these magazines are replicated in widely shared images and videos. The role of children has become highly newsworthy in Western news media with events such as the Manchester Bombing and the U.S. January failed raid in Yemen dominating the media landscape; an analysis of how these events are covered by *jihadist* groups across media platforms would be conducive to further understanding the role of children in these conflicts.

Notes

1. Brandon Colas, "What Does *Dabiq* Do? ISIS Hermeneutics and Organizational Fractures within *Dabiq* Magazine," *Studies in Conflict & Terrorism* 40, no. 3 (2016), 173–190; Haroro Ingram, "An Analysis of Islamic State's Dabiq Magazine," *Australian Journal of Political Science* 51, no. 3 (2016), 458–477; Julian Droogan and Shane Peattie, "Reading Jihad: Mapping the Shifting Themes of Inspire Magazine," *Terrorism and Political Violence* 30, no. 4 (2016), 684–717; Anthony Lemieux, Jarret Brachman, Jason Levitt, and Jay Wood, "Inspire Magazine: A Critical Analysis of Its Significance and Potential Impact through the Lens of the Information, Motivation, and Behavioral Skills Model," *Terrorism and Political Violence* 26, no. 2 (2014), 354–371; Susan Sivek, "Packaging Inspiration: Al Qaeda's Digital Magazine Inspire in the Self-Radicalization Process," *International Journal of*

Communications 7 (2013), 584–606; Haroro Ingram, "An Analysis of the Taliban in Khurasan's Azan (Issues 1–5)," *Studies in Conflict & Terrorism* 38 (2015), 560–579.

2. Droogan and Peattie, "Reading Jihad"; Christoph Gunther, "Presenting the Glossy Look of Warfare in Cyberspace—The Islamic State's Magazine Dabiq," 9, no. 1 (2015); Haroro Ingram, "Analysis of Islamic State's Dabiq Magazine," *Australian Journal of Political Science* 51, no. 3 (2016), 458–477; Haroro Ingram, "An Analysis of Inspire and Dabiq: Lessons from AQAP and Islamic State's Propaganda War," *Studies in Conflict & Terrorism* 40, no. 5 (2016), 357–375; Haroro Ingram, "An Analysis of the Taliban in Khurasan's Azan (Issues 1-5), *Studies in Conflict & Terrorism* 39, no. 7 (2015), 560–579; Anthony F. Lemieux, Jarret M. Brachman, Jason Levitt, and Jay Wood, "Inspire Magazine: A Critical Analysis of its Significant and Potential Impact Through the Lens of the Information, Motivation, and Behaviour Skills Model," *Terrorism and Political Violence* 26, no. 2 (2014), 354–371; Celine M. I. Novernario, "Differentiating Al Qaeda and the Islamic State Through Strategies Publicized in the Jihadist Magazines," *Studies in Conflict & Terrorism* 39, no. 11 (2016), 953–967.
3. Kyle J. Greene, "ISIS: Trends in Terrorist Media and Propaganda," *International Studies Capstone Research Papers,* 3 (2015), 1–57; Maura Conway, Jodie Parker, and Seán Looney, "Online Jihadi Instructional Content: The Role of Magazines, in ed. Maura Conway, Lee Jarvis, Orla Lehane, Stuart Macdonald, and Lella Nouri, *Terrorists' Use of the Internet: Assessment and Response* (Amsterdam: IOS Press, 2017), 182–193.
4. Carol K. Winkler, Kareem El Damanhoury, Aaron Dicker, and Anthony F. Lemieux, "The Medium is Terrorism: Transformation of the About to Die Trope in Dabiq,"*Terrorism and Political Violence* (2016), 1–20.
5. Anthony Lemieux, Jarret Brachman, Jason Levitt, and Jay Wood, "Inspire Magazine: A Critical Analysis of Its Significance and Potential Impact through the Lens of the Information, Motivation, and Behavioral Skills Model," *Terrorism and Political Violence* 26, no. 2 (2014), 354–371.
6. Julian Droogan and Shane Peattie, "Reading Jihad: Mapping the Shifting Themes of Inspire Magazine," *Terrorism and Political Violence* 30, no. 4 (2016), 684–717; Brandon Colas, "What Does *Dabiq* Do? ISIS Hermeneutics and Organizational Fractures within *Dabiq* Magazine," *Studies in Conflict & Terrorism* 40, no. 3 (2016), 173–190.
7. Noman Benotman and Nikita Malik, "The Children of Islamic State," *The Quilliam Foundation* (2016), 1-100.
8. George Stenberg, "Conceptual and Perceptual Factors in the Picture Superiority Effect," *European Journal of Cognitive Psychology* 18, no. 6 (2006), 813–847.
9. Wayne Wanta and Virginia Roark, "Cognitive and Affective Responses to Newspaper Photographs," Paper presented to the Visual Communication Division at the Association for Education in Journalism and Mass Communication annual conference, Kansas City, MO (1993).
10. Dolf Zillmann, Silvia Knobloch, and Hong-sik Yu, "Effects of Photographs on the Selective Reading of News Reports," *Media Psychology* 3, no. 4 (2001), 301–324.
11. Nicole Smith Dahmen and Daniel Morrison, "Place, Space, Time: Media Gatekeeping and Iconic Imagery in the Digital and Social Media Age," *Digital Journalism* 4, no. 5 (2016), 658–678; Vicki Goldberg, *The Power of Photography: How Photographs Changed our Lives,* (New York: Abbeville Press, 1991); David Perlmutter, *Visions of War: Picturing Warfare from the Stone Age to the Cyber Age* (New York: St. Martin's Press; New York: Oxford University Press, 1999); Barbie Zelizer, *About to Die: How News Images Move the Public* (Oxford University Press, 2010).
12. Maxine Rhodes, "Approaching the History of Childhood: Frameworks for Local Research," *Family & Community History* 3, no. 2 (2000), 121–134, at 125.
13. Ibid.
14. Ibid.
15. Mia Bloom, John Horgan, and Charlie Winter, "Depictions of Children of Youth in the Islamic State's Martyrdom Propaganda 2015–2016," *CTC Sentinel* 9, no. 2 (2016), 29–32.

16. Noman Benotman and Nikita Malik, "The Children of Islamic State," *The Quilliam Foundation* (2016), 1–100.
17. Agathe Christien, "The Representation of Youth in the Islamic State's Propaganda Magazine Dabiq," *Journal of Terrorism Research* 7, no. 3 (2016), 1–8.
18. Maxine Rhodes, "Approaching the History of Childhood: Frameworks for Local Research," *Family & Community History* 3, no. 2 (2000), 121–134.
19. Ibid.
20. Virginia Morrow, "Understanding Children and Childhood," *Centre for Children and Young People Background Briefing Series, no. 1.* (2nd ed.). Lismore: Centre for Children and Young People, Southern Cross University (2011).
21. Joanne Faulkner, *The Importance of Being Innocent: Why We Worry about Children* (Cambridge: Cambridge University Press, 2010).
22. Francesca Capone, "'Worse' than Child Soldiers? A Critical Analysis of Foreign Children in the Ranks of ISIL," *International Criminal Law Review* 17 (2017), 161–185.
23. Peter Singer, *Children at War* (Berkeley: University of California Press, 2006).
24. Kara Anderson, "'Cubs of the Caliphate': The Systematic Recruitment, Training, and Use of Children in the Islamic State," *International Institute for Counter-Terrorism* (2016), 1–46; Capone, "'Worse' than Child Soldiers?"
25. Ibid.
26. Ibid.
27. Cole Pinheiro, "The Role of Child Soldiers in a Multigenerational Movement," *CTC Sentinel* 8, no. 2 (2015), 11–13.
28. Ibid.
29. Ibid.
30. Ibid.
31. Christien, "The Representation of Youth in the Islamic State's Propaganda Magazine Dabiq."
32. Ibid.
33. Ibid.
34. Priyanka Motaparthy, "'Maybe We Live and Maybe We Die': Recruitment and Use of Children by Armed Groups in Syria," *Human Rights Watch* (2014).
35. Pinheiro, "The Role of Child Soldiers in a Multigenerational Movement," 11–13.
36. Noman Benotman and Nikita Malik, "The Children of Islamic State," *The Quilliam Foundation* (2016), 1–100.
37. Cathy Otten, "Yazidis Tell How Fearful Isis Kept Them on Move," *The Independent*, 10 April 2015, http://www.independent.co.uk/news/world/middle-east/yazidis-tell-how-fearful-isis-kept-them-on-move-10169024.html (accessed January 2017)
38. Charlie Winter, "Women of the Islamic State: A Manifesto on Women by the Al-Khansaa Brigade," *Quilliam Report* (2015), 1–41.
39. Peter Singer, *Children at War* (University of California Press, 2006).
40. Anderson, "Cubs of the Caliphate.'"
41. Cole Pinheiro, "The Role of Child Soldiers in a Multigenerational Movement," *CTC Sentinel* 8, no. 2 (2015), 11–13.
42. As none of the images came with age information, the researchers made the decision to only include children whom we were confident visually looked younger than 18 years old; however, we cannot be completely certain that no mistakes were made.
43. United Nations Humans Rights Office of the High Commissioner (1990) Convention on the Rights of the Child, http://www.ohchr.org/EN/ProfessionalInterest/Pages/CRC.aspx (accessed January 2018).
44. The term "fulfilled" has come from Macdonald and Lorenzo-Dus who used "fulfilled" as a category in their *jihadist* image study: Stuart Macdonald and Nuria Lorenzo-Dus, "Visual Jihad: Constructing the 'Good Muslim' in Online Jihadist Magazines," *Under Consideration* (2018).

45. Monika Bednarek and Helen Caple, "'Value Added': Language, Image and News Values," *Discourse, Context & Media* 1, no. 2 (2012), 103–113.
46. Ibid.
47. Ibid.
48. Ibid.
49. John Richardson, *Analysing Newspapers: An Approach from Critical Discourse Analysis* (Basingstoke, England: Palgrave Macmillan, 2007), 94.
50. Bednarek and Caple, "'Value Added.'"
51. Ibid.
52. Ibid.
53. Ibid.
54. Ibid., 104
55. Ibid.
56. Christien, "The Representation of Youth in the Islamic State's Propaganda Magazine Dabiq"; Priyanka Motaparthy, "Maybe We Live and Maybe We Die': Recruitment and Use of Children by Armed Groups in Syria," *Human Rights Watch* (2014); Pinheiro, "The Role of Child Soldiers in a Multigenerational Movement," 11–13; Noman Benotman and Nikita Malik, "The Children of Islamic State," The Quilliam Foundation (2016), *pp.* 1-100; Cathy Otten, "Yazidis Tell How Fearful Isis Kept Them on Move," *The Independent*, 10 April 2015, http://www.independent.co.uk/news/world/middle-east/yazidis-tell-how-fearful-isis-kept-them-on-move-10169024.html (accessed January 2017); Charlie Winter, "Women of the Islamic State: A Manifesto on Women by the Al-Khansaa Brigade," *Quilliam Report* (2015), 1–41.
57. Francesca Capone, "'Worse' than Child Soldiers? A Critical Analysis of Foreign Children in the Ranks of ISIL," *International Criminal Law Review* 17 (2017), 161–185.
58. Christien, "The Representation of Youth in the Islamic State's Propaganda Magazine Dabiq.".

OPEN ACCESS

Disrupting Daesh: Measuring Takedown of Online Terrorist Material and Its Impacts

Maura Conway, Moign Khawaja, Suraj Lakhani, Jeremy Reffin, Andrew Robertson, and David Weir

ABSTRACT

This article contributes to public and policy debates on the value of social media disruption activity with respect to terrorist material. In particular, it explores aggressive account and content takedown, with the aim of accurately measuring this activity and its impacts. The major emphasis of the analysis is the so-called Islamic State (IS) and disruption of their online activity, but a catchall "Other *Jihadi*" category is also utilized for comparison purposes. Our findings challenge the notion that Twitter remains a conducive space for pro-IS accounts and communities to flourish. However, not all *jihadists* on Twitter are subject to the same high levels of disruption as IS, and we show that there is differential disruption taking place. IS's and other *jihadists'* online activity was never solely restricted to Twitter; it is just one node in a wider *jihadist* social media ecology. This is described and some preliminary analysis of disruption trends in this area supplied too.

In the aftermath of the London Bridge attack in June 2017, the British prime minister, Theresa May, warned social media companies, including Twitter and Facebook, that they must eradicate extremist "safe spaces."[1] She reiterated this in her speech to the World Economic Forum at Davos in January 2018, stating "technology companies still need to do more in stepping up to their responsibilities for dealing with harmful and illegal online activity. Companies simply cannot stand by while their platforms are used to facilitate … the spreading of terrorist and extremist content."[2] Prime Minister May's concerns about the use of the Internet, particularly social media, by violent extremists, terrorists, and their supporters are shared by an assortment of others, including academics, policymakers, and publics. Much of this is due to apparent connections between the consumption of, and networking around, violent extremist and terrorist online content and the internalization[3] of extremist ideology (i.e., "(violent) online radicalization");

Color versions of one or more of the figures in the article can be found online at www.tandfonline.com/uter.

recruitment into violent extremist or terrorist groups or movements; and/or attack planning and preparation. Apparently easy access to large volumes of potentially influencing violent extremist and terrorist content on prominent and heavily trafficked social media platforms is a cause of particular anxiety. The micro-blogging platform, Twitter, has been subject to particular scrutiny, especially regarding their response (or alleged lack of same) to use of their platform by the so-called Islamic State (IS), also known as Daesh or Da'ish.

Internet companies have responded both individually and collectively. On 26 June 2017, Facebook, Microsoft, Twitter, and YouTube jointly announced, via an agreed text posted on each of their company's official blogs, the establishment of the Global Internet Forum to Counter Terrorism (GIFCT).[4] They described the purpose of the GIFCT as "help[ing] us continue to make our hosted consumer services hostile to terrorists and violent extremists" and went on to state: "We believe that by working together, sharing the best technological and operational elements of our individual efforts, we can have a greater impact on the threat of terrorist content online."[5] In terms of individual companies' responses, in November 2017 Facebook published a blog post in their "Hard Questions" series addressing the question "Are We Winning the War on Terrorism Online?" Facebook announced in the post that it is able to remove 99 percent of IS and Al Qaeda material prior to it being flagged by users "primarily" due to advances in artificial intelligence techniques. Once Facebook becomes aware of a piece of terrorist material, it removes 83 percent of "subsequently uploaded copies" within an hour of their being uploaded, the company said.[6] Missing from the update however were figures on how much terrorist content (e.g., posts, images, videos) is removed from Facebook on a daily, weekly, or monthly basis. Twitter is much less reticent on this point.

According to the section "Combating Violent Extremism" in Twitter's twelfth *Transparency Report*, published in September 2017, in the period 1 January to 30 June 2017:

> … a total of 299,649 accounts were suspended for violations related to promotion of terrorism, which is down 20% from the volume shared in the previous reporting period. Of those suspensions, 95% consisted of accounts flagged by internal, proprietary spam-fighting tools, while 75% of those accounts were suspended before their first tweet.[7]

All told, Twitter claim to have suspended a total of 1,210,357 accounts for "violations related to the promotion of terrorism" in the period from 1 August 2015 to 31 December 2017.[8]

A disparity therefore exists between the assertions of policymakers, on the one hand, and major social media companies, on the other, as regards the levels and significance of their disruption activity. Although Twitter claims severe disruption of IS is occurring on their platform, detailed description and analysis of the precise nature of this disruption activity and, importantly, its effects are sparse,[9] particularly within the academic literature. This article aims to contribute to public and policy debates on the value of disruption activity, particularly aggressive account and content takedown, by seeking to accurately measure this activity and its impacts. The research findings challenge the notion that Twitter remains a conducive space for IS accounts and communities to flourish, although IS continue, to some lesser extent, to distribute propaganda through the channel. Not all *jihadists* on Twitter are subject to the same high levels of disruption as IS; however, this research demonstrates that a level of differential disruption is taking place. Additionally, and critically, the online presence of IS and other *jihadists* is not restricted to Twitter. The platform is merely one node in a wider *jihadist* online ecology. The article describes and discusses this, and supplies some preliminary analysis of disruption trends in this area too.

Social Media Monitoring

Methodology

To undertake the research, a semi-automated methodology for identifying pro-*jihadist* accounts on Twitter was developed (see Figure 1) and implemented using the social media analysis platform known as Method 52.[10] In the first instance, a number of candidate accounts of interest were identified. The approach was grounded in finding tweets that contained specific terms of interest (i.e., "seed search terms"), and/or the identification of accounts that were, in some way, related to other accounts known to be of interest (i.e., "seed accounts") (see step (i) in Figure 1).

If a tweet matched these search criteria, it was automatically analyzed to determine if it was relevant, using a machine-learning classifier trained to mimic the classification decisions of a human analyst.[11] A key task of the relevancy classifier was to separate target Twitter accounts from other Twitter accounts using similar language, such as those held by journalists or researchers, for example. If the tweet was deemed as relevant, further historic tweets were automatically extracted for the candidate account and assessed for relevancy (see step (ii) in Figure 1), providing the system with an aggregate view of the tweet history of the account. This overview of the tweet history was combined with other account metadata that could be extracted. These pieces of information were scored automatically and candidate Twitter accounts that exceeded the set thresholds were presented to a human analyst for decision (see step (iii) in Figure 1). As portrayed

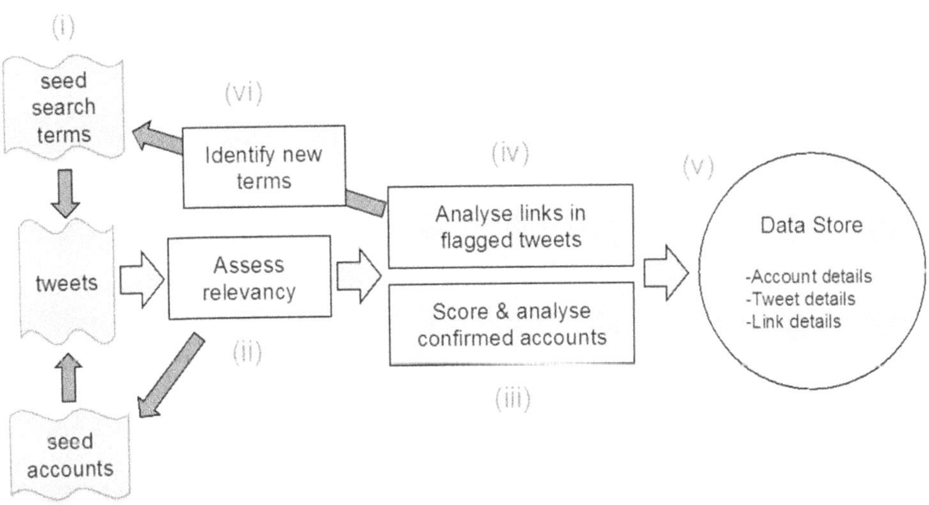

Figure 1. Detailed flow diagram for semi-automated social media analysis.

in step (iv) in Figure 1, if one of the research analysts on the project confirmed that the account was pro-*jihadist*, then the out-links contained in all of the account's tweets were automatically analyzed, and details of the account, its tweets, and its links were stored in the database (see step (v) in Figure 1).

Information from new confirmed accounts was used by the system in a feedback loop to continually improve its efficiency, thereby identifying new seed search terms (see step (vi) in Figure 1) and providing additional seed accounts (see step (ii) in Figure 1).

Caveats

There were, however, a number of caveats attached to the data-collection that deserve mention. First, the bulk of the data was gathered over two months in early 2017 (February to April). The system to implement the semi-automated methodology was created, tested, and evolved throughout this period. The online accounts returned by the system were integrated with those found via traditional, manual search for accounts of interest. The overall approach was, therefore, a combination of automated and manual, and snowball and purposive sampling methods.

Second, not all available data were captured. There were some periods of downtime for the semi-automated system throughout this period as the methodology was developed and modified. In addition, certain accounts found via automated means were unable to be included due to them being taken down before the human analyst could assess and confirm their affiliation,[12] providing an early indication of the high levels of disruption taking place. By the end of the research, when the system was working optimally, 100 percent of these accounts were identified by the software as pro-IS, again reflecting the high level of disruption of IS-related accounts (discussed in further detail below).

Third, the semi-automated system primarily focused on pro-IS accounts operating in English and Arabic (or some combination of these languages). There is, then, the possibility that accounts tweeting primarily in, for example, Bahasa,[13] Russian, or Turkish were overlooked. This is worth noting, but probably negligible as the system's effectiveness improved as the research team learned more about pro-IS users' Twitter activity and refined the methodology accordingly. By early April 2017, for example, the software was able to detect accounts directly distributing IS propaganda with very high precision, regardless of what language was used. In addition, it is believed that the system also identified the majority of accounts linking to that propaganda.

Data

The research dataset comprised 722 pro-IS accounts (labeled Pro-IS hereafter) and 451 other *jihadist* accounts (labeled "Other *Jihadist*" hereafter), with at least one follower[14] active on Twitter at any point between 1 February and 7 April 2017 (see Table 1). Accounts were determined to be Pro-IS if their avatar or carousel images contained explicitly pro-IS imagery and/or text, and/or at least one recent tweet by the user (i.e., not a retweet) contained explicitly pro-IS images and/or text, such as referring to IS as "Dawlah" or their fighters as "lions." Accounts maintained by journalists, academics, researchers, and others who tweeted, for example, Amaq News Agency content for

Table 1. Description of final dataset.

	Pro-IS	Other *jihadist*
Number of accounts	722	451
Number of tweets	57,574	62,156
Number of out-links	7,216	7,928
Percentage of tweets containing out-links	12.5	13

Table 2. Location and identification of Twitter accounts.

	Pro-IS		Other *jihadist*	
	No.	Percent	No.	Percent
Manually identified	193	27	332	74
Semi-automated	218	30	119	26
Advanced semi-automated	311	43	—	—
Total	722		451	

informational purposes, were manually excluded. The Other *Jihadist* category included, among others, those supportive of Hay'at Tahrir al-Sham (HTS), Ahrar al-Sham, the Taliban, and al-Shabaab. Similar parameters were employed to categorize these accounts.

Accounts in the research database were located and identified in three different ways (see Table 2). The first set of accounts was manually identified by the research team, principally by examining known *jihadi* accounts (or those known to be of interest to *jihadi* supporters) and inspecting accounts within their networks (i.e., those following or being followed by them). A second group of accounts was identified "semi-automatically"—that is, automatically by the above-described social media monitoring system and then manually inspected by a human analyst who confirmed: (a) whether or not they were *jihadist* accounts; and (b), if they were, of what type. Several approaches were used to identify or generate seed accounts. This included analyzing vocabulary used in known *jihadi* accounts that were active during the time period studied or had recently been active. This enabled the team to determine which terms were being used much more often than would be expected statistically, and searching for tweets that contained these terms. These candidates were then winnowed based on the relevancy of their tweets in general (see above) and other metadata. Finally, a third set of accounts was identified automatically by the social media monitoring system, based on the presence of known IS propaganda links (i.e., Uniform Resource Locators [URLs] linking to official IS content hosted on some other platform or in some database on the Internet). These links were first identified through other tracking procedures, including (but not limited to) being spotted in confirmed IS tweets.

It is important to underline here that the Pro-IS account dataset is as close as possible—taking into account the caveats already made—to a full dataset of explicitly IS-supportive accounts with at least one follower for the period studied. On the other hand, the Other *Jihadist* dataset is a convenience sample of non-IS *jihadist* Twitter accounts collected for comparison purposes and in no way reflects the actual number of these accounts present on Twitter.

Measuring Disruption and Its Effects

Twitter was one of the most preferred online spaces for IS and their "fans,"[15] even prior to the establishment of their so-called caliphate in June 2014. It was estimated that there were between 46,000 and 90,000 pro-IS Twitter accounts active in the period September to December 2014.[16] However, their activity was subject to disruption by Twitter from mid-2014 and, although initially low level and sporadic, significantly increasing levels of disruption were instituted throughout 2015 and 2016. From mid-2015 through January 2016, for example, Twitter claimed to have suspended in the region of 15,000 to 18,000 IS-supportive accounts per month. From mid-February to mid-July 2016, this increased to an average of 40,000 IS-related account suspensions per month,[17] according to the company.[18] Despite the growing costs attached to remaining on Twitter (such as greater effort to maintain a public presence while relaying diffused messages and deflated morale), during this period IS supporters routinely penned online missives exhorting "Come Back to Twitter."[19] The question raised here is whether, in 2017, it was any longer worthwhile for pro-IS users to continue to seek to retain a presence on the platform?

Until now, the small amount of publicly available research on the online disruption of IS has focused on the impact of Twitter's suspension activities on follower numbers for reestablished accounts.[20] As well as updating these data, this research also examined the longevity or survival time of accounts, and compared Pro-IS to Other *Jihadist* accounts on both measures (i.e., follower numbers and longevity). The overall finding was that IS-supportive accounts were being significantly disrupted, which in turn has effectively eliminated IS's once vibrant Twitter community. Differential disruption is taking place, however, meaning Other *Jihadist* accounts were subject to much less pressure.

Account Longevity

This section addresses the survival time of accounts in the research database. All were active at the point they were identified and classified as Pro-IS or Other *Jihadist*. Once an account was added to the database, its status was monitored and the system recorded when it was suspended, if this subsequently occurred. This enabled the research team to measure the age of each account (i.e., the time elapsed since the account's creation) at the date of suspension. Worth underlining here is that the below-described survival rates of Pro-IS accounts would likely have been considerably shorter if the analysis included those accounts suspended—often within minutes of creation—before they could be captured by the research team for inclusion in the dataset.

Figure 2 depicts the estimated cumulative suspension rate for all Twitter accounts in the dataset, outlining the probability of an account being suspended against its age (represented in days) for the 722 Pro-IS accounts and 451 Other *Jihadist* accounts. The majority—around 65 percent—of Pro-IS accounts were suspended before they reached 70 days since inception. At the same time point, less than 20 percent of Other *Jihadist* accounts had been suspended. In fact, in terms of differential disruption, more than 25 percent of Pro-IS accounts were suspended within five days of inception; a negligible number (less than 1 percent) of Other *Jihadist* accounts were subject to the same swift response.

The categorization of these accounts as *jihadist* in orientation was necessarily subjective. It is possible that others may disagree with our decisions. To address this possibility, Figure 3 focuses on those accounts in the dataset that were eventually suspended:

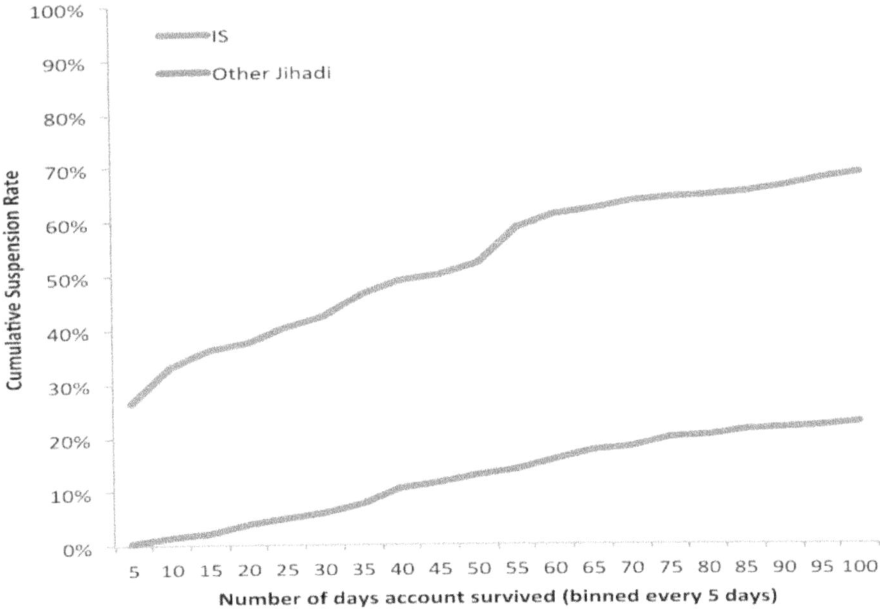

Figure 2. Cumulative suspension rate for all accounts in database.

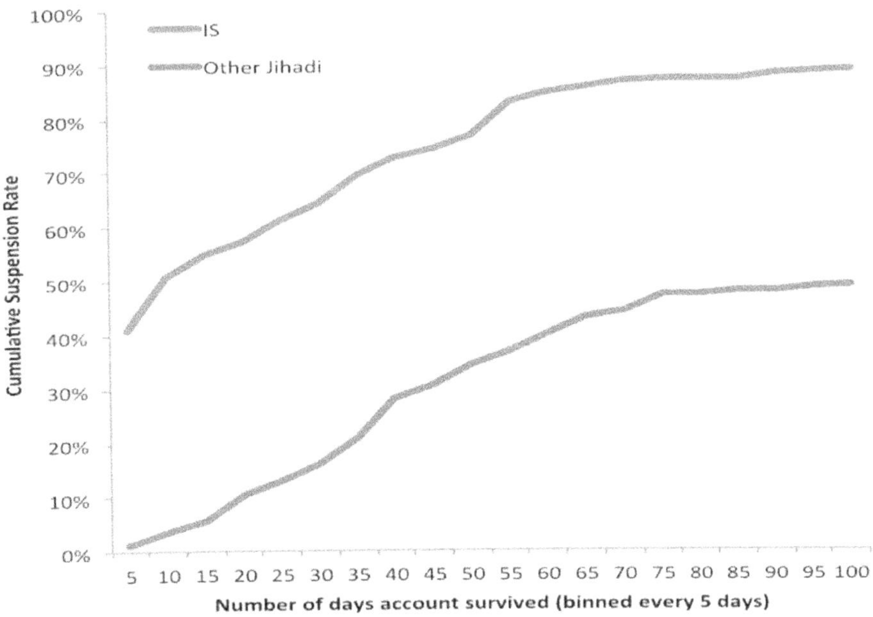

Figure 3. Cumulative suspension rate for accounts eventually suspended.

455 Pro-IS accounts and 163 Other *Jihadist* accounts. The rationale is that these accounts were independently judged to have breached Twitter's terms of service. Again, regarding differential disruption, the data illustrates that 85 percent of Pro-IS accounts were suspended within the first 60 days of their life, compared to 40 percent of accounts falling into the Other *Jihadist* category. Further, more than 30 percent of Pro-IS

accounts were suspended within two days of their creation; less than 1 percent of Other *Jihadist* accounts met the same fate.

Further analysis of suspended accounts revealed that the three subsets of Pro-IS accounts (i.e., those identified manually, semi-automatically based on general tweet content, and advanced semi-automatically as a result of linking to official IS propaganda) also displayed different survival and activity patterns. From the 722 Pro-IS accounts in the dataset, the manually identified accounts (27 percent) survived disruption for longer periods and were primarily tweeting about general IS and non-IS related news. The accounts identified through semi-automated means (30 percent) had a somewhat shorter lifespan and were tweeting content generically related to IS involvement in the Syria conflict, including daily battle updates from several of what were then IS frontlines, such as Mosul, Al-Bab, Deir Ez-Zor, and eastern Aleppo. Accounts located via advanced semi-automated means (43 percent) experienced the shortest lifespans. They were initially identified as a result of sending at least one tweet specifically disseminating "official" IS propaganda (e.g., from the Amaq News Agency). Many were thus found to be exclusively tweeting links to official IS propaganda.

Mini-Case Study: Intervention Effectiveness

Throughout the period of data collection, IS operated a 24-hour "news cycle," disseminating a new batch of propaganda on a daily basis via Twitter and other online platforms, using links to content hosted elsewhere on the Internet. These were probably "*ghazwa*" or social media "raids" orchestrated using an alternative online platform, such as Telegram.[21] The rapid takedown of Twitter accounts sending tweets containing links to official IS propaganda is seen in greater detail in this case study, which shows the effectiveness of intervention over a single 24-hour period. Figure 4 depicts survival curves for those Twitter accounts in the research database that disseminated links to one or more pieces of official IS propaganda produced on Monday, 3 April 2017[22] (based on data collected on Monday, 3 April and Tuesday, 4 April 2017).[23]

On Monday, 3 April 2017, IS uploaded its daily propaganda content to a variety of social media and online content-hosting platforms. This content generally included videos (in daily news format and other propaganda videos), "picture stories" (a photo montage that tells a story), brief pronouncements similar to short press releases, radio podcasts, and other documents (e.g., magazines). Over the course of Monday afternoon and evening, 153 unique Twitter accounts were identified that sent a total of 842 tweets with links to external (non-Twitter) Web pages, each loaded with an item or items of IS propaganda. It was found that only 10 of those Twitter accounts (7 percent) were independent, third-party "mainstream" accounts. The balance of accounts was identified as pro-IS. Fifty of these appeared to be throwaway accounts (i.e., accounts with no followers set up solely to distribute propaganda and sending only IS propaganda tweets until suspended) created on Monday evening.

Method 52 was used to track all accounts disseminating this propaganda—those sending one or more tweets with a 3 April propaganda link at some point prior to 06.00 GMT on the morning of Tuesday, 4 April 2017. Figure 4 shows the survival curves for

Figure 4. Case study of intervention effectiveness.

all 153 Twitter accounts tweeting IS propaganda from Monday, 3 April and for the subset of 50 throwaway accounts specifically created on the Monday evening. The data shows that at 07.00 GMT on Tuesday, 4 April 2017, 100 percent of these accounts were active. However, by 13.00 GMT, this figure had reduced to just 73 percent, falling to 58 percent by 23.00 GMT. This then dropped sharply to 35 percent surviving un-suspended by midnight on Tuesday. Very few of these surviving accounts were suspended over the subsequent 48 hours tracked. The fifty throwaway accounts created on Monday evening specifically to disseminate propaganda were suspended or deleted even faster: by 13.00 GMT only 52 percent were still active, falling to 34 percent by 23.00 GMT and 24 percent by midnight on Tuesday.

This demonstrates that the response to official IS propaganda being distributed via Twitter was reasonably effective in terms of identifying and taking down disseminator accounts in the first 24 hours after they linked to official IS content. Pro-IS accounts disseminating this official IS propaganda were taken down at a higher rate, compared to those Pro-IS accounts not disseminating it. However, it must be borne in mind that some Pro-IS accounts were operating on a 24-hour "news cycle" and a large number of accounts were created daily to disseminate this propaganda. As these accounts were being taken down during Tuesday, a similar number of fresh accounts were being created and used to distribute the next day's official IS content. Therefore, it could be argued that, while efforts to remove permanent traces of IS propaganda links from Twitter were relatively successful, pro-IS users were still able to broadcast links to its daily propaganda using Twitter in 24-hour bursts during the research period.

Table 3. Median number of tweets, followers, and friends for accounts not yet suspended.

	Tweets	Followers	Friends
Pro-IS	51	14	33
Other *jihadist*	320	189	122

Community Breakdown

What are the effects of this disruption on IS-supportive users and accounts? The truncated survival rates for Pro-IS accounts meant that their relationship networks were much sparser than for the Other *Jihadist* accounts in the dataset and compared to previously mapped IS-supporter networks on Twitter. Taking a qualitative perspective, this means that the pro-IS Twitter community was virtually non-existent during the research period.

To demonstrate this, Table 3 compares the median number of tweets, followers, and friends[24] of Pro-IS accounts versus those of *Other Jihadists*. The short lifespan of Pro-IS accounts meant that many had only a small window in which to tweet, gain followers, and follow other accounts. This meant *Other Jihadist* accounts had the opportunity to: send six times as many tweets; follow or "friend" four times as many accounts; and importantly, gain 13 times as many followers as the Pro-IS accounts. An even more stark comparison is between median figures for Pro-IS accounts in 2017 versus those recorded for similar accounts in 2014. The median number of followers for pro-IS accounts in 2017 was 14 versus 177 in 2014,[25] a decrease of 92 percent. The median number of accounts followed by IS supporters in 2014 was 257, whereas this research found a median of thirty-three "friends" per pro-IS account—a decrease of 87 percent.[26] In an analysis of 20,000 IS supporter accounts in a five-month period between September 2014 and January 2015, Berger and Morgan observed suspension of just 678 accounts,[27] a total loss of 3.4 percent. In the research dataset outlined in this article, the total loss of Pro-IS accounts in just four months (between January and April 2017) was conservatively 63 percent.

Throughout what may be referred to as the IS Twitter "Golden Age" in 2013 and 2014, a variety of official IS "fighter" and an assortment of other IS "fan" accounts were accessible with relative ease. For the uninitiated user, once one IS-related account was located, the automated Twitter recommendations on "who to follow" accurately supplied others.[28] For those "in the know," pro-IS users were easily and quickly identifiable through their choice of carousel and avatar images, along with their user handles and screen names. Thus, if one wished, it was quick and easy to become connected to a large number of like-minded other Twitter users. If sufficient time and effort was invested, it was also relatively straightforward to become a trusted—even prominent—member of the IS "Twittersphere."[29] Not only was there a vibrant overarching pro-IS Twitter community in existence at this time, but also a whole series of strong and supportive language (e.g., Arabic, English, French, Russian, Turkish) and/or ethnicity-based (e.g., Chechens or "al-Shishanis") and other special interest (e.g., females or "sisters"[30]) pro-IS Twitter sub-communities. Most of these special interest groups were a mix of: a small number of users on the ground in the "caliphate"; a larger number of users wanting to travel to the "caliphate" (or with a stated preference to do so); and an even larger number of "jihobbyists."[31] The latter had no formal affiliation to any *jihadist* group, but spent their time lauding fighters, celebrating suicide attackers and other "martyrs," and networking around and disseminating IS content.

In 2014, pro-IS accounts were already experiencing some pressure from Twitter; for example, official IS accounts were some of the first to be suspended that summer. Twitter's disruption activity increased significantly over time, forcing pro-IS users to develop and institute a host of tactics to allow them to maintain their Twitter presences, remain active, and preserve their communities of support on the platform.[32] For example, the group employed particular hashtags, such as #baqiyyafamily ("*baqiyya*" means "remain" in Arabic), to announce the return of suspended users to the platform, in an attempt to regroup after their suspension. Twitter eventually responded by including these hashtags in their disruption strategies. Interestingly, this increased disruption only strengthened some IS supporters' resolve and they became more determined to reestablish their accounts, even after repeated suspensions. During this time, suspension was, for some, considered to be a "badge of honor." Thus, although disruption may have resulted in decreased numbers of pro-IS users, it may also have contributed to the generation of more close-knit and unified communities, as those who remained needed a high level of commitment and virtual community support to do so.[33]

Eventually, however, the costs of remaining on Twitter began to outweigh the benefits. Research from 2016 shows that "the depressive effects of suspension often continued even after an account returned and was not immediately re-suspended. Returning accounts rarely reached their previous heights,"[34] in terms of numbers of followers and friends. This was probably due to the eventual discouragement of many IS supporters subjected to rapid and repeated suspension. Even those who persisted were forced to take countermeasures such as locking their accounts so they were no longer publicly accessible, or diluting the content of their tweets so their commitment to IS was no longer so readily apparent. By April 2017, these measures had taken such hold that the vast majority of Pro-IS account avatar images were default "eggs" or other innocuous images, and many of the account user handles and screen names were meaningless combinations of letters and numbers (see Table 4).[35] A conscious, supportive, and influential virtual community is almost impossible to maintain in the face of loss of access to such group or ideological symbols and the resultant breakdown in commitment. As a result, IS supporters have re-located their online community-building activity elsewhere, primarily to Telegram, which is no longer merely a back-up for Twitter.[36]

From a quantitative perspective, the data discussed in this section demonstrate three key findings. First, IS and their supporters were being significantly disrupted by Twitter, where the rate of disruption depended on the content of tweets and out-links. Second, although all accounts experienced some type of suspension over a period of time, Pro-IS accounts experienced this at a much higher rate compared to the Other *Jihadist*

Table 4. Changes in account name types due to disruption activity.*

Typical user handles 2014–2015	Typical user handles 2017
Mujahid1985	4iM7EjZphT3OXYG
BintSham	5Asdf68
ukhtialalmani	Omar_00
Khilafah78	t7dYqgYMaSB4Ecl
ShamGreenbird	GilUllul

Note. *These are not "real" account screen names but composite examples constructed for illustration purposes.

accounts in the dataset. Third, this severely affected IS's ability to develop and maintain robust and influential communities on Twitter. As a result, pro-IS Twitter activity has largely been reduced to tactical use of throwaway accounts for distributing links to pro-IS content on other platforms, rather than as a space for public IS support and influencing activity.

Beyond Twitter: The Wider *Jihadi* Online Ecology

Research on the intersections of violent extremism and terrorism and the Internet have, for some time, been largely concerned with social media. Studies have often had a singular focus on Twitter due to its particular affordances (e.g., ease of data collection due to its publicness, the nature of its application programming interface), which is problematic.[37] For example, Europol's Internet Referral Unit reported that, as far back as mid-2016, they had identified "70 platforms used by terrorist groups to spread their propaganda materials."[38] This section of the article is therefore concerned with the wider online ecology where IS supporters and other non-IS *jihadist* users operate, with a particular focus on out-links from Twitter.

Owing partly to its character limit,[39] Twitter can function as a "gateway"[40] platform to other social networking sites and a diversity of other online spaces. In 2014, it was estimated that one in every 2.5 pro-IS tweets contained a Uniform Resource Locator (URL). It was acknowledged at the time that it would be useful to analyze these links, but this was not undertaken due to complications around Twitter's URL-shortening practices.[41] The roll-out of auto-expanding link previews by Twitter in July 2015 remedied this difficulty. In terms of link activity in the data collected for this research, most links were not out-links, but rather in-links (i.e., within Twitter): 8,086 or 14 percent for Pro-IS and 4,650 or 7.5 percent for Other *Jihadist* tweets. Of the Pro-IS and Other *Jihadist* Twitter accounts identified, one in eight (around 13 percent) contained non-Twitter URLs or out-links. This is a considerable reduction from the 40 percent of tweets reportedly containing URLs in 2014. Analysis of Twitter out-links nonetheless provides an interesting snapshot of the Top 10 platforms linked to by Pro-IS and Other *Jihadist* accounts during our data-collection period (see Table 5).

YouTube was the top linked-to platform for both Pro-IS and Other *Jihadist* accounts, pointing to the overall importance of the site—and of video generally in Web 2.0—in the *jihadist* online scene. Facebook does not appear in the Top 10 out-links for Pro-IS accounts, albeit a recent report claims that IS content and IS-supportive users are still easily locatable on Facebook.[42] What our findings indicate is that, like Twitter, Facebook is engaged in differential disruption as it is the second most preferred platform for out-linking by Other *Jihadists*. The somewhat obscure justpaste.it content upload site has been known for some time as a core node in the "jihadisphere,"[43] and its high-ranking status for both Pro-IS and Other *Jihadist* accounts is thus relatively unsurprising.

Other content upload destinations preferred by Pro-IS users, including Google Drive, Sendvid, Google Photos, and the Web Archive, do not appear in the Other *Jihadist* Top 10. One particular reason for this is probably the focus of Other *Jihadists* on linking to traditional proprietary websites, such as the Taliban's suite of sites. It is worth

Table 5. Top 10 other platforms (based on out-links from Twitter).

Pro-IS			Other *jihadist*		
Platform	*Number*	*Percent of all Pro-IS tweets*	*Platform*	*Number*	*Percent of all Other* jihadist *tweets*
1. YouTube	1,330	2.3	1. YouTube	2,488	4.0
2. Google Drive	792	1.4	2. Facebook	1,294	2.1
3. justpaste.it	472	0.82	3. justpaste.it	479	0.77
4. Google Photos	431	0.75	4. Islamic prayers website	316	0.51
5. sendvid.com	410	0.71	5. Taliban news website	244	0.39
6. archive.org	353	0.61	6. Official Taliban website	228	0.37
7. archive.is	243	0.42	7. Taliban's official Urdu language website	208	0.33
8. "Unofficial" Bahasa language IS fan site	198	0.34	8. Hizb ut-Tahrir website	189	0.30
9. medium.com	155	0.27	9. Telegram	111	0.18
10. "Unofficial" Arabic language IS news site	139	0.24	10. Taliban's official English language website	103	0.17

mentioning that, while Telegram slips into the Top 10 for Other *Jihadists*, only twenty (0.04 percent) of all tweets from Pro-IS accounts contained a telegram.me link. The paucity of such links caused us to explore further; we were surprised to find that just two of 722 Pro-IS users' biographies and two of 451 Other *Jihadist* users' biographies contained Telegram links. Neither group of accounts were using Twitter to advertise ways into Telegram.

Case Study: Destinations of Official IS Propaganda

As mentioned, during the research period, IS was operating a 24-hour "news cycle," disseminating a daily batch of new official propaganda via social media channels, including Twitter. Links to this propaganda were circulated through tweets and other means. These links pointed to a wide variety of other social media and content hosts that contained newly uploaded propaganda daily. A sample of these propaganda destinations were analyzed at three time points: 4–8 February, 4–8 March (excluding 7 March, see below), and 4–8 April 2017. The research team obtained the full daily roster of IS propaganda and the sites where it appeared for each of these time periods. This allowed the identification of the most frequently linked-to platforms, along with how many pieces of propaganda were posted by host domains, and what proportion of these URLs were subsequently taken down (see Figure 5).

Overall, over these three time periods, Pro-IS users linked to thirty-nine different third-party platforms or sites, as well as IS running its own server[44] to host its propaganda material. It is important to note that the former were exclusively, it is believed, "leaf" destinations. That is, they contained content but no links to other sites, so did not have a networking or community-building aspect. Someone visiting such a page would not be able to discover more about the network of other sites. Important exceptions to this were YouTube and a small number of other sites that algorithmically

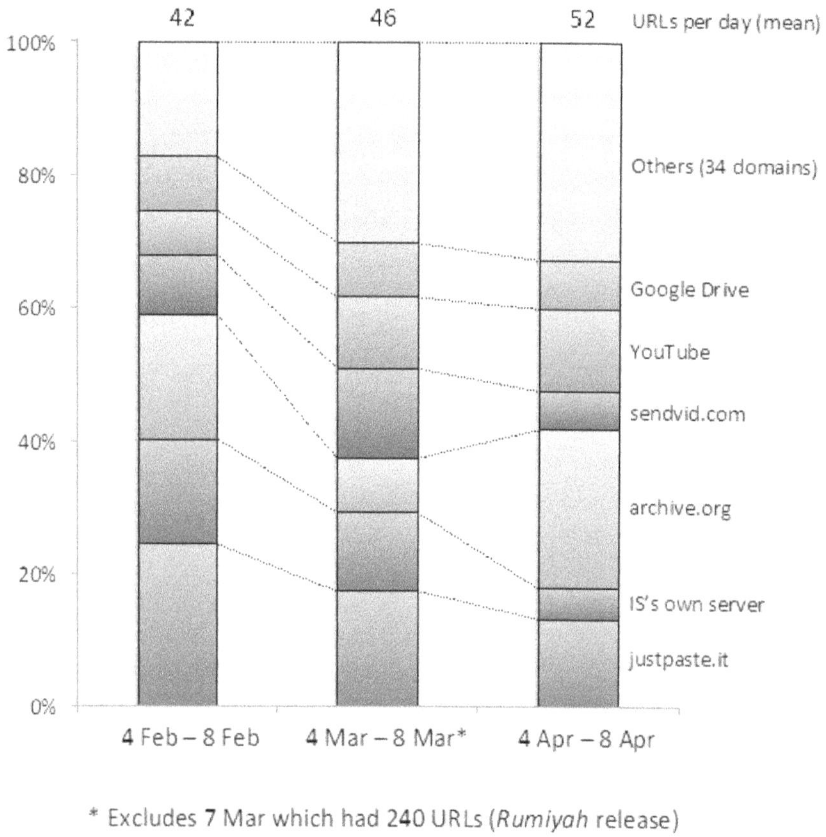

Figure 5. Destinations of official IS propaganda: Number of URLs and URL destinations February to April 2017.

"recommend" similar content in their inventory, which may have resulted in their pointing to other available IS propaganda.[45] During the period of the research, the average number of URLs populated rose from forty-two per day in February to fifty-two per day in April. This hints at increasing fragmentation and dispersal, possibly in response to takedown activity by a variety of platforms and sites. However, there was a large inter-day variation (twenty to sixty-five) and one outlier day on 7 March was excluded, as it was the publication date of issue 7 of IS's *Rumiyah* online magazine. On this day, IS pushed 240 separate URLs, a quarter of which contained direct reference to *Rumiyah* in the link, and many more that probably linked to the new issue of the magazine.[46]

Of the forty domains used (thirty-nine external, one internal server), a consistent "big 6" became apparent across the three time periods: justpaste.it; IS's own server; archive.org; sendvid.com; YouTube; and Google Drive. These six domains accounted for 83 percent, 70 percent, and 67 percent of the URLs in the February, March, and April sampling periods, respectively. However, there was a noticeable declining trend in the use of justpaste.it and IS's own servers. Between them, this accounted for 40 percent of URLs in February declining to only 18 percent by April. At around that time the Amaq News Agency website had come under repeated attack, which may have been responsible for its relative downgrading.[47] Use of sendvid.com and archive.org varied across the time periods, while Google Drive and YouTube were consistently heavily used. In fact, YouTube use showed an increasing trend (7 percent, 11 percent, and 12 percent, respectively). The remaining URLs (17 percent in February rising to 33 percent of URLs by April) were spread across a wide variety of mainly, although not exclusively, content upload sites (thirty-four in total).

The proportion of IS propaganda successfully taken down was also analyzed. The takedown rate (as of 12 April, 2017) was 72 percent, 66 percent, and 72 percent for the February, March, and April samples, respectively. Overall, 30 percent of links were still live on 12 April. This suggests that takedown activity was relatively rapid (occurring over a matter of days after propaganda was posted) and widespread (across a multiplicity of sites and platforms).

Conclusion

The costs for most pro-IS users of engaging on Twitter (in terms of deflated morale, diffused messages and persistent effort needed to maintain a public presence) now largely outweigh the benefits. This means that the IS Twitter community is now almost non-existent. In turn, this means that radicalization, recruitment, and attack planning opportunities on this platform have probably also decreased. However, a hard core of users remain persistent. In particular, a subset of established throwaway disseminator accounts pushed out "official" IS content in a daily cycle during our data-collection period and continue to do so. These accounts were generally suspended within 24 hours, but not before they promoted links to content hosted on other platforms.

This article was mainly concerned with pro-IS Twitter accounts and their disruption. However, IS are not the only *jihadists* active on Twitter, and a host of other violent *jihadists* were shown to be subject to much lower levels of disruption by Twitter. Also, IS and other *jihadist* groups remain active on a wide range of other social media platforms, content hosting sites and other cyberspaces, including blogs, forums, and dedicated websites. While it appears that official IS content is being disrupted in many of these online spaces, the extent is yet to be fully determined.

The Telegram messaging application was mentioned a number of times in this article and is worth treating here in slightly more depth as it is IS supporters' currently most preferred platform. Telegram is as yet a lower profile platform than Twitter—and obviously also Facebook—with a smaller user base and higher barriers to entry (e.g., provision of a mobile phone number to create an account, time-limited invitations to join channels[48]). These are probably positive attributes from the perspective of cutting down on the numbers of users exposed to IS's online content and thereby in a position to be violently radicalized by it. On the negative side, this may mean that Telegram's pro-IS community is more committed than its Twitter variant. Also, while IS's reach via Telegram is less than it was via Twitter, the echo chamber effect may be greater as the "owners" of Telegram channels and groups have much greater control over who joins and contributes to these than on Twitter. Another aspect of Telegram that's doubtless also attractive to pro-IS users is its in-platform content upload and cloud storage function(s). While Telegram restricts users from uploading files larger than 1.5GB—roughly a two-hour movie—it provides seemingly unlimited amounts of storage.

In terms of proactive steps taken by Telegram with respect to IS and their supporters' use of their service, in December 2016, Telegram established a dedicated "ISIS Watch" channel, which provides a running tally of numbers of "ISIS bots and channels banned" by them. On 11 March, 2017 a message on the channel stated "Our abuse team actively bans ISIS content on Telegram. Following your reports, an average of 70 ISIS channels are terminated each day before they reach any traction." Between January and May 2018, the average number of terminations per days had jumped sixfold to 422. All told, Telegram claims to have banned 106,573 "ISIS bots and channels" in the period December 2016 to 31 May 2018, with May 2018 (9,810) having the highest number of bans yet recorded.[49] While it is clear therefore that Telegram routinely bans pro-IS users, channels, and bots, interpreting the numbers that Telegram has supplied is difficult absent knowing the overall numbers of users, channels, and bots actually active on the platform at any given time. Also worth pointing out is that in addition to exploiting the channels feature, IS began taking advantage of Telegram's groups function around summer 2017. So-called Supergroups allow for intra-group communication among up to 30,000 members[50] and like all other group chats on Telegram are private among participants; Telegram does not, in other words, process requests, including termination requests, related to them.[51]

Recommendations

The recommendations arising from this analysis are threefold. First, modern social media monitoring systems have the ability to dramatically increase the speed and effectiveness of data gathering, analysis, and (potentially) intervention. To work effectively, however, they must deploy a combination of suitable technology solutions, including analytical systems, with trained human analysts who are versed in the relevant domain(s) and preferably also the appropriate languages. This is particularly the case where an adversary is actively trying to evade tracking efforts. Technology such as Method52 assists by allowing the analyst to rapidly develop new analytical pipelines that take into account day-to-day changes in modes of operation. However, technology cannot detect such changes; these can generally only be spotted by a human well-versed in the particular domain of interest.

Second, some IS supporters remain active on Twitter. Content disseminators using throwaway accounts could probably be degraded further—although this may have both pros (e.g., detrimental impact on last remaining significant IS supporter Twitter activity) and cons (e.g., further degradation of Twitter as a source of data or open source intelligence on IS). Like all disruption activity, whether this is viewed positively or negatively depends on one's perspective and institutional interests. For example, law enforcement tends to favor this approach, whereas free-speech advocates warn against corporate policing of political speech, even if that speech is deeply objectionable. Some intelligence professionals, on the other hand, advocate for greater attention to social media intelligence.[52]

Third, the focus of this article has not just been Twitter, but the importance of the wider *jihadist* online ecology was also pointed to. The analysis was also not restricted to IS users and content; the presence and often uninterrupted online activity of non-IS *jihadists* was underlined too. In recent years, many counterterrorism professionals tasked with examining the role of the Internet in violent extremism and terrorism have narrowed their focus to IS. Scholarly researchers have acted similarly, many narrowing their focus further to IS Twitter activity. Continued analytical contraction of this sort should be guarded against. Maintenance of a wide-angle view of online activity by diverse other *jihadists* across a variety of social media and other online platforms is recommended. This is particularly important due to the shifting fortunes of IS and HTS on the ground in Iraq and Syria. In the face of increasing loss of physical territory, the continued—and potentially increasing— importance of online "territory" should not be underestimated. It is not that a focus on IS should be dispensed with, but the significantly less-impeded online activity of HTS is surely an important asset for them and worth monitoring. Because data collection and analysis of other terrorist groups and their online platforms has been neglected, very few historical metrics are available for comparative analyses; this should be guarded against in future too.

Future research

Finally, some comments as regards future research. Our Other *Jihadist* category was a convenience sample of non-IS *jihadist* accounts. It is therefore proposed to replicate the present research, but with a larger and more equal sample of HTS, Ahrar al-Sham, and Taliban accounts. This would allow for a more systematic and comparative analysis of the disruption levels for a range of non-IS *jihadists*, including those with a significant international terrorism footprint (i.e., HTS), groups with a significant national and regional terrorism profile (i.e., Taliban), and a party to the Syria conflict (i.e., Ahrar al-Sham).[53] Such an analysis could help to ascertain the vibrancy of their contemporary Twitter communities and Twitter out-linking practices, and allow their preferred other online platforms to be identified.

Additional research is also clearly warranted into the wider violent *jihadist* online ecology. Wider and more in-depth research into the following is therefore recommended:

1. patterns of use, including community-building and influencing activity;
2. levels of disruption on other platforms besides Twitter, including other major platforms such as YouTube, but also other smaller or more obscure platforms, such as justpaste.it and others.

Analysis of pro-IS and other violent *jihadist* activity on Telegram and comparing this with our present findings is suggested too. It would also be worthwhile analyzing out-linking trends on Telegram to determine how the functionalities of different platforms have an impact on linking practices.

Notes

1. George Parker, "Theresa May Warns Tech Companies: 'No Safe Space' for Extremists," *Financial Times*, 4 June 2017, https://www.ft.com/content/0ae646c6-4911-11e7-a3f4-c742b9791d43?mhq5j=e3 (accessed 1 Oct. 2018).
2. Theresa May, "PM's Speech at Davos 2018," Prime Minister's Office, 25 January 2018, https://www.gov.uk/government/speeches/pms-speech-at-davos-2018-25-january (accessed 1 Oct. 2018).
3. For a detailed discussion on "internalization" see Herbert C. Kelman, "Compliance, Identification and Internalization: Three Processes of Attitude Change," *The Journal of Conflict Resolution* 2, no. 1 (1958), 51–60; in relation to radicalization and violent extremism, see Suraj Lakhani, *Radicalisation as a Moral Career: A Qualitative Study of How People Become Terrorists in The United Kingdom*, Ph.D. thesis (Universities Police Science Institute: Cardiff University, 2014).
4. Facebook, "Facebook, Microsoft, Twitter and YouTube Announce Formation of the Global Internet Forum to Counter Terrorism," *Facebook Newsroom*, 26 June 2017, https://newsroom.fb.com/news/2017/06/global-internet-forum-to-counter-terrorism/ (accessed 1 Oct. 2018).
5. Ibid.
6. Monika Bickert, "Hard Questions: Are We Winning the War on Terrorism Online?" *Facebook Newsroom*, 28 November 2017, https://newsroom.fb.com/news/2017/11/hard-questions-are-we-winning-the-war-on-terrorism-online/ (accessed 1 Oct. 2018).
7. Twitter, "Government TOS Reports: January to June 2017," *Twitter Transparency*, n.d., https://transparency.twitter.com/en/gov-tos-reports.html (accessed 1 Oct. 2018).
8. Twitter Public Policy, "Expanding and Building #TwitterTransparency," *Twitter Blog*, 5 April 2018, https://blog.twitter.com/official/en_us/topics/company/2018/twitter-transparency-report-12.html (accessed 1 Oct. 2018).
9. J. M. Berger and Jonathan Morgan, "The ISIS Twitter Census: Defining and Describing the Population of ISIS Supporters on Twitter," The Brookings Project on U.S. Relations with the Islamic World, Analysis Paper #20 (2015), https://www.brookings.edu/wp-content/uploads/2016/06/isis_twitter_census_berger_morgan.pdf (accessed 1 Oct. 2018).
10. Method52 was developed by the TAG Laboratory at the University of Sussex. For more information, see www.taglaboratory.org (accessed 1 Oct. 2018).
11. Classifiers were trained using supervised machine-learning approaches. Method52 provides components that enable this to be done swiftly and in a manner that is bespoke to a project.
12. Berger and Morgan, "The ISIS Twitter Census," 41 and 44.
13. J. M. Berger and Heather Perez, "The Islamic State's Diminishing Returns on Twitter: How Suspensions are Limiting the Social Networks of English-speaking ISIS Supporters," Washington DC: George Washington University Program on Extremism, 2016, 6, https://cchs.gwu.edu/sites/cchs.gwu.edu/files/downloads/Berger_Occasional%20Paper.pdf (accessed 1 Oct. 2018).
14. The data from the latter stages of this project suggest that fifty or more throwaway IS accounts were produced daily. These accounts appeared to be set up solely to distribute propaganda, typically had no followers, and sent only IS propaganda tweets until they were suspended. If the throwaway accounts from across the whole research period had been included in the dataset, the total number could have reached as many as 2,000–3,000.
15. Walid Magdy, Kareem Darwish, and Ingmar Weber, "#FailedRevolutions: Using Twitter to Study the Antecedents of ISIS Support," Doha: Qatar Foundation, 2015, 3, https://arxiv.org/abs/1503.02401 (accessed 1 Oct. 2018).
16. Berger and Morgan, "The ISIS Twitter Census," 9.
17. Twitter, "Combating Violent Extremism," *Twitter Blog*, 5 February 2016, https://blog.twitter.com/2016/combating-violent-extremism (accessed 1 Oct. 2018).
18. Twitter, "An Update on our Efforts to Combat Violent Extremism," *Twitter Blog*, 18 August 2016, https://blog.twitter.com/2016/an-update-on-our-efforts-to-combat-violent-extremism (accessed 1 Oct. 2018).
19. Cole Bunzel, "'Come Back to Twitter': A Jihadi Warning Against Telegram," *Jihadica*, 18 July 2016, www.jihadica.com/come-back-to-twitter/ (accessed 1 Oct. 2018).

20. Berger and Perez, "The Islamic State's Diminishing Returns on Twitter."
21. Nico Prucha, "IS and the Jihadist Information Highway: Projecting Influence and Religious Identity via Telegram," *Perspectives on Terrorism* 10, no. 6 (2016), 51–52.
22. By early April 2017, the research had reached the stage where there was complete access to IS's main Twitter propaganda apparatus. This enabled the semi-automated system to determine what IS and supporter tweets would be linking to before those tweets were sent. It is thought that this occurred several hours before Twitter themselves become aware of these accounts and their tweets. Much of this may have been due to the research team being able to access data and intelligence across multiple sites, allowing early prediction of tweet material, where Twitter's disruption team were likely restricted to monitoring their own platform only. The system was thus able to immediately identify when an account disseminated one of these propaganda links on Twitter. It was then possible to capture the rate and speed of suspension.
23. It should be noted that this date was chosen at random. Propaganda represented in this graph had no relation to the chemical attack on the town of Khan Shaykhun, also on 4 April, as content was produced by IS on Monday 3 April 2017.
24. The term "friends" refers to accounts the Pro-IS accounts were following.
25. Berger and Morgan, "The ISIS Twitter Census," 30.
26. BerIbid.
27. Ibid.
28. Online recommender systems present content to users of specific platforms that they might not otherwise locate based on, for example, prior search or viewing history on that platform; see Derek O'Callaghan, Derek Greene, Maura Conway, Joe Carthy, and Pádraig Cunningham, "Down the (White) Rabbit Hole: The Extreme Right and Online Recommender Systems," *Social Science Computer Review* 33, no. 4 (2015), 459–478.
29. See, for example, the extensive media coverage of Twitter user @ShamiWitness who, in December 2014, was revealed to be Mehdi Biswas, a 24-year-old Bangalore-based business executive, who prior to his arrest was one of the most prominent IS supporters on social media. Interestingly, his Twitter account was only suspended in early 2017, despite being dormant since his arrest. At the time of writing Biswas is awaiting trial in India.
30. Pearson, "Wilayat Twitter and the Battle Against Islamic State's Twitter Jihad."
31. Jarret M. Brachman, *Global Jihadism: Theory and Practice* (Abingdon: Routledge, 2009), 19.
32. For examples, see Berger and Perez, "The Islamic State's Diminishing Returns on Twitter," 15–18.
33. Pearson, "Wilayat Twitter and the Battle Against Islamic State's Twitter Jihad." See also Elizabeth Pearson, "Online as the New Frontline: Affect, Gender, and ISIS-takedown on Social Media," *Studies in Conflict & Terrorism* 5 (September 2017).
34. Berger and Perez, "The Islamic State's Diminishing Returns on Twitter," 9.
35. Such meaningless combinations of letters and numbers are also characteristic of "bots" (i.e., automated social media accounts that pose as real users). See Ben Nimmo, Digital Forensics Research (DFR) Lab, "#BotSpot: Twelve Ways to Spot a Bot: Some Tricks to Identify Fake Twitter Accounts," Medium, 28 August 2017, https://medium.com/dfrlab/botspot-twelve-ways-to-spot-a-bot-aedc7d9c110c (accessed 1 Oct. 2018).
36. Berger and Perez, "The Islamic State's Diminishing Returns on Twitter," 15.
37. Maura Conway, "Determining the Role of the Internet in Violent Extremism and Terrorism: Six Suggestions for Progressing Research," *Studies in Conflict and Terrorism* 40, no. 1 (2017), 9 and 12.
38. EUROPOL, "EU Internet Referral Unit: Year One Report," EUROPOL (2016), 11, www.europol.europa.eu/content/eu-internet-referral-unit-year-one-report-highlights (accessed 1 Oct. 2018).
39. Twitter's character limit per tweet was 140 when this research was undertaken. It was increased to 280 characters per tweet platform-wide on 7 November, 2017.
40. Derek O'Callaghan, Derek Greene, Maura Conway, Joe Carthy, and Pádraig Cunningham, "Uncovering the Wider Structure of Extreme Right Communities Spanning Popular Online

Networks," in *WebSci 13: Proceedings of the 5th Annual ACM Web Science Conference* (New York: ACM Digital Library, 2013), 276–285.

41. Berger and Morgan, "The ISIS Twitter Census," 21.
42. Gregory Waters and Robert Postings, "Spiders of the Caliphate: Mapping the Islamic State's Global Support Network on Facebook," New York and London: Counter Extremism Project, 2018, https://www.counterextremism.com/sites/default/files/Spiders%20of%20the%20Caliphate%20%28May%202018%29.pdf (accessed 1 Oct. 2018).
43. The term "Twittersphere" is used to refer to Twitter users as a collectivity. The term "jihadisphere" has been used to refer to online *jihadis* as a collectivity; see Benjamin Ducol, "Uncovering the French-speaking Jihadisphere: An Exploratory Analysis," *Media, War & Conflict* 5, no. 1 (2012).
44. Due to the domain names experiencing rapid removal, this server had five names over the three research periods studied.
45. O'Callaghan et al., "Down the (White) Rabbit Hole," 37.
46. For a detailed accounting of Twitter activity around the release of an issue of *Rumiyah*'s precursor publication, *Dabiq*, see Daniel Grinnell, Stuart Macdonald, and David Mair, "The Response Of, and On, Twitter to the Release of *Dabiq* Issue 15," paper presented at the 1st European Counter Terrorism Centre (ECTC) conference on online terrorist propaganda, 10–11 April 2017, Europol Headquarters, The Hague, Netherlands, https://www.europol.europa.eu/publications-documents/response-of-and-twitter-to-release-of-dabiq-issue-15 (accessed 1 Oct. 2018).
47. Lizzie Dearden, "ISIS Losing Ground in Online War Against Hackers After Westminster Attack Turns Focus on Internet Propaganda," *The Independent*, 1 April 2017, http://www.independent.co.uk/news/world/europe/isis-islamic-state-propaganda-online-hackers-westminster-whatsapp-amaq-cyber-attacks-paranoia-a7662171.html (accessed 1 Oct. 2018).
48. Mia Bloom, Hicham Tiflati, and John Horgan, "Navigating ISIS's Preferred Platform: Telegram," *Terrorism and Political Violence* (July) Vol. 29, pp.'s 1–13.
49. The previous highest number of bot and channel terminations took place in October 2017 and amounted to 9,270.
50. Telegram, "Q: What's the Difference Between Groups, Supergroups, and Channels?" *Telegram FAQ*, n.d., https://telegram.org/faq#groups-supergroups-and-channels (accessed 1 Oct. 2018).
51. Telegram, "Q: There's Illegal Content on Telegram. How do I Take it Down?" *Telegram FAQ*, n.d., https://telegram.org/faq#q-what-are-your-thoughts-on-internet-privacy. See also Maura Conway, with Michael Courtney, "Violent Extremism and Terrorism Online in 2017: The Year in Review," Dublin, VOX-Pol, 2018, 4, http://www.voxpol.eu/download/vox-pol_publication/YiR-2017_Web-Version.pdf (accessed 1 Oct. 2018).
52. David Omand, Jamie Bartlett, and Carl Miller, "Introducing Social Media Intelligence (SOCMINT)," *Intelligence and National Security* 27, no. 6 (2012).
53. Nationally, Syria, Russia, Iran, Egypt, and the UAE have designated Ahrar al-Sham as a terrorist organization. Internationally, the United States, Britain, France, and Ukraine blocked a May 2016 Russian proposal to the United Nations to take a similar step.

Acknowledgment

This article is a slightly revised and updated version of the VOX-Pol report with the same title, available at http://www.voxpol.eu/download/vox-pol_publication/DCUJ5528-Disrupting-DAESH-1706-WEB-v2.pdf.

Funding

This research was supported by funding from the UK Home Office and the European Union's Framework Programme 7 [Grant number 312827: VOX-Pol Network of Excellence].

OPEN ACCESS

Informal Countermessaging: The Potential and Perils of Informal Online Countermessaging

Benjamin J. Lee

ABSTRACT

Online countermessaging—communication that seeks to disrupt the online content disseminated by extremist groups and individuals—is a core component of contemporary counterterrorism strategies. Countermessaging has been heavily criticized, not least on the grounds of effectiveness. Whereas current debates are focused on the role of government and large organizations in developing and disseminating countermessages, this article argues that such approaches overlook the informal production of countermessages. Recognizing the appetite for "natural world" content among those engaged in countermessaging, this article highlights some of the potential benefits of informal approaches to countermessaging. At the same time, the article also acknowledges the risks that may result from closer working between countermessaging organizations and informal actors.

Online countermessaging (hereafter "countermessaging")—communication that seeks to disrupt the messages disseminated by extremist groups and individuals—is a core component of contemporary counterterrorism strategies. Thus far, formal programs, often directed by governments or civil society organizations, have dominated the discussion of countermessaging. This article seeks to expand this discussion by highlighting the potential for informally produced countermessages to contribute to wider policy goals. The article concentrates on some of the potential benefits and risks of countermessaging by informal actors. Informal content has the potential to be seen as more credible by audiences, as well as to be more aggressive in its messages, for example by isolating and ridiculing individual extremists and organizations. This comes at a cost, as informal content creates increased risk of backlash against creators, and of potentially encouraging hate speech as countermessaging tips over into abuse.

Theoretically, this article builds on insights from nodal governance theory that see security as being increasingly provided by networks that include public, private, and citizen actors.[1] It is also a direct response to the move by some formal organizations engaged in countermessaging to use informally produced content rather than producing their own in-house material.[2] This article does not suggest that informally produced countermessages are superior to formally produced ones, or that informal messages can be relied on as a substitute for formal approaches. However, any understanding of countermessaging is incomplete without acknowledging the potential of content produced by informal creators, and the damage that may result from co-opting it into a formal campaign. Although governments have taken a hand in both directly producing countermessages, and mobilizing wider networks of influencers, these attempts have drawn criticism from both the press and political activists.[3]

What Is Countermessaging?

Countermessaging fits loosely under the heading of countering violent extremism (CVE), a broad policy area that encompasses a range of activities. Harris-Hogan et al. aim to use public health models to frame CVE for policymakers, identifying primary, secondary, and tertiary interventions.[4] Tertiary interventions seek to enable disengagement from violent extremist networks, for example through deradicalization and disengagement programs.[5] Secondary interventions aim to intervene where individuals are displaying "symptoms" of radicalization.[6] Given that individuals targeted by these interventions are unlikely to have committed any offense secondary interventions are prone to being the most controversial. Primary interventions are preventative and aim through training and education to reduce the prevalence of violent extremism.[7] Countermessaging can be seen as a form of both primary and secondary CVE depending on intended audiences. In many cases it is aimed at both those already engaged with violent extremism and those at risk of engagement.[8] There is also further differentiation over the goals of countermessaging, varying between changing minds and changing behavior.[9]

Countermessages seek to undermine the messages presented by extremist groups. Existing literature on the subject reveals a broad range of understandings and different terms in use. Peter Neumann, writing on potential responses to online radicalization in the United States, identified countermessages as a potential tactic to reduce demand for violent extremist material.

> Broadly speaking, counter-messaging may involve challenges to the violent extremists' ideology and to their political and/or religious claims; messages that aim to "mock, ridicule or somehow undermine their credibility"; contrasts between violent extremists' grandiose claims and the reality and/or consequences of their actions; or positive alternatives that cancel out or negate the violent extremists' ideology or lifestyle.[10]

Within this definition there are multiple types of messages: disputing claims, undermining extremist groups, contrasting rhetoric and reality, and promoting positive alternative ideologies. Other approaches have concentrated more heavily on media and the delivery of messages, including making specific references to social media, as well as religious authority. Setting out elements of a countermessaging strategy designed for use against Islamic State of Iraq and Syria (ISIS), Pelletier et al describe some core components:

> Defeating ISIS will be a multi-faceted long-term effort to delegitimize the movement and undermine its radical interpretation of Islamic Law, while inhibiting their ability to persuade and inspire followers. As with messaging, effective counter-messaging is as much

a technique as it is a process, and a counter-messaging (CM) strategy also involves a combination of written/oral communications, reinforced by actions and behaviors and then propagated through the effective use of social media."[11]

Others have varied the terminology. In particular, narrative and counternarrative have been the main descriptors used in many settings. A narrative refers to a set of events in sequence, however, and is more expansive than a message, which can be isolated claims.[12] Ferguson differentiates between counternarratives as a term deployed in the "CVE literature" and "alternative" strategies focusing on existing media and journalism, including drama.[13] Even beyond message and narrative, there are a plurality of descriptions for the activities described here, including the concept of "alter-messaging" focusing on "alternative content to the ideology of terrorism."[14] In this article, the use of the term countermessaging is intended to enable a broad analysis. Subsequent discussion of informal countermessages and messaging will demonstrate how diverse that content can be, but with little of it fitting the description of a narrative, with producers instead often focusing on specific messages as opposed to longer sequences of connected events.

One common thread in discussions of countermessaging is a lack of specificity in describing audiences. Leuprecht et al., for example, suggest differentiating between individuals who are closer to the top of the "pyramid" (of radicalization) or are likely to be so, and those further down who are seen as higher risk;[15] Neumann talks about audiences that are "potentially vulnerable to becoming radicalised." [16] There is little consideration of the impact of countermessages beyond audiences who may potentially be vulnerable to radicalization, despite the impact of extremist messaging, most notably terrorism, on both potential victims and wider society.[17]

In practice, countermessaging campaigns can manifest in many different forms, but analysis tends to be confined to campaigns that have some kind of formalized support. Examples include Abdullah-X, a cartoon avatar that features in online "comics," as well as in a series of twenty-two YouTube videos. Titles include *The Real Meaning of Jihad* and *Freedom of Speech vs Responsibility*. The site and videos are well presented, and feature references to media engagement by the content creator, reportedly a former extremist. The project is listed as "made possible by jigsaw," an incubator within Google's parent company, Alphabet.[18] No new videos have been produced since October 2016, however. The Global Survivors Network focuses on testimony from victims of terrorism. The network produced the documentary film *Killing in the Name*, which was nominated for an Oscar in 2011. The network also had a presence on YouTube, Facebook, and a website. The latter is now defunct and the Facebook page has not been updated since November 2015. A case study by the Institute for Strategic Dialogue describes the project as "seeded" following a September 2008 UN symposium, with the aim of sharing victim testimonies with vulnerable communities.[19] Both of these campaigns now appear defunct, although the content they have produced persists online.[20]

Critiques of Countermessaging

There have been three main related critiques of countermessaging: strategic effectiveness, normative, and capability-based.

Much of the criticism of countermessaging has stemmed from a perceived lack of strategic effectiveness. This can be framed as questioning the role of messaging in general. The basis of this critique is that policymakers have over-estimated the importance of propaganda in driving violent extremism, and therefore assume that the solution is to promote the alternate view.[21] Glazzard, in a paper for the International Counter Terrorism Centre, excoriates "counter-narrative theory," noting the extent to which government, think tanks, and advocacy organizations are organizationally committed to the idea and the limited evidence base.[22] Other critiques of effectiveness dwell on the scale of the task, suggesting that the volume of extremist material makes developing countermessages a drop in the ocean.[23]

These criticisms are further compounded by the difficulties in measuring the effectiveness of countermessaging campaigns. Although raw metrics are often used to support arguments for effectiveness, knowing the final impact of exposure to countermessages is very difficult, particularly in a real-world setting.[24] Not least because, depending on the intended targets of countermessaging campaigns, effective outcomes can be based on nonevents. In the preventative space, for example, this could mean dissuading an individual from engaging with an extremist organization at all.

These are valid criticisms. However, much depends on what countermessages are expected to achieve. Involvement in extremist organizations is dynamic and granular. At any one point there are multiple audiences inside and outside an extremist milieu. Some may be committed activists, others may be wavering, others still contemplating deeper engagement. There may also be potential members who are yet to even hear of a group, a largely indifferent public, fearful potential victims, and ideological opponents that may even be involved in their own forms of extremism. Despite an assumed ability to micro-target content, countermessaging campaigns are not limited to a single audience, and leakage from campaigns has the potential to impact unintended audiences. This potential only becomes greater when material is published online where it can be re-posted and remixed to different effects. The effects of countermessaging on these audiences are not well understood, but there at least needs to be a recognition that despite the stated aims of countermessaging campaigns, that they will impact a variety of audiences. In addition to these considerations, we might also consider the alternative of remaining silent, and the ramifications of allowing extremist messages to go (formally at least) uncontested.

As well as questioning the effectiveness of countermessaging campaigns to date, there are deeper questions on the normative aspects of government involvement. Although few would question the role of government in confronting terrorism, the indistinct margins between radical milieus and support for violence raise awkward questions around the extent to which interventions are warranted.[25] Richards, for example, argues for a distinction between "extremism of thought" and "extremism of method."[26] Conflating nonviolent ideology with violent methods is problematic from a policy angle, but equally distinguishing between nonviolent and violent ideology, and crucially the trajectories between the two, is also extremely difficult. These nuanced and at times invisible distinctions create extremely muddy waters for governments looking to either counter extremist ideologies directly, or do so through proxies. Countermessaging sits awkwardly on the dividing line between legitimate counterterrorism and publicly unacceptable ideological engineering. More recent shifts in U.K. government policy, including the 2015 UK Counter Extremism Strategy, seem to indicate an increasing focus on extremism as opposed to violent extremism.[27] This focus has been criticized by the Joint Committee on Human Rights for being based on an "escalator" between extremism and terrorism.[28]

Countermessaging runs the risk of being equated with propaganda. Propaganda has historically been seen in democratic states as the preserve of undemocratic opponents.[29] In the aftermath of World War I, the term propaganda became synonymous with dishonesty.[30] In some accounts propaganda is used in democratic states either for dubious ends,[31] or as part of everyday communication.[32] Some make the case that promotional culture is now pervasive, and consequently the term propaganda has served its usefulness.[33] Despite the normalization of propaganda, recent incidents have also showcased public alarm at both CVE policy and countermessaging. In the United Kingdom, Prevent, the government's official CVE strategy, has already been much maligned both by the press and civil society organizations on the grounds that it unfairly targets Muslims, causes alienation, and is ultimately counterproductive.[34] Focusing specifically on countermessaging, the Home Office-based Research Information and Communication Unit (RICU) was heavily criticized for their *Help for Syria* campaign, which distributed leaflets and targeted student events without identifying itself as being government backed.[35] Clearly in this case, it was felt that acknowledging government involvement would immediately sour audiences on the message, but the revelation may have done further damage to the U.K. government's credibility, suggesting the campaign may even have been counterproductive. Examples of RICU's work have been seized on by anti-Prevent campaign organizations, including the highly partisan pressure group CAGE, which in 2016 published a report *We Are Completely Independent*, in which claims of covert government support were made against several campaigns. The overall tone of the report is highly critical.[36] The risks of "sock-puppet" organizations (i.e., organizations claiming to be independent but working to advance specific agendas), have been identified as including worsening trust in government over time, as well as undermining the credibility of other organizations without official ties.[37]

A final criticism stems from the lingering doubts about the capabilities of countermessaging actors to produce material that will resonate with audiences. One account of countermessaging in the United States identifies a "preachy" tone as being a key problem with audiences.[38] Meanwhile, governments are seen by many as having a "credibility gap" with target audiences, and efforts to engage may be dismissed out of hand, or even potentially entrench extremist beliefs.[39] Writing on countering ideological support for terrorism, Herd and Aldis argue:

> This [countering ideological support for terrorism] is not an appropriate task for governments to undertake, but on the evidence of our case studies appears best carried out by indigenous religious or other civil society organizations. Too obvious governmental efforts in this field, too close cooperation with moderate religious associations within a region or state, will only serve to delegitimize them in the eyes of the population.[40]

Civil society organizations are not tainted with the same lack of credibility that governments are; however, civil society organizations are very often aligned with governments, seeking to obtain favor and resources. The perception (often ideologically skewed) is potentially one of a counterextremism industry, composed of charities, think tanks, and other organizations, all seeking to engage with high-priority counterterror efforts. Schmid suggests that many civil society organizations are dependent on government for funding, and are staffed by employees who move between governmental and nongovernmental organizations (NGOs).[41] Likewise, Tierney argues that governments are still seen as the "ultimate drivers" of CVE efforts.[42] To illustrate this point, the Abdullah X campaign (described above) was described in one (highly ideological) blog as follows:

> With further research one realises that the connections of the "Abdullah-X" project reaches [sic] into the global counter-radicalisation industry which promotes neoconservative, Zionist aims.[43]

Informal Countermessaging

It is fair to say that analysis of countermessaging, along with CVE more broadly, thus far has been focused almost entirely on organized programs, often those with financial connections to government and larger NGOs. The presence of government funding in this space has led to a focus on discrete programs undertaken by identifiable organizations with measurable outcomes.[44] The need to justify the use of public money and measure success funnels funding to programs that can produce measurable results.[45] This focus on formal programs risks ignoring some of the most potentially useful contributions to countermessaging.

In contrast to the current academic and policy fixation, much countermessaging work is done informally by citizens with no connection with government security policy or any wider community organizations. At the micro level this means conversations with friends and family, discussions around the dinner table, in clubs, community centers, and in the back rooms of pubs. Research based in Indonesia has highlighted the informal role of women in challenging extremism, suggesting that they constitute an important resource that has been allowed to go "under the radar."[46] Although these micro countermessages remain difficult to access, the ease and availability of digital communication platforms has resulted in a corpus of readily accessible countermessages in formats including video and social media accounts. In effect, alongside government and NGO efforts at countermessaging, there is an informal sector of actors producing digital content that is critical of extremist messages. Based on the existing criticism of government-aligned countermessaging, there is good reason to believe that informal countermessages are likely to differ significantly from more formalized approaches to countermessaging.

Probably the most infamous example of informal messaging in the United Kingdom emerged following a 2011 demonstration by the counter-*jihadist* street group the English Defense League (EDL). At the event, Press TV interviewed a (possibly drunk) EDL supporter during the demonstration asking why he was protesting. His reply was garbled and slurred. One reference, possibly to "Islamic rape gangs," was heard as "muslamic ray guns," and this became the hook of a music video created by auto-tuning the original interview.[47] The resulting video, produced by Alex Vegas, attracted over 1.9 million views. The song and the phrase became a running joke at the expense of the

EDL and is available to buy as a t-shirt. Defending himself in the comment section of the original video, creator Alex Vegas said: "All I did was make him sing, I didn't change what he said."

While "Muslamic Ray Guns" serves as perhaps the best known, there are additional examples of countermessaging that have received less attention. The YouTube channel Veedu Vids was established in 2015 with the motto "let's beat bigotry with a smile." At the time of writing the channel has over 2,300 subscribers, and features thirty videos ranging from one minute and 30 seconds to 6 minutes and 45 seconds long. The videos deal primarily with topics around Islam and Islamist extremist narratives and speakers, but also feature some videos focusing on "alt-light" figure Milo Yiannopoulous, as well as controversial evolutionary biologist Richard Dawkins. Titles include *ISIS Appeal: Don't mock ISIS*; *Milo Yiannopoulos VS Anjem Choudary: Is Islam compatible with the West?*; and *Zakir Naik: Are Nursery Rhymes Halal? (PARODY)*. Videos tend to focus on parody and imitation with the protagonist (presumably the channel owner) taking on all the roles in short sketches. An early video—*Abu Haleema Trailer (PARODY)* centers on a montage of shots set to music (*Carmina Burana*) in which the protagonist seemingly imitates the London-based militant Islamist Abu Haleema. The parody of Haleema featured his trademark beard and hand gestures. Haleema rose to some prominence following a Channel Four Documentary—*The Jihadis Next Door*—which followed Haleema through various legal troubles and gave some insight into the production of YouTube videos. Despite the media exposure, Abu Haleema's now seemingly deleted YouTube account had around 1,600 subscribers (in early 2017).

In addition to video, social media accounts have also been a source of informal countermessaging. In some cases these can take the form of parody accounts such as 'Britain Furst', a successful Facebook page parodying the far-right group Britain First.[48] The page specialized in developing alternative versions of the Facebook memes that helped to popularize Britain First on social media. Other social media presences are more straightforward in their opposition such as Exposing Britain First, which has accounts on multiple social networks, and the Facebook group Muslims against Daesh. One important caveat on these examples is the tendency of government and society actors to conceal the source of countermessaging campaigns. Given these practices, it is not possible to say for certain that any of these examples constitutes genuine countermessaging and is not a component of a broader government or civil society initiative.

The Potential for Formal and Informal Collaboration

Despite the inherent murkiness of the communications environment, at this juncture there is little evidence of coordination between producers of formal and informal countermessaging. However, the informal sector has been identified as a potential source of content that could be co-opted by formal organizations. A 2016 report by the Institute for Strategic Dialogue, a prominent counterextremism organization, recommended that "natural world" content could be used to get around the bottlenecks presented by the need to create high-quality original content.[49] A later report on the extreme-right also argued for greater counterculture-specific knowledge:

> They [counterspeech measures] must penetrate alternative platforms and burst extreme-right bubbles with campaigns that build on a thorough understanding of internet culture and counter-cultures.[50]

Likewise, the Jigsaw-backed "Re-direct method" advises against the creation of original content in service of new countermessaging campaigns:

> Campaigns to confront online extremism don't necessitate new content creation. The best part of the research beyond identifying ISIS's recruiting narratives and the content categories most likely to debunk them was that it surfaced hundreds of online videos in English and Arabic that were already uploaded to YouTube, and that would not be be [sic] rejected outright by our target audience.[51]

There is also a strong theoretical case for building closer ties between formal and informal content creators. Closer cooperation between security practitioners and private citizens has been identified as a possible model of security provision. In a cyber-security context, nodal governance models have been applied as tools for analyzing the actions of citizens who have used technology to take on the role of criminal investigators.[52] The concept has also been directly applied to a citizen-led terrorism investigation. The investigation into the 2013 Boston marathon bombing initiated by a number of "digilantes" using the social media site Reddit provided examples of ad-hoc organization, deployment of specialist resources to analyze the devices used, and crowdsourced investigations into the identities of suspects.[53] Ultimately, the Reddit-based investigation earned some interest from the Federal Bureau of Investigation, but identified the wrong suspect. Nevertheless, the Reddit affair stands as an example not only of the public's willingness to use technology to intervene in security matters, in this case an investigation, but also the extent to which authorities are powerless to stop them.

> … the proverbial genie is out of the bottle: the Internet has created an environment in which the public can and will choose to play a role in public criminal and other investigations that capture its interest.[54]

Nodal security frameworks identify individual actors or groups—nodes—which then form networks, each node able to apply its own capital to a collective problem.[55] Capital can include technology, political and social relationships, and resources.[56] In the case of the investigation into the Boston Marathon Bombing, Reddit users were observed to contribute specialist knowledge to the investigation, as well as to pick through media (e.g., photographs) associated with the attacks.[57] Applying this framework to countermessaging, informal content creators bring both symbolic capital, in the form of legitimacy, social capital through their relationships with audiences, and cultural capital stemming from the content they produce. When combined with the critiques of existing formal countermessaging the benefits of informally produced countermessages, in the form of credibility and content, become apparent.

Credibility

The leading critique of formalized countermessaging has been credibility. This applies both to direct communication by government, and to indirect attempts to gain influence through allied groups.[58] Literature on online persuasive communication emphasizes the importance of source credibility in persuasiveness.[59] Analyzing the evidence on persuasive communication online, Wathen and Burkell identified twenty-six factors under five headings: source, receiver, message, medium, and context, that could affect persuasion.[60] They further argued that credibility was a multidimensional concept, composed primarily of perceptions of a source's "trustworthiness" and "expertise," but also including the source's presentation (dynamism, likeability, and goodwill).

Source credibility factors can also interact with aspects of the message itself. Where persuasive messages differ extensively from already held beliefs, the persuasive effect of messages can be reduced.[61] This confirms more theoretical accounts that have long held that successful persuasive attempts are ones that work with established attitudes, rather than directly contradicting them.[62] Persuasive materials that were too firmly rooted in the interests of the message originator, and not the audience, were unlikely to find favor. Analysis of U.S. attempts at countering misinformation has raised the problem of "the credibility deficit opened up by the tension between rhetoric and practice in the US War of Ideas."[63] For many audiences, supporting, being insufficiently critical of, or failing to address government policy, is likely to be a turn off.

In contrast, audiences may be making different judgments about source credibility in response to content from informal actors than formally aligned ones. Whereas formal countermessaging risks being labeled as biased, or out of touch, informal actors can present themselves as free from bias (at least bias toward the government line), and more in touch with their audiences. In part, some of this credibility may come from accepting assumptions that are incompatible with government support; for example, conservative religious positions, or attitudes toward foreign policy. Given the scope and scale of the potential countermessaging space, the most credible spokespeople are unlikely to align themselves with formal countermessaging programs. The ones that do may risk longer-term damage to their credibility.

Content

Schmid has suggested that being one step removed from government allows civil society organizations greater leeway in terms of the content that they produce.[64] In the informal countermessaging space there are no checks and no standards. Countermessages produced by nonaligned actors are free to include personal attacks on specific individuals, use humor, and even sympathize explicitly with extreme political views. One potential strategy is to discredit violent extremist organizations, or to target individual extremists for ridicule.[65] This strategy may be difficult for larger organizations to engage with without being perceived as bullying, and risking adding legitimacy to extreme actors by acknowledging them and their claims. Some researchers have called for a more robust approach to content creation to match the content produced by extreme groups (i.e., "to fight fire with fire").[66]

As well as the freedom to produce coarser content, informal countermessaging actors are also free to experiment with different forms of content. While Internet memes have come to mean something different from the original use of the term meme, the idea of harnessing the power of seemingly ephemeral trends to sway the public mind has been advocated by several campaigners.[67] Memes, according to Shifman, are characterized by three factors: they spread through interpersonal contact but influence wider culture, they reproduce through imitation but not through exact replication, and they compete for survival with one another.[68] In the past, the concept of meme warfare has also found favor with anti-corporate groups. Kalle Lasn used the term "meme wars" and "meme warriors" to set out his vision of a second, anti-corporate, American revolution. Mainstream political parties have copied the form, if not the underlying philosophy, of memes in their production of online political posters designed to be shared on social media platforms such as Facebook.[69]

Meme-inspired approaches may also have value for countermessaging. Laura Huey analyzed the production of messages on the social media platform Twitter during the 2015 kidnapping of two Japanese citizens by ISIS. Huey highlights the satirical nature of "political jams" by focusing on the trend of responding to the videoed ransom demand by reconfiguring images to show the kidnappers and the hostages in various absurd situations: serving sushi, carving kebab meat, and reversing the position of kidnappers and hostages.[70] In particular, Huey identifies the role of these images as allowing audiences to respond to fear with humor. Muslamic ray guns has also arguably attained the status of a meme.

In contrast. where government-backed communication has attempted to replicate this style of communication it has been less successful. A video produced by the Centre for Strategic Counterterrorism Communications, in the U.S. State Department called "Run, Don't Walk to ISIS Land," featured footage produced by ISIS itself, including executions. The tone of the video was sarcastic, intended to highlight the hypocrisy of ISIS's behavior, in particular its treatment of Muslims. The video provoked a public backlash, criticized on the successful HBO show *Last Week Tonight* as "ironic propaganda."[71] The ensuing criticism caused the Centre to change direction, limiting themselves to a more fact-based approach to countermessaging.[72]

Collaboration and Risk

On paper, there is much to gain from greater collaboration between formal and informal content creators. However, it is not clear what form any formalized support for informal countermessaging actors would take. It may be possible that strategies such as the re-direct method intend to co-opt content produced by others, promoting it through paid advertising, without building any more concrete relationship with creators. Alternative models could theoretically range from building loose relationships, provision of tools and training, to incorporating content creators into existing organizations. However, any closer working would entail risk. These risks can be further divided into four types: personal risks, risks to targets, strategic risks, and reputational risks.

First, informal actors are often getting down and rolling in the mud with extreme political actors and groups. In highly localized contexts they may risk their own safety; for example, in one video in which the protagonist confronts Abu Haleema and challenges his messages, the protagonist is clearly concerned for his safety. The protagonist is audibly nervous, and the video is filmed entirely from the protagonist's point of view while concealing his identity.[73] The channel the video is posted on contains only that one video and there is no further way to contact the producer. In addition to physical security, nonaligned actors also open themselves up to responses from extreme actors online. Veedu Vidz composed a video in which he responded to negative comments received online. Comments included: "Son of a bitch, everyone start reporting this arsehole production."

A second risk is the risk to specific targets of content. Parody videos of Abu Haleema for example stimulated dehumanizing language in comments sections, and calls for his death. This risk can be, at least in part, be viewed as being a component of reciprocal radicalization or cumulative extremism. This is the hypothesized interaction between extreme political and religious groups, in which different forms of extremism fuel each other.[74] Content designed to ridicule extreme political and religious positions, in particular content that singles out individuals, may raise tensions within communities and contribute to escalations in the form of either rhetoric or violence.[75] Analysis of countermessages posted on the social networking site Facebook, for example, found a high proportion of "non-constructive counter speech" on some pages.[76] The trend for some extreme movements to present themselves as moderate opposition groups to other extreme movements is another good illustration of this problem.[77] The dividing line between countermessage, and in some cases hate speech, is heavily trafficked, and the difference between counterspeech and provocation is not always immediately apparent.

The third risk plays out on a broader strategic level. Isolation and distance from wider society has been seen as a potential factor in the move toward violence among some groups. Everton's analysis of the 11 September 2001 attackers, the so-called Hamburg cell, for example, uses the concept of sociocultural tension as a factor in network closure: the hiving off of extreme clusters of actors in networks into their own echo chambers.[78] Countermessaging risks exacerbating and increasing the sense of isolation for those already engaging with extreme groups. While the intention to "de-cool" extreme groups may be viable for those who have not yet engaged, for others that already identify with extreme groups, or who are already actively involved, then ridicule will likely do little to persuade them to desist. This contrast is a good example of the complexities of CVE. In this instance one form of CVE—primary countermessaging—could well negatively impact secondary and tertiary CVE—attempts to either persuade extreme actors to disengage, or to rehabilitate those who have already engaged in violence.

Finally, the value of informal countermessaging content is precisely its perceived distance from a broader policy agenda. Closer working relationships raise similar risks to closer working between government and civil society: that informal creators will be branded as cogs in the wider CVE machine by audiences. While the investigatory capacity of citizen actors in the Reddit affair was relatively stable even during their involvement with the authorities, the source credibility enjoyed by informal countermessaging actors is much more likely to be damaged as a result of collaboration, or even unwitting co-option, by more "establishment" agencies. There is the risk that harnessing countermessaging produced by informal actors will risk damaging the effectiveness of content itself.

Reputational risk also goes both ways. While government-backed countermessages need to serve government policy, informal actors have unknown motivations, and may even be actively hostile to wider CVE policy agendas. In some cases, content may not be produced for explicitly political ends, but instead it may emerge from a range or mixture of motivations, including commercial gain and entertainment. *Father Daughter Ad*, produced by long running U.S. comedy institution *Saturday Night Live*, is arguably an example of countermessaging content produced for commercial ends.[79] In other cases those creating countermessaging content may be closer to agents of chaos. Interviews with an actor on a social media account mocking the far-right, reveals that they were motivated by "shits and giggs" rather than by any political conviction.[80] Even where content is produced for political ends, this does not mean that the ideological outlook of activists producing the content is compatible with collaboration with state-backed agencies. Consider for example antifascist movements that can be simultaneously opposed to far-right extremism, but equally committed to opposition to unjust state practices. For example, Unite Against Fascism has been critical of the Prevent strategy, which, it argues, "places an eye of suspicion" on Muslim communities.[81]

Conclusions

There will always be ambiguity surrounding the effectiveness of countermessaging as a tool for challenging violent extremism. Primarily, the challenges of countermessages come from the indistinct audiences. Although some level of targeting is possible, there is no way to know if exposure to countermessages serves to reduce future involvement in violent extremism. Despite this, challenging the narratives of violent extremists remains a policy goal. In the United Kingdom, the government has invested significant resources into supporting countermessaging both by large civil society actors as well as from smaller community groups.

The analysis here is inevitably focused only on mediated communication because it is accessible to a researcher outside of the space. This analysis does not include the work being undertaken beneath this level in families and communities. The primary argument of this article is that, in addition to this acknowledged level of countermessaging, there exists an informal level of nonprofessionals creating countermessaging content. In some cases actors are likely just speaking their minds and have little idea of how the content they produce may align (or not) with broader policy goals. What's more, given the proximity of these creators to potential audiences, and the lack of restrictions on the content they produce, there is the possibility that informal countermessaging content may differ from government-supported content. This article has suggested that, in some cases, the independence of informal actors compared to government aligned ones may boost their credibility. Not only are informal actors more independent, but they are likely to be seen as more authentic by audiences. Key examples have also raised the possibility of content based around memes, humor, and personal attacks that may become harder the more bureaucratized content creation becomes. Equally, official content is ultimately tied to policy goals and societal norms that many members of target audiences, not just violent extremists, reject.

The price for this edgier and potentially more influential content is risk. Non-aligned countermessaging creates risks for both actors and their targets. Ridiculing an extreme figure or group may potentially inflame tensions and risks giving support to opposed extreme views, even where authors do not intend it. Likewise, "de-cooling" extreme groups may work for those in the audience that are yet to engage, but it may risk further alienating those already involved. Research on group radicalization suggests that isolation from wider social networks may be a factor in the move toward violence. For some audiences, informal countermessaging may be counterproductive.

There are good theoretical and practical reasons to expect that officially aligned organizations may move to co-opt at least some informal content. Citizen actors, supported by communications technology, are free to bring their own resources to bear on problems, and state agents are likewise able to make use of these. The nodal governance argument is, however, heavily dependent on actors sharing goals that may not always be the case for countermessaging actors. Also, the resources of informal countermessaging actors, specifically their credibility and their free-wheeling content, may not be appreciated or survive in organizations that need to account for themselves publicly.

Finally, it is worth considering the policy ramifications of this research area. Although it is tempting to speculate about the potential for informal content to inject fresh life into officially recognized countermessaging efforts, more research is needed to better understand the experience of informal countermessaging actors, whatever they may call themselves. Specifically of interest are their motivations and how they see themselves in relation to questions of extremism, terrorism, and policy. Although there is clearly interest from some groups in co-opting "natural" content, no one has asked how content producers would feel about this. It's also not clear what level of support can be offered if the benefits of informal activism are to be preserved. At what point will informal content become similarly inauthentic? These risks need to be understood and managed if closer working is to serve wider policy aims.

Perhaps a more important point, however, is to remind ourselves of the inevitability of countermessaging. Extreme groups are by definition in the minority. Societies will always react negatively to extreme messages, and given the tools to express their opinions some citizens will do so. Furthermore, it is likely that countermessaging content is regulated to some extent by the size of perceived threats. Where extreme content goes viral and breaks into mainstream networks, then members of those networks will respond. Where extreme content remains confined to obscure networks of supporters, then there will be fewer critical responses created. Informal countermessaging exists in equilibrium with extremist messaging, regardless of government policy.

Funding

This work was funded by the Centre for Research and Evidence on Security Threats (CREST). CREST is commissioned by the Economic and Social Research Council (ESRC Award: ES/N009614/1) with funding from the UK Intelligence Community.

Notes

1. Johnny Nhan, Laura Huey, and Ryan Broll, "Digilantism: An Analysis of Crowdsourcing and the Boston Marathon Bombings," *British Journal of Criminology* 57, no. 2 (2015), 341–361; Laura Huey, Johnny Nhan, Ryan Broll, "'Uppity Civilians' and 'Cyber-Vigilantes': The Role of the General Public in Policing Cyber-Crime," *Criminology & Criminal Justice* 13, no. 1 (2012), 81–97; Benoît Dupont, "Security in the Age of Networks," *Policing and Society* 14, no. 1 (2004), 76–91.
2. Tanya Silverman, Christopher J. Stewart, Zahed Amanullah, and Jonathan Birdwell, *The Impact of Counter-Narratives: Insights From a Year-Long Cross-Platform Pilot Study of Counter-Narrative Curation, Targeting, Evaluation and Impact* (London: Institute for

Strategic Dialogue, 2016); Moonshot CVE, Quantum Communications, Valens Global & Nadia Oweidat, and Jigsaw, *The Redirect Method: A Blueprint for Bypassing Extremism* (n.d.).

3. Ben Hayes, and Asim Qureshi, "We Are Completely Independent: The Home Office, Breakthrough Media and the PREVENT Counter Narrative Industry" (London: CAGE, 2016).
4. Shandon Harris-Hogan, Kate Barrelle, and Andrew Zammit, "What is Countering Violent Extremism? Exploring CVE Policy and Practice in Australia," *Behavioral Sciences of Terrorism and Political Aggression* 8, no. 1 (2016), 6–24.
5. Daniel Koehler, *Understanding De-Radicalization* (Oxford: Routledge, 2016).
6. Harris-Hogan, Barrelle, and Zammit, "What is Countering Violent Extremism?"
7. Ibid.
8. Omar Ashour, "Online De-Radicalization? Countering Violent Extremist Narratives: Message, Messenger and Media Strategy," *Perspectives on Terrorism* 4, no. 6 (2010), 15–19.
9. Rachel Briggs and Sebastian Feve, *Review of Programs to Counter Narratives of Violent Extremism* (London: Institute for Strategic Dialogue, 2013); Pizzuto, *Alter-Messaging.*
10. Peter Neumann, "Options and Strategies for Countering Online Radicalization in the United States," *Studies in Conflict & Terrorism 36*, no. 6 (2013), 447. Neumann draws on a working paper from the Institute for Strategic Dialogue for the wording here.
11. Ian R. Pelletier, Leif Lundmark, Rachel Gardner, Gina Scott Ligon, and Ramazan Kilinc, "Why ISIS' Message Resonates: Leveraging Islam, Socio-Political Catalysts and Adaptive Messaging," *Studies in Conflict & Terrorism* 39, no. 10 (2016), 891.
12. Andrew Glazzard, *Losing the Plot: Narrative, Counter-Narrative and Violent Extremism* (The Hague: International Centre for Counter-Terrorism, 2017).
13. Kate Ferguson, *Countering Violent Extremism Through Media and Communication Strategies* (University of East Anglia: Partnership for Conflict, Crime & Security Research, 2016).
14. Michael Pizzuto, *Alter-Messaging: The Credible, Sustainable Counterterrorism Strategy* (Goshen, IN: Centre on Global Counterterrorism Cooperation, 2013).
15. Christian Leuprecht, Todd Hataley, Sophia Moskalenko, and Clark Mccauley, "Containing the Narrative: Strategy and Tactics in Countering the Storyline of Global Jihad," *Journal of Policing, Intelligence and Counter Terrorism* 5, no. 1 (2010), 42–57.
16. Neumann, "Options and Strategies for Countering Online Radicalization in the United States."
17. Alexander Schmid and Janny De Graaf. *Violence as Communication: Insurgent Terrorism and the Western News Media* (Beverly Hills, CA: Sage, 1982).
18. Jigsaw, "Disrupt Online Radicalization and Propaganda" (n.d.), https://jigsaw.google.com/projects/#abdullah-x (accessed 4 October 2017).
19. Institute for Strategic Dialogue, "Global Survivors Network," https://www.counterextremism.org/resources/details/id/415/global-survivors-network (accessed 4 October 2017).
20. Although outside the scope of this article, where countermessaging campaigns are reliant on time-limited support from organizations, they can appear transient and short term. This is a marked contrast with the larger and more persistent libraries of content that seem to be developed by both informal countermessengers and extremists.
21. Ferguson, *Countering Violent Extremism Through Media and Communication Strategies.*
22. Glazzard, *Losing the Plot.*
23. Tom Holt, Joshua Freilich, Steven Chermak, and Clark McCauley, "Political Radicalization on the Internet: Extremist Content, Government Control, and the Power of Victim and Jihad Videos," *Dynamics of Asymmetric Conflict 8*, no. 2 (2015), 107–120.
24. Silverman et al., *The Impact of Counter-Narratives.*
25. Stefan Malthaner and Peter Waldmann, "The Radical Milieu: Conceptualizing the Supportive Social Environment of Terrorist Groups," *Studies in Conflict & Terrorism* 37, no. 12 (2014), 979–998.
26. Anthony Richards, "From Terrorism to 'Radicalization' to 'Extremism': Counterterrorism Imperative or Loss of Focus?" *International Affairs* 91, no. 2 (2015), 371–380.

27. Secretary of State for the Home Department, *Counter Extremism Strategy* (October 2015), https://www.gov.uk/government/publications/counter-extremism-strategy (accessed 5 May 2017). See also: Martin Innes, Colin Roberts, and Trudy Lowe, "A Disruptive Influence? 'Prevent-ing' Problems and Countering Violent Extremism Policy in Practice," *Law & Society Review* 51, no. 2 (2017), 252–281.
28. Joint Committee on Human Rights, *Counter Extremism,* (July 2016), https://publications.parliament.uk/pa/jt201617/jtselect/jtrights/105/10502.htm (accessed 12 May 17).
29. Ferguson, *Countering Violent Extremism Through Media and Communication Strategies.*
30. Steven A. Seidman, *Posters, Propaganda, and Persuasion in Election Campaigns Around the World and Through History* (Oxford: Peter Lang, 2008).
31. Edward Herman and Noam Chomsky, *Manufacturing Consent: The Political Economy of the Mass Media* (New York: Vintage, 1995).
32. Edward L. Bernays, *Propaganda* (New York: Ig, 2005).
33. John Corner, "Mediated Politics, Promotional Culture and the Idea of 'Propaganda,'" *Media, Culture & Society* 29, no. 4 (2007), 669–677.
34. BBC, "Muslim Council Says Prevent Anti-Terror Scheme has 'Failed'" (2014), http://www.bbc.co.uk/news/uk-28934992 (accessed 21 September 2016).
35. Ian Cobain, Alice Ross, Rob Evans, and Mona Mahmood, "Help for Syria: The 'Aid Campaign' Secretly Run by the UK Government" (2016), https://www.theguardian.com/world/2016/may/03/help-for-syria-aid-campaign-secretly-run-by-uk-government (accessed 26 May 2017).
36. Ben Hayes and Asim Qureshi, *We Are Completely Independent: The Home Office, Breakthrough Media and the PREVENT Counter Narrative Industry* (London: CAGE, 2016)
37. Tim Aistrope, "The Muslim Paranoia Narrative in Counter-Radicalization Policy," *Critical Studies on Terrorism* 9, no. 2 (2016), 182–204.
38. Michael Tierney, "Combating Homegrown Extremism: Assessing Common Critiques and New Approaches for CVE in North America," *Journal of Policing, Intelligence and Counter Terrorism* 12, no. 1 (2017), 66–73.
39. Briggs and Feve, *Review of Programs to Counter Narratives of Violent Extremism*; Ferguson, *Countering Violent Extremism Through Media and Communication Strategies*; Alex Schmid, *Al- Qaeda's "Single Narrative" and Attempts to Develop Counter- Narratives: The State of Knowledge* (The Hague: International Centre for Counter Terrorism, 2014).
40. Graeme Herd and Anne Aldis, "Synthesizing Worldwide Experiences in Countering Ideological Support for Terrorism (CIST)," in *The Ideological War on Terror: Worldwide Strategies for Counter Terrorism*, ed. Anne Aldis and Graeme Herd (London: Routledge, 2016), 247.
41. Schmid, *Al-Qaeda's "Single Narrative" and Attempts to Develop Counter-Narratives.*
42. Tierney, "Combating Homegrown Extremism."
43. Coolnessofhind, "Abdullah-X or Abdul-Neocon?" (2015), https://coolnessofhind.wordpress.com/2015/05/06/abdullah-x-or-abdul-neocon/ (accessed 4 October 2017).
44. Ashour, "Online De-Radicalization?"
45. Herd and Aldis, "Synthesizing Worldwide Experiences in Countering Ideological Support for Terrorism (CIST)"; Sarah Marsden, "Conceptualising 'Success' with those convicted of terrorism Offences: Aims, Methods, and Barriers to Reintegration," *Behavioral Sciences of Terrorism and Political Aggression* 7, no. 2 (2015), 143–165.
46. Jacqui True and Sri Eddyono, "Preventing Violent Extremism: Gender Perspectives and Women's Roles," Monash University, n.d.
47. The original interview can be heard here: https://www.youtube.com/watch?v=kjuNuqIev8M and the auto-tune version can be heard here: https://www.youtube.com/watch?v=AIPD8qIIhtVU
48. James Walsh, "Britain Furst: The Halal Ray-Ban-Wearing Far Right Facebook Mockers" (2014), https://www.theguardian.com/media/2014/jun/20/britain-furst-the-halal-ray-ban-wearing-far-right-facebook-mockers (accessed 26 May 2017).

49. Tanya Silverman, Christopher J. Stewart, Zahed Amanullah, and Jonathan Birdwell, *The Impact of Counter-Narratives: Insights From a Year-Long Cross-Platform Pilot Study of Counter-Narrative Curation, Targeting, Evaluation and Impact* (London: Institute for Strategic Dialogue, 2016).
50. Jacob Davey and Julia Ebner, *The Fringe Insurgency: Connectivity, Convergence and Mainstreaming of the Extreme Right* (London: Institute for Strategic Dialogue, 2017), 6.
51. The Redirect Method, "The Redirect Method: A Blueprint for Bypassing Extremism," https://redirectmethod.org/ (accessed 19 October 2017).
52. Huey, Nhan, and Broll, "'Uppity Civilians' and 'Cyber-Vigilantes.'"
53. Nhan, Huey and Broll, "Digilantism."
54. Ibid., 342.
55. Benoît Dupont, "Security in the Age of Networks," *Policing and Society* 14, no. 1 (March 2004): 76–91.
56. Huey, Nhan, and Broll, "'Uppity Civilians' and 'Cyber-Vigilantes.'"
57. Nhan, Huey and Broll, "Digilantism."
58. Aistrope, "The Muslim Paranoia Narrative in Counter-Radicalization Policy."
59. Adrian Cherney, "Designing and Implementing Programmes to Tackle Radicalization and Violent Extremism: Lessons from Criminology," *Dynamics of Asymmetric Conflict* 9, no. 1–3 (2016), 82–94.
60. C. Nadine Wathen and Jacquelyn Burkell, "Believe It or Not: Factors Influencing Credibility on the Web," *Journal of the American Society for Information Science and Technology* 53, no. 2 (2002), 134–144.
61. Wathen and Burkell, "Believe It or Not."
62. Jacques Ellul, *Propaganda: The Formation of Men's Attitudes* (New York: Vintage, 1973).
63. Aistrope, "The Muslim Paranoia Narrative in Counter-Radicalization Policy."
64. Schmid, *Al- Qaeda's "Single Narrative" and Attempts to Develop Counter-Narratives.*
65. Herd and Aldis, "Synthesizing Worldwide Experiences in Countering Ideological Support for Terrorism (CIST)."
66. Tierney, "Combating Homegrown Extremism."
67. Richard Dawkins, *The Selfish Gene* (Oxford: Oxford University Press, 1989); Limor Shifman, "Memes in a Digital World: Reconciling with a Conceptual Troublemaker," *Journal of Computer-Mediated Communication 18*, no. 3 (2013), 362–377.
68. Shifman, "Memes in a Digital World."
69. Benjamin Lee and Vincent Campbell, "Looking Out or Turning In?: Organizational Ramifications of Online Political Posters on Facebook," *The International Journal of Press/Politics* 21, no. 3 (2016), 313–337.
70. Laura Huey "This is Not Your Mother's Terrorism: Social Media, Online Radicalization and the Practice of Political Jamming," *Journal of Terrorism Research* 6, no. 2 (2015), 1–16.
71. For the full video, see: https://www.youtube.com/watch?v=o3VDDbh5dXw
72. Greg Miller and Scott Higham, "In a Propaganda War Against ISIS, the US Tried to Play by the Enemies Rules," *The Washington Post* 8 May 2015, https://www.washingtonpost.com/world/national-security/in-a-propaganda-war-us-tried-to-play-by-the-enemys-rules/2015/05/08/6eb6b732-e52f-11e4-81ea-0649268f729e_story.html (accessed 14 June 2017).
73. See: https://www.youtube.com/watch?v=tMPfJJNeZUI
74. Roger Eatwell, "Community Cohesion and Cumulative Extremism in Contemporary Britain," *The Political Quarterly* 77, no. 2 (2006), 204–216.
75. Joel Busher and Graham Macklin. "Interpreting 'Cumulative Extremism': Six Proposals for Enhancing Conceptual Clarity," *Terrorism and Political Violence* 27, no. 5, 884–905.
76. Jamie Bartlett and Alex Krasodomski-Jones, *Counter-Speech Examining Content that Challenges Extremism Online* (London: Demos, 2015).
77. Benjamin Lee, "A Day in the 'Swamp': Understanding Discourse in the Online Counter-Jihad Nebula," *Democracy & Security* 11, no. 3, 248–274.
78. Sean Everton "Social Networks and Religious Violence," *Review of Religious Research*, 58, no. 2 (2016), 191–217.

79. The sketch can be viewed at https://www.youtube.com/watch?v=_L2fazw5Y9k (accessed 14 June 2017).
80. Interview with research participant (2017).
81. Zac Cochrane "Islamophobia Awareness Training in Schools" (2016), http://uaf.org.uk/2016/07/islamophobia-awareness-training-in-schools/ (accessed 19 June 2017).

Social Media and (Counter) Terrorist Finance: A Fund-Raising and Disruption Tool

Tom Keatinge and Florence Keen

ABSTRACT

The proliferation of social media has created a terrorist finance vulnerability due to the ease with which propaganda can be spread, promoting fund-raising for a certain cause. Social media companies recognize the importance of preventing violent extremist and terrorist content, but less attention is paid to their fund-raising role. As well as presenting a threat, the movement of terrorist fund-raising activities online creates a disruption opportunity. This article argues that social media companies need to display greater awareness of their vulnerability to supporting terrorist financing and greater collaboration with law enforcement and financial institutions to strengthen the integrity of the system against abuse.

In recent years, social media has proved to be an empowering force for those seeking to promote both positive and extremist messages. Such promotion seeks to spread awareness of ideas and campaigns, attract followers to a particular cause, and solicit their support in the form of material funds. The ease with which social media can be used to propagate messages and garner supporters makes it an ideal platform through which to raise finances.

Activists of all types take advantage of the power of social media. Charities raising funds for famine relief; individuals promoting their marathon running or mountain climbing; or terrorist groups and their supporters—all make use of the profile and access social media provides, with their followers and those that chose to share their call for funds promoting the use to which their valuable donations will be put. In the case of Islamist extremist and terrorist financing, the combination of support for the cause, religious messaging, and social media has proved to be a powerful means of raising funds. Finance is the lifeblood of any terrorist organization, regardless of specific beliefs, and thus the intersection between social media and terrorist finance requires far greater examination than it has received to date.

While the use of social media may boost terrorist fund-raising possibilities, the move online also presents identification and disruption opportunities for those in law enforcement and the private sector responsible for policing their activities. Social media intelligence (SOCMINT[1]) could play an important role in assisting with gathering the financial information needed to develop a clearer picture of terrorist fund-raising methodologies and developing strategies to disrupt their finances.

This article explores the role of social media as both a fund-raising and a disruption tool, drawing on the experience of the financial sector as an example of the way in which the private sector already shares information with law enforcement in order to enhance financial investigations.

This article argues that given the rising use of social media by terrorist groups to support their fund-raising ambitions, counterterror finance (CTF) efforts need to embrace the currently neglected social media companies themselves. Unlike the financial sector, these companies are not governed by any formal regime requiring them to detect and report terrorist financing (TF) activity on their networks. This lack of oversight may be hampering the international community's ability to tackle TF as it increasingly occurs online.

Given the use of social media by terrorist groups and their supporters and the rise in fatal attacks across Europe, it is inevitable that the role of social media companies in the fight against terrorism is increasingly questioned. At a meeting in Paris in June 2017, British Prime Minister Theresa May and French President Emmanuel Macron agreed on the "French-British Action Plan on Internet Security."[2] Of note, this plan prioritizes the removal of illegal content from the Internet, placing a responsibility on companies to establish an "industry-led forum" that will automate the detection and suspension or removal of content, as well as improving country-access to data for investigative purposes. What followed was the launch of the Global Internet Forum to Counter Terrorism (GIFCT), a collaboration of Facebook, Microsoft, Twitter, and YouTube.[3] The forum has stated its intention to focus on technology-driven solutions and partnership across the sector to tackle and remove terrorist and violent extremist content from their platforms.

The focus of the GIFCT is yet to be clearly determined; however, social media providers are certainly beginning to respond to this political pressure. This increased receptiveness also provides a window of opportunity for engagement with the CTF regime, much of which is increasingly founded on cooperation with private sector financial institutions, and from which, therefore, lessons can be learned. This article seeks to contribute to this evolving debate by making the case for social media companies to become more active contributors to the global effort to combat TF. It provides specific policy recommendations that should be considered if the response to terrorism in the digital age is to reflect the creativity of those that take advantage of the power of social media to act as an increasingly important TF tool.

Background

The extent to which terrorist groups have used social media to promote their ideology and encourage violent extremism has been extensively documented and reviewed.[4] The power these online tools give terrorists to attract supporters to their cause is immense and the subject of constant and increasing scrutiny from leaders and policymakers. What has been far less studied is the role of social media as a fund-raising tool for terrorist groups. This is despite references to the potential vulnerabilities in various UN

Security Council Resolutions, including paragraph 7 of United Nations Security Council Resolution (UNSCR) 2178,[5] which:

> Expresses its strong determination to consider listing pursuant to resolution 2161 (2014) individuals, groups, undertakings and entities associated with Al-Qaida who are financing, arming, planning, or recruiting for them, or otherwise supporting their acts or activities, including through information and communications technologies, such as the internet, social media, or any other means;

As well as paragraph 23 of UNSCR 2368,[6] which:

> Urges Member States to remain vigilant about the use of information and communication technology for terrorist purposes and act cooperatively to prevent terrorists from recruiting and raising funds for terrorist purposes, and to counter their violent extremist propaganda and incitement to violence on the Internet and social media, including by developing effective counter narratives, while respecting human rights and fundamental freedoms and in compliance with obligations under international law, and *stresses* the importance of cooperation with civil society and the private sector in this endeavour.

The 2017 G7 Leaders' Taormina Statement on the fight against terrorism and violent extremism increased pressure on social media companies to act, committing to "combat the misuse of the Internet by terrorists" and calling on "Communication Service Providers and social media companies to substantially increase their efforts to address terrorist content ... promoting incitement to violence."[7] The failure to connect social media with TF is illuminated by the same G7 Leaders' Statement. It includes taking action "to cut off sources and channels of TF and the financing of violent extremism"[8] as one of its three main priorities alongside tackling the misuse of the Internet by terrorists and managing the risk posed by foreign fighters, yet fails to connect disrupting terrorist financing with the threat posed by social media.

This is a considerable oversight when, as noted in 2014 by former US Treasury Under-Secretary for terrorism and financial intelligence David Cohen "social media allows anyone with an Internet connection to set himself up as an international terrorist financier."[9] Indeed just a few months after Cohen's speech, the U.S. Treasury sanctioned three key financiers of the Al Qaeda affiliated al-Nusrah Front and the Islamic State of Iraq and the Levant (ISIL, also known as Islamic State of Iraq and Syria or Daesh). According to the U.S. Treasury, these three individuals had been using social media and financial networks to organize fund-raising appeals in support of terrorists fighting in Syria and Iraq.[10]

As this article will explore, social media can be used in a number of innovative ways by those seeking to raise finance for terrorist groups: promoting a terrorist group's cause and an associated call for funding in support; as a payment platform or for directing donors and funders to a particular payment platform; raising funds for a terrorist group by advertising services, for example via YouTube videos; as a medium to direct users onto more encrypted channels via the Dark Web to share terrorist finance strategies; and to facilitate the sale of products in support of terrorism.

As terrorists' affairs have increasingly moved online, the opportunities for law enforcement and intelligence agencies to exploit the rich source of data they leave behind have grown. SOCMINT is proving to be a particularly fruitful resource for those seeking to disrupt criminal activity through online methods.[11] Yet one area where the potentially valuable use of SOCMINT is less prominent is for the development of financial intelligence, specifically in the context of CTF. As this article will demonstrate, the growing role social media plays in TF means that this marriage could be transformative in enhancing the ability of authorities to disrupt those soliciting and providing such funding. Although the financial transactions themselves may occur via covert or encrypted channels, the promotion of causes and calls for funding are necessarily overt and open to monitoring by security authorities.

The marriage of SOCMINT with CTF encompasses a range of stakeholders. Law enforcement and security agencies are not the only actors at play; indeed, the wealth of information held by the private sector, namely, those providing financial services as well as the social media organizations themselves, has the potential to enrich and transform CTF operations. Evidence suggests that financial institutions and financial technology (FinTech) firms are beginning to draw on social media as a source of intelligence themselves to verify identities when signing up customers to their products to ensure compliance with their regulatory responsibilities.[12] Furthermore, social media platforms are increasingly offering customers their own online payments services. For example, Facebook has partnered with payment platform TransferWise[13] to allow users to send money internationally without paying foreign exchange fees. The social media giant also facilitates charitable donations through its platform[14] allowing donations in just a matter of a few clicks.[15]

This intersection of actors in the terrorist finance and social media space poses a number of questions, from two opposing and yet interconnected perspectives: that of the terrorist financiers who use social media to fund their objectives; and that of law enforcement and private sector entities responsible for disrupting terrorist finance. What are the vulnerabilities and opportunities in social media platforms that terrorists are managing to exploit for fund-raising efforts? How can public and private actors use social media as financial intelligence to better combat terror finance? And what responsibility do social media platforms have more broadly within the CTF architecture?

A greater understanding of the role social media plays in TF is becoming ever more pertinent. Since the conquest by ISIL of large tracts of Syria and Iraq, the focus of CTF efforts has been on reducing the group's access to oil and tax revenue. As the group's territorial hold has diminished, access to these sources of funding has declined significantly. The group will necessarily adapt, relying to a greater extent on other sources of funding to support its activities. ISIL has proved to be a sophisticated user of social media to promote its ideology and attract supporters; using social media likewise to attract funding for its cause is an inevitable development. The importance of understanding the extent to which social media can also be exploited to improve insights into, and ultimately disrupting this development, is thus at the core of this article.

Definitions and Methodology

In formulating this argument, it is important to first clarify what we mean when referring to "terrorism" for which there is no internationally recognized definition or interpretation. For the purpose of this article, we will use Hoffman's definition of terrorism as: inherently political and ineluctably about power in order to achieve political change, using violence, or the threat of violence in order to pursue these aims.[16]

The term "social media" encompasses a broad range of activities; in this article, we follow the 2017 Merriam-Webster definition of social media as "forms of electronic communication (such as websites for social networking and microblogging) through which users create online communities to share information, ideas, personal messages and other content (such as videos)."[17] When we refer to social media in this article, we thus include platforms such as Facebook, Twitter, LinkedIn, YouTube and Instagram. We do not include applications such as WhatsApp, WeChat, and Telegram (often conflated as social media), categorizing them as "communications technology"— and therefore not directly relevant to the article. Omand et al.'s term "SOCMINT," the harvesting of both open and closed sources of social media, is also referred to frequently, and is increasingly used as an additional weapon in the fight against organized crime and terrorism.

This article first reviews the current literature on terrorism and social media identifying the clear gap that exists in relation to terrorist finance—both in its use as a fund-raising tool and in contributing to its identification and disruption. It then considers the extent to which, and the means by which, social media increasingly contributes to fund-raising campaigns, including for terrorist groups and their activities. It then explores the opportunities for exploiting social media as part of the broader and established responsibilities placed on law enforcement, intelligence authorities and private sector actors that facilitate payments, to identify and disrupt TF. The collaboration of these actors with social media companies to exploit the wealth of financial information that they can amass between them could prove invaluable for developing a comprehensive strategy against modern forms of TF. Finally, this article proposes means by which the status quo can be strengthened, reflecting the role social media plays in facilitating TF and the increased responsibility that must be felt by those social media companies that, like financial institutions, facilitate the raising and transferring of funds in support of terrorist activity.

To assess the degree to which social media can be utilized in order to better understand and ultimately disrupt terrorist finance, this article draws on academic literature, policy documents, and media reporting relating to the subject matter, supplemented by interviews with relevant personnel in law enforcement and the private sector who are faced with the challenge of disrupting TF. The purpose of the interviews was to assess the extent to which social media presents a TF vulnerability, as well as a disruption opportunity.

Literature Review

The CTF Regime

As a relatively new policy objective, conceived in its current, globally coordinated form following the 11 September 2001 (9/11) attacks on New York and Washington, D.C., CTF has been studied far less extensively by the academic community than terrorism more broadly. Since 9/11 recognition that the disruption of TF and the gathering of financial intelligence may play a critical role in counterterrorism responses has garnered more attention. For example, in the immediate aftermath of 9/11 the Financial Action Task Force (FATF)[18] added a further nine "Special Recommendations"[19] to its existing forty combating money-laundering. As Gardner states, terrorism experts recognize money as the "Achilles heel of criminal activity" and as a crucial pressure point in terrorist organizations, and points to the FATF as one of the most effective mechanisms in the modern international system for disrupting and seizing the financial resources of terrorist actors.[20] Biersteker and Eckert have also emphasized the importance of CTF alongside a military strategy as among the most powerful tools deployed by the international community, not only to limit available resources to terrorists, but also to diminish the impact of attacks that cannot be prevented.[21]

The role of private actors, particularly financial institutions, in the fight against TF has been considered to some extent. As Pieth states, the concept of "customer due diligence" (CDD) came about in the late 1980s with the Basel Committee on Banking Supervisions Principles, which introduced the concept of *know your customer* as a means of financial institutions managing and reducing the risks of uncontrolled money flows. The events of 9/11 were seen to galvanize legislators into action, prioritizing CDD as a means of detecting terrorist actors in the system.[22] Bures explores this increased burden placed on banks to implement Anti-Money Laundering and CTF controls as part of the international strategy to disrupt financial crime. His analysis, however, finds that the dominant CTF models constructed through the United Nations and the FATF may no longer be applicable for the nature of many contemporary terrorist groups. He also argues that the responsibility placed on the private sector by public entities is often not matched with necessary intelligence from government partners.[23] This is a debate worth bearing in mind as we explore later in the article the extent to which public–private partnerships have been developed to tackle these threats and have become more efficient and central to the global response in recent years. In view of this rise in cross-sector collaboration it is, however, important to scrutinize this response framework as we consider social media companies as additional private sector actors in the intelligence picture.

With unprecedented advances in technology since the CTF framework came into force, most pertinently the proliferation of social media, it is arguable that the traditional financial intelligence response that focuses predominately on transactions through the formal sector is out-dated. Some have criticized the "financial war on terrorism" pointing out that most operations cost relatively little, and therefore that focus on finance may not be efficient.[24] This may indeed be true, particularly with an increase in lone-actor attacks in recent years that have proven to cost even smaller sums of money.[25] Lemieux and Prates go further, arguing that the CTF architecture is a predominately Western construct, failing to view terrorist organizations as the entrepreneurial sophisticated entities that they are. They posit that enforcement measures targeting suspicious transactions fail to take into account the entire financial chain, and may therefore be inappropriate.[26] Neumann has also questioned the efficacy of the regime,[27] positing that terrorist organizations have more money than ever before, and that the current focus on cutting off terrorist access to the formal financial system is inappropriate given that large amounts of the funds simply avoid the formal system altogether. His assertion is correct: attempting to "cut off funding" in absolute is impossible.

Money will always find a way to flow. It does, however, strengthen the case for an intelligence-led approach to CTF that incorporates the full range of available information, including from social media.

Social Media and Terrorism

The use of social media by citizens and terrorists has been extensively documented. Social media tools were well established as a means of sharing news and promoting causes when the Syrian conflict began as an antigovernment protest in the southern Syrian city of Deraa in March 2011. But it was the so-called Arab Spring—the series of protests that swept across North Africa and the Middle East beginning in Tunisia in December 2010, leading to the ousting of leaders in Tunisia and Egypt—that cemented the use of social media as a tool by which antigovernment groups could effectively organize protests and share and reveal details of the persecution they suffered in reprisal for their actions.[28] Thus, it was via Twitter, Facebook, and other platforms that the arrest, torture, and shooting of protestors in Deraa, Syria was rapidly spread around the world, just as it was being used across the Middle East and North Africa in defiance of rulers and leaders.[29]

At the same time as antigovernment protests were being promoted and orchestrated via social media, ISIL was itself creating a social media strategy that would become fundamental to the group's development. ISIL's effective use of the medium in many ways mirrors the broad tenets of how to employ social media effectively in support of a successful awareness-raising and promotional campaign—be it as a business or a terrorist group. ISIL understands the power of "branding," demonstrating sophistication far beyond the capabilities of similar terrorist groups such as Al Qaeda, through the way it reaches out to sympathizers worldwide, driving an unprecedented flow of foreign fighters into Syria and Iraq, in addition to inspiring homegrown attackers to commit atrocities if they are unable to reach the Caliphate. Their online campaigns reveal them to be slick operators, producing high-quality YouTube videos[30] pitting Islamic State fighters as warriors against the failing regimes of Syria and Iraq.

The group uses trusted members within the Caliphate to cultivate relationships with Western supporters via channels such as Telegram and Surespot, becoming *jihadi* "celebrities" and "influencers" among sympathetic circles.[31] This strategy would not be out of place among a startup, or sports brand trying to promote a new product. It indicates an intelligent, tech-literate demographic, in which information technology graduates and social media strategists are as valuable to the group as a suicide bomber. The group even had a designated information minister, Wa'il Adil Hasan Salman al-Fayad, who oversaw the production of its propaganda videos (until his death in September 2016).[32] ISIL has thus managed to combine the modernity of the digital age with its medieval brand of religious barbarism, re-writing the playbook for terrorists to come.

The Research Gap

As indicated above, there is a growing body of research into the expansion of social media, and how this has re-shaped terrorist organizations in terms of publicity and support. Separately, the traditional CTF regime (to a lesser extent) has been discussed, including the role of financial institutions. Less documented however, are the specific ways in which social media has been instrumental in raising funds, and how actors (both public and private) can exploit this to develop intelligence to assist with disruption.

The CTF regime has come a long way since 2001, and yet it would be wrong to claim that we are "winning" the war against terror finance. Terrorists continue to commit atrocities in all parts of the world, dependent on the funds they are able to raise—be it lone actors with small sums, or self-proclaimed proto-states such as ISIL. This does not, however, mean the international community should abandon the current mechanisms that already exist to combat terror finance. It points to the need for a more creative strategy, building on the public–private infrastructure already in place. It is at this juncture we posit that SOCMINT is relevant and underutilized.

Without a clear understanding of the ways in which terrorist groups use social media to fund-raise, policymakers and law enforcement risk missing important disruption opportunities. The next section therefore seeks to address this gap by considering the fund-raising power of social media and the ways in which this ability has been harnessed by terrorist groups in support of their fund-raising activity.

The Fund-raising Power of Social Media

Before considering the extent to which terrorist groups use social media to raise finance in support of their campaigns, it is worth pausing to consider the power of social media as a fund-raising tool in general. This capability has been extensively studied by academics and the business community alike[33] and has been harnessed to great effect by the voluntary sector as it seeks to raise funding in support of its various causes.[34] This use of social media has contributed to a rapid rise in the use of online means of fund-raising by charities. According to the Charity Commission for England and Wales, online giving rose by 7.9 percent in 2016, and donations made via websites, social media, and apps account for 26 percent of donations in the United Kingdom. They also report that 17 percent of all donations in 2016 were made using a mobile device.[35]

Expert companies that mount social media fund-raising campaigns recommend a number of ways in which charities can maximize the success of their online fund-raising appeals. Key among them are: the importance of identifying the target audience and developing a clear understanding of the social media platforms they use; employing links to websites, photos, and videos to engage with potential supporters and create impact on platforms that often limit space for the use of text (e.g., Twitter limits post lengths to just 280 characters); conveying urgency by providing real-time updates on the cause being promoted—again, photos, and videos can be powerful in this regard—the progress the campaign is making and the remaining donations needed to meet the fund-raising goal; focusing on the impact that each donation will have by linking it to a specific deliverable (e.g., every £100 donated will vaccinate a certain number of children); and finally, including a "call to action," exhorting followers to become "an army" and promote the campaign to their own contacts and followers, undertaking their own fund-raising efforts.[36]

As this article will demonstrate, while these factors are devised to support the promoting of awareness and the raising of funding for "good causes" the power of social media to drive interest in, and raise funding for, causes that are espoused by terrorist groups is equally, if not more applicable. While there are no available statistics regarding the amounts raised or the proportion of terror groups' financing conducted via social media—indeed its often-covert nature makes this near-impossible—there are a growing number of cases being revealed, pointing to an upward trend in the exploitation of social media as a TF tool, as the next section will explore.

Social Media as a TF Tool

Among a very limited body of literature, the FATF's October 2015 report, *Emerging Terrorist Financing Risks*,[37] provides the most extensive consideration of the role social media plays in TF, including some simple case studies provided by member states. As the report notes, "The widespread access to and anonymity of the Internet and especially the rapid expansion of social media, have been exploited by terrorist groups to raise funds from sympathetic individuals globally and represents a growing TF vulnerability."[38] This opportunity to raise funds complements the broad and frequent use made of social media by terrorist organizations to promote their propaganda and to document and advertise their experiences and achievements. This latter point has been used with particularly compelling effect by those foreigners who have traveled to Syria and Iraq to join ISIL. For example, the Twitter hashtag #FiveStarJihad was used to promote the cause of *jihad* in Syria and Iraq and attract others to join the excitement that those that had already traveled were purportedly enjoying,[39] even "posing with chocolate bars or jars of Nutella to prove that they can still access their home comforts on the Syrian front line."[40]

A further report from the FATF, *Financing of Recruitment for Terrorist Purposes*, provides more evidence of the role social media can play in TF. In a case provided by the Russian Federation, calls via social media were used both to recruit for ISIL as well as solicit donations to fund their travel.[41]

Indonesian authorities have also noted greater use of social media for terrorist fund-raising purposes. A White Paper published in October 2017 reportedly classifies fund-raising via social media as a high security risk—downgrading previously popular fund-raising tools such as illegal drug trading and motorcycle theft. The report notes that "The rise of the use of social media is because it is easy to open a social media account and anyone can use a bogus identity easily, giving the authorities challenges to identify and trace. The reach of social media is so vast, that the potential of the terror cells to raise funds is huge."[42]

And finally, a fund-raising effort called Al-Sadaqah, aimed at raising money for weapons and other necessary resources from Muslims in the West, has reportedly recently been circulating on social media platforms linked to Al Qaeda.[43] This case is interesting for two reasons. First, it appears that while this campaign has been shut down by Facebook, it continues to operate on Telegram, highlighting the discrepancy between the response of different social media platforms in responding to cases of suspected TF. Second, this is one of the few cases where Bitcoin (or any other form of cryptocurrency) is accepted as payment for donations. Equally notable is the very limited response this campaign has achieved in its call for cryptocurrency donations, suggesting that thus far the ease and anonymity of cash continue to outweigh the complexities, volatility, and questionable operational security of cryptocurrencies.

As the FATF notes, "Social networks are being also used to coordinate fund-raising campaigns. Large-scale and well-organized fund-raising schemes aimed at TF may involve up to several thousand 'sponsors' and may raise significant amounts of cash."[44] The reach of social media and the numbers of online "followers" gathered by many leading supporters of ISIL in particular, and *jihadi* preachers more generally, lends credence to this claim. But perhaps more relevant than the number of followers that terrorist financiers have on social media is the message they convey, underpinned by Islamic texts that support their call for funding.

Financing Jihad

It is not just for the promoting of ideology, the sharing of grievances, and the calling for brothers "to make hijrah to the Islamic State" that Twitter and other social media have been used during the Syrian conflict. Fund-raising campaigns in support of terrorist causes have also been widely promoted, tapping into the concept of "financial Jihad," motivated by the emphasis provided by the Qu'ran of the importance of giving generously to the cause of Jihad.[45]

A commonly referenced approach is to emphasize "*Tajheez al-Ghazi*," the act of equipping a fighter. Those, such as women, who are less able to join the physical fight, can achieve the reward of waging *jihad* by funding fighters. Donations and sponsorship are encouraged, for "He who prepares a Ghazi going in Allah's Cause is (given a reward equal to that of) a *Ghazi*; and he who looks after properly the dependents of a Ghazi going in Allah's Cause is (given a reward equal to that of) *Ghazi*."[46] ISIL's online *Rumiyah* magazine also emphasizes the importance of waging *jihad* with one's wealth as "wealth is used initially in order to prepare equipment and arm the troops."[47] In contrast to physical fighting, from which some are exempt, there is no excuse "for anyone whom Allah has enriched from His bounty and who has yet to spend."[48]

This concept can be seen clearly in various fund-raising initiatives promoted via social media in the early stages of the Syrian conflict. Involving nineteen leading public, religious, and political figures, the *Ramadan Campaign* conducted in Kuwait in 2013 aimed "to prepare 12,000 jihadists for the sake of Allah."[49] According to posters supporting the campaign, a donation of US$2,500 would equip one fighter for battle. One evening of fund-raising for this campaign raised US$350,000. A further campaign reported by the *New York Times* and run by a Syria-based Saudi sheikh close to Al Qaeda, called "Wage Jihad With Your Money," promised donors that they would earn "silver status" by giving US$175 for fifty sniper bullets, or "gold status" by giving twice as much for eight mortar rounds.[50] And yet another campaign, reported by the *Washington Post*, calls for the US$2,400 needed to fund the travel, arming, and training of foreign fighters.[51]

A selection of three further examples provided by the Investigative Project on Terrorism[52] include:

- A call for funding by the Nafir al Aqsa Campaign of US$2,500 to "equip a mujahid" with a Kalshnikov, ammunition vest, military clothing, ammunition, and military boots
- Another post from the same Twitter account (@Nafeer_aqsa100, now suspended) solicits funding for a range of weapons: sniper rifle, US$6,000; rocket propelled grenade launcher, US$3,000; and a PK machine gun, US$5,500
- A call for funding to help buy weapons in a campaign connected with the al-Nusra Front to support the "Islamic battalions" led by Saudi Sheikh Abdullah Mhesne, including prices for eight mortar shells (100 Kuwaiti Dinars or 1,300 Saudi or Qatari Riyals) as well as both Kalashnikov and sniper bullets (50 Kuwaiti Dinars or 650 Saudi or Qatari Riyals for 150 and 50 rounds, respectively). As with other such fund-raising drives, WhatsApp numbers are included via which the donor can receive the necessary payment details. The call for funding is also supported by an extract from the Qu'ran that underlines the importance of charity. In this case 47:38 stating "Behold, you are those who are called upon to spend in Allah's Way, but some of you are niggardly. Whoever is niggardly is in fact niggardly to himself. For Allah is All-Sufficient, whereas it is you who are in need of Him. If you turn away, He will replace you by a people other than you, and they will not be like you."

As noted previously, the conflict in Syria has witnessed extensive, sophisticated, and expanding use of social media, including for fund-raising purposes. Investigating the activity of those individuals designated by the United States in August 2014, the Camstoll Group underlines the extent to which social media can be used for financing purposes.[53] The ability of such individuals to continue operating following their addition to terrorist sanctions lists by the United States and the United Nations reveals one of the weaknesses of the global response to social media as a TF tool.

The Case of Hajjaj Fahd Al-Ajmi

Prior to his designation in August 2014, Hajjaj al-Ajmi's role as a fund-raiser for Al Qaeda operations in Syria was promoted by a number of Twitter accounts including those related to Al Qaeda affiliate the al-Nusra Front, designated as a terrorist group by the United States and the United Nations in 2012 and 2013, respectively. Al-Ajmi had also set up a fund-raising organization called the "Popular Commission in Support of the Syrian Revolution." This organization called for funding to support the purchase of weapons and artillery for *jihadi* groups in Syria and "raised hundreds of thousands of dollars to finance Syrian rebel groups" according to the *Washington Post*.[54]

Al-Ajmi also supported other fund-raising initiatives including the "Mobilization of the People of Qatar Campaign for the Levant." Once again, this campaign included the use of social media to support communication and promotion of the campaign including the distribution of videos of beneficiaries thanking donors and in some cases renaming their group in honor of al-Ajmi.

Following his designation in August 2014, Twitter suspended the account of Hajjaj al-Ajmi, but inevitably, "within hours" a new account was opened including his name and photo and was being widely promoted by his supporters using the hashtag #Campaign_for_a_million_followers_for_Hajjaj_AlAjmi urging people to "follow" this new Twitter account. According to the Camstoll Group, "within two days, Hajjaj al-Ajmi recouped nearly 42,000 followers, and as of early April 2016, Hajjaj al-Ajmi's new Twitter account was still active and had garnered more than 176,000 followers."[55] Furthermore, the Camstoll Group also reports that his Instagram page, followed by more than 1.3 million accounts, likewise remained active as of April 2016.

As will be reviewed in more detail below, this case highlights some key considerations for policymakers, including the need for social media companies to be alert to, and react to, sanctions designations and the ability of those subject to sanctions to adapt to the blocking and suspension of their accounts. These cases also raise the question of whether those that promote the accounts and activity of designated individuals are providing "material support"[56] and should thus have their accounts likewise suspended or be added to sanctions lists.

The Case of Babar Ahmad

According to the U.S. National Terrorist Financing Risk Assessment 2015, U.S. authorities have "observed foreign persons directly soliciting US residents for financial and non-cash contributions to terrorist groups, frequently using social media."[57] One such case cited by the risk assessment involves U.K. resident Babar Ahmad, "a pioneer of internet jihad,"[58] who used social media and websites, known as Azzam Publications, to solicit funding. The websites promoted "the rhetoric of violent jihad … solicited the donation of funds, equipment, and personnel for terrorists, including the Taliban."[59] Babar Ahmad was extradited from the United Kingdom to the United States in 2012 and in December 2013, Babar Ahmad pleaded guilty to terrorism charges and was sentenced to 12.5 years in jail.[60] Given the length of time he had spent in detention in the United Kingdom, he was released in July 2015.[61]

The Inquiry into Adeel Ul-Haq

In an investigation by the Charity Commission for England and Wales into an individual known as Mr. Adeel Ul-Haq, it was found that charitable funds had been solicited by the individual via a Twitter account between July 2013 and April 2014. Ul-Haq had made public statements on the platform that the funds would be sent to Syria for humanitarian purposes, stating, "If you want to donate money InshaAllah to aid those in Syria DM or @ me for a follow back. 100% donation policy." Over the course of this period, funds in excess of £12,370 were raised, some of which were spent on a professional laser pen, a water-resistant security pouch, and night vision scope. These purchases raised a suspicion that the funds were not being used for charitable purposes, and in February 2016 Ul-Haq was convicted of TF offenses under both section 5 the Terrorism Act 2006 and section 17 of the Terrorism Act 2000.[62]

Exploiting Charitable Giving

The charitable sector has often found itself at the center of TF concerns. For example, the 9/11 Commission revealed the extent to which Osama bin Laden used charities to raise and move funding in support of his activities.[63] More recently, William Shawcross, chairman (at the time of writing) of the Charity Commission for England and Wales, warned that terrorism and extremism represent "one of the most deadly threats faced by some charities today."[64] The issue of charities and TF is a contentious one.[65] Following 9/11, the FATF, global standard-setter for anti-money laundering and counterterror finance, was tasked with developing a response to terrorist finance. The FATF quickly produced nine new Special Recommendations[66] focused on TF to supplement its existing forty. In the FATF's view, charities "possess characteristics that make them particularly attractive to terrorists or vulnerable to misuse for terrorist financing" including the fact that they enjoy public trust, have access to considerable sources of funds, and operate cash-intensive activities across borders, often in or near areas where designated terrorist groups are based or operate.[67]

This wording has been extensively criticized, as in many places this alleged vulnerability to abuse by terrorist groups was used to impose restrictions on civil society organizations "to ensure that they cannot be misused."[68] Responding to this concern, since 2013 the FATF has moderated its advice.[69] In June 2016, the reference to charities being "particularly vulnerable" to terrorist abuse was removed from the relevant FATF Recommendation and the accompanying Interpretive Note was updated.[70]

Notwithstanding the moderation of the FATF's guidance, in its National Terrorist Financing Risk Assessment 2015,[71] the U.S. government asserts that "Private donations from individuals and charitable organizations have continued to provide terrorist groups with a consistent flow of funds" with "hundreds of millions of dollars [collected] through regular fundraising events held at homes or mosques and through social media pleas."[72] In his March 2014 speech, then–U.S. Under Secretary for Terrorism and Financial Intelligence David Cohen was explicit, saying that:

> Our ally Kuwait has become the epicenter of fundraising for terrorist groups in Syria. A number of Kuwaiti fundraisers exploit the charitable impulses of unwitting donors by soliciting humanitarian donations from both inside and outside the country, cloaking their efforts in humanitarian garb, but diverting those funds to extremist groups in Syria. Meanwhile, donors who already harbor sympathies for Syrian extremists have found in Kuwait fundraisers who openly advertise their ability to move funds to fighters in Syria.[73]

Cohen also criticized Qatar for its failure to curb "fundraisers aggressively [soliciting] donations online from supporters in other countries, notably Saudi Arabia, which have banned unauthorized fundraising campaigns for Syria." He claimed that "Private fundraising networks in Qatar, for instance, increasingly rely upon social media to solicit donations for terrorists and to communicate with both donors and recipient radicals on the battlefield."[74]

Underlining these assertions, the U.S. State Department noted in August 2014 that "Private fundraising networks increasingly rely upon social media to solicit donations and communicate with donors and recipient opposition groups or terrorist organizations. It also enables fundraisers to solicit donations from supporters in countries where otherwise it would be banned, such as Saudi Arabia."[75]

It is not surprising that much of the focus of the social media fund-raising activity in support of terrorist organizations is couched in charitable terms. As mentioned above, charities are highly effective vehicles for fund-raising, whether licit or illicit and whether such illicit fund-raising is willingly undertaken[76] or the identity and trust of a charitable organization is abused.[77]

In its *Emerging Terrorist Financing Risks* report, the FATF also provides case studies of overt and covert calls for funding that are framed in humanitarian language. For example:

> In Germany in 2013, an explicit call for funding was made in a Facebook group on recipes for women by one of the users. A fighter in Syria was mentioned (no name indicated) who urgently needed "equipment, food and pharmaceuticals." There was time to collect funds until "Thursday," in order to "dispatch" the requested material by "Friday." The user also provided the details of an account held with a German bank where the funds were to be sent. It is unknown if the author of the Facebook call for funds is also the person responsible for this initiative. The owner of the account is a convert, who is suspected of coordinating this advertising campaign.[78]

Another example that once again highlights the failure of social media companies to react to the designation of individuals and entities is provided by the case of James McLintock and the al-Rahmah Welfare Organization.

Al-Rahmah Welfare Organization

In March 2016, James Alexander McLintock, president, chief executive officer, and chairman of the Pakistan-based Al-Rahmah Welfare Organization (RWO) was designated by the U.S. Treasury pursuant to Executive Order 13224, which targets terrorists and those providing support to terrorists or acts of terrorism. RWO was designated at the same time in light of its close connection with McLintock.[79]

The U.S. Treasury assessed that RWO had solicited funding in support of supposed work with orphans that was in fact destined for extremists in support of *jihadi* operations. This was a concerted effort of deception, using photos of children, Afghan identity documents, and cell phone numbers to create dossiers for soliciting donations for RWO supported by social media activity. Through his connections, McLintock and the RWO are believed to have provided funding for the activities of Al Qaeda, the Taliban, and Lashkar-e-Taibah.

Of particular note, the U.S. Treasury asserts that:

> Since May 2012, McLintock has provided support to the Taliban by using RWO and his other non-governmental organizations (NGOs) to receive large amounts of money from British donors who were not aware of the NGOs' Taliban ties. According to publicly available information, between April 2011 and April 2012 RWO received the equivalent of approximately $180,000 from donors in the United Kingdom. RWO has also received financial support from charities in the Persian Gulf and the United Kingdom.

According to the Camstoll Group, despite the designation of RWO and McLintock, as of early April 2016, social media accounts linked to both were still active and soliciting donations.[80] The extent to which social media companies should comply with sanctions designations, as the financial institutions that receive the donations gathered by these designated entities must certainly do, is considered further in this article.

Crowd-Funding

A key benefit of social media is that it allows fund-raisers to reach thousands of potential donors in an efficient and targeted manner. Followers of particular social media accounts are typically already favorably disposed to the narrative and ideology of the person they are following. It is thus likely that a call for funding will be received positively. As the FATF observes, "Individuals and organizations seeking to fundraise for terrorism and extremism support may claim to be engaging in legitimate charitable or humanitarian activities and may establish NPOs [the term used by FATF for charities] for these purposes."[81] Fund-raising via a large number of small donations, or as it is known more commonly, "crowd-funding," has been—or has the potential to be—successfully exploited by terrorist organizations at a time when the fund-raising routes that were traditionally used by groups such as Al Qaeda—charities and deep-pocketed donors moving money through the formal banking system[82]—are under considerable concerted global pressure. Although some anti-fraud measures are taken, crowd-funding websites can be used to set up fund-raising pages quickly with limited due diligence checks on the fund-raiser or the legitimacy of the cause that is being promoted.

In the United Kingdom, the first *National Risk Assessment of Money Laundering and Terrorist Financing* published in October 2015 did not consider money laundering (ML) and TF threat from crowd-funding.[83] However, the second edition, published in November 2017, noted that "Economic crime risks have been identified where platforms can be used to launder money, while other crowdfunding activities could facilitate fraud," observing further that "Crowdfunding, in particular peer to peer lending or donation sites, also has the potential to be used as a TF tool, though this has not been observed to date in the UK."[84]

Leading security officials elsewhere in the world have been more direct. In a speech in November 2015, the then-chief executive of the Australian Financial Intelligence Unit (FIU), AUSTRAC, Paul Jevtovic observed that "Terrorism financing continues to manifest itself in so many different ways with more recent developments coming in the form of the use of the largely unregulated space of social media by terrorist groups such as ISIL for crowdfunding."[85]

The challenges posed to the authorities by such approaches to fund-raising are also highlighted by the Canadian FIU, FINTRAC. It reportedly notes that although cross-border payments greater than C$10,000 must be reported to the authorities, intelligence gaps often exist with regard to the source of these funds, "especially when trying to flag individuals supporting a crowdfunding campaign that may be suspected of being (TF)-related by an investigative authority" as the contributions are most often less than C$10,000 and are therefore not individually subject to legal reporting requirements.[86]

Disrupting Terrorist Financing

Having established that the combination of humanitarian or religiously inspired giving and social media has proven to be highly effective for those seeking to fund terrorism, we will now consider the ways in which the moving of TF operations online presents opportunities for law enforcement, intelligence, and private sector actors to develop deeper knowledge of TF networks. As observed by the RAND Corporation in an extensive study examining the use of Twitter by ISIL and opposition groups, the use of social networks, while being advantageous for the terrorist group themselves, gives the public a "unique window" into the networks of terrorists and their supporters. Such insight can be valuable in the development of disruption strategies through an improved understanding of their architecture. It also supports the creation and targeting of counternarrative strategies for the digital space that are essential in any counterterrorism response.[87] SOCMINT is proving not only to be practical in terms of insight and counternarratives, but is beginning to demonstrate tangible disruptive capabilities; in Israel, Israeli Defense Forces algorithms are known to monitor the social-media accounts of suspected individuals and their networks, to look for early terrorist warning signs.[88]

This article posits that we can and should extend this logic to the development of CTF strategies. Financial intelligence has long played a critical role in disrupting the activity of illicit actors; given the ubiquity of social media, the intelligence that can be gleaned from it should be considered and exploited. The tools and technologies to monitor social media for this purpose are developing rapidly; challenges, however, remain in navigating some of the technical and legal issues around using that information.[89] Intelligence gathering and information sharing for the purposes of financial crime disruption is something that the financial sector has been harnessing for years, and important lessons could therefore be learned.

Since the creation of the FATF in 1989 and the obligation it places on states to ensure that banks and other entities handling or facilitating the movement of finance (such as lawyers and accountants), financial institutions have been placed on the frontline of the fight against illicit finance. In this role, they are required to monitor their customers and screen transactions for "suspicious activity" and report any such suspicions to their national Financial Intelligence Unit in the form of a suspicious transaction report.[90]

Following 9/11, although targeting the financing of terrorists was not new—for example, the United Kingdom had invested considerable resources in seeking to disrupt the finances of the Provisional Irish Republican Army—a coordinated, global effort certainly was. 9/11 exposed the significant vulnerabilities of the U.S. domestic and international approaches and architecture for disrupting TF. Furthermore, given the extent to which finance moves internationally, the lack of an effective, transnational response was a significant weakness.

In 1999, the UN had introduced the *International Convention on the Suppression of the Financing of Terrorism*, stating:

> Any person commits an offense within the meaning of this Convention if that person by any means, directly or indirectly, unlawfully and willingly, provides or collects funds with the intention that they should be used or in the knowledge that they are to be used, in full or in part, in order to carry out [terrorist acts] ...[91]

However, this initiative was treated as a low priority by most member states. As of 9/11, only four states—the United Kingdom, Botswana, Sri Lanka, and Uzbekistan—had actually adopted this convention.[92]

The 9/11 attacks on New York and Washington, DC intensified the burden on states and their "obliged entities" as the FATF added nine further "Special Recommendations" dealing specifically with TF to its existing forty. Ever since 9/11, and with increased intensity since the emergence of ISIL in summer 2014, banks and other financial institutions such as large money remittance companies have dedicated considerable resources to efforts to identify TF along with financial activity that might be indicative of terrorist activity.[93] Yet this mission proves, in most cases, fruitless as the ability of banks to identify the small amounts of (most often) clean money associated with TF is near impossible. As the 9/11 Commission's *Monograph on Terrorist Financing* acknowledged in 2004, "Although financial institutions lack information that can enable them to identify terrorists, they have information that can be absolutely vital in finding terrorists."[94] Richard Barrett, the former coordinator of the UN al-Qaeda and Taliban Monitoring Team concurs, asserting that "States cannot expect the private sector to have a better idea of what TF looks like than the states themselves,"[95] particularly when modern technology is increasingly moving money flows out of traditional banking channels.

In recent years, the greater involvement of the private sector as partners in efforts to disrupt TF has been well-established via information-sharing mechanisms such as the United Kingdom's Joint Money Laundering Intelligence Taskforce.[96] The inclusion of SOCMINT in the response framework must certainly be explored as an augmentation to the existing disruption strategy. The next section will look at the ways in which social media intelligence is already being used as financial intelligence, and question how it could be more effectively married with the CTF regime as a whole.

SOCMINT as Financial Intelligence

It is pertinent to first emphasize that when considering the use of SOCMINT as financial intelligence, different actors will be able to make varying uses of this source, depending on their level of access. For example, in the United Kingdom, whereas security services and police forces have the ability to access communications data when it is needed to facilitate investigations, so long as such access is deemed "necessary and proportionate,"[97] most often, private sector access to social media is limited to "open" networks.

Based on interviews with leading financial institutions, the use of social media to check customers is growing, particularly in cases of enhanced due diligence when a customer has been classified as "high-risk." It is, however, important to caveat that while social media may form part of the wider intelligence picture when a customer is under scrutiny, it is rarely used as standalone evidence for a number of reasons: the data sets are large and unstructured, meaning that patterns and interpretations are often false; data can be unreliable due to multiple and fake accounts; many users have the same name with no further unique identifying features; and users operate in multiple languages, complicating the intelligence picture further. Ultimately, it is highly challenging to validate whether social media posts are true.[98] Thus, SOCMINT will currently most often be used to corroborate and strengthen existing evidence. That being said, given the extensive use made of social media by terrorists and the emerging use financial institutions make of open source access to customer social media profiles, there is clear potential in considering developing a more formal strategy that brings SOCMINT and financial intelligence together.

This concept is not new. In 2013 the FATF explicitly cited social media as a means of verifying the accuracy of customers' personal declarations regarding their sources of wealth.[99] A discrepancy, for example, in declared wealth and online evidence could be evidence of criminality. The Canadian FIU FINTRAC also reportedly scrutinizes Facebook and other social media platforms in order to enhance their financial intelligence picture. FINTRAC's spokesperson Renee Bercier stated, "It is important to remember that the perpetrators of these crimes (ML/TF) have an online presence and actively use the web, including social media to connect with associates, facilitate their activities, and in the case of terrorism financing, even raise funds."[100]

Interviews with FinTech companies reveal even more innovation in this regard. The sector offers customers new financial products and services as an alternative to those traditionally offered by incumbent financial institutions. As most of these platforms offer services entirely online, digital procedures are built into their business model, including the verification and screening of transactions. Based on interviews with some of the United Kingdom's leading FinTech firms, it is clear that social media screening forms a core part of their financial crime risk management. Sites monitored include Facebook, LinkedIn, and Twitter, in order to gather information on customers, proving to be a useful source when verifying new customers and conducting the necessary due diligence checks to ensure they are not using the platform for financial crime purposes.[101]

Law enforcement's use of SOCMINT when conducting financial investigations is evolving. Digital policing is on the rise,[102] particularly when investigating missing persons and child sexual exploitation. However, evidence suggests that at the FIU level and in units responsible for financial investigations, SOCMINT is not yet incorporated as a core investigative tool. This is in part due to the validity and reliability of what can be found online, as well as the extra resources needed to monitor social media and networking platforms. As social media continues to proliferate, however, the onus on law enforcement to make use of these platforms as financial intelligence may grow. As proven by the private sector, it can be a fruitful exercise, and should be considered as a creative way to exploit terrorists' online presence but may almost certainly require the collaboration of the social media companies themselves.

Taking Responsibility

As we have demonstrated, social media platforms are critically important for terrorists to assist with planning, communicating, or equipping their activities, yet they are seemingly immune from the level of responsibility placed on FATF-obliged entities such as banks. The ongoing debate about the responsibility of social media platforms such as Facebook, Twitter, and YouTube reveals the extent to which this lack of obligation presents security vulnerabilities.

It would be wrong to suggest that high-profile social media platforms take no action. Twitter's "Government Terms of Service" reports disclose the extent to which the company has responded to requests from governments to remove content that violates Twitter's terms of service against the promotion of terrorism[103]—in the period from January to June 2017, Twitter received reports related to 1,200 accounts believed to be in contravention. Of these reports, 92 percent were addressed via account suspension. This number is dwarfed by the 299,649 accounts in total that Twitter suspended during that period for violations related to the promotion of terrorism, identified primarily by Twitter's own filtering systems.

Facebook has a team focused on terrorist content, ensuring that users who support terror groups are quickly removed and posts by their friends are investigated.[104] Regarding their online payments services, like banks, social media firms are also required to file suspicious transaction reports with national FIUs, and thus employ financial crime compliance specialists to ensure sanctions and counterterrorism legislation are not being contravened.[105] Facebook's public statement, "Hard Questions: How We Counter Terrorism,"[106] attempts to respond to increasing pressure on the tech industry in the wake of recent terror attacks. Here, they outline their use of artificial intelligence combined with human expertise and industry cooperation to demonstrate their commitment to countering the use of their platform for terrorist purposes. Indeed, they believe "technology, and Facebook can be part of the solution." This belief is further emphasized via the creation of the previously referenced GIFCT, a collaboration between Facebook, Microsoft, Twitter, and YouTube. The forum has stated its intention to focus on technology-driven solutions and partnership across the sector to tackle and remove terrorist and violent extremist content from their platforms.

Less information, however, is available on how to prevent the financial element of terrorism through their platforms, which is in large part because there is no formal financial crime reporting regulatory obligation, beyond those in almost all countries outlawing the provision of "material support or resources" to individuals or groups designated, proscribed, or sanctioned as terrorists. This contrasts sharply with the financial services industry, which has experienced significant enforcement action for failing to comply with sanctions issued by the UN or national bodies such as the U.S. Treasury Department's Office of Foreign Assets Control.[107] Given the extent to which social media tools provide a platform for these sanctioned groups and individuals, this apparent failure to place social media companies under a similar regime of responsibility to that experienced by financial institutions would appear to be a significant oversight. For example, the Camstoll Group highlights that despite being subject to U.S. and UN sanctions designations, terrorist financiers Shafi al-Ajmi, Hajjaj al-Ajmi, and Abd al-Rahman al-Anizi ensured that via social media their fund-raising beneficiaries continued to receive support from their co-facilitators who still used the designated individual's profiles to assist with soliciting donations.[108]

Strengthening the Status Quo

As David Cohen has noted, "fundraisers can now use social media handles instead of face-to-face solicitations, and sympathetic donors can bypass a risky rendezvous in favor of a simple and remote hashtag search."[109] The extent to which social media has changed the TF landscape argues for an urgent reassessment of the status quo. Traditional approaches to tackling TF were developed following 9/11, in a time before the proliferation of social media. Indeed, Facebook and Twitter were not created until 2004 and 2006, respectively.

We therefore propose the following approaches to tackling the increasing prevalence of social media as a TF tool:

- **Multilateral and domestic organizations** issuing sanctions should ensure that social media companies and related social media activity are covered by designations. Social media can clearly be exploited by terrorist groups for fund-raising purposes and should thus be explicitly covered by TF-related designations, including social media handles and account names. Furthermore, those that promote the social media feeds of sanctioned individuals should likewise be subject to sanction.
- It would appear that the payment platforms of **social media companies** endeavor to comply with regulations to ensure customers are not using their services for financial crime. However, the compliance of **social media companies** with domestic or internationally mandated sanctions regimes by closing down accounts identified as related to designated individuals and entities appears limited. While continued operation of accounts may assist with intelligence gathering in some cases, the prevalence of accounts remaining active long-after their owners are sanctioned seems unlikely to explain all apparent oversights. In addition, those that promote designated individuals and entities should also have their accounts closed as their support is arguably "material" and therefore in contravention of sanctions legislation.
- While it is positive that the major platforms have established the GIFCT, little has been said regarding the responsibility of platforms to comply with CTF. **Social media companies** must demonstrate greater commitment to terrorism reporting and sanctions designations programs. The definition of "terrorist financing" has been increasingly broadly drawn to include the provision of support or assistance. For example, the United Kingdom's Terrorism Act 2000 imposes a duty of disclosure on anyone who "believes or suspects that another person has committed a [terrorist fund-raising] offense."[110] Broad definitions of TF suggest that terrorist-related fund-raising campaigns via social media should be reported to the authorities as "suspicious transactions."
- **Social media companies** need to demonstrate ownership of the risk of their platforms being abused for TF purposes. First, lessons should be learned from the approach taken to require Internet service providers to "expeditiously" remove content related to child pornography from their sites if they wish to be protected from liability.[111] Similar responsibilities should apply to TF-related material. Second, **social media companies** should form active information-sharing and partnership mechanisms that ensure that those that are identified as abusing their services are made known to other providers and disrupted from moving to other social media platforms.

- **Crowd-funding platforms** should also be included in these initiatives to strengthen the overall integrity of the digital fund-raising space.
- In line with FATF's Recommendation 15, **national regulatory authorities** need to demonstrate that they are alert to the TF risks posed by all forms of new technology, including social media. For example, they should ensure that social media companies are filing suspicious transaction reports with regard to the financial transactions they facilitate through their payment platforms.
- **Security authorities** should take advantage of the prevalence of social media not only to promote counternarratives but, where legislation allows, create covert social media profiles, and fund-raising campaigns that attract TF supporters in order to identify key funders and promoters of financing campaigns. Similar techniques have been used successfully to tackle child sexual exploitation.[112] While social media can indeed avoid "risky rendezvous" it can also encourage bad actors to display their allegiance and support in public, a vulnerability that security authorities can exploit. The early 2017 direction, reportedly from ISIL to its supporters forbidding the use of social media sites, highlights this vulnerability.[113] Furthermore, the ability to map networks of supporters and their activities within social media is powerful. It is thus possible to identify networks and disrupt their fund-raising activity by suspending their accounts and remaining alert to signs that they have opened new accounts to which supporters are directing previous followers. In addition, where fund-raising campaigns are identified, **security authorities** should seek to covertly solicit the associated bank account details to support counterterrorism operations.
- Although the responsibility for monitoring terrorist finance–related social media content lies with the social media companies themselves, **financial institutions** should also endeavor to monitor open-source social media activity to identify financial activity that they can potentially block or report. SOCMINT gathered must, however, be corroborated by traditional forms of intelligence due to the caveats that we have already addressed regarding the validity and reliability of information found online. They should also be aware that the accounts terrorist financiers use for social media–based funding campaigns are likely to be regional banks to which global banks are exposed via correspondent relationships.
- As previously noted, there are no official statistics that reference the proportion of TF that is conducted through social media. **Quantifying the challenge would strengthen the case** that social media platforms should take greater ownership of the issue. It is thus crucial that more research into the linkages is undertaken, starting with content that the social media companies themselves have identified and taken down.
- And finally, as with all security issues that cross over between the public and private sectors, **greater collaboration and partnership is needed**. In a number of countries, public–private information-sharing partnerships are being established to enable a more effective response to financial crime. The Joint Money Laundering Intelligence Taskforce (JMLIT) in the United Kingdom and the Fintel Alliance in Australia are two such examples.[114] A forum that promotes greater information sharing between law enforcement, social media companies,

and financial institutions would significantly strengthen the integrity of the system against abuse for TF.

Conclusion

The power of social media to communicate news, advertising, or propaganda rapidly and broadly is immense. The use of social media has transformed the ability of terrorist groups to garner online supporters, some of whose actions have extended to leaving their homes to join *jihadi* groups in Syria, Iraq, and elsewhere or conducting acts of murderous violence in their own countries. Social media has also allowed terrorist groups to attract funding from those that either wish to support their cause or those who, via the support of seemingly worthy charitable organizations, have made unwitting donations.

In contrast to the banking sector that is legally obliged to deploy resources in an effort to identify, report, and disrupt TF, social media companies face far less onerous responsibilities. Indeed, many question the commitment of social media companies to limiting the use to which terrorist groups put their services.[115]

The research conducted to date into the use of social media by terrorist groups has focused substantially on its effective exploitation for the purposes of recruitment, promoting ideology, and spreading propaganda, and on the efforts made by governments to use social media as a means of promoting a counternarrative. Study of the extent to which social media is deployed as a TF tool is limited, a failing that we believe is shortsighted. Although individual terrorist attacks may be cheap to conduct, in order to grow and sustain, terrorist organizations need funding. The apparent failure to document and quantify the extent to which terrorists accrue funding via social media, and address this financing route with the same rigor that is applied to other, more established funding approaches are a gap and vulnerability that need to be addressed.

Notes

1. David Omand, Jamie Bartlett, and Carl Miller, "Introducing Social Media Intelligence (SOCMINT)," *Intelligence and National Security* 27, no. 6 (2012): 801–823.
2. "French-British Action Plan: Internet Security," French-British Action Plan: Internet Security—GOV.UK, https://www.gov.uk/government/publications/french-british-action-plan-internet-security (accessed 19 June 2017).
3. "Launch of Global Internet Forum to Counter Terrorism—Tech Against Terrorism," *Techagainstterrorism.Org*, https://www.techagainstterrorism.org/2017/07/26/launch-of-global-internet-forum-to-counter-terrorism/ (accessed 11 December 2017).
4. Ali Fisher, "How Jihadist Networks Maintain a Persistent Online Presence," *Perspectives on Terrorism* 9, no. 3 (2015); Nico Prucha and Ali Fisher, "Tweeting for the Caliphate: Twitter as the New Frontier for Jihadist Propaganda," *CTC Sentinel* 6, no. 6 (2013): 19–23; Scott Gates and Sukanya Podder, "Social Media, Recruitment, Allegiance and the Islamic State," *Perspectives on Terrorism* 9, no. 4 (2015).
5. United Nations Security Council Resolution 2178, http://www.un.org/en/sc/ctc/docs/2015/SCR%202178_2014_EN.pdf (accessed 20 June 2017).
6. United Nations Security Council Resolution 2368, http://unscr.com/en/resolutions/doc/2368 (accessed 20 June 2017).

7. "G7 Taormina Statement on the Fight against Terrorism and Violent Extremism." Consilium. 26 May 2017, http://www.consilium.europa.eu/en/press/press-releases/2017/05/26/statement-fight-against-terrorism/ (accessed 20 June 2017).
8. Ibid.
9. "Remarks of Under Secretary for Terrorism and Financial Intelligence David Cohen before the Center for aNew American Security on 'Confronting New Threats In Terrorist Financing.'" Treasury.Gov. https://www.treasury.gov/press-center/press-releases/Pages/jl2308.aspx (accessed 20 June 2017).
10. U.S. Department of the Treasury, "Treasury Designates Three Key Supporters of Terrorists in Syria and Iraq," https://www.treasury.gov/press-center/press-releases/Pages/jl2605.aspx (accessed 18 June 2017).
11. "Social Media Use in Law Enforcement: Crime Prevention and Investigative Activities Continue to Drive Usage," Lexis Nexis. November 2014, https://www.lexisnexis.com/risk/downloads/whitepaper/2014-social-media-use-in-law-enforcement.pdf (accessed 20 June 2017).
12. "Disrupting Financial Crime: Best Practice in Customer Due Diligence Among FinTechs." Fintech Fincrime Exchange. May, 2017, https://static1.squarespace.com/static/57ea58d4cd0f685ecfe1a0c4/t/5909a4bd2e69cf1c8523e29c/1493804231393/FFE+CDD+Paper_03052017.pdf (accessed 10 June 2017).
13. Bonnie Christian, "Facebook Messenger Bots Let You Send Money with TransferWise," WIRED, 21 February 2017. http://www.wired.co.uk/article/transferwise-launches-facebook-messenger-bot (accessed 20 June 2017).
14. Claire Zilman, "Facebook Just Made It Easier to Ask Friends for Charitable Donations." *Fortune.* http://fortune.com/2016/06/30/facebook-donations-fundraising-charitable-giving/ (accessed 30 June 2017).
15. Ben Fox Rubin, "Sorry GoFundMe. Facebook Wants to Steal Your Business, Too." CNET. 24 May 2017, https://www.cnet.com/uk/news/sorry-gofundme-facebook-wants-to-steal-your-business-too/ (accessed 18 June 2017).
16. Bruce Hoffman, *Inside Terrorism* (Rev. ed.) (New York: Columbia University Press, 2006).
17. "Social Media," Merriam-Webster, 2017, https://www.merriam-webster.com/dictionary/social%20media (accessed 5 January 2018).
18. The FATF is the body responsible for setting global standards against money laundering, terrorist financing, and proliferation finance.
19. "XI Special Recommendations," FATF. 2001, http://www.fatf-gafi.org/publications/fatfrecommendations/documents/ixspecialrecommendations.html (accessed 16 June 2017).
20. Kathryn L. Gardner, "Terrorism Defanged: The Financial Action Task Force and International Efforts to Capture Terrorist Finances," *Uniting against Terror: Cooperative Nonmilitary Responses to the Global Terrorist Threat*, in *Uniting Against Terror: Cooperative Nonmilitary Responses to the Global Terrorist Threat*, ed. David Cortight and George A. Lopez (Boston, MA: MIT Press, 2007), 159–186.
21. Thomas J. Biersteker and Sue E. Eckert, eds., *Countering the Financing of Terrorism* (New York: Routledge, 2007).
22. Mark Pieth, "Financing of Terrorism: Following the Money," in *Financing Terrorism* (Dortrecht: Springer Netherlands, 2002), 115–126.
23. Oldrich Bures, "Private Actors in the Fight against Terrorist Financing: Efficiency versus Effectiveness," *Studies in Conflict & Terrorism* 35, no. 10 (2012): 712–732.
24. Martin S. Navias, "Finance Warfare as a Response to International Terrorism," *The Political Quarterly* 73, no. s1 (2002): 57–79, in Lawrence Freedman, ed., *Superterrorism: Policy Responses* (London: Wiley-Blackwell, 2002).
25. Tom Keatinge and Florence Keen, "Lone-Actor and Small Cell Terrorist Attacks: A New Front in Counter-Terrorist Finance?" *RUSI Occasional Papers.* 2017.
26. Frédéric Lemieux and Fernanda Prates, "Entrepreneurial Terrorism: Financial Strategies, Business Opportunities, and Ethical Issues," *Police Practice and Research* 12, no. 5 (2011): 368–382.

27. Peter R. Neumann, "Don't Follow the Money," *Foreign Affairs*. 24 July 2017, https://www.foreignaffairs.com/articles/2017-06-13/dont-follow-money
28. Yasmeen Serhan, "The Killing of ISIS's Information Minister," *The Atlantic*, 16 September 2016, https://www.theatlantic.com/news/archive/2016/09/the-killing-of-isis-information-minister/500432/ (accessed 13 June 2017); Jeffrey Ghannam, "Social Media in the Arab World: Leading up to the Uprisings of 2011," *Center for International Media Assistance* 3 (2011): 19–34.
29. Nicholas Blanford, "On Facebook and Twitter, Spreading Revolution in Syria," *The Christian Science Monitor*, 8 April 2011, http://www.csmonitor.com/World/Middle-East/2011/0408/On-Facebook-and-Twitter-spreading-revolution-in-Syria (accessed 10 June 2017).
30. Charlie Winter, "*The Virtual'Caliphate": Understanding Islamic State's Propaganda Strategy* (London: Quilliam, 2015).
31. Brendan I. Koerner, "Why ISIS Is Winning the Social Media War," Wired. 1 May 2017, https://www.wired.com/2016/03/isis-winning-social-media-war-heres-beat/ (accessed 15 June 2017).
32. Yasmeen Serhan, "The Killing of ISIS's Information Minister," *The Atlantic*. 16 September 2016. 2017. https://www.theatlantic.com/news/archive/2016/09/the-killing-of-isis-information-minister/500432/ (accessed 13 June 2017).
33. Richard D. Waters, Emily Burnett, Anna Lamm, and Jessica Lucas, "Engaging Stakeholders through Social Networking: How Nonprofit Organizations are using Facebook," *Public Relations Review* 35, no. 2 (2009): 102–106; Gregory D Saxton and Lili Wang, "The Social Network Effect: The Determinants of Giving through Social Media," *Nonprofit and Voluntary Sector Quarterly* 43, no. 5 (2014): 850–868.
34. For example, the #NoMakeUpSelfie campaign run by Cancer Research UK raised £8 million in six days in 2014: "No-Makeup Selfies Raise £8m for Cancer Research UK in Six Days," *The Guardian*, 25 March 2014, https://www.theguardian.com/society/2014/mar/25/no-makeup-selfies-cancer-charity (accessed 18 December 2017).
35. "Charitable Giving Statistics in the United Kingdom," NPT Donor Advised Funds | National Philanthropic Trust, http://www.npt-uk.org/philanthropic-resources/uk-charitable-giving-statistics (3 January 2018).
36. Charitable Giving Statistics in the UK (as of 2015): "8 Ways to Boost Nonprofit Fundraising using Social Media," FrontStream, 7 February 2017, https://www.frontstream.com/8-ways-boost-nonprofit-fundraising-using-social-media/ (accessed 18 May 2017).
37. "Emerging Terrorist Finance Risks," FATF. October 2015, http://www.fatf-gafi.org/media/fatf/documents/reports/Emerging-Terrorist-Financing-Risks.pdf (accessed 18 June 2017).
38. Ibid., 30.
39. Aris Roussinos, "Jihad Selfies: These British Extremists in Syria Love Social Media," *Vice*, 5 December 2013, https://www.vice.com/en_us/article/syrian-jihadist-selfies-tell-us-a-lot-about-their-war (accessed 10 May 2017).
40. Shiraz Maher, "From Portsmouth to Kobane: The British Jihadis Fighting for Isis," *New Statesman*. http://www.newstatesman.com/2014/10/portsmouth-kobane (accessed 10 May 2017).
41. "Financing of Recruitment for Terrorist Purposes," FATF, January 2018, http://www.fatf-gafi.org/media/fatf/documents/reports/Financing-Recruitment-for-Terrorism.pdf (accessed 20 January 2018).
42. Wahyudi Soeriaatmadja, "Donations Via Social Media Now Main Source of Terrorism Funding in Indonesia," *The Straits Times*, 18 October 2017, http://www.straitstimes.com/asia/se-asia/donations-via-social-media-now-main-source-of-terrorism-funding-in-indonesia (accessed 3 January 2018).
43. Yaya Fanusie, "Terrorist Networks Eye Bitcoin as Cryptocurrency's Price Rises," *The Cipher Brief*, 20 December 2017, https://www.thecipherbrief.com/terrorist-networks-eye-bitcoin-cryptocurrencys-price-rises (accessed 3 January 2018).
44. "Emerging Terrorist Financing Risks," FATF: 31.

45. See for example, "... and wage *Jihad* with your wealth and your lives in the cause of God," Qur'an 9:41; "The ones who have believed, emigrated and striven in the cause of Allah with their wealth and their lives are greater in rank in the sight of God. And it is those who are the recipients of his reward," Qur'an 9:20.
46. Sahih al Bukhari 2843, Book 56, Hadith 59: https://sunnah.com/bukhari/56/59 (accessed 10 January 2018).
47. *Rumiyah*, Issue 1, 18.
48. Ibid., 18.
49. Elizabeth Dickinson, "Playing with Fire: Why Private Gulf Financing for Syria's Extremist Rebels Risks Igniting Sectarian Violence at Home," *Analysis Paper* 16.
50. Ben Hubbard, "Private Donors' Funds Add Wild Card to War in Syria," *The New York Times*, 12 November 2013, http://www.nytimes.com/2013/11/13/world/middleeast/private-donors-funds-add-wild-card-to-war-in-syria.html?_r=2 (accessed 15 May 2017).
51. Joby Warrick, "Private Donations Give Edge to Islamists in Syria, Officials Say," *Washington Post*, 21 September 2013, http://www.washingtonpost.com/world/national-security/private-donations-give-edge-to-islamists-in-syria-officials-say/2013/09/21/a6c783d2-2207-11e3-a358-1144dee636dd_story.html (accessed 12 May 2017).
52. Shankar Abha, "Social Media Emerges as a Valuable Terrorist Fundraising Tool," *Investigative Project on Terrorism*, 20 April 2016, https://www.investigativeproject.org/5314/social-media-emerges-as-a-valuable-terrorist# (accessed 30 May 2017).
53. "Use of Social Media by Terrorist Fundraisers & Financiers," The Camstoll Group, April 2016, https://www.camstoll.com/wp-content/uploads/2016/04/Social-Media-Report-4.22.16.pdf (accessed 11 June 2017).
54. Warrick, "Private Donations Give Edge to Islamists in Syria, Officials Say."
55. Ibid., 7. Note: as of May 2017, these accounts do now appear to be suspended.
56. "Material support" is a broadly defined legal term in U.S. law referring to support provided to designated terrorist groups. Full details can be found in title 18 of the United States Code, sections 2339A and 2339B.
57. "National Terrorist Financing Risk Assessment." 12 June 2015. U.S. Treasury Department, https://www.treasury.gov/resource-center/terrorist-illicit-finance/Documents/National%20Terrorist%20Financing%20Risk%20Assessment%20–%2006-12-2015.pdf (20 June 2017).
58. Philip Sherwell, "Babar Ahmad Sentenced to 12.5 Years for Supporting Islamic Terrorists," *The Telegraph*, 16 July 2014. http://www.telegraph.co.uk/news/worldnews/northamerica/usa/10971189/Babar-Ahmad-sentenced-to-12.5-years-for-supporting-Islamic-terrorists.html (16 July 2017).
59. Michael Taxay, "Trends in the Prosecution of Terrorist Financing and Facilitation," *United States Attorneys Bulletin* 62 (2014): 2.
60. Sherwell, "Babar Ahmad Sentenced to 12.5 Years for Supporting Islamic Terrorists."
61. Robert Verkaik, "The Trials of Babar Ahmad: From Jihad in Bosnia to a US Prison via Met Brutality," *The Observer*, 19 March 2016, https://www.theguardian.com/uk-news/2016/mar/12/babar-ahmad-jihad-bosnia-us-police-interview (accessed 3 January 2018).
62. "Terror Trial: Men who Helped Teen Go to Syria Jailed," BBC News. 10 February 2016, http://www.bbc.co.uk/news/uk-wales-south-east-wales-35491802 (accessed 3 January 2018).
63. John Roth, Douglas Greenburg, and Serena Wille, "National Commission on Terrorist Attacks Upon the United States," *Monograph on Terrorist Financing* (2004).
64. "Tackling Abuse and Mismanagement 2014–15—Full Report," https://www.gov.uk/government/publications/tackling-abuse-and-mismanagement-2014-15/tackling-abuse-and-mismanagement-2014-15-full-report (accessed 3 January 2018).
65. For a detailed examination of this issue, see Tom Keatinge, "Uncharitable Behaviour" (London: Demos, 2014); Victoria Metcalfe-Hough, Tom Keatinge, and Sara Pantuliano, "UK Humanitarian Aid in the Age of Counter-Terrorism: Perceptions and Reality" (Overseas Development Institute, 2015); Tom Keatinge and Florence Keen, "Humanitarian Action and Non-State Armed Groups: The Impact of Banking Restrictions on UK NGOs" (Chatham House, 2017); Peter Romaniuk and Tom Keatinge (forthcoming), "Protecting

Charities from Terrorists … and Counter Terrorists: FATF and the Global Effort to Prevent Terrorist Financing through the Non-Profit Sector," *Crime, Law and Social Change* (2018).

66. "FATF IX Special Recommendations," FATF, October 2001, http://www.fatf-gafi.org/media/fatf/documents/reports/FATF%20Standards%20-%20IX%20Special%20Recommendations%20and%20IN%20rc.pdf (accessed 2 January 2018).
67. "Terrorist Financing," FATF, 29 February 2008, www.fatf-gafi.org/media/fatf/documents/reports/FATF%20Terrorist%20Financing%20Typologies%20Report.pdf (accessed 14 June 2017).
68. For a good explanation of this growing awareness, see Ben Hayes, *Counter-Terrorism, "Policy Laundering' and the FATF: Legalising Surveillance, Regulating Civil Society.* Transnational Institute, 2012.
69. The FATF has produced a number of documents considering this issue and providing a more nuanced analysis of the challenge including: "Risk of Terrorist Abuse in Non-Profit Organisations," FATF, 18 June 2014, http://www.fatf-gafi.org/media/fatf/documents/reports/Risk-of-terrorist-abuse-in-non-profit-organisations.pdf (accessed 10 June 2017); "Best Practices Paper on Combating the Abuse of Non Profit Organisations," FATF, June 2015, http://www.fatf-gafi.org/media/fatf/documents/reports/BPP-combating-abuse-non-profit-organisations.pdf (accessed 18 May 2017).
70. "FATF Revises Recommendation 8." Global NPO Coalition on FATF. http://fatfplatform.org/announcement/fatf-revises-recommendation-8/ (2 June 2017).
71. U.S. Treasury Department, "National Terrorist Financing Risk Assessment" (2015).
72. Ibid., 16.
73. U.S. Department of the Treasury, "Remarks of Under Secretary for Terrorism and Financial Intelligence David Cohen before the Center for a New American Security on 'Confronting New Threats in Terrorist Financing,'" https://www.treasury.gov/press-center/press-releases/Pages/jl2308.aspx (accessed 3 January 2018).
74. Ibid.
75. "Daily Press Briefing: August 21, 2014." U.S. Department of State. 21 August 2014. https://2009-2017.state.gov/r/pa/prs/dpb/2014/08/230798.htm (3 January 2018).
76. For example, see Elizabeth J. Shapiro, "The Holy Land Foundation for Relief and Development: A Case Study," *United States Attorneys Bulletin* 62 (2014): 23.
77. For example, in 2011 U.K. police and security forces uncovered a plot to detonate explosives across Birmingham. Physical surveillance revealed that the architects of the plot had financed themselves by posing as charity workers for Muslim Aid, gathering £12,000 in donations. See Dominic Casciani, "Terror Plot: Jail Terms for Birmingham Bomb Plotters," BBC News. 26 April 2013, http://www.bbc.co.uk/news/uk-22290927 (accessed 15 May 2017).
78. Provided by Germany to the FATF report, "Emerging Terrorist Financing Risks" (2015).
79. U.S. Department of the Treasury, United States and Saudi Arabia Designate Terrorist Fundraising and Support Networks, https://www.treasury.gov/press-center/press-releases/Pages/jl0400.aspx (accessed 18 May 2018).
80. As of 30 May 2017, the Twitter accounts @YaqubRWO and @AlRahmahWelfare were both still active although had not posted content since respectively 31 December 2015 and 2 April 2016.
81. "Emerging Terrorist Financing Risks," FATF: 31.
82. Roth et al., "National Commission on Terrorist Attacks Upon the United States,"
83. "UK National Risk Assessment of Money Laundering and Terrorist Financing," October 2015. HM Treasury & Home Office, https://www.gov.uk/government/uploads/system/uploads/attachment_data/file/468210/UK_NRA_October_2015_final_web.pdf (accessed 11 June 2017).
84. "UK National Risk Assessment of Money Laundering and Terrorist Financing" October 2017. HM Treasury & Home Office, https://www.gov.uk/government/uploads/system/uploads/attachment_data/file/655198/National_risk_assessment_of_money_laundering_and_terrorist_financing_2017_pdf_web.pdf (accessed 10 November 2017).

85. Susan McDonald, "Islamic State 'using Social Media to Crowdfund Terrorist Activities,'" ABC News, 16 November 2015, http://www.abc.net.au/news/2015-11-17/is-using-social-media-to-crowdfund-terrorist-activities/6948374 (accessed 1 June 2018).
86. Alexandra Posadzki, "Hard to identify Crowdfunding Platforms Financing Terrorism," Thestar.com. 18 May 2017, https://www.thestar.com/business/2017/05/18/hard-to-identify-crowdfunding-platforms-financing-terrorism.html (accessed 3 January 2018).
87. Elizabeth Bodine-Baron, "Fighting the Islamic State on Social Media," RAND Corporation, 11 October 2016, https://www.rand.org/blog/2016/10/fighting-the-islamic-state-on-social-media.html (10 June 2018).
88. "How Israel Spots Lone-Wolf Attackers," *The Economist*, 8 June 2017, http://www.economist.com/news/international/21723113-algorithms-monitor-social-media-posts-palestinians-how-israel-spots-lone-wolf-attackers (17 June 2017).
89. Interview conducted with private sector official.
90. For further details, see Recommendations 20, and accompanying Interpretative Note, of the FATF Recommendations.
91. United Nations, *International Convention for the Suppression of the Financing of Terrorism*, December 1999, http://treaties.un.org/doc/db/Terrorism/english-18-11.pdf.
92. United Nations, *United Nations Treaty Collection*, 2012, http://treaties.un.org/Pages/ViewDetails.aspx?src=IND&mtdsg_no=XVIII-11&chapter=18&lang=en (12 June 2018).
93. Tom Keatinge, "Identifying Foreign Terrorist Fighters: The Role of Public-Private Partnership, Information Sharing and Financial Intelligence," RUSI Occasional Papers (2015).
94. Roth et al., "National Commission on Terrorist Attacks Upon the United States," 58.
95. Richard Barrett, "Preventing the Financing of Terrorism," *Case Western Reserve Journal of International Law* 44, no. 3 (2013), 730.
96. For a full description of the U.K.'s JMLIT, see http://www.nationalcrimeagency.gov.uk/about-us/what-we-do/economic-crime/joint-money-laundering-intelligence-taskforce-jmlit
97. See for example the UK Investigatory Powers Act 2016, para. 89.
98. Interview conducted by author.
99. FATF, "FATF Guidance: Politically Exposed Persons" (Recommendations 12 and 22) (2013).
100. Elizabeth Thompson, "Large Cash Transactions Alert Authorities to Look at Your Facebook, Social Media," CBCnews, 12 March 2017, http://www.cbc.ca/news/politics/facebook-twitter-privacy-moneylaundering-1.4020638 (accessed 16 June 2017).
101. "Disrupting Financial Crime: Best Practice in Customer Due Diligence Among FinTechs," Fintech Fincrime Exchange.
102. NPCC Digital Policing http://www.npcc.police.uk/NPCCBusinessAreas/ReformandTransformation/Digitalpolicing.aspx (accessed 22 June 2017) and Metropolitan Police Digital Policing Strategy 2017–2020. February 2017, 2017. https://beta.met.police.uk/globalassets/downloads/about-the-met/one-met-digital-policing-strategy-2017-2020.pdf (accessed 20 June 2017)
103. "Government TOS Reports," Twitter, https://transparency.twitter.com/en/gov-tos-reports.html (23 February 2018).
104. Natalie Andrews and Deepa Seetharaman, "Facebook Steps Up Efforts Against Terrorism," *The Wall Street Journal*, 11 February 2016, https://www.wsj.com/articles/facebook-steps-up-efforts-against-terrorism-1455237595 (accessed 9 June 2017).
105. Interview conducted by the author.
106. Monika Bickert and Brian Fishman, "Hard Questions: Are We Winning the War On Terrorism Online?" Facebook Newsroom, https://newsroom.fb.com/news/2017/11/hard-questions-are-we-winning-the-war-on-terrorism-online// (accessed 4 December 2017).
107. See, for example, "BNP Paribas Agrees to Plead Guilty and to Pay $8.9 Billion for Illegally Processing Financial Transactions for Countries Subject to U.S. Economic Sanctions," The United States Department of Justice, 30 June 2014, http://www.justice.gov/opa/pr/bnp-paribas-agrees-plead-guilty-and-pay-89-billion-illegally-processing-financial (accessed 3

January 2018) and "HSBC Holdings Plc. and HSBC Bank USA N.A. Admit to Anti-Money Laundering and Sanctions Violations, Forfeit $1.256 Billion in Deferred Prosecution Agreement," The United States Department of Justice, 11 December 2012, http://www.justice.gov/opa/pr/hsbc-holdings-plc-and-hsbc-bank-usa-na-admit-anti-money-laundering-and-sanctions-violations (accessed 3 January 2018).

108. "Use of Social Media by Terrorist Fundraisers & Financiers," The Camstoll Group: 4–5
109. Cohen, "Remarks of Under Secretary for Terrorism and Financial Intelligence David Cohen before the Center for a New American Security on 'Confronting New Threats In Terrorist Financing.'"
110. Terrorism Act 2000, 9.
111. See for example, European Commission (2016), *Report from the Commission to the European Parliament and the Council Assessing the Implementation of the Measures Referred to in Article 25 of Directive 2011/93/EU of 13 December 2011 on Combating the Sexual Abuse and Sexual Exploitation of Children and Child Pornography.*
112. For example, Norfolk Police in the United Kingdom have run operations where officers go undercover in online forums and chatrooms to identify and disrupt offenders, http://www.apccs.police.uk/latest_news/apcc-response-first-tranche-bids-awarded-funding-201718-police-transformation-fund/?cookie_dismiss=true
113. As translated by Aymenn al-Tamimi, the proclamation states "The enemies of the religion have adopted all means to penetrate the ranks of the monotheists, get in on their secrets and among those means is social media, for the spread of the use of these sites among the soldiers of the Islamic State has great harm on the group, especially as they are ignorant that it was established by the enemies of God and His Messenger and it is monitored night and day. For so many mujahideen have been killed because of it and so many bases have been destroyed. Therefore beginning from the date of this statement for distribution, it is absolutely forbidden to use social media sites, and every violator will expose himself to inquiry and being held accountable.: See Aymenn Jawad Al-Tamimi, "Archive of Islamic State Administrative Documents (Continued… Again)," http://www.aymennjawad.org/2016/09/archive-of-islamic-state-administrative-documents-2 (accessed 9 June 2017).
114. For a full description of the UK's JMLIT, see http://www.nationalcrimeagency.gov.uk/about-us/what-we-do/economic-crime/joint-money-laundering-intelligence-taskforce-jmlit; and for the Fintel Alliance see: www.austrac.gov.au/about-us/austrac/fintel-alliance
115. "Tech Giants are under Fire for Facilitating Terrorism," *The Economist*, 8 June 2017, https://www.economist.com/news/international/21723106-some-criticism-unfair-there-more-they-could-do-tech-giants-are-under-fire (accessed 10 June 2017).

A Storm on the Horizon? "Twister" and the Implications of the Blockchain and Peer-to-Peer Social Networks for Online Violent Extremism

Gareth Mott

ABSTRACT

"Twister," developed by Miguel Freitas, is a social network platform centered around micro-blogging, much like Twitter. However, rather than relying on centralized servers owned and maintained by a single firm, Twister users operate a blockchain combined with distributed hash table (DHT)–like and BitTorrent-like protocols to both make posts and send private messages, and also to receive entries from other users. Twister's *raison d'etre* is that it offers a social networking platform that cannot be censored and cannot itself censor. The software does not record the Internet Protocol addresses users use to access the service, nor does it notify other users of an account's online/offline status. Growing adoption of blockchain services means that it is possible that the concept of decentralized social networks could become a norm. It is suggested in this article that blockchain-based peer-to-peer social networks present challenges to the current counterextremist practices for content removal and censorship. While there are methods to disrupt usage of blockchain-based peer-to-peer services, these approaches may have the net harm of curtailing bona fide use of legal and novel technologies. Given this opportunity cost, non-transitory online violent extremist content may need to be tolerated.

While the online social media landscape is today dominated by technology giants, such as Facebook with its roughly 1.94 billion monthly users,[1] this does not necessitate that the centralized, advertising revenue model of social networking will remain the norm. This centralized architecture, in which a service is offered in exchange for valuable data, is not the only viable means for social interaction and virtual community building mediated via the Internet. A social media space does not need to be hosted at a centralized Web domain. The World Wide Web *is* already decentralized; indeed, decentralization and resilience are core tenets of the Web's *raison d'etre*. If the contemporary Web can be described as "centralized," this is socially constructed, rather than preordained.

Using Miguel Freitas's novel micro-blogging social network "Twister" as a case study, this article considers the challenges that are presented by peer-to-peer blockchain-based social networks to the counterextremism practice of content removal. The article is divided into four sections. The first section draws from the existing literature on violent extremist usage of social media to highlight: the extent to which violent extremists are deemed to be interested in using social media generally; the effectiveness of counterextremist measures against this usage; and the propensity of violent extremists to migrate to social media services where such counterextremist measures become more difficult. The second section details the unique aspects of Twister's methods for user registration and content dissemination. The third section examines the utility of peer-to-peer, blockchain-based microblogging for violent extremists. Last, the fourth section considers viable means by which state-based authorities could attempt to mitigate violent extremist activity on such networks, and suggests that a transition from content *removal* to content *contention* may be necessary.

Violent Extremism and Social Media: Existing Literature

A considerable literature exploring the utility of Web communication, particularly social media, platforms for violent extremists already exists. However, this is a developing field and research gaps are present. In particular, as Conway has identified, there has been a general focus on particular online violent extremist content, but "not its producers or consumers, *distribution mechanisms*, or its functioning and effects."[2] Similar sentiment had been expressed by Zelin, who argued that research on the "conduits" through which violent extremist material is disseminated has been insufficient.[3] It is in this context that this article is written. It is useful, it is argued herein, to consider the utility of peer-to-peer, blockchain-based social networks for violent extremists because violent extremists have expressed interest in alternative social media. It is also useful to consider the means by which other users of alternative social media and counterextremist agencies could mitigate the use of such an online communication platform for violent extremist purposes.

It is suggested in this article that Twister is a novel platform for creating virtual communities and disseminating content because of the challenge of censoring material hosted on it. Nevertheless, from a violent extremist perspective, Twister as a microblogging service shares some limitations of online communication platforms more broadly. As Burke suggests, social media can be used to facilitate propaganda dissemination and can provoke people to offer financial support, but it will not kinetically alter on-the-ground power relations in a given violent conflict.[4] Power exhibited among a given online virtual community does not, by default, automatically translate to "real" power.[5] It is also worth recognizing that access to the Internet and social media services is not universal. In some cases, not only violent extremists but general populations may be prohibited from accessing social media because of restrictive local laws, the absence of affordable Internet service provision, or indeed a dearth of reliable electricity.[6]

Nonetheless, violent extremists are unlikely to use social media arbitrarily. It has been suggested elsewhere that violent extremists use Internet-mediated virtual communities for the planning of terrorist attacks,[7] for recruiting personnel,[8] establishing the possibility of a leaderless organization,[9] and for teaching recruits in "virtual classrooms."[10] Social media could be said to have lowered the cost of participating in violent extremist and terrorist activity,[11] even if cases of self-recruitment as a result of purely online content consumption could be considered rare.[12] At the very least, for a violent extremist, the acquisition of online "followers" and the receipt of supportive messages from them is likely to provide a sense of political or ideological validation that, under certain circumstances, may be less forthcoming in their immediate "real world" circles.[13] With text-based online mediums composed of information rather than matter, distinctions of identity and imbalances of power are "deferred, if not effaced"; as Peter Steiner captured in his *New Yorker* cartoon, on the Internet, nobody knows you're a dog.[14]

While violent extremist individuals and groups have precedent in maintaining Web presences through the use of dedicated basic hypertext markup language websites and forums, today such groups may span several networks and social media platforms.[15] In 2016, Europol's Internet Referral Unit noted that they had identified in excess of seventy platforms used by terrorist organizations to spread propaganda materials.[16] Separate two-day joint Europol operations in 2017 identified violent extremist content disseminated across forty-one and fifty-two platforms, respectively.[17] In 2018, the United Kingdom's Home Office revealed that Islamic State supporters had been found to use in excess of 400 online platforms during 2017.[18] These findings would suggest that the dissemination of violent extremist online material relies on an increasingly diverse ecosystem. The hosting of a dedicated website or forum posed some drawbacks. For instance, even prior to the Snowden revelations in 2012, it is known that violent extremists were aware that their online spaces were likely to be monitored and they conditioned their own behavior on this basis.[19] Users of some dedicated forums were warned against posting sensitive information on how to travel to a conflict zone, or construct an explosive, unless this was considered to already exist in the public domain.[20] Forcible seizure of a server by law enforcement can reveal not only the content of forum messages and blog posts, but also private messages between users. It has been noted elsewhere that for violent extremists, the maintenance of a stable, persistent Web presence has proven challenging.[21]

For the violent extremist, outsourcing their Web presence to popular social media platforms does not guarantee a persistent online presence. Research in this field has, for example, shown that violent extremist accounts on Twitter have become increasingly transitory. When Berger and Morgan analyzed 20,000 Islamic State–supporting Twitter accounts in the period September 2014 to January 2015, they found that just 3.4 percent of these accounts were suspended over the five months.[22] Conversely, Conway et al.'s *Disrupting Daesh* report analyzing Islamic State–supporting accounts and broader *jihad*-supporting accounts operational on Twitter between 1 February and 7 April 2017 highlighted that Twitter's anti-extremist operations had gained significant traction since 2014, with conservatively 65 percent of Islamic State–supporting accounts suspended during this period.[23] The authors noted that by April 2017, Islamic State–supporting Twitter accounts had increasingly adopted meaningless usernames of jumbled letters and numbers, and either left their avatars as the default "egg" or uploaded a benign image.[24] Conway et al. proposed that Islamic State supporters were likely to be migrating their operations to Telegram, given that "a conscious, supportive and influential virtual community" had become "almost impossible to maintain"[25] on Twitter. Far-right extreme groups have also experienced censorship and account suspension on Twitter's services, following changes to the Twitter User Agreement that came into force on 18 December 2017.[26]

It is in this context—a hardening social media environment for the outspoken violent extremist—that this article is written. Telegram, an encrypted communication program released in 2013 for smartphones and computers is, of course, not the only alternative to the dominant communication platforms that has attracted interest from violent extremists. One notable alternative social media platform is Diaspora, which launched in 2010. Diaspora is a distributed social networking service that allows users to establish their own "pods," which can either be public or closed. Control of the content hosted on a given pod is governed by the owner of the server, known as the "podmin." In August 2014, it was reported on the Diaspora blog that an unspecified number of Islamic State–supporting accounts had been established on the main Diaspora pod, "JoinDiaspora.com," as well as other pods on the Diaspora network.[27] From the perspective of the violent extremist, however, Diaspora inherits limitations shared by the more prominent mainstream centralized social media networks. The "podmin" of a Diaspora server has read and write privileges over unencrypted data of the users on their pod. While this issue may be partially assuaged in the case of a closed Diaspora pod operated by an individual empathetic to a given violent extremist cause, it remains that their server is a fixed and vulnerable point of attack or seizure by law enforcement. Furthermore, the continued and uninterrupted operation of a given pod relies on the continual operation of the podmin's server. Bielenberg et al. "crawled" the Diaspora network between June and November 2011, and found that over 35 percent of the servers that they pinged were never online across the period of 150 days, half of the servers had less than 50 percent uptime, and only the top 20 percent of servers were able to maintain an uptime in excess of 90 percent.[28] A hypothetical pod that is amenable to a violent extremist presence may not be able to foster a vibrant virtual community if it is not able to sustain a persistent uptime. Were a given pod to unexpectedly go offline, users might assume that the server had been seized by law enforcement and may therefore not entrust it with their proscribed communications if it were to return online.

Diaspora and Twister are two alternative social media networks among many. Sharing similarities with Diaspora, Mastodon[29] is a "federated" social media microblogging network. Scuttlebutt is a social network that uses a Bitcoin-like blockchain to register users similarly to Twister's model.[30]

Twister—or a similar alternative—may offer a partial fix for this inherent tradeoff of privacy, trust, and persistence that violent extremists engage with in order to sustain online virtual communities. Twister's implementation consciously adopted the microblogging format that has made Twitter a popular "universalised"[31] form of online communication. Unlike Diaspora, however, Twister's network is not compartmentalized into independently run servers. Instead, each Twister user operates a "node" that helps to ensure the continued persistence of the network. Twister offers an encrypted platform for the construction of virtual communities with no single point of attack. The next section describes the technologies that have made a peer-to-peer, blockchain-based social network possible and have given rise to potential virtual communities built on what can be termed "trustless trust."

Twister, BitTorrent, and the Blockchain

One of the core technologies that enables Twister to function as a fully decentralized, continually operational social network is the "blockchain." While Twister's blockchain is patched and unique to the social network, other blockchains exist. Indeed, among other uses, blockchains can be used to share data between health providers and indefinitely store contracts and land registries.[32] However, the seminal utility of the blockchain was demonstrated by Bitcoin. In October 2008, someone—or several persons—using the pseudonym "Satoshi Nakamoto" posted a white paper to the Cryptography Mailing list. This white paper detailed the outline of a digital currency called "Bitcoin."[33] Bitcoin, which is essentially a computer program, serves two core functions: first, it is an electronic commodity, and second, it is an open source protocol for pseudo-anonymous trading. While other digital currencies have existed, it was the blockchain that made Bitcoin unique. Bitcoin's blockchain is a distributed public ledger of all transactions that have ever occurred via the Bitcoin protocol. Bitcoins are not printed or distributed by a central bank in the same way that fiat currencies are produced; instead, a computer algorithm ensures that new Bitcoins are created roughly every ten minutes. "Miners" compete for these freshly minted Bitcoins with their computing power, by directing their machines to multiply large numbers in the search for a unique "hash."[34] These miners serve two core functions for the Bitcoin protocol; first, their mining power serves to secure the existence of the network, and second, each successful "hash" that they find creates a new "block" on the blockchain. Each new block incorporates transactions that Bitcoin users are attempting to make, and once a transaction is included into a block and disseminated across the Bitcoin network it is considered "confirmed."

Initially, miners were rewarded with fifty Bitcoins for each block that they successfully generated; however, over time, this reward "halves," until eventually, in around the year 2140, the finite limit of 21 million mined Bitcoins will have been reached and no more can be generated.[35] Miners are currently rewarded with twelve Bitcoins, and the next "halving" is set to occur in 2020. Given that, at the time of writing, a Bitcoin trades for around $15,283,[36] there is a substantial motivation for Bitcoin miners to outcompete their competitors. The extent of this mining competition, which substantially secures the network, is relatively exceptional. As will be detailed later, the incentive to mine the Twister network is exponentially lower. During the outset of Bitcoin's introduction, when a Bitcoin would have been worth fractions of a cent, it was possible to successfully mine blocks with the CPU of a domestic laptop or desktop computer. Competition for reward Bitcoins produced an arms race of computing power, however, which caused miners to begin using graphics cards for their mining operations, until these were replaced by purpose-built "ASICs,"[37] industrial computers whose sole purpose is to churn out as many hash calculations as their silicon permits. Today it is impossible to profitably mine Bitcoins with a non-ASIC machine. The mining "difficulty"[38] has to increase to match the computing power of the network, so that the roughly ten-minute rate of block generation can be maintained. In February 2018, the hash rate of the entire network is in excess of 21.5 trillion GH/s; in the same month the year before, it was just over 3.1 trillion GH/s.[39] Concentrated in regions that offer low ambient temperatures and inexpensive electricity—notably mountainous China[40] and Chelan County in Washington State, USA[41]—the electricity demanded by global computing power underpinning the Bitcoin network is said to exceed the energy consumption of Nigeria or the Republic of Ireland.[42] The computational power underpinning the Twister network is exponentially lower.[43] As will be discussed later with reference to two mining experiments conducted by this author, the low difficulty democratizes the ability to benefit from Twister's mining reward implementation, but also makes Twister's blockchain theoretically easier to corrupt.

Twister is a social network developed by Miguel Freitas and released in 2014. It is currently at the "beta" stage of live development, but is freely available to download, compile, and use.[44] Twister is a microblogging platform that shares similarities with the model offered by Twitter; users can upload character-limited posts for other users to view, "follow" other users, read their posts, and send direct messages between themselves. However, rather than relying on centralized servers to record user activity and disseminate content, Twister is novel in that it uses the blockchain, Kademlia-like DHT, and BitTorrent-like protocols to connect users and distribute data between them. A DHT is a decentralized distribution system that provides a lookup service between nodes; in this case each Twister user represents a unique node. The BitTorrent protocol facilitates a peer-to-peer network for disseminating computer files, including but not limited to: music, films, software, and 3-D printing designs.[45] Computer scientists had, for some time, sought to implement bona fide peer-to-peer networks.[46] However, overcoming the challenges of data storage and user authentication had proven challenging. Three years into its lifespan, the Twister network purportedly comprises 1,819,510 posts, or "twists."[47]

In order to function as a virtual community in which posts are tied to specific accounts, a social network has to record a given identity for its users. This serves two purposes. First, if a user has registered a particular username, they do not have to register a unique identity each time that they access the service or post content. Second, registering a given username prevents other users from using the same identity and falsely posting content under the guise of another user. Rather than registering usernames to a central database, the Twister network uses its own blockchain to keep the records. Accordingly, when a user installs the software onto their computer and has downloaded the full copy of the blockchain, they can input a username that they would like to use, which their "node" will check against the blockchain. If the username is available, the name is broadcast to other nodes on the Twister network, and the user waits until the name is included in a "block." A private encryption key is generated and stored on the user's hard drive; this private key provides the user access to their account in much the same way that a Bitcoin user retains access to their wallet addresses. The private key can be copied by the user and used on other devices to access the same account. Once the username is included into a block, this block is disseminated across the network and other nodes will become aware of the account's existence. Unlike Bitcoin, there is no direct financial incentive for miners to expend electricity and computational power to generate blocks. However, miners on the Twister network are rewarded by entering a lottery for free advertising. These free adverts are disseminated to all nodes, although a user should only encounter one such advert in any given 24-hour period.

The Twister network blockchain would be an inefficient means of distributing post content. Were the blockchain used as the content database, all users would have to indiscriminately download a potentially very large blockchain, irrespective of whether they were interested posts' content. Using the blockchain for content dissemination would also be unsatisfactory for users who wish to post and access content instantaneously, given that posts would need to wait for a new block to be generated before being accepted by the network. Instead, Kademlia-like DHT and BitTorrent-like protocols are used; when a user sends a request to view a given user's feed, the content should be received almost instantly. There is some precedent for violent extremist usage of the BitTorrent protocol. Violent extremists have used the BitTorrent protocol to access and disseminate extremist material, ideological documents, and guidance manuals for bomb-making.[48] It is also worth noting that micro-blogging is not the only utility that is made possible through the combination of blockchain and BitTorrent technology. "Zeronet" is a peer-to-peer, blockchain-based network for the hosting of static and dynamic websites.[49] Instead of associating a website with a given Internet Protocol (IP) address, websites that are hosted on the Zeronet network are associated with public addresses listed on the blockchain; much like the public-facing addresses of a Bitcoin wallet. So long as at least one computer is "seeding" a given Zeronet webpage, other users will be able to access it. In theory, Zeronet offers the possibility of technical resilience against traditional means of pressure for content removal, such as Digital Millennium Copyright Act (DMCA) takedown notices. Samata Ullah—jailed in the United Kingdom in May 2017 on five terrorism offenses including membership of Islamic State and the preparation of terrorist acts—had admitted researching Zeronet and had authored a blog hosted on the network.[50]

Miguel Freitas, Twister's creator, has noted in interviews that while he is fond of Twitter and actively uses its services,[51] he became concerned that its utility for quickly disseminating information during a potential future Brazilian riot could be reduced if the Brazilian state or Twitter itself decided that it would be expedient to shut down the free flow of information. Freitas expressed similar alarm about the British government's rhetoric regarding Internet communication freedom amid the 2011 London riots.[52] For Freitas, the notion of curtailing information flows was "totally against the idea of the internet, where you are supposed to have no single point of failure."[53]

Twister is a technical solution to resist blocking and censorship of online content and communications. The technical novelty of a blockchain-based peer-to-peer network proffers some legal considerations. Because it does not rely on central hosting by a unitary entity, there is no single figure or organization for authorities to pursue for content removal. Twister's source code is released and distributed under a Massachusetts Institute of Technology and Berkeley Software Distribution (MIT/BSD) license.[54] This, the creator has suggested, protects Twister "from most, if not all legal procedures meant to shut it down."[55] The source code could not be made illegal, and even if legal action were to be pursued against the network's creator, the network would continue to function as a court could not successfully enforce its shutdown. Enforcing legal measures against open-source peer-to-peer blockchain technology in general may be impracticable, whether the blockchain is for the Twister, Zeronet, Bitcoin, Ethereum, Litecoin, or indeed other network. In order for there to be potential for successful enforcement against a disseminated blockchain, "joint liability" would need to be introduced and imposed.[56] As Low and Teo point out, however, such enforcement would be highly impractical, because copies of a given blockchain are likely to be held across multiple jurisdictions, and users cannot be obligated to update their copy to a particular version.[57] As has been demonstrated by the experience of the Ethereum cryptocurrency, two or more communities operating nodes on a blockchain can use differing code to force a "hard fork."[58] However, a hard fork on a given network does not overwrite an original blockchain with a new one; the new and old blockchains can continue operating independently with separate communities of nodes adhering to different code.

The Twister network does not have a central administrator who can delete user accounts or suspend their ability to make posts, send private messages, and commit computational power to compete for advertising. Furthermore, unlike Twitter and Facebook, Twister does not apply an algorithm to filter the content that users see; content is delivered to nodes instantaneously, as-is. While filtering could be implemented, this would be a local filter, configured by a user on their personal node, much like a spam filter on a Post Office Protocol (POP3) and Internet Message Access Protocol (IMAP) e-mail client.[59] As a social network, Twister is novel because users are not obligated to trust a third party in the same way that they would when using Twitter, Facebook, or a federated service such as Diaspora. Trust is a central component of successful human interaction in a contemporary society;[60] as human beings, we are able to trust other people on the basis of what we know about them, our family ties to them, and information garnered about a given person from other sources that we trust, but this kind of trust is limited. If an inter-subjectively valued "radius of trust" does not exist, every social interaction descends into a prisoner's dilemma. In order for the "radius of trust" to expand sufficiently to nurture a functional society, a "trust architecture" needs to exist.[61] Werbach argued that until the invention of the blockchain, "there were two primary trust architectures: Leviathan (deference to a central enforcement authority) and peer-to-peer (reliance on social norms and other governance mechanisms in tight-knit communities)."[62]

Werbach suggested that "trustless trust"—epitomized in software form by the blockchain— made it "possible to trust the outputs of a system without trusting any actor within it."[63] Granted, the code underpinning the Twister network's blockchain is subjectively rather than objectively written given that human beings authored it. However, because the source code is open source, anyone with the requisite knowledge can review the code, make alterations, and submit them to peer-review, which diminishes—although does not eradicate—the perceived risks of trusting the network's development community.

It is this condition of "trustless trust" that presents the potential utility of peer-to-peer blockchain-based social networking to political dissidents and violent extremists alike. Similarly, it is the condition of "trustless trust" that may force a rethink of current counterextremism efforts that rely on the cooperation of a "trusted" figure such as a central administrator or domain owner.

A Storm on the Horizon? The Utility of Blockchain-Based Social Networks for Violent Extremists

As has been noted above, Twister's current content base is small.[64] Assessing whether any of these posts relate to violent extremist content is difficult. A researcher interested in combing through Twitter user data can do so either through Twitter's search function, or by requesting data from the Application Programming Interface (API). Twister, conversely, does not have this user-friendly functionality. Twister's "search" bar provides a user limited search functionality to find user names registered to the blockchain, but one cannot search for post content. TwisterIO.com and Twistnik.ru are advertised as search engines for the Twister network, but at the time of writing, they appear to have limited functionality. In theory, clicking on another user's name will instantly display their posts, in date order. However, not all posts will necessarily be immediately accessible, particularly if they are older posts. On-demand retrieval of historical post content relies on a computer already in possession of the content that can "seed" it on request via the BitTorrent protocol. This article has *not* been written on the basis of concrete evidence pointing to the existence of violent extremist virtual communities on the Twister network. Nevertheless, given that violent extremists have expressed interest in alternative social media, it is useful to consider the utility of a peer-to-peer, blockchain-based social network for the violent extremist. Similarly, it is useful to consider the means by which other users of alternative social media and counterextremist agencies could mitigate the use of such an online communication platform for violent extremist purposes.

As discussed above, online communication platforms have offered a degree of utility for violent extremists who wish to disseminate propaganda material relatively quickly and inexpensively. Benson has noted that Internet-mediated communication has allowed violent extremists the attractive prospect of dividing their "operational" wing from their "propaganda" wing.[65] The "operational" wing can be afforded the anonymity that may be necessary to carry out successful on-the-ground maneuvers, while the online platforms empower the "propaganda" wing, which can disseminate material without even having any tangible contact with their kinetically violent counterparts. This broad division structures the ensuing discussion. It is suggested here that a peer-to-peer, blockchain-based microblogging platform could be useful for both the "propaganda" and "operational" components of violent extremist activity.

For an "operational" community of violent extremists, there is one core utility that Twister could prove useful for. This is Twister's direct messaging function, which could serve as an alternative to the popular "Bitmessage" service, an encrypted peer-to-peer communication service that violent extremists have been encouraged to use.[66] A violent extremist could create a seemingly innocuous Twister account, using a randomized combination of letters and numbers, and pass this to their peers. These associates, who could have similar accounts, would then be able to "follow" this account, which they can elect to do publicly or privately. Once two accounts are following one another, they are able to send and receive direct messages between themselves. Users can also create "groups" for group messaging. The end-to-end encrypted message will not be visible to any user other than the intended recipient. Direct messages between Twister users are not "stored" or retrospectively viewable in plaintext in the same way that a Twitter direct message, or a conventional e-mail might be. The only means by which a direct message can be accessed is to be in possession of the private key to the sending or recipient account. Additional security may be offered if the users are connecting to the network through a virtual private network (VPN) and storing their private keys on a discrete or hidden removable storage device. The extremist could zero-out the removable storage device and smash it apart, or re-use it to store new keys. In principle, this could make the direct messaging service of a peer-to-peer, blockchain-based microblogging platform a feasible means of communicating instantly across long distances, with a degree of plausible deniability. Given that the only direct cost to a user who uses their node to broadcast a request for a new account is the time expended waiting for the name to be included in the next mined block, "operational" violent extremists could discard accounts much like they may discard inexpensive "burner" mobile phones. The tangible cost of creating new accounts—the mining of the requisite block—is shouldered by those voluntarily choosing to commit computational power to mining and is manifest in their electricity consumption and hardware wear and tear.

A peer-to-peer, blockchain-based microblogging service may also be useful for the "propaganda" wing of a violent extremist organization. Propaganda can only serve its purpose if it is seen and digested by an audience. If violent extremist online content—and the user accounts used to upload and re-broadcast the content—are transitory because of active censorship by the host platform, the utility of the content may be limited. Violent extremists would need to play a whack-a-mole game with the administrators and moderators of the host platform. A hosted item of violent extremist content does not necessarily exist in a vacuum. From the perspective of the violent extremist, censorship may be a particular nuisance not just for "out-links" (links to platforms outside of the host platform), but also for "in-links" (links within the host platform). Research by Conway et al. regarding Islamic State and other *jihadist* use of Twitter identified that 14 percent of pro–Islamic State and 7.5 percent of *Other Jihadist* tweets included an in-link.[67] Such in-linking provides moderators with the ability to map pathways between suspected violent extremist accounts.

A peer-to-peer, blockchain-based microblogging service such as Twister mitigates the necessity for the violent extremist to play the whack-a-mole game in order to maintain a persistent presence. So long as a Twister user retains the private key linked to their public address that registered their account in the blockchain, their free access to their account and their ability to post content is assured. While the overall content base of the Twister network is small, especially vis-à-vis mainstream proprietary social networks, it is possible that a Twister account could serve as a useful violent extremist propaganda resource on several fronts. First, an account could be used as a resilient, non-transitory space for the blogging of updates on the progress of a given violent extremist cause. Particularly of interest for violent extremists who are keen to produce and disseminate video outputs,[68] posts need not necessarily be limited to text. In May 2016, experimental WebTorrent media embedding was introduced to the Twister network, making video and image hosting possible.[69] Second, while in-linking is not yet implemented in the network, Twister could already provide a service for the archiving of shortened out-links to content elsewhere on the internet.

A third and novel utility draws on Twister's mining-reward implementation. As noted previously, unlike the Bitcoin network which rewards its mining community with the opportunity to win a diminishing supply of freshly minted Bitcoins, the Twister network rewards its miners with the opportunity to win free advertising. An "advert" is a single post of 140 characters. When a miner successfully mines a new block to the network's blockchain, a "promoted" post of their authorship is disseminated and attached—by their choosing—either to their username or to the anonymous "nobody" tag. Twister users can select a tab on the graphical user interface to specifically view "promoted" posts in descending chronological order. In addition, miners enter a lottery for "pushed" advertising, in which there is a chance that their promoted message may be shown to other Twister users on their generic timeline feed.

Because the mining-reward advertising discriminates on the basis of the computational power that a miner commits to calculating hashes, rather than on the content of a promoted message, a violent extremist might find mining to be a useful mechanism for disseminating propaganda. There was an instance on 1 June 2017 when a miner using the anonymous "nobody" tag successfully mined blocks and was rewarded with five promoted antisemitic messages.[70] The next day, a Twister user flagged this to Freitas, who responded publicly with the post "hmmm, I have yet to see these assholes you're talking about. Content filtering, freedom x anonymity x abuse is always a tricky business."[71]

On 18 December 2017, this author committed a desktop computer with a quad-core Intel 5 processor, 8GB of RAM, and a GeForce GTX 650ti graphics card to mining on the Twister network. This experiment was run to observe the hardware power that a violent extremist might require if they wished to make promoted posts to the network and potentially benefit from the advertising lottery. The computer mined for four hours, between 1630 and 2030 GMT, when the stated mining "difficulty" was 0.00355891 and the latest mined block was block 216068. The author set any promoted posts to be distributed under the guise of the anonymous "nobody" tag, and the text of promoted posts were manually inputted quotes from the popular television sitcom, *Seinfeld*. At 1709:20 GMT, the computer had successfully mined its first block, number 216070. Over the four-hour period, the computer was rewarded with a total of eleven promoted *Seinfeld* quotes. The interface for chronological "promoted messages" avoids displaying duplicate consecutive promoted messages and the latest identical promoted message subsumes those before it, so the actual number of blocks successfully mined by the computer may be marginally more than eleven. The mining difficulty is set and adjusted by the protocol so that in theory, a new block is added to the blockchain roughly every ten minutes. On paper, over a four-hour period, one would expect that approximately twenty-four blocks may be added to the blockchain. In this case, thirty-three blocks were added to the blockchain over the four-hour period, which is an unexceptional fluctuation. The Intel 5 processor was therefore able to mine at least one third of the blocks generated during the running of the experiment. It was apparent that blocks were also mined by three people other than the author. On 21 December 2017, the author ran the experiment a second time between 1130 and 1530 GMT, using the same computer. The mining difficulty was the same as it had been during the initial experiment. The latest mined block before the experiment began was 216538. Over the four hours, a total of thirty-two blocks were added to the blockchain. The computer successfully mined ten of these blocks, the first of which was block 216543 at 1216:14 GMT, and from these the computer was rewarded with seven manually inputted promoted *Seinfeld* quotes. During the running of the second experiment, it was apparent that the mining community was slightly more diverse; blocks were mined by five accounts other than the author, three of whom were the same accounts who had successfully mined blocks during the first experiment.

While these data are anecdotal, it does suggest that three years into its lifespan, the computational power underpinning the Twister network's blockchain is small. For comparison, the Bitcoin network's mining operation, with a difficulty of 1,590,896,927,258 on 21 December 2017,[72] would have ignored the computer that the author used for the mining experiments. The Twister network's mining difficulty at the time of the experiments was lower than it had been in June 2017, when the author had initially written this article for the *Terrorism and Social Media* conference at Swansea University.[73] The weakness of the computational power underpinning the mining process of the Twister network has implications for the opportunities afforded to both the hypothetical violent extremist and the counterextremist.

From the perspective of the hypothetical violent extremist, the opportunity is relatively obvious; at the time of writing, with just one unexceptional processor, they could commit computational power to the network and receive a sizeable proportion of the promoted posts afforded to successful miners. Such messages could be disseminated to hundreds or thousands of active users. One use for promoted messages might be to alert potentially like-minded individuals that they could join an extremist community by sending the promoter a private message. Alternatively, given that the Twister network supports hashtags, promoted messages could notify potentially like-minded individuals that they can engage in real-time discussions on extremist matters if they used a particular hashtag. Even if the general user population were not remotely interested in extremist material—and indeed may reject it—the appearance of pushed promoted extremist content could serve as a digital "graffiti tag," demonstrating a violent extremist's willingness to engage with alternative social media.

While this author does not suggest that a Twister-like platform would *replace* the online platforms currently used by violent extremists, it is apparent that the Twister network may have some utility for a violent extremist's purposes. Particularly because of the censorship-free nature of the network, it has been suggested that violent extremists could be attracted to the possibility of escaping a "whack-a-mole" operation that they may need to routinely employ in reaction to moderation activity on proprietary, censored platforms. The next section details approaches that could be used by counterextremists as part of an operation to mitigate hypothetical violent extremist usage of a peer-to-peer, blockchain-based microblogging platform.

Countering Violent Extremist Usage of Blockchain-Based Social Networks

This section considers some approaches that could be undertaken by counterextremists against peer-to-peer, blockchain-based microblogging platforms. There are some windows of opportunity, which draw on the same opportunities afforded to the hypothetical violent extremist, that are worth considering. It has been remarked by others that technological development is outpacing institutional change and the resources committed to *developing* new technologies exceed those dedicated to *governing* new technologies.[74] While it may once have been possible to prevent the movement of encrypted technology across borders,[75] today peer-to-peer, encrypted communication services fit with the increasing privatization and proliferation of consumer-targeted empowering technologies, many of which were once the solely the domain of national defense departments. Such technologies include consumer-oriented drones, 3 D printing, driverless cars and cyber-offense toolkits, among myriad other technologies. It is in this context that the counterextremist would approach the task of policing or attempting to exert influence over a peer-to-peer, blockchain-based microblogging platform.

One window of opportunity for the counterextremist would be to use accounts on the network to post information relating to their endeavor (e.g., promote a link to their anti-extremism website or content). Second, while violent extremists may be able to use Twister's "hashtag" functionality, there would be nothing stopping counterextremists commandeering such hashtags to offer banal or countering narratives.[76] Third, given that non-direct message posts are publicly viewable, the counterextremist could identify prolific "propaganda" accounts and collect associated data for intelligence purposes. The counterextremist might code a bot specifically for this purpose, which could automatically follow all accounts on the network and download all publicly available posts. While the counterextremist could not delete these posts nor lobby a central domain owner for their removal, the data could prove useful from open source intelligence (OSINT) and signals intelligence (SIGINT) perspectives.

Just as the mining process does not discriminate against the hypothetical violent extremist, the computational weakness of the mining operation underpinning the Twister network could also present opportunities to counterextremists. Again, one opportunity is obvious: a counterextremist could commit some computational power to mining on the network and use any rewarded promoted posts to refute an extremist narrative and provide a shortened out-link to a website or e-mail address for reporting extremist content. This approach would not undermine the network. Alternatively, however, there is the potential to cause disruption against the network itself. This could be achieved by exploiting a vulnerability inherent to decentralized, nondiscriminatory peer-to-peer blockchains, which is the risk that they may be undermined by a "51 percent attack." A "51 percent attack," sometimes known as a "majority attack," would be a betrayal of the pillar of "trustless trust" that the blockchain relies on. In order to conduct a majority attack, a perpetrator would need to modify the code running their "node." The attack would be more likely, and sustained, for each percentage point majority that the perpetrator could achieve. The Bitcoin community has expressed concern about the potential of a majority attack, given that in June 2014, the mining pool "Ghash.io" controlled 51 percent of the hash power on the network.[77] A successful perpetrator of a majority attack against the Bitcoin network would have the opportunity to reverse recent transactions and double-spend Bitcoins. An attack on the Bitcoin network may be unlikely, because of the profits that a successful attacker would forego as a result of the sabotage.[78] With the microblogging platform, however, the successful perpetrator of a majority attack could have the opportunity to retrospectively delete some recently created accounts, or, perhaps more significantly, prevent new users from creating accounts by intentionally mining empty blocks. However, because the blockchain is used for account registration and not the dissemination of posts, the successful majority attacker could not prevent existing accounts from making public posts or from sending private messages. As a result, it is suggested here that this would be an ineffective counterextremist measure. The intentional prevention of new account creation would prove irritating to a hypothetical violent extremist looking to join the network, and to those who may wish to replace an existing account with a new "burner" account, but the net harm of this approach is that *all* potential new users would be prevented from creating accounts. Disgruntled developers would not be structurally prevented from modifying the code and releasing a new version of a peer-to-peer microblogging platform.

Internationally, there appears to be growing official rhetoric regarding the necessity for proprietary mainstream platforms to make greater financial and staffing efforts to prevent their profit-making services from being used for violent extremist purposes.[79] As has been indicated by the literature considered earlier in this article,[80] and by the reports of organizations such as the U.K. and EU Internet Referral Units,[81] there is evidence that content removal on such online platforms has gained traction. However, in the future, today may be retrospectively viewed as a "golden age" for the feasibility of online content removal. As open-source encrypted peer-to-peer technologies become increasingly adopted, the dominance of closed, proprietary online communication platforms that extract advertising revenue from the private data of the individual may not be assured. Within the foreseeable future, counterextremist organizations such as the United Kingdom's Internet Referral Unit may not be afforded the luxury of a central authority that they can pressure for content removal. If a given item of offensive violent extremist content is disseminated through BitTorrent-like protocols on services such as Twister or Zeronet, the content is likely to remain accessible for as long as at least one person is willing to "seed" the relevant torrent file with their computer. In this sense, while certain items of violent extremist content may be proscribed under the domestic laws of a given jurisdiction, successfully enforcing these laws may not be possible in all cases. With encrypted, fully peer-to-peer hosting, the law of computer code[82] may override legislated regulation. In an era of decentralized, diffuse technology, "code is law" can be actioned by both state and nonstate agents. Just as "code is law" enabled, for instance, MI5, MI6, and Government Communications Headquarters (GCHQ) to "unlawfully" collect the online communication data of British citizens for 17 years,[83] the motivated individual— extremist or otherwise—is empowered to make efforts to evade online surveillance and online censorship.

A hypothetical violent extremist could significantly improve the privacy of their seeding operations by connecting to their desired peer-to-peer services through a VPN. However, as has been noted regarding the feasibility of prosecuting music, film, and game BitTorrent filesharers,[84] even if the perpetrator were to use their true IP address, the evidence collected by monitoring the IP address would tie the activity to a given Internet address but not a particular individual. On the basis of IP data alone, a prosecution could not be assured success. A risk of prosecution has not prevented relatively widespread use of BitTorrent services for illicit activity. In 2009, 15 percent of Americans polled by Pew admitted to illicit file-sharing using BitTorrent software.[85] Research in 2015 by Sandvine found that the overall share of bandwidth in North America used by BitTorrent data had declined due to the increasing popularity of bandwidth-heavy services such as Netflix and YouTube, but BitTorrent traffic still represented 26.83 percent of "upstream" data, a decline from 36.35 percent two years earlier.[86]

While violent extremist content hosted in an encrypted peer-to-peer manner may have the potential to be *technically* resilient, this does not necessarily make it *socially* resilient. The ability to host and access difficult-to-remove violent extremist content through use of encrypted peer-to-peer channels does not mean that the material will be compelling. There is perhaps a risk that fetishizing online violent extremist content could artificially manufacture a compelling narrative to the content through overt reactions by law enforcement and policymaking communities. Conway has suggested that "there is no yet proven connection between consumption of and networking around violent extremist online content and adoption of extremist ideology and/or engagement in violent extremism and terrorism."[87] Notwithstanding perceived online causality of violent extremism, the notion of "radicalization" itself has not been without controversy. In particular, "radicalization" as a concept has been criticized for possessing an ambiguous, subjective definition and for lacking empirical data linking causality to violent behavior.[88]

If online extremist content is an ideological "virus" of sorts[89] that cannot be eradicated altogether but that may, or may not, have the potential to incite people into committing acts of violence, citizens should be encouraged to develop the effective antibody of a critical mind. When violent extremists elect to use social media to further their agenda—whether the platforms are mainstream or alternative—they give their narrative(s) visibility and open a space for them to be critiqued.[90] On Twister, for instance, just as with Twitter, YouTube, and Facebook, there is nothing structurally preventing non-extremist users from responding to extremist content with satire and ridicule.[91] When 4chan users reproduced imagery of Islamic State fighters by superimposing rubber ducks and toilet brushes onto them, the bravado of the images was replaced with disarming humor.[92] This is, of course, not to promote flippancy or disregard for online material that could be extremely offensive or which could, in some circumstances, provoke individuals to align with a violent cause. However, this author agrees with the suggestion of Bartlett and Krasodomski-Jones; in a context of limited counterextremist resources, the most worthwhile approach may be to develop users' critical faculties so that ideologies can be rejected and ensure that top-down human resources are best placed to prevent violent behavior, rather than chase uncomfortable propaganda around the Internet.[93] The greater the pressure applied to proprietary, mainstream services to enact counterextremist censorship measures on their services, the faster these platforms will become untenable for sustaining viable violent extremist communities, which will likely encourage them to migrate to services that offer them technical resilience against disruptive censorship, rather than give up on Internet-mediated communication altogether.

Conclusion

Technology and software have empowered individuals to communicate seamlessly across borders either with the assistance of centralized, privately owned platforms, or without them. 2017 was an exceptional year for the blockchain's most prominent case study, the Bitcoin cryptocurrency, with a surge in public and media interest. According to Google, "How to buy Bitcoin" was the second most-asked "How to" question of

2017, and "What is Bitcoin" was the fourth most-asked "What is" question.[94] The encrypted peer-to-peer blockchain-based cat is out of the bag.

This article has argued that violent extremists experiencing difficulty maintaining viable, persistent presences on social media platforms may elect to eschew mainstream platforms on which they are increasingly censored, in favor of alternative platforms where they are not. A violent extremist who made a conscious decision to operate a node on the Twister network, for instance, could retain sovereignty over the content that they post and access. It has been suggested that a network such as Twister could offer utility for both "operational" and "propaganda-producing" violent extremists. Policing and moderating violent extremist communities on alternative social media platforms is likely to present challenges for counterextremist organizations such as the United Kingdom's Internet Referral Unit, which rely on the cooperation of domain owners and ISPs for content removal. Encryption and Internet-mediated communication has significantly bolstered the U.K. economy,[95] which makes disrupting the technologies that enable peer-to-peer blockchain-based online platforms to exist an untenable approach to counterextremism. It is plausible that counterextremist practices toward online content may, not through preference but through necessity, need to shift from a focus on content *removal*, to content *contention*.

Notes

1. Jessica Guynn, "Facebook's Ad Sales Machine Roars," *USA Today*, last modified 3 May 2017, https://www.usatoday.com/story/tech/news/2017/05/03/facebook-first-quarter-2-billion-users-topped-revenue-estimates/101254122/ (accessed 19 May 2017).
2. Maura Conway, "Determining the Role of the Internet in Violent and Extremism and Terrorism: Six Suggestions for Progressing Research," *Studies in Conflict and Terrorism* 40, no. 1 (2017): 82, emphasis added.
3. Aaron Zelin, *The State of Global Jihad Online: A Qualitative, Quantitative, and Cross-Lingual Analysis* (Washington, DC: New America Foundation, 2013), 1.
4. Jason Burke, "Al-Shabab's Tweets won't Boost its Cause," *The Guardian*, last modified 16 December 2011, https://www.theguardian.com/commentisfree/2011/dec/16/al-shabab-tweets-terrorism-twitter (accessed 13 December 2017).
5. Walter Laqueur, *The New Terrorism: Fanaticism and the Arms of Mass Destruction* (Oxford: Oxford University Press, 1999), 262.
6. Christina Archetti, "Terrorism, Communication and New Media: Explaining Radicalisation in the Digital Age," *Perspectives on Terrorism* 9, no. 1 (2015), 54–55.
7. Timothy Thomas, "Al Qaeda and the Internet: The Danger of 'Cyberplanning,'" *Parameters: US Army War College* 33, no. 1 (2003), 112–123.
8. Gabriel Weimann, *Terror on the Internet: The New Arena, the New Challenges* (Washington DC: United States Institute of Peace Press, 2006). See also Gabriel Weimann, "Using the Internet for Terrorist Recruiting," in *NATO Security through Science Series: Hypermedia Seduction for Terrorist Recruiting* ed. Boaz Ganor (Amsterdam: IOS Press, 2007).
9. Marc Sageman, *Leaderless Jihad: Terror Networks in the Twenty-First Century* (Philadelphia: University of Pennsylvania, 2008).
10. David Cole, "Virtual Terrorism and the Internet E-learning Options," *E-Learning* 4, no. 2 (2007), 116–127.
11. Javier Argomaniz, "European Union Responses to Terrorist Use of the Internet," *Cooperation and Conflict* 50, no. 2 (2015), 253.
12. Anja Dalgaard-Nielsen, "Violent Radicalisation in Europe: What we Know and What we do not Know," *Studies in Conflict and Terrorism* 33, no. 9 (2010), 797–814; Tim Stevens and

Peter Neumann, *Countering Online Radicalisation: A Strategy for Action* (London: ICSR, 2009).

13. Lorraine Bowman-Grieve, "Exploring 'Stormfront': A Virtual Community of the Radical Right," *Studies in Conflict and Terrorism* 32, no. 11 (2009), 989–1007; Jerold Post, Kevin Ruby, and Eric Shaw, "From Car Bombs to Logic Bombs: The Growing Threat from Information Terrorism," *Terrorism and Political Violence* 12, no. 2 (2000), 97–122.
14. Lisa Nakamura, *Cyber Types: Race, Ethnicity, and Identity on the Internet* (New York: Routledge, 2002), 35. See also Judith Donath, "Identity and Deception in the Virtual Community," in *Communities in Cyberspace*, ed. Peter Kollock and Marc Smith (London: Routledge, 1999). See comments by Peter Steiner in Glenn Fleishman, "Cartoon Captures Spirit of the Internet," The New York Times, last modified 14 December 2000, https://www.nytimes.com/2000/12/14/technology/cartoon-captures-spirit-of-the-internet.html (accessed 20 September 2018).
15. Derek O'Callaghan et al., "Uncovering the Wider Structure of Extreme Right Communities Spanning Popular Online Networks," proceedings of the 2010 International Conference on Advances in Social Networks Analysis and Mining (2010), https://arxiv.org/pdf/1302.1726.pdf (accessed 13 December 2017). See also Stewart Bertram and Keith Ellison, "Sub Saharan African Terrorist Groups' use of the Internet," *Journal of Terrorism Research* 5, no. 1 (2014), 5–26.
16. Europol, *EU Internet Referral Unit: Year One Report Highlights* (The Hague: Europol, 2016), 5.
17. See Europol, "Europol Coordinates Joint Action Days to Flag Online Terrorist Content," *Europol Newsroom*, last modified 27 February 2017, https://www.europol.europa.eu/newsroom/news/europol-coordinates-joint-action-days-to-flag-online-terrorist-content (accessed 19 December 2017); Europol, "Europol Coordinates EU-wide Hit Against Online Terrorist Propaganda," *Europol Newsroom*, last modified 2 May 2017, https://www.europol.europa.eu/newsroom/news/europol-coordinates-eu-wide-hit-against-online-terrorist-propaganda (accessed 19 December 2017).
18. Home Office, "New Technology Revealed to Help Fight Terrorist Content Online," *Gov.uk*, last modified 13 February 2017, https://www.gov.uk/government/news/new-technology-revealed-to-help-fight-terrorist-content-online (accessed 23 February 2018).
19. Anne Stenersen, "The Internet: A Virtual Training Camp?," *Terrorism and Political Violence* 20, no. 2 (2008), 215–233.
20. Ibid.
21. Manuel Soriano, "The Vulnerabilities of Online Terrorism," *Studies in Conflict and Terrorism* 35, no. 4 (2012), 268.
22. J. M. Berger and Jonathan Morgan, *The ISIS Twitter Census: Defining and Describing the Population of ISIS Supporters on Twitter* (Washington, DC: Brookings, 2015), 33.
23. Maura Conway et al., *Disrupting Daesh: Measuring Takedown of Online Terrorist Material and its Impacts* (Dublin: Vox-Pol, 2017), 5.
24. Ibid., 30. While the choice of an avatar may seem banal, users of online communication services develop associations with their avatars and can view them as extensions of themselves. See Edward Castronova, *Synthetic Worlds: The Business and Culture of Online Games* (Chicago: University of Chicago Press, 2005), 45. See also William Bainbridge, *The Warcraft Civilisation: Social Science in a Virtual World* (London: MIT Press, 2010), 181.
25. Ibid., 30. See also Nico Prucha, "IS and the Jihadist Information Highway: Projecting Influence and Religious Identity via Telegram," *Perspectives on Terrorism* 10, no. 6 (2006), 48–58.
26. See Lorand Bodo, "Account Suspended: Twitter and Extreme Right-wing Groups in the UK," *VOX-Pol*, last modified 20 December 2017, http://www.voxpol.eu/account-suspended-twitter-extreme-right-wing-groups-uk/ (accessed 23 December 2017). See Twitter's rules at Twitter, "The Twitter Rules," https://help.twitter.com/en/rules-and-policies/twitter-rules (accessed 23 December 2017). See also DFRLab, "Alt-Right and Alt-Social Media," *Medium*,

last modified 8 September 2017, https://medium.com/dfrlab/alt-right-and-alt-social-media-4fa23eb2fbd1 (accessed 23 December 2017).

27. Diaspora Foundation, "Islamic State Fighters on Diaspora," *Diaspora*, last modified 20 August 2014, https://blog.diasporafoundation.org/4-islamic-state-fighters-on-diaspora (accessed 14 December 2017). See also Samuel Gibbs, "Islamic State Moves to other Social Networks after Twitter Clampdown," *The Guardian*, last modified 21 August 2014, https://www.theguardian.com/technology/2014/aug/21/islamic-state-isis-social-media-diaspora-twitter-clampdown (accessed 14 December 2017); BBC News, "Islamic State Shifts to New Platforms after Twitter Block," *BBC News*, last modified 21 August 2014, http://www.bbc.co.uk/news/world-middle-east-28843350 (accessed 14 December 2017); Sophie Curtis, "Islamic State Invades Diaspora Social Network after Twitter Ban," *The Telegraph*, last modified 22 August 2014, http://www.telegraph.co.uk/technology/social-media/11050712/Islamic-State-invades-Diaspora-social-network-after-Twitter-ban.html (accessed 14 December 2017).
28. Ames Bielenberg, "The Growth of Diaspora—A Decentralised Online Social Network in the Wild," *IEEE*, last modified 3 May 2012, http://ieeexplore.ieee.org/document/6193476/ (accessed 14 December 2017).
29. Mastodon, https://joinmastodon.org/ (accessed 22 December 2017).
30. Scuttlebutt, https://www.scuttlebutt.nz/ (accessed 22 December 2017).
31. Colin Koopman, *Genealogy as Critique: Foucault and the Problems of Modernity* (Bloomington: Indiana University Press, 2013), 19.
32. See Udit Sharma, "Blockchain in Healthcare: Patient Benefits and More," *IBM*, last modified 30 October 2017, https://www.ibm.com/blogs/blockchain/2017/10/blockchain-in-healthcare-patient-benefits-and-more/ (accessed 23 December 2017); Frederick Reese, "Land Registry: A Big Blockchain use Case Explored," *Coindesk*, last modified 19 April 2017, https://www.coindesk.com/blockchain-land-registry-solution-seeking-problem/ (accessed 23 December 2017); Coindesk, "How do Ethereum Smart Contracts Work?," https://www.coindesk.com/information/ethereum-smart-contracts-work/ (accessed 23 December 2017).
33. "Satoshi Nakamoto," "Bitcoin: A Peer to Peer Electronic Cash System," *Bitcoin.org*, https://bitcoin.org/bitcoin.pdf (accessed 23 December 2017).
34. In essence, this is simply a very long number. The Bitcoin protocol rewards the mining computer that successfully finds the correct number of binary zeros at the beginning of the number.
35. In theory, the Bitcoin protocol accommodates for the reality that miners are self-interested rather than altruistic. In the absence of a "reward" of fresh Bitcoins, it is envisaged that miners would still compete for the "transaction fee" that users set and include with their transaction. When a miner successfully generates a new block, they are able to retain the transaction fees of all the transactions included within that block. As miners will prioritize the transactions with the highest fee, the fee system simultaneously serves to reward miners post-2140 and to discourage "spam" transactions on the network.
36. XE, "XE Currency Converter: XBT to USD," http://www.xe.com/currencyconverter/convert/?Amount=1&From=XBT&To=USD (accessed 23 December 2017).
37. An "application specific integrated circuit."
38. An increase in the mining difficulty increases the number of binary zeros at the beginning of the sought-after hash for a given block generation.
39. BitcoinWisdom, "Bitcoin Difficulty and Hashrate Chart," https://bitcoinwisdom.com/bitcoin/difficulty (accessed 23 February 2018).
40. Simon Denyer, "The Bizarre World of Bitcoin 'Mining' Finds a New Home in Tibet," *The Washington Post*, last modified 12 September 2016, https://www.washingtonpost.com/world/asia_pacific/in-chinas-tibetan-highlands-the-bizarre-world-of-bitcoin-mining-finds-a-new-home/2016/09/12/7729cbea-657e-11e6-b4d8-33e931b5a26d_story.html (accessed 23 December 2017).
41. Chelan County, with a population of ~76,000, has three hydroelectric plants on the Columbia River. United States Census Bureau, "Chelan County, Washington," https://www.census.gov/quickfacts/table/PST045215/53007 (accessed 23 December 2017).

42. Peter Martinez, "Bitcoin Mining Consumes More Energy than 159 Countries," *CBS News*, last modified 27 November 2017, https://www.cbsnews.com/news/bitcoin-mining-energy-consumption/ (accessed on 23 December 2017).
43. Twister Network, 127.0.0.1:28332/network.html (accessed 23 December 2017).
44. Miguel Freitas, "Download," *Twister*, post 24 November 2013, http://twister.net.co/?page_id=23 (accessed 23 December 2017).
45. Anna Leach, "The Pirate Bay Torrents Printable 3D Objects," *The Register*, last modified 25 January 2012, https://www.theregister.co.uk/2012/01/25/pirate_bay_3d_printer_files/ (accessed 23 December 2017). See also Anne Lewis, "The Legality of 3D Printing: How Technology is Moving Faster than the Law," *Tulane Journal of Technology and Intellectual Property* 17 (2014), 303–318.
46. For instance, see Markus Ackermann et al., "Helloworld: An Open Source, Distributed and Secure Social Network," WC3 Workshop on the Future of Social Networking-Position Papers (2008), https://www.w3.org/2008/09/msnws/papers/HelloWorld_paper.pdf (accessed 17 December 2017); David Koll, Jun Li, and Xiaoming Fu, "SOUP: An Online Social Network by the People, for the People," *ACM Press* (2014), https://dl.acm.org/citation.cfm?doid=2663165.2663324&preflayout=flat (accessed 17 December 2017), 193–204; Alireza Mahdian, "MyZone: A Next-Generation Online Social Network," *arXiv.org* (2011), https://arxiv.org/abs/1110.5371 (accessed 17 December 2017); Robert Gehl, "Alternative Social Media: From Critique to Code," *SSRN* (2015), https://papers.ssrn.com/sol3/Delivery.cfm/SSRN_ID2955827_code2077148.pdf?abstractid=2955827 (accessed 17 December 2017).
47. Data taken from MaximAL, "Twistnik: About," *Twistnik*, https://twistnik.ru/about (accessed 23 February 2018).
48. Paul Gill et al., *What are the Roles of the Internet in Terrorism: Measuring Online Behaviours of Convicted UK Terrorists* (Dublin: Vox-Pol, 2015), 21. See also Donald Holbrook, "A Critical Analysis of the Role of the Internet in the Preparation and Planning of Acs of Terrorism," *Dynamics of Asymmetric Conflict* 8, no. 2 (2015), 126.
49. For information, FAQs and installation instructions, see "Zeronet," https://zeronet.io/ (accessed 18 December 2017).
50. *The Guardian*, "Cardiff Terrorist who Hid Extremist Data on Bond-Style Cufflink is Jailed," last modified 2 May 2017, https://www.theguardian.com/uk-news/2017/may/02/cardiff-terrorist-extremist-data-bond-style-cufflink-jailed-samata-ullah (accessed 18 December 2017).
51. Klint Finley, "Out in the Open: An NSA-Proof Twitter, Built with Code from Bitcoin and BitTorrent," *Wired*, last modified 13 January 2014, https://www.wired.com/2014/01/twister/ (accessed 23 December 2017).
52. For instance, see Josh Halliday anmd Juliette Garside, "Rioting Leads to Cameron Call for Social Media Clampdown," *The Guardian*, last modified 11 August 2011, https://www.theguardian.com/uk/2011/aug/11/cameron-call-social-media-clampdown (accessed 17 December 2017); Christopher Williams, "Cameron Told not to Shut Down Internet," *The Telegraph*, last modified 1 November 2011, http://www.telegraph.co.uk/technology/news/8862335/Cameron-told-not-to-shut-down-internet.html (accessed 17 December 2017).
53. See interview transcript at Robert Gehl, "Building a Better Twitter: A Study of the Twitter Alternatives GNU Social, Quitter, rstat.us, and Twister," *SSRN* (2015), https://papers.ssrn.com/sol3/papers.cfm?abstract_id=2595247 (accessed 17 December 2017), 9.
54. See Open Source Initiative, "The MIT License," https://opensource.org/licenses/MIT (accessed 17 December 2017).
55. Robert Gehl, "Building a Better Twitter," 12.
56. See Kelvin Low and Ernie Teo, "Bitcoins and Other Cryptocurrencies as Property?" *Law Innovation and Technology* 9, no. 2 (2017), 235–268.
57. Ibid., 264.
58. For an overview of the Ethereum blockchain fork, see Alyssa Hertig, "Ethereum's Two Ethereums Explained," *Coindesk*, last modified 28 July 2017, https://www.coindesk.com/ethereum-classic-explained-blockchain/ (accessed 18 December 2017). The Bitcoin cryptocurrency experienced its own hard fork in August 2017, when "Bitcoin Cash" split

from the "Bitcoin" network. See Alyssa Hertig, "Bitcoin Cash: Why it's Forking the Blockchain and what that Means," *Coindesk*, last modified 26 July 2017, https://www.coindesk.com/coindesk-explainer-bitcoin-cash-forking-blockchain/ (accessed 18 December 2017).

59. See interview transcript as Robert Gehl, "Alternative Social Media," 10.
60. Francis Fukuyama, *Trust: The Social Virtues and the Creation of Prosperity* (New York: Free Press, 1995).
61. Kevin Werbach, "Trust, but Verify: Why the Blockchain Needs the Law," *SSRN* (2017), https://papers.ssrn.com/sol3/papers.cfm?abstract_id=2844409 (accessed 23 December 2017), 4.
62. Ibid., 4–5.
63. Ibid., 4–5.
64. Data taken from MaximAL, "Twistnik: About."
65. David Benson, "Why the Internet is not Increasing Terrorism," *Security Studies* 23, no. 2 (2014), 299.
66. See "Amreeki," "Al-Khilafah Aridat The Caliphate has Returned: Remaining Anonymous Online," *Wordpress*, last modified 20 August 2014, https://alkhilafaharidat.wordpress.com/2014/08/20/remaining-anonymous-online/comment-page-1/ (accessed 20 December 2017). See also Jamie Bartlett and Alex Krasodomski-Jones, *Online Anonymity Islamic State and Surveillance* (London: Demos, 2015).
67. Maura Conway et al., *Disrupting Daesh: Measuring the Takedown of Online Terrorist Material and its Impacts*, 33.
68. Virginie Andre, "The Janus Face of New Media Propaganda: The Case of Patani Neojihadist Youtube Warfare and its Islamophobic Effect on Cyber-Actors," *Islam and Christian-Muslim Relations* 25, no. 3 (2014), 335–356; Imogen Richards, "'Flexible Capital Accumulation in Islamic State Social Media," *Critical Studies on Terrorism* 9, no. 2 (2016), 205–225; James Farwell, "The Media Strategy of ISIS," *Survival* 56, no. 6 (2014), 49–55.
69. See Miguel Freitas, "File Attachment and WebTorrent Support," *Twister News*, post 9 May 2016, http://twister.net.co/?page_id=215 (accessed 22 December 2017).
70. These objectionable messages posted on 1 June 2017 read: "GAS THE KIKES RACE WAR NOW!!!"
71. See Miguel Freitas "@mfreitas," http://127.0.0.1:28332/home.html#profile?user=mfreitas, post 7 June 2017 (accessed 20 December 2017). [requires Twister to be installed and running].
72. BitcoinWisdom, "Bitcoin Difficulty and Hashrate Chart," https://bitcoinwisdom.com/bitcoin/difficulty (accessed 21 December 2017).
73. Twister Network, 127.0.0.1:28332/network.html (accessed 21 June 2017).
74. Ben FitzGerald and Jacqueline Parziale, "As Technology goes Democratic, Nations Lose Military Control," *Bulletin of the Atomic Scientists* 73, no. 2 (2017), 106.
75. See Wystan Ackerman, "Encryption: A 21st Century National Security Dilemma," *International Review of Law, Computers and Technology* 12, no. 2 (1998), 371–394.
76. Russian authorities have deployed this strategy in the past against protestors who had been using Twitter. See BBC News, "Russian Twitter Political Protests 'Swamped by Spam,'" last modified 8 March 2012, http://www.bbc.co.uk/news/technology-16108876 (accessed 27 December 2017). A similar approach was taken by Mexican authorities, see Klint Finley, "Pro-Government Twitter Bots try to Hush Mexican Activists," *Wired*, last modified 23 August 2015, https://www.wired.com/2015/08/pro-government-twitter-bots-try-hush-mexican-activists/ (accessed 27 December 2017). Similar strategies have been deployed in Morocco, Syria, Bahrain, Egypt and Iran. See Jillian York, "Syria's Twitter Spambots," *The Guardian*, 21 April 2011, https://www.theguardian.com/commentisfree/2011/apr/21/syria-twitter-spambots-pro-revolution (accessed 27 December 2017).
77. Members of the mining pool withdrew their computing power from the group in order to avoid the majority stake persisting. See Alex Hern, "Bitcoin Currency could have been Destroyed by '51%' Attack," *The Guardian*, last modified 16 June 2014, https://www.

theguardian.com/technology/2014/jun/16/bitcoin-currency-destroyed-51-attack-ghash-io (accessed 23 December 2017).

78. Frederick Reese, "As Bitcoin Halving Approaches, 51% Attack Question Resurfaces," *Coindesk*, last modified 6 July 2017, https://www.coindesk.com/ahead-bitcoin-halving-51-attack-risks-reappear/ (accessed 23 December 2017).
79. For instance, see Home Affairs Committee, *Hate Crime: Abuse, Hate and Extremism Online* (London: Prevent Directorate, 2017); Mike Wright, "Facebook 'Reviewing' Britiain First Page after Twitter Suspends Far-right Group's Accounts," *The Telegraph*, last modified 19 December 2017, http://www.telegraph.co.uk/technology/2017/12/19/facebook-reviewing-britain-first-page-twitter-suspends-far-right/ (accessed 23 December 2017); Committee on Oversight and Government Reform House of Representatives, *Radicalization: Social Media and the Rise of Terrorism* (Washington, DC: US Government Publishing Office, 2015); Cara McGoogan, "Germany to Fine Facebook and Youtube €50m if they Fail to Delete Hate Speech," *The Telegraph*, last modified 30 June 2017, http://www.telegraph.co.uk/technology/2017/06/30/germany-fine-facebook-youtube-50m-fail-delete-hate-speech/ (accessed 23 December 2017).
80. Maura Conway et al., *Disrupting Daesh*.
81. The Counter Terrorism Internet Referral Unit removes more than 1,000 pieces of content from the Internet each week. See Gov.uk, "Guidance: Online Radicalisation," last modified 26 November 2015, https://www.gov.uk/government/publications/online-radicalisation/online-radicalisation (accessed 23 December 2017). In 2013, 17.541 items were removed, in 2015, 55,556 items were removed, and in 2016 this figure had reached around 100,000. See Vikram Dodd, "Counter-Terrorism Drive for Public to Report Online ISIS Propaganda," *The Guardian*, last modified 14 April 2016, https://www.theguardian.com/uk-news/2016/apr/15/police-launch-crackdown-on-isis-internet-extremism (accessed 23 December 2017). From July 2015, the CTIRU was superceded by the European Internet Referral Unit at the European level. This unit had removed 12,000 pieces of terrorist-related content by October 2016. See Ben Wallace, "Terrorism: Social Media Written Question 48934," *Parliamnet.uk*, answered 2 November 2016, https://www.parliament.uk/business/publications/written-questions-answers-statements/written-question/Commons/2016-10-17/48934/ (accessed 23 December 2017).
82. Lawrence Lessig, "Code is Law," *Harvard Magazine*, last modified 1 January 2000, hhttps://harvardmagazine.com/2000/01/code-is-law-html (accessed 22 December 2017). See also Lawrence Lessig, *Code* (New York: Basic Books, 2006), 1–8.
83. Alan Travis, "UK Security Agencies Unlawfully Collected Data for 17 Years, Court Rules," *The Guardian*, last modified 17 October 2016, https://www.theguardian.com/world/2016/oct/17/uk-security-agencies-unlawfully-collected-data-for-decade (accessed 22 December 2017).
84. BBC News, "BitTorrent Study Finds Most File-Sharers are Monitored," last modified 4 September 2012, http://www.bbc.com/news/technology-19474829 (accessed 22 December 2017).
85. Mary Madden, "The State of Music Online: Ten Years after Napster," *Pew*, last modified 15 June 2009, http://www.pewinternet.org/2009/06/15/the-state-of-music-online-ten-years-after-napster/#footnote9 (accessed 22 December 2017).
86. Sarah Perez, "Netflix, HBO Streaming Video Traffic Increases as BitTorrent Declines," *TechCrunch*, last modified 28 May 2015, https://techcrunch.com/2015/05/28/netflix-hbo-streaming-video-traffic-increases-as-bittorrent-declines/ (accessed 22 December 2017). See also Sandvine, *Global Internet Phenomena Report* (Waterloo: Sandvine, 2013), 6.
87. Maura Conway, "Determining the Role of the Internet in Violent Extremism and Terrorism," 77.
88. See Anthony Richards, "The Problem with 'Radicalisation': The Remit of 'Prevent' and the Need to Refocus on Terrorism in the UK," *International Affairs* 87, no. 1 (2011), 143–152; Charlotte Heath-Kelly, "Counter-Terrorism and the Counterfactual: Producing the 'Radicalisation' Discourse and the UK PREVENT Strategy," *The British Journal of Politics and International Relations* 15 (2013), 394–415; Jonathan Githens-Mazer, "Rethinking the

Causal Concept of Islamic Radicalisation: Political Concepts," Committee on Concepts and Methods Working Paper Series, 42 (2010); Jonathan Githens-Mazer and Robert Lambert, "Why Conventional Wisdom on Radicalisation Fails: The Persistance of a Failed Discourse," *International Affairs* 86, no. 4 (2010), 889–901; Michael King and Donald Taylor, "The Radicalisation of Homegrown Jihadists: A Review of Theoretical Modles and Social Psychological Evidence," *Terrorism and Political Violence* 23, no. 4 (2011), 602–622; Mark Sedgwick, "The Concept of Radicalisation as a Source of Confusion," *Terrorism and Political Violence* 22, no. 4 (2010), 479–494; Charlotte Heath-Kelly, "Algorithmic Autoimmunity in the NHS: Radicalisation and the Clinic," *Security Dialogue* 48, no. 1 (2016), 29–25.

89. Norman Bettison, "Preventing Violent Extremism: A Police Response," *Policing* 3, no. 2 (2009), 129–138.
90. Soriano calls this a "peril" of Web 2.0. See Manuel Soriano, "The Vulnerabilities of Online Terrorism," 272–274.
91. Charlotte Heath-Kelly, "Can we Laugh Yet? Reading post-9/11 Counterterrorism Policy as Magical Realism and Opening a Third Space of Resistance," *European Journal of Criminal Policy and Research* 18 (2012), 343–360.
92. Joel Gunter, "ISIS Mocked with Rubber Ducks as Internet Fights Terror with Humour," *The Guardian*, last modified 28 November 2015, https://www.theguardian.com/world/2015/nov/28/isis-fighters-rubber-ducks-reddit-4chan (accessed 22 December 2017).
93. Bartlett and Krasodomski-Jones, *Online Anonymity Islamic State and Surveillance*, 17.
94. Margi Murphy, "Bitcoin Mania: Google's Top Searches in 2017 Dominated by Digital Currency Craze," *The Telegraph*, last modified 13 December 2017, http://www.telegraph.co.uk/technology/2017/12/13/bitcoin-mania-googles-top-searches-2017-dominated-digital-currency/ (accessed 22 December 2017).
95. The United Kingdom was identified as a net exporter of e-commerce goods in 2009, exporting £2.80 for every £1 imported. See Carl Kalapesi, Sarah Willersdorg and Paul Zwillenberg, *The Connected Kingdom: How the Internet is Transforming the UK Economy*, (Boston: Boston Consulting Group, 2010), 5. In 2016, the Internet economy was estimated to account for 12.4 percent of British Gross Domestic Product, a figure that would have characterised the United Kingdom as more reliant on internet-mediated commerce than all of its G20 counterparts, with South Korea at 8 percent and the United States at 5.4 percent. See David Dean et al., *The Internet Economy in the G20: The $4,2 Trillion Growth Opportunity* (Boston: Boston Consulting Group, 2012), 9. By 2016, 45.9 million people, or 87.9 percent of the British population, were regarded as Internet users. See Office for National Statistics, "Internet Users in the UK: 2016," last modified 20 May 2016, https://www.ons.gov.uk/businessindustryandtrade/itandinternetindustry/bulletins/internetusers/2016/ (accessed 22 December 2017).

Index

Note: **Bold** page numbers refer to tables; *italic* page numbers refer to figures and page numbers followed by "n" denote endnotes.

For Product Safety Concerns and Information please contact our EU
representative GPSR@taylorandfrancis.com
Taylor & Francis Verlag GmbH, Kaufingerstraße 24, 80331 München, Germany

www.ingramcontent.com/pod-product-compliance
Ingram Content Group UK Ltd.
Pitfield, Milton Keynes, MK11 3LW, UK
UKHW050756180926
475701UK00007B/1082

* 9 7 8 1 0 3 2 0 8 1 7 9 3 *